I0836581

THE REVISED

COMPENDIUM OF METHODISM

EMBRACING

THE HISTORY AND PRESENT CONDITION OF ITS VARIOUS BRANCHES IN ALL COUNTRIES;

WITH

A DEFENCE OF ITS DOCTRINAL, GOVERNMENTAL, AND PRUDENTIAL PECULIARITIES.

BY REV. JAMES PORTER, D. D.,

AUTHOR OF "THE TRUE EVANGELIST," "REVIVALS OF RELIGION," "CHART OF LIFE," "WINNING WORKER," ETC.

"Prove all things, hold fast that which is good."—*Paul.*

NEW YORK: HUNT & EATON.
CINCINNATI: CRANSTON & STOWE.

PREFACE.

In offering this volume to his Wesleyan brethren, the author deems it appropriate to mention some of the considerations that have influenced him in its publication. One is, that many of the difficulties which have occurred in the church owe their existence to misapprehension. Most of the attempts at revolution are attributable to this cause. Had the reformers been better acquainted with the various church arrangements of different sects, and especially of their own, they would have remained quiet and useful members. But they imagined evils that never existed, and conceived beautiful schemes, that, in their opinion, would open a better era; not knowing that similar experiments had repeatedly proved unsuccessful in abler hands. Besides, many fail to work our plan as effectually as they might, for the want of a proper understanding and appreciation of it. And to this we may add, that much of the prejudice of other sects against us is attributable to the same general cause. They have no just conception either of our system or their own, and know little of our operations or success.

The object of the writer has been to adapt himself to this state of things, and present a view of the whole subject, sufficiently full and comprehensive to supply the information necessary, in a single volume of moderate size and *expense*. If he has succeeded as he intended, the thousands of young people who annually join us on trial, will be able, by reading it, to get quite an idea of our history, doctrines, government, and prudential economy, — the points of difference among Methodists, — and the grounds of their dissent from older denominations. Thus they will be prepared, on graduating to full connection, to give a reason for their preference, and to maintain our peculiarities against the popular prejudices with which they may be assailed. Should other sects happen to read it, we trust it may rectify their misconceptions, and lead to that charitable consideration of our claims to which we are entitled.

The materials for the work have been gathered from the most authentic sources. We have derived particular assistance from the Life of Mr. Wesley, and his Works; Grinnod's Compendium; Dr. Bangs' "History of the M. E. Church," and "Original Church of Christ," and Stevens' "Church Polity." For the statistics we are considerably indebted to Rev. William Butler, author of "The Land of the Veda," recently issued. They have cost us great labor and perplexity, but we are quite sure that they form the most perfect exhibit of Methodism ever published. There is, however, a little disparity between the tabular views on page 194 and some of the numbers given in the preceding pages. This is attributable to the fact that the table was the last thing stereotyped, and gives the statistics for 1874 in the cases referred to, instead of those for 1873. The chapter of official decisions has been transcribed from books, periodicals, conference journals, and private manuscripts. Our aim has been to portray Methodism in its true character and relations — not to *mend* it. However successful the effort may prove, it cannot exceed the author's high sense of the intrinsic excellence of the system, or of the obligations of society to it for the civil and religious privileges it enjoys.

Finally, we commend the work to the kind examination of all Methodists. Please to read it carefully, and lend it to your prejudiced neighbors. It may correct some of their errors, and promote better feelings. If any are thinking to leave us, and enter into other church relations, it may lead them to inquire where they are more needed, or can be more useful. May the divine presence accompany it, and make it the instrument of good to many souls

THE AUTHOR.

NEW YORK, *March*, 1875.

CONTENTS.

PART FIRST.

HISTORICAL SKETCH OF METHODISM FROM ITS RISE TO THE PRESENT TIME.

PART SECOND

DOCTRINAL VIEWS OF METHODISTS AS DISTINGUISHED FROM THOSE OF OTHER DENOMINATIONS.

PART THIRD.

OF GOVERNMENT, PARTICULARLY THAT OF THE METHODIST EPISCOPAL CHURCH.

PART FOURTH.

PRUDENTIAL ARRANGEMENTS PECULIAR TO DIFFERENT SECTS OF WESLEYANS.

TOPICAL INDEX.

PART FIRST.

HISTORICAL SKETCH OF METHODISM FROM ITS RISE TO THE PRESENT TIME.

CHAPTER I.

THE ORIGIN OF METHODIST SOCIETIES.

THE REV. JOHN WESLEY, the distinguished founder of Methodism, was born at Epworth, in England, in the year of our Lord 1703, O. S. If others have been more fortunate in respect to the secular wealth and honor of their pedigree, few have had equal facilities for a thorough education. His father, Rev. Samuel Wesley, was a man of great practical wisdom and piety, and spared no pains to train his children for the highest attainments in knowledge and virtue. His mother, Susannah Wesley, was a woman of extraordinary worth. She was the daughter of Dr. Samuel Annesley, and inherited much of his genius. Her education, and deep concern for the welfare of her children, endowed hei with superior qualifications to fit them for distinction in the ranks of usefulness and honor.

United in piety and solicitude for the proper training of their offspring, these parents early impressed them with sentiments of reverence for the Author of their being. At the age of eleven John was placed under that eminent scholar, Dr. Walker, Principal of the Charter-house School. Here he had some rather severe experience, though a favorite with his tutors; but such was his application, at the age of *sixteen*, he was elected to Christ's Church, Oxford. Here he was placed under Dr. Wigan, a gentleman of great classical knowledge, and pursued his studies with much energy. His natural temper, it is said, was gay and sprightly, with a turn for wit and humor. Mr. Babcock observes of him, that "when he was about twenty-one years of age he appeared the very sensible and acute theologian, — a young fellow of the finest classical taste, of the most liberal and manly sentiments. His perfect knowledge of the classics gave a smooth polish to his wit, and an air of superior elegance to all his compositions."

Being about tc enter into deacon's orders, his attention was called to the nature and importance of the work, and the motives and qualifications necessary to its successful prosecution. Reflection led to some just perception of the magnitude of the undertaking, and that to farther investigation. He now began to study divinity with a new zest, and became more anxious than ever to enter into orders. Some of the books that occupied his attention were among the most spiritual and heart-searching of the age, such as "*The Imitation of Christ*," by Kempis, and Bishop Taylor's "*Rules of Holy Living and Dying*." These made a deep impression, and aroused his whole soul to the subject. If Kempis and Taylor were right, he was wrong. In his extremity, like a true son, not spoilt by a college course, he wrote to his parents, stating his difficulties, and received very able and interesting responses from each of them. This correspondence drew out the best thoughts of both pupil and teachers; but while it indicates deep interest in the subject of religion generally, it betrays a want of knowledge and experience in salvation by faith.

Having fully prepared himself for the holy office, according to the standard of the age, he was ordained deacon on the 19th of September, 1725, by Dr. Potter, then Bishop of Oxford. This only increased his interest in the study of divinity and the classics, and such became his standing for character and learning that, on the 17th of March, 1726, he was elected Fellow of Lincoln College, an appointment of no inconsiderable honor or profit, and one that was not without its influence on the work for which Providence was preparing the way.

The following summer he spent at Epworth and Wroote, reading prayers, preaching twice on the Sabbath, and otherwise assisting his father in the various duties of his parish. This situation was highly favorable to his interests, not only as it gave him an opportunity to cultivate the pastoral office under the paternal tuition of an experienced master, but to mature his knowledge of experimental and practical theology by frequent conversations with his esteemed parents, which he did not fail to improve. On the 21st of September he returned to Oxford, and was soon chosen Greek Lecturer and Moderator of the classes, though but little more than twenty-three years of age, and not yet advanced to the Master's degree.

His advancement in religious tendencies was not less marked. Writing to his mother about this time, he says: "The conversation of one or two persons whom you may have heard me speak of (I hope never without gratitude) first took off my relish for most other pleasures, so far that I despised them in comparison of that. I have since proceeded a step farther, to slight them absolutely. And I am so little at present in love with even company, the most elegant entertainment next to books, that, unless the persons have a religious turn of thought, I am much better pleased without them. I think it is the settled temper of my soul, that I should prefer, at least for some time, such retirement as would seclude me from all the world, to the station I am now in. Not that this is by any means unpleasant to me, but I imagine it would be more improving to be in a place where I might confirm or implant in my mind what habits I would, without interruption, before the flexibility of youth is over."

How to dispose of himself in accordance with these predilections was not easy to determine. He first thought of a school in Yorkshire, which fell into the hands of another who stepped in before him. His father, having two livings, and not finding it convenient to obtain an assistant to his mind, now invited him to become his curate, which he did. In July, 1728, he was inducted into the office of priest, and soon after left his curacy at the call of the rector of his college, and returned to Oxford. Here he found his brother Charles standing vigorously up against the tide of infidelity which was setting in upon the students on all sides, and united with him in the pursuit of learning, and in doing good. Besides attending to the duties of his office, he became tutor to various pupils placed under his care, and labored assiduously for their welfare. His address to the tutors of the university indicates the objects and spirit of his endeavors. "Ye venerable men," said he, "who are more especially called to form the tender minds of youth, to dispel thence the shades of ignorance and error, and train them up to be wise unto salvation; are you filled with the Holy Ghost? With all those fruits of the Spirit which your important office so indispensably requires? Is your heart whole with God? Full of love and zeal to set up his kingdom on earth? Do you continually remind those under your care that the one rational end of all our studies is to know, love, and serve the only true God, and Jesus Christ whom he hath sent? Do you inculcate upon them, day by day, that love alone never faileth? Whereas, 'whether there be tongues, they shall fail,' or philosophical knowledge, 'it shall vanish away;' and that without love all learning is splendid ignorance, pompous folly, vexation of spirit? Has all you teach an actual tendency to the love of God, and all mankind for his sake? Have you an eye to this end in whatsoever you prescribe touching the kind, the manner, and the measure of their studies; desiring and laboring that wherever the lot of these young soldiers of Christ is cast they may be so many burning and shining lights, adorning the gospel of Christ in all things? And permit me to ask, do you put forth all your strength in the vast work you have undertaken? Do you labor herein with all your might? Exerting every faculty of the soul? Using every talent which God hath lent you, and that to the uttermost of your power?"

The process by which his mind had reached this intensity of religious devotion is best stated in his own words, which are as follows: "In the year 1725, being in the twenty-third year of my age, I met with Bishop Taylor's '*Rules and Exercises of Holy Living and Dying.*' In reading several parts of this book, I was exceedingly affected with that part in particular which relates to *purity of intention.* Instantly I resolved to dedicate all my life to God: all my thoughts, and words, and actions: being thoroughly convinced there was no medium, but that every part of my life must either be a sacrifice to God, or to myself, that is, in effect, to the devil.

"In the year 1726 I met with '*Kempis's Christian Pattern.*' The nature and extent of inward religion, the religion of the heart, now appeared to me in a stronger light than ever it had done before. I saw that giving even all my life to God, would profit me nothing, unless I gave my heart, yea, all my heart, to him. I saw that simplicity of intention, and purity of affection, one design in all we speak or do, and one desire, ruling all our tempers, are indeed the wings of the soul, without which we can never ascend to the mount of God.

"A year or two after, Mr. Law's '*Christian Perfection*' *and* '*Serious Call*' were put into my hands. These convinced me more than ever of the absolute impossibility of being half a Christian. And I determined through his grace to be all devoted to God, to give him all my soul, my body, and my substance. In 1729 I began not only to read, but to study the Bible, as the one, the only, standard of truth, and the only model of pure religion. Hence I saw, in a clearer light, the indispensable necessity of having the mind which was in Christ, and of walking as Christ also walked; even of having, not some part only, but all the mind which was in him, and of walking as he walked, not only in many, or in most respects, but in all things. And this was the light wherein at this time I generally considered religion, as a uniform following of Christ, an entire inward and outward conformity to our Master."

Under these convictions he entered more fully into the work of God. Conversing with his brother Charles, afterwards with Mr. Morgan, Mr. Hervey, (one of his pupils, and author of the Meditations,) Mr. Whitefield, and others, they agreed to meet and read divinity on Sunday evenings. The next summer they began to visit the prisoners in the Castle, and the sick and poor in the town. By degrees their meetings assumed a more religious character, and embraced in their exercises the careful examination of the Greek Testament, and close personal conversation on the deep things of God. To these means of spiritual improvement they added the observance of the Wednesday and Friday fasts, and the weekly sacrament. They were fifteen in number, and, as Mr. Wesley observed, "*all of one heart and mind.*"

Such a spectacle could but attract attention, especially as religion was in a low state; there being little of it in the community, except the form, and scarcely enough of that to meet the claims of the municipal law, or the rules of the University. Every one spake of the young men according to his particular fancy; some well, some ill. A rude youth, of Christ's Church, observing the exact regularity of their lives and studies, characterized them as "*a new set of Methodists*," in allusion to a class of ancient physicians distinguished by that name. The same spirit of reproach which suggested the title gave it popularity, and immortalized the young men it designed to crush. Taking no offence at any thing, and, withal, perceiving that their new cognomen expressed in a word exactly what they would be in life and godliness, they responded to it in all cheerfulness, as their successors have done, hoping never to dishonor it by the least departure from the ways of well-doing.

The history of this little company is full of interest, and may be found detailed in "Moore's Life of Wesley." It is a checkered page, exposing the enmity of the carnal mind, and illustrating the truth of the declaration, "all that will live godly in Christ Jesus shall suffer persecution;" but not more fully than it confirms the encouraging announcement of the Holy Spirit, "He that goeth forth and weepeth, bearing precious seed, shall doubtless come again with rejoicing, bringing his sheaves with him." The conflict was severe, but they succeeded. Many were benefited by their endeavors, and they received a hundred fold in discipline for the more difficult achievements of coming days.

Mr. Wesley was the master spirit of the band. His absence from Oxford, only for a few weeks, was attended with serious consequences in several instances, which compelled him to see the importance of his presence to its growing interests. Hence, when urged to accept his declining father's place at Epworth, a sense of duty required him to resist, and still cleave to his pupils and the little society with which he was surrounded.

But he had only escaped the importunities of his friends, by the assignment of the Epworth living to another, when he was designated as the most suitable person to come over to the Georgia Colony, as a missionary, both to the colonists and the Indians. Whether he ought to accept this call was too grave a question to settle hastily. Therefore he took time to consider, and immediately wrote to his mother and other friends, as he was wont to do on all questions of magnitude. His mother replied in these memorable words: "Had I twenty sons, I should rejoice that they were all so employed, *though I should never see them more.*" His brother Samuel acquiesced in the measure, as did his eldest sister, and some others; but still he hesitated. At length, however, after reasonable deliberation, he determined to leave Oxford and go to America. His brother Charles signifying his willingness to accompany him, arrangements were made for that purpose, and they commenced their voyage about the middle of October, 1735. "Not to avoid want," says Mr. John Wesley, "God having given us plenty of temporal blessings; nor to gain the dung and dross of riches and honor; but singly this, to save our souls, and to live wholly to the glory of God."

Their labors in Georgia were not as successful as they anticipated, particularly among the Indians, and their conflicts and sufferings were considerable. But they made the best of every thing for almost one year and nine months, and returned to England wiser and better men than when they left. Anxious as Mr. Wesley had been to be wholly the Lord's, profound as he was in divinity, and scrupulously as he had lived in all godliness, and honesty, he was ignorant and inexperienced in justification by faith, and the renewing of the Holy Ghost. He had worked and suffered for salvation, but had not *believed* with a heart unto righteousness. He *hoped* that he was a Christian, but had no joyful assurance of it, and therefore was more of a *servant* than a *son* of God, and was influenced more by *fear* than *love*. And yet, according to the prevailing theology of the day, in its brightest and purest aspects, he lacked nothing but continuance in well doing to ensure him the highest enjoyments of religion here, and an inheritance with the saints hereafter.

But light awaited him, as it does every diligent and honest inquirer after truth, and its revelation to his heart was the chief advantage of his mission to America. But this was reflected through a medium that human wisdom would not have suggested, yet in admirable accordance with the simplicity of the divine plan of humbling the pride of man, and of securing all the glory of his salvation to Him to whom it rightfully belongs.

When he embarked for Georgia, he found twenty-six Germans on board, all members of the Moravian Church, and deeply experienced in the things of God. Observing their Christian deportment, Mr. Wesley set himself to learn the German language, that he might converse with them. The existence of fear in his own heart, and the exhibition of peculiar graces in the Moravians, gave him much trouble. Referring to them, he said: "I had long observed the great seriousness of their behavior. Of their humility they had given a continual proof, by performing those servile offices for the other passengers which none of the English would undertake, for which they desired, and would receive, no pay, saying, 'It was good for their proud hearts, and their loving Saviour had done more for them.' And every day had given them occasion of showing a meekness which no injury could move. If they were pushed, struck, or thrown down, they rose again and went away, but no complaint was found in their mouths. There was now an opportunity of trying whether they were delivered from the spirit of fear, as well as from that of pride, anger, and revenge. In the midst of the Psalm wherewith their service began the sea broke over, split the mainsail in pieces, covered the ship, and poured in between the decks as if the great deep had already swallowed us up. A terrible screaming began among the English. The Germans calmly sung on. I asked one of them afterwards, 'Was you not afraid?' He answered, 'I thank God, no.' I asked, 'But were not your women and children afraid?' He mildly replied, 'No; our women and children are not afraid to die.'"

The result of all his study and observation during his absence, on his own heart, is stated in his journal. Jan. 8, 1738, he wrote: "By the most infallible of proofs, inward feeling, I am convinced, 1. Of unbelief; having no such faith in Christ as will prevent my heart from being troubled. 2. Of pride, throughout my past life, inasmuch as I thought I had what I find I have not. 3. Of gross irrecollection; inasmuch as in a storm I cry to God every moment, in a calm not. 4. Of levity and luxuriancy of spirit; appearing by my speaking words not tending to edify; but most, by the manner of my speaking of my enemies. Lord, save, or I perish! Save me, 1. By such a faith as implies peace in life and death. 2. By such humility as may fill my heart from this hour forever with a piercing, uninterrupted sense, that hitherto I have done nothing. 3. By such a recollection as may enable me to cry to thee every moment. 4. By steadiness, seriousness, sobriety of spirits, avoiding, as fire, every word that tendeth not to edify, and never speaking of any who oppose me, or sin against God, without all my own sins set in array before my face."

A few days after, as he was nearing the English shore, he wrote: "I went to America to convert the Indians; but O! who shall convert me? Who is he that will deliver me from this evil heart of unbelief? I have a fair summer religion; I can talk well, nay, and believe myself while no danger is near; but let death look me in the face, and my spirit is troubled. Nor can I say, '*to die is gain.*'

'I have a sin of fear, that when I've spun
My last thread, I shall perish on the shore.'"

On arriving home, and reviewing his whole life in the light of divine truth, and the developments of Christian experience he had observed in his German friends, he wrote again: "And now, it is upwards of two years since I left my native country, in order to teach the Georgian Indians the nature of Christianity; but what have I learned myself in the meantime? Why, what I least of all suspected, that I, who went to America to convert others, was never converted myself. *I am not mad*, though I thus speak; but speak the words of truth and soberness; if haply some of those who still dream may awake, and see that as I am so are they. Are they read in philosophy? So am I. In ancient or modern tongues? So was I also. Are they versed in the science of divinity? I too have studied it many years. Can they talk fluently upon spiritual things? The very same I could do. Are they plenteous in alms? Behold, I give all my goods to feed the poor. Do they give of their labor as well as of their substance? I have labored more abundantly than they all. Are they willing to suffer for their brethren? I have thrown up my friends, reputation, ease, country: I have put my life in my hand, wandering into strange lands; I have given my body to be devoured of the deep, parched up with heat, consumed by toil and weariness, or whatsoever God shall please to bring upon me. But does all this (be it more or less, it matters not) make me acceptable to God? Does all I ever did, or can know, say, give, do, or suffer, justify me in his sight? Yea, or the constant use of all the means of grace? (which, never theless, is meet, right, and our bounden duty,) or that I am, as touching outward righteousness, blameless? Or, (to come closer yet,) the having a rational conviction of all the truths of Christianity? Does all this give me a claim to the holy, heavenly, divine character of a Christian? By no means. If the oracles of God be true, if we are still to abide by the law and the testimony, all these things, though when ennobled by faith in Christ they are holy, and just, and good, yet without it are '*dung and dross*.'

"This, then, I have learned in the ends of the earth, that I am '*fallen short of the glory of God;*' that my whole heart is '*altogether corrupt and abominable;*' and consequently my whole life, (seeing it cannot be that '*an evil tree*' should 'bring forth good fruit,') that my works, my own sufferings, my own righteousness, are so far from reconciling me to an offended God, so far from making any atonement for the least of those sins, which 'are more in number than the hairs of my head,' that the most specious of them need an atonement themselves, or they cannot abide his righteous judgment; that having the sentence of death in my heart, and having nothing in or of myself to plead, I have no hope but that of being justified freely 'through the redemption that is in Jesus;' I have no hope but that if I seek I shall find the Christ, and 'be found in him, not having my own righteousness, but that which is of God by faith.'

"If it be said I have faith, (for many such things have I heard from many miserable comforters,) I answer, so have the devils a sort of faith; but still they are strangers to the covenant of promise. So the apostles had even at Cana in Galilee, when Jesus first 'manifested forth his glory;' even then they, in a sort, '*believed on him;*' but they had not then 'the faith that overcometh the world.' The faith I want is '*a sure trust and confidence in God that, through the merits of Christ, my sins* are forgiven, and I reconciled to the favor of God.' That faith which enables every one that hath it to cry out, '*I live not; but Christ liveth in me: and the life which I now live I live by faith in the Son of God, who loved me and gave himself for me.*' I want that faith which none has without *knowing* that he hath it, is 'freed from sin, the whole body of sin is destroyed' in him. He is freed from fear, '*having peace with God through Christ, and rejoicing in the hope of the glory of God.*' And he is freed from doubt, '*having the love of God shed abroad in his heart, through the Holy Ghost which is given unto him; which Spirit itself beareth witness with his spirit that he is a child of God.*'"

With these views of his spiritual state, Mr. Wesley left no means unemployed to obtain the blessing he so earnestly desired. Count Zinzendorf, the founder and protector of the Moravian Society, a man of learning and deep experience, coming into the country about that time, Mr. Wesley consulted with him, as he did with one Peter Boehler, another pious Moravian. They kindly listened to all his difficulties, and endeavored to impart such advice as his case required. It was difficult for one of his mental structure, education, and religious notions, tc come directly to the point. The idea of depending on nothing but Christ, and on him, *now*, for salvation, and the correlative idea of instantaneous conversion, — a sentiment generally discarded in the church, — gave him great trouble. Still he kept inquiring and praying with all his heart. Thinking that, perhaps, he ought to quit preaching until he should realize what he now saw to be necessary, he asked his friend Boehler whether he should not, who replied: "By no means; preach faith *till* you have it; and then, because you have it, you *will* preach faith." "Accordingly," says he, "I spake clearly and fully, at Blendon, to Mr. Delamotte's family, of the nature and fruits of Christian faith. Mr. Broughton and my brother were there. Mr. Broughton's great objection was, 'he could never think that I had not faith, who had done and suffered such things.' My brother was very angry, and told me 'I did not know what mischief I had done by talking thus.' And, indeed, it did please God then to *kindle a fire* which I trust shall never be extinguished."

Mr. Wesley now felt deeply for others who were still seeking to be justified by the works of the law. Some to whom he spake received the word gladly, and found rest to their souls by faith; but many doubted. Nevertheless, he committed his whole being to the work, and by labors, and watchings, and tears, such as alarmed his friends, and brought down upon him the reproaches of even many who professed better things, to say nothing of others, he spread the truth of what he believed to be the power of God unto salvation. His brother Charles resisted for a time, but at last yielded the point, confessed himself without God and without hope in the world, and earnestly sought redemption in the blood of the Lamb, even the forgiveness of sins. "May 21st," says Mr. Moore, "he waked in hope and expectation of soon attaining the object of his wishes. At nine o'clock his brother and some friends came in, and sung a hymn. When they left, he betook himself to prayer. Soon afterwards, a person came and said in a very solemn manner, 'Believe in the name of Jesus of Nazareth, and thou shalt be healed of all thine infirmities.' The words went through his heart, and animated him with confidence. He looked into the Scriptures, and read, '*Now, Lord, what is my hope? truly, my hope is even in thee.*' He then cast his eyes on these words, '*He hath put a new song into my mouth, even a thanksgiving unto our God; many shall see it and fear, and put their trust in the Lord.*' Afterwards he opened upon Isaiah xl. 1, 'Comfort ye, comfort ye my people, saith your God; speak ye comfortably to Jerusalem, and cry unto her that her warfare is accomplished, that her iniquity is pardoned, for she hath received of the Lord's hand double for all her sins.' In reading these passages of Scripture he was enabled to view Christ as '*set forth to be a propitiation for his sins, through faith in his blood*,' and received, to his unspeakable comfort, that peace and rest in God which he had so earnestly sought.

"The next morning he waked with a sense of the Divine goodness and protection, and rejoiced in reading the 107th Psalm, so nobly descriptive, he observes, of what God had done for his soul. Yet he had no self-confidence. 'This day,' says he, 'I had a humbling view of my own weakness, but was enabled to contemplate "*Christ in his power to save to the uttermost all those who come unto God by him.*"'"

Though Mr. John Wesley had not yet realized the fulness of what he was urging upon the acceptance of others, he was still panting after it. May 24th, about five in the morning, according to his own account, he opened his Testament on these words, "*There are given unto us exceeding great and precious promises, that by these ye might be partakers of the divine nature.*" "Just as I went out," says he, "I opened it again on these words, '*Thou art not far from the kingdom of God.*' In the afternoon I was asked to go to St. Paul's. The anthem was, 'Out of the deep have I called unto thee, O, Lord; Lord, hear my voice. O, let thine ears consider well the voice of my complaint. If thou, Lord, wilt be extreme to mark what is done amiss, O, Lord, who may abide it! But there is mercy with thee, therefore thou shalt be feared. O, Israel, trust in the Lord; for with the Lord there is mercy, and with him is plenteous redemption: and he shall redeem Israel from all his sins.'

"In the evening I went very unwillingly to a society in Aldersgate street, where one was reading Luther's Preface to the Epistle to the Romans. About a quarter before nine, while he was describing the change which God works in the heart through faith in Christ, *I felt my heart strangely warmed. I felt I did trust in Christ, Christ alone, for salvation; and an assurance was given me that he had taken away my sins, even mine, and saved me from the law of sin and death.*"

This was the crisis toward which God had been drawing him for years — the luminous point he must reach to be properly endowed for his high calling. It was indispensable for him to *know* the things whereof he affirmed. This revelation of God to his soul assured him that what he had believed was the truth as it is in Jesus, and enabled him to declare it with a degree of confidence he never had done before. It revealed to him the *nature* and evidences of religion with the clearness of light, and gave him the power of patient endurance in well doing that was necessary to the position which he was to occupy.

Witnesses to the truth of instantaneous justification by faith had now become sufficiently numerous to show that it was no cunningly devised fable. The line of demarcation between the Wesleys and other clergy was distinctly drawn, the point of attainment in religious experience defined, and the standard of genuine religion established. Following the instincts of their new state, no less than the dictates of a sound policy, they had already organized themselves into a society for mutual improvement, and agreed to these regulations: —

"1 That they would meet together once a week, to 'confess their faults one to another, and pray one for another, that they might be healed.'

"2. That the persons so meeting should be divided into several bands, or little companies, none of them consisting of fewer than five, or more than ten persons.

"3. That every one, in order, should speak as freely, plainly, and concisely as he could, the real state of his heart, with his several temptations and deliverances since the last time of meeting.

"4. That all the bands should have a conference at eight every Wednesday evening, begun and ended with singing and prayer.

"5. That any who desire to be admitted into this society should be asked, What are your reasons for desiring this? Will you be entirely open, using no kind of reserve? Have you any objection to any of our orders?

"6. That when any new member was proposed, every one present should speak clearly and freely whatever objection he might have to him.

"7. That those against whom no reasonable objection appeared, should be, in order for their trial, formed into one or more district bands, and some person agreed on to assist them.

"8. That after two months' trial, if no objection then appeared, they should be admitted into the society.

"9. That every fourth Saturday should be observed as a day of general intercession.

"10. That on the Sunday seven-night following, there should be a general love-feast, from seven till ten in the evening.

"11. That no particular member should be allowed to act in any thing contrary to any order of the society; and that if any persons, after being therein admonished, should not conform thereto, they should not longer be esteemed as members."

This took place in London, May 1st, 1738, and has been regarded the *origin* of Methodism. Using the term in one very common sense of it, this is a mistake; but if it be used to designate existing Methodist societies, it is no doubt true. Mr. Wesley refers its origin to three distinct periods. He says, "The first rise of Methodism was in November, 1729, when four of us met together at Oxford. The second was at Savannah, in April, 1736, when twenty or thirty persons met at my house. The last was at London, on this day, [May 1, 1738,] when forty or fifty of us agreed to meet together every Wednesday evening, in order to free conversation, begun and ended with singing and prayer." The reader can place the origin to suit his own judgment. But if we mistake not, place it where he will, he will recognize God as its author; his glory, and the best good of man, its tendency and aim.

CHAPTER II.

EARLY PROGRESS OF METHODISM, GIVING THE ORIGIN OF SEVERAL OF ITS PECULIARITIES.

THE Wesleys were now objects of special attention. They had been generally considered "over-much righteous" for several years, though they had not entirely broken loose from the prevailing errors of their times. But now that they had imbibed sentiments which, if true, involved nearly the whole church in condemnation — branded their righteousness as "filthy rags," and their long cherished hopes as vain and deceptive, they were supposed to be crazy. And the more so, because they professed to have demonstrated the truth of their doctrine by a joyful experience of its provisions in their own souls. Men care little about cold opinions, but, as one writer observes, "speak of faith in such a manner as makes Christ a saviour to the utmost, a most universal help and refuge; in such a manner as takes away glorying, but adds happiness to wretched man; as discovers a greater pollution in the best of us than we could before acknowledge, but brings a greater deliverance from it than we could before expect; if any one offers to talk at this rate, he shall be heard with the same abhorrence as if he was going to rob mankind of their salvation, their Mediator, or their hopes of forgiveness."

But nothing moved them. Mr. John Wesley soon took a tour in Germany, for the confirmation of his faith by intercourse with the Moravians, to whom he was much indebted already; while his brother Charles contended earnestly for the faith among formalists at home. Both obtained the object of their earnest desire, viz.: clearer views and deeper experience. And they were not without success in bringing some into the same blessed state. Their word was accompanied by divine power. The utterance of a few simple truths, whether from the Bible, or personal experience, was like fire, "and like a hammer that breaketh the rock in pieces." Professional men, full of pride and conceit, became as little children.

Mr. Wesley had been refused to preach in many of the churches of London some time before, but now more especially. He therefore preached as the providence of God opened his way. "In several places, while he was expounding the Scriptures, many persons trembled and fell down before him. Some cried aloud, and others appeared convulsed as in the agonies of death. Many of these were afterwards eminent professors of the holiness and happiness of religion, and declared they had at the time such a deep sense of the nature of sin, and of the just wages of it, that they were constrained to cry aloud for the disquietude of their heart." Writing to a friend, Oct. 14th of the year of his conversion, he remarked: —

"Though my brother and I are not permitted to preach in most of the churches in London, yet, thanks be to God, there are others left, wherein we have liberty to speak the truth as it is in Jesus. * * * Nor hath he left himself without witnesses of his grace and truth. Ten ministers I know now in England, who lay the right foundation, '*The blood of Christ cleanseth us from all sin.*' Over and above whom I have found one Anabaptist, and one, if not two, of the teachers among the Presbyterians here, who, I hope, love the Lord Jesus Christ in sincerity, and teach the way of God in truth."

This was encouraging, but still the way of these good men was hedged up. What could they do? Various plans were suggested, but they seemed to look more to this world than to the next, and were therefore rejected. Mr. Whitefield had now returned from America, and united with the brothers in the work of God. But were could he preach? Not in the churches, for they were closed; not in private dwellings, for they were too small. Hence he betook himself to the fields and highways, and thus attracted thousands to hear the gospel who would not have gone to the churches had they been open. Mr. Wesley hesitated a little at this seeming irregularity, but when he came to consider the example of Christ, and that he was excluded from the churches, "I submitted," says he, "to be yet more vile, and proclaimed in the highways the glad tidings of salvation, speaking from a little eminence in a ground adjoining to the city [Bristol] to about three thousand people." He did not *choose* this position; he was rather averse to it; but he accepted it as the best that offered to preach Christ and save souls. And God evidently approved, for "many who had set all laws, human and divine, at defiance, and were utterly without God in the world, now fell before the majesty of heaven, and acknowledged that 'a prophet was sent among them.' Cries and tears on every hand frequently drowned his voice, while many exclaimed, in the bitterness of their soul, 'What must I do to be saved?' Not a few of these were soon '*filled with peace and joy in believing*,' and evidenced that the work was really of God, by holy, happy, and unblamable walking before him. Blasphemies were now turned to praise, and the voice of joy and gladness was found where wickedness and misery reigned before."

The result of this *new measure* was the formation of a society in Bristol like the one in London. The object of their association was to build each other up in the faith of Christ, in order to which they agreed to meet together. But here was a difficulty, they had no place sufficiently large to accommodate them. This suggested the idea of building a room, which, having expanded into a plan of a house to accommodate such as wished to be present at the *preaching* as well as the society meetings, the corner-stone of the first Methodist meeting-house the world ever saw was laid on Saturday, May 12th, 1739.

The peculiar settlement of this house, and the circumstances which led to it, and justified it, explain a feature in Methodist economy that has not been well understood. We will give Mr. Wesley's account of the matter in his own words: "I had not at first," says he, "the least apprehension or design of being personally engaged either in the expense of the work, or in the direction of it; having appointed eleven feoffees, on whom I supposed these burdens would fall, of course. But I quickly found my mistake: first, with regard to the expense; for the whole undertaking must have stood still had not I immediately taken upon myself the payment of all the workmen; so that before I knew where I was I had contracted a debt of more than a hundred and fifty pounds; and this I was to discharge how I could, the subscriptions of both societies not amounting to one-quarter of the sum. And as to the direction of the work, I presently received letters from my friends in London, Mr. Whitefield in particular, backed with a message by one just come from thence, that neither he nor they would have any thing to do with the building, nor contribute any thing towards it, unless I would instantly discharge all feoffees, and do every thing in my own name. Many reasons they gave for this; but one was enough, viz.: 'That such feoffees would always have it in their power to control me, and, if I preached not as they liked, to turn me out of the room I had built.' I accordingly yielded to their advice, and, calling all the feoffees together, cancelled [no man opposing] the instruments made before, and took the whole management into my own hands. Money, it is true, I had not, nor any human prospect or probability of procuring it. But I knew 'the earth is the Lord's and the fulness thereof,' and in his name set out, nothing doubting."

From this time the work of God spread in every direction, triumphing over the prejudices and opposition of men of various ranks and conditions, and effecting such results on the hearts and lives of many as had never been seen before; and societies were formed in many places. Says Mr. Wesley: "Such a work this hath been in many respects as neither we nor our fathers had known. Not a few whose sins were of the most flagrant kind, drunkards, swearers, thieves, whoremongers, adulterers, have been brought *from darkness unto light, and from the power of Satan unto God.* Many of these were rooted in their wickedness, having long gloried in their shame, perhaps for a course of many years, yea, even to hoary hairs. Many had not so much as a rational faith, being Jews, Arians, Deists, or Atheists. Nor has God only made bare his arm in these last days in behalf of oper publicans and sinners, but many of the Pharisees also have believed on him; of the righteous, that seemed to need no repentance; and having received the sentence of death in themselves, have then heard the voice that raiseth the dead; have been made partakers of an inward, *vital religion,* even righteousness, peace and joy in the Holy Ghost.

"The *manner* wherein God hath wrought this work is as strange as the work itself. In any particular soul it has generally, if not always, been wrought in one moment. As the lightning shineth from heaven, so was the coming of the Son of Man, either to bring peace or a sword; either to wound or to heal; either to convince of sin, or to give remission of sins in his blood. And the other circumstances attending it have been equally remote from what human wisdom would have expected. So true is that word, 'My ways are not as your ways, nor my thoughts as your thoughts.' These extraordinary circumstances seem to have been designed by God for the further manifestation of his work, to cause his power to be known, and to awaken the attention of a drowsy world."

Not satisfied to confine the gospel within the limits of his own country, Mr. Wesley visited Wales, where, finding the churches shut against him, as at home, he preached Jesus in the streets and private dwellings with his usual power, and many were converted, and united together to run the race set before them.

By this time Mr. Charles Wesley had overcome his scruples about preaching out of church, and had joined with his brother and Mr. Whitefield in calling after sinners in the highways and hedges. But he was not a little annoyed by the attempt of a layman, a Mr. Bowers, to speak after he had closed, which was so palpable a breach of church order that both he and Mr. Whitefield declared against it. The necessity of such efforts had not yet appeared, nor had these men of God become so weaned from their church notions as to countenance the movement in any event not involving the command of God. This was the first attempt at lay preaching among them, and it met with so much opposition that Bowers soon confessed his errors and acquiesced in the judgment of his superiors. But the spirit that throbbed in his bosom was destined to speak out.

About this time the society in London fell into dangerous errors, by means of the Moravians, with whom they were intimately connected. This led to an able discussion of the points of difference, and finally to the division of the society, and the separation of Mr. Wesley from the Moravian body. These differences, together with the multiplication of societies, suggested the importance of having some definite basis of union; which, while it should invite all serious persons to the highest privileges of the gospel, would authorize the pastors of the flock to eject such from their fellowship as should prove themselves unworthy of confidence. This necessity was supplied by the adoption of that most excellent code in our Discipline, entitled, "*The General Rules of our United Societies*." [See *Dis.*, *pp.* 30–31.

Things now seemed to be settling into a more systematic and permanent state. The Wesleys were seeing eye to eye as they had not always done. Mr. Whitefield, and various others of the regular clergy, were with them in spirit and in effort, as far as it was practicable in their different circumstances; and other appearances were flattering. But no slight shade was soon cast over their prospects by an occurrence the least anticipated. Mr. Whitefield departed from the faith. Having made a second tour in America, and been cordially received by many of the Calvinistic clergy, who held almost the entire religious influence in the northern States at the time, he had been induced to read their writings and adopt their creed. The consequence was just what might have been expected, viz.: debate and alienation. It is impossible for men to avoid being influenced by their opinions. Having embraced Calvinism, how could he coöperate with Mr. Wesley as before? His new opinions positively forbade it. He could avoid controversy, and he did so, to considerable extent. But his friends and sympathizers felt it their duty to explode the Arminian heresy, as Methodism was called, and they were not always scrupulous about the means they employed to do it.

Says Mr. Moore: "The disturbance which this opinion occasioned at Bristol, and the parts adjacent, was not so soon or so easily quieted. Mr. Wesley had permitted an excellent young man, Mr. Cennick, afterwards a minister of the Moravian Church, to pray with and exhort the society at Kingsword, as well as to superintend the school during his absence. Mr. Cennick now embraced the doctrine of the decrees; and soon after seems to have lost all love and respect for his former friend, speaking against him and his doctrine with much contempt and bitterness. The consequence was that, after some fruitless efforts to heal the breach, Mr. Cennick departed, and carried off with him about *fifty* of the society, whom he formed into a separate connection. Mr. Wesley mourned over this young man in such a manner as evinced that he held him in high esteem."

Fearing nothing for the cause, and especially from contention, all things being ordained from everlasting, those who sympathized with Mr. Whitefield improved every opportunity to make converts to their new opinions. This occasioned no little disquietude. If the doctrines of Whitefield and his followers were true, Methodism must be false. Being diametrically opposed to each other at the same point, both could not be true.

To meet the emergency, Mr. Wesley printed a sermon on Predestination, exposing the absurdity of the particular views contended for by the Calvinists. This gave considerable offence, and led to a separation of the two parties, an event much to be regretted in many respects; but which, considering the doctrinal differences existing among them.

was indispensable to the success of either. The truth is, the two systems are antagonistic to each other. It is not possible to harmonize them. One of them is essentially false, and cannot coöperate with the other without creating a controversy. This is true, whether we look at the subject in the light of facts, philosophy, or religion. And hence we regard all attempts to effect an amalgamation of religious elements, thus radically discordant, as worse than in vain. The *best*, we believe, that can be done in such cases, is what Wesley and Whitefield (bating the use of some few emphatic expressions) did, viz.: to separate, and work out their respective systems with all possible energy; but still, so to love each other as Christians, and the cause of God, as to rejoice in each other's success in winning souls to Christ, and contribute to each other's comfort and efficiency as far as practicable without impairing his own.

This these two men of God did in a high degree. True, they spake very, perhaps too plainly to each other, in a few letters that passed between them; but, after all, they loved as brethren; and Mr. Wesley closed the controversy by saying, "How easy it were for me to hit many other palpable blots, in that which you call an answer to my sermon! And how above measure contemptible would you then appear to all men, either of sense or learning? But I spare you; mine hand shall not be upon you. The Lord be judge between me and thee! The general tenor both of my public and private exhortations, when I touch thereon at all as even my enemies know, if they would testify, is, '*Spare the young man, even Absalom, for my sake.*'"

How kindly these remarks were received is indicated by the following words, in a letter from Mr. Whitefield, written some months after: "I long to hear from you, and write this hoping to have an answer. I rejoice to hear the Lord blesses your labors. May you be blessed in bringing souls to Christ more and more! I believe we shall go on best when we only preach the simple gospel, and do not interfere with each other's plan. * * * Brother Charles has been pleased to come and see me twice. Behold, what a happy thing it is for brethren to dwell together in unity! That the whole Christian world may all become of one heart and one mind; and that *we*, in particular, though differing in judgment, may be examples of mutual, fervent, undissembled affection, is the hearty prayer of, reverend and dear sir, your most affectionate, though most unworthy, younger brother in the kingdom and patience of Jesus." This letter was answered in the same brotherly spirit, and the mutual regard of these excellent men suffered no diminution to the last. So that Mr. Whitefield found it in his heart to record in his last will and testament, "I leave a mourning ring to my honored and dear friends, and distinguished fellow laborers, the Rev. Messrs. John and Charles Wesley, in token of my indissoluble union with them, in heart and Christian affection, notwithstanding our difference in judgment about some particular points of doctrine." Under the impulse of the same feeling, he often expressed a wish to have Mr. Wesley preach his funeral sermon, should he die first, which he did, and in which he gave a full proof of profound love for the partner of his youthful conflicts.

Another necessity to be provided for, arising from the growing state of the societies, was the increasing demand for laborers. Mr. Wesley's desire was that the established clergy should watch over such as he and his associates had brought to repentance, and encourage them in faith and practice, as their spiritual interests required. But they did no such thing. They conducted towards them, in most cases, more like *wolves* than *shepherds*, ridiculing their religion, repelling them from the Lord's table, and otherwise hindering rather than helping them. The result was, many turned back to the world, and plunged into sin, as their legal pastors had taught them.

How to remedy this difficulty was a question. Every society needed a pastor; but the pastors were few, and these must travel all over the kingdom. This suggested the selection of some one from among themselves, of deep piety, and sound judgment in divine things, and request him to meet the others and confirm them, by reading, conversation, and prayer, as he might be able. No other plan seemed at all practicable, and this would not always serve well, for the want of the right style of men, as we have seen in the case of Mr. Cennick, who was one of the first appointed to this office, and the very first to divide the society and set up an independent meeting.

The society in London had suffered much by false teaching, and been considerably scattered. Therefore, as Mr. Wesley was about to leave the city, he appointed a young man, a Mr. Maxfield, whom he considered sound in the faith, to meet it at the usual times, and, by such means as were suitable for a layman, to encourage the members to stand forth in the liberty wherewith Christ had made them free. Being fervent in spirit, and mighty in the Scriptures, he pleased and profited the people greatly, and demonstrated the wisdom of the lay pastorate involved in this novel scheme.

But Providence had designs beyond the mere establishment of the little flock. The talent and energy of Maxfield attracted many to his meetings, whose attention indicated that they were a people prepared for the Lord. This led him a little further than he at first designed, or than was consistent with the prevailing notions of church order at that time. He began to *preach*. But notwithstanding it was not quite orderly, the Lord blessed the effort, and many were deeply awakened and brought to the joyful knowledge of the truth. This, however, did not justify the "*irregularity*" in the esteem of some. There are individuals in most places who hold church order above every other consideration. God must work by their rules, and sinners be converted in their way, or there will be trouble. So it was in this case. While not a few rejoiced in the glorious results of this strange innovation, many trembled for the honor of the priestly office, and complaint was rife on all sides. Mr. Wesley, being directly informed of the *disorder*, hastened to London to arrest it. But before he came to the immediate agent of the trouble, the timely advice of his ever considerate and pious mother moderated his displeasure, and suggested the propriety of an examination, which at first was not thought necessary. Seeing, on his arrival, that something troubled him, she inquired what it was; to which he abruptly replied, "Thomas Maxfield has turned preacher, I find." Looking him attentively in the face, "John," said she, "you know what my sentiments have been. You cannot suspect me of favoring readily any thing of this kind. But take care what you do with respect to that young man, for he is as surely called of God to preach as you are. Examine what have been the fruits of his preaching, and hear him for yourself." He did so, and was constrained to say, "*It is the Lord. Let him do what seemeth to him good.*"

"In other places, also," says the biographer of Mr. Wesley, "the same assistance was afforded." But he submitted to it with reluctance. His high church principles stood in his way. But, such effects were produced, he frequently found himself in the condition of Peter, who, being questioned in a matter somewhat similar, could only relate the fact, and say, "*What was I, that I could withstand God.*"

"But the Lord was about to show him greater things than these. An honest man, a mason, of Bristol, in Yorkshire, whose name was John Nelson, coming up to London to work at his trade, heard that word which he found to be the '*power of God unto salvation.*' Nelson had full business in London, and large wages. But from the time of making his peace with God it was continually on his mind that he must return to his native place. He did so about Christmas, in the year 1740. His relations and acquaintances soon began to inquire 'what he thought of this new faith? And whether he believed there was any such thing as a man's knowing that his sins were forgiven?' John told them, point blank, 'that this new faith, as they called it, was the old faith of the gospel; and that he himself was as sure that his sins were forgiven as he could be of the shining of the sun.' This was soon noised abroad, and more and more came to inquire concerning these strange things. Some put him upon the proofs of the great truths which such inquiries naturally led him to mention. And thus he was brought unawares to quote, explain, compare, and enforce several parts of Scripture. This he did, at first sitting in his house, till the company increased so that the house could not contain them. Then he stood at the door, which he was commonly obliged to do in the evening, as soon as he came from work. God immediately set his seal to what was spoken; and several believed, and therefore declared that God was merciful also to their unrighteousness, and had forgiven all their sins.

"Here was a preacher, and a large congregation, many

of whom were happy partakers of the faith of the gospel, raised up without the direct interference of Mr. Wesley. He therefore now fully acquiesced in the order of God, and rejoiced that the thoughts of God were not as his thoughts."

Thus we have the origin of lay preaching, to which Methodism, under God, is so much indebted. Who that is not blinded by Popish notions of apostolic succession, can fail to see that it was a divine conception, and owes its existence to the direct appointment of Providence! Though the ministry has greatly increased since, it has not yet superseded the necessity of this appliance, because the people have increased also, and, after all, there are fields of ministerial usefulness to be occupied that it is not in the power of the regular clergy to supply. But more of this hereafter.

This new development introduced Mr. Wesley to Yorkshire, where he labored much, and where religion has taken deeper root than in almost any other part of England. And it opened the way to other fields, and so the work of God spread; but not without other difficulties than those already mentioned. Since Mr. Wesley's separation from the Moravians, some of his old friends had left him and gone over to them; but what was most painful of all, his brother Charles manifested strong tendencies in the same direction. This was a trying circumstance. But still he trusted in the Lord, having no separate interest to promote, and wrote his brother a pathetic letter, in which we find these words: "O! my brother, my soul is grieved for you; the poison is in you; fair words have stolen away your heart. 'No English man or woman is like the Moravians!' So the matter is come to a fair issue. Five of us did stand together a few months since, but two are gone to the right hand,

(Hutchins and Cennick,) and two more to the left, (Mr. Hall and you.) Lord, if it be thy gospel which I preach, arise and maintain thine own cause."

This letter took effect, and brought his brother more fully into union with himself and into the itinerant work. He immediately proceeded to Oxford, and from thence to Gloucester, and elsewhere, preaching Jesus in various places, but chiefly in the highways and hedges, from Whitefield's pulpit—the stone wall; and thousands flocked to hear him, upon whom God wrought with power. Convictions were often quick and distressing, and conversions sudden and clear as the meridian sun. To show that God is no respecter of person or rank, the work extended to all grades of society, if we except those of the highest fashion and folly, who generally avoid the gospel altogether. The poor colliers especially drank deep at the fountain of life, and manifested the most astonishing improvement that grace ever produced. June 22d, says Mr. Wesley: "I went again to learn Christ among our colliers, and drink into their spirit. We rejoiced for the consolation. God knows their poverty; but they are rich, and daily entering into his rest. They do not hold it necessary to deny weak faith in order to get strong. Their souls truly wait upon God in his ordinances. Ye many masters, come learn Christ of these outcasts; for know that, except ye be converted and become like these little children, ye cannot enter into the kingdom of heaven."

The new religion also gave its subjects wonderful victory over death. Speaking of a sister Hooper, says Mr. Wesley: "I asked her whether she was not in great pain? 'Yes,' she answered, 'but in greater joy. I would not be without either.' 'But do you not prefer either life or death?' She replied, 'All is alike to me; let Christ choose; I have no will of my own.' I spoke with her physician, who said he had little hope of her recovery; 'only,' he added, 'she has no dread upon her spirits, which is generally the worst symptom. Most people die for fear of dying; but I never met with such people as yours. They are none of them afraid of death; but calm, and patient, and resigned to the last.'"

The glorious effects of these itinerant labors extorted concessions from Dr. Whitehead which his prejudices would not have allowed under ordinary circumstances. He observes: —

"Viewing *itinerant* preaching in this light, we see its importance, and must acknowledge that the authors of it deserve great praise; especially as they introduced it by their own example, under great difficulties and hardships. Their prospects in life, from their learning, their abilities, and their rank in society, were all sacrificed to the plan of itinerancy. They had every thing to lose by it, reputation, health, and the esteem of their friends; and nothing in this world to gain, but great bodily fatigue, ill usage from the mob, and general contempt. And as only three persons united together in the plan, they could not expect to form any extensive or permanent establishment. It is evident from their writings that these three servants of God did not look to any distant consequences of their proceedings. They contented themselves with doing as much good as possible in the way which opened before them; and they truly labored also for their own continuance in the faith, knowing that unfaithfulness to their calling would impair, and in the issue destroy it."

This brings us to consider another necessity of the cause and its supply. Mr. Wesley had been induced to form his followers into societies, from observing that where they were not thus formed they soon relapsed into their former habits; and the experiment showed the wisdom of the measure. A little reflection also convinced him that this was the very course pursued from the beginning of Christianity. He had been constrained to preach in the highways, and other unconsecrated places, by the closing of the churches against him, and he had felt compelled to allow pious laymen to exhort, and even *preach*, by the refusal of the regular clergy to do their duty and watch over the souls of inquirers, and give them such instructions as they needed.

But still there were frequent defections which brought great scandal upon the cause, and yet no remedy appeared. "At length," Mr. Wesley remarks, "while we were thinking of quite another thing, we struck upon a method for which we have cause to bless God ever since. I was talking with several of the society in Bristol concerning the means of paying the debts there; when one stood up and said, 'Let every member of the society give a *penny* a week till all are paid.' Another answered, 'But many are poor and cannot afford to do it.' 'Then,' said he, 'put eleven of the poorest with me, and if they can give any thing, well. I will call on them weekly, and if they can give nothing, I will give for them as well as for myself. And each of you can call on eleven of your neighbors weekly; receive what they give, and make up what is wanting.' It was done. In a while some of these informed me, 'they found such and such a one did not live as he ought.' It struck me immediately, 'this is the thing, the very thing we have wanted so long.' I called together all the leaders of the classes, [so they called the collectors,] and desired that each would make a particular inquiry into the behavior of those whom he saw weekly. They did so. Many disorderly walkers were detected. Some turned from the evil of their ways. Some were put away from us. Many saw it with fear, and rejoiced unto God with reverence."

The same arrangement was soon adopted in London, and in all the other societies, with the happiest effect. Each leader was required to see every member of his class once a week, at least, to inquire after the prosperity of their souls; to advise, reprove, or exhort, as it was found necessary; to receive what they were disposed to give for the relief of the poor; and to meet the minister, and stewards, &c., as at the present time. This arrangement, we believe, has never been abrogated in any branch of the Methodist family, and it is to be hoped that it never will be. But at first the leaders visited the members at their own houses. This was soon found to be very inconvenient, and in some cases impracticable. Hence it was agreed that the members of each class should meet together once a week, and the leader was required to visit only those who might be absent. So much for the history of our classes.

About this time intelligence reached Mr. Wesley that the brethren at Kingswood had fallen into the practice of occasionally spending the greater part of the night in prayer and praise. At the same time he was advised to put an end to it, as a disorder that could not be tolerated without danger to the cause. But the fact that it was a new measure was not sufficient to satisfy him that it might not be right and useful, nor the other fact that it was opposed. He took time, therefore, to "weigh the thing thoroughly," and finding a practice among the early Christians of much the same character, he could not persuade himself to forbid it. For the sake of obtaining fuller information as to the meetings themselves, he sent word to the watching brethren that he would watch with them on the Friday nearest the full moon. He did so, preaching at eight or nine, and con tinuing the exercises a little beyond midnight, praying and praising God amid a throng of spectators. The effect was good. God so wrought by this means that it was introduced in other places, and continued once a month for a long time. Some of the opposers thought the effect attributable to the novelty of the thing, or, perhaps, to the silence of the night, to which Mr. Wesley wisely replied, "I am not careful to answer in this matter. Be it so. However, the impression then made on many souls has never since been effaced. Now, allowing that God did make use of either the novelty or any other indifferent circumstance, in order to bring sinners to repentance, yet they are brought; and herein let us rejoice together."

Thus, our *watch meetings* originated, like lay preaching, in what was regarded the excessive zeal of individuals; and though by no means as serviceable to the cause, they have no doubt proved an efficient auxiliary in saving souls from death.

It was about this time also that another custom was started, viz.: the giving of quarterly tickets to the faithful of the flock. It happened on this wise: as the society increased, Mr. Wesley saw the necessity of greater care to separate the precious from the vile; and determined to converse with each member once in three months personally. In carrying this purpose into effect, it occurred that it might be well for him to give such as he found walking in the truth some testimonial of character and connection with the society. For this purpose he prepared a ticket, which, being publicly explained, had all the form of a full length recommendation. Those who bore these *tessera*, as the ancients called them, were acknowledged by their brethren of other societies, and received with cordiality. They also found ready access to all the society meetings; while those whose conduct had been such as to render them unworthy of receiving the quarterly tickets were excluded.

The practice thus started has been of excellent service in more ways than one. Though it has not been rigidly carried out, particularly in this country, it is nevertheless among our regulations, and will vary in its application and utility just as the ministry varies in its pastoral fidelity. Originating in an effort to be more critical in watching over the flock, and defending it from the corrupting influence of unworthy characters, it will always be found useful in the execution of this holy design.

The same grand pursuit suggested the *band meetings* also. Many were anxious for a more intimate union. They had conflicts it would not be proper to detail in a promiscuous society, but in relation to which they needed counsel no less than on other points. "In compliance with their desire," says Mr. Wesley, "I divided them into smaller companies; putting the married or single men, and married or single women, together. In order to increase in them a grateful sense of all the mercies of the Lord, I desired that one evening in a quarter they should all come together, that we might '*eat bread*' (as the ancient Christians did) *with gladness and singleness of heart*." This was the origin of our *love feasts*, of the nature and influence of which we shall speak more particularly in another place.

Thus we see that these peculiarities of Methodism were of providential origin, springing out of the spiritual necessities of the pious, and of perishing sinners. There seems to have been no planning, no human ingenuity, no speculation. Mr. Wesley's plans were the *plans of the Episcopal Church*. He *knew* no other, he *wanted* no other, till the necessity appeared, and the measure stood up before him like a real *presence;* and then he adopted it for the sake of the cause, though in doing so he had to depart from a long cherished system of operations, to which he had adhered with undeviating tenacity.

Mr. Wesley had now a number of helpers after his own heart; besides many class and band leaders, whose services were indispensable to his benevolent designs. The preaching of the word was with power. It was generally extemporaneous, and directly adapted to the circumstances of the people, as the sermons of other clergy were not. The hearers, even the low and despised, listened with astonishment, and, regarding it as a message from God to them, made haste to " repent and be converted." Several soldiers of the British army, whom the Holy Spirit had conquered, going into Germany, began to preach Jesus to the army, and great was the power of God that attended them.

Mr. Haime, writing to Mr. Wesley, says. " We remained in this camp eight days, and then removed to a place called Arsk. Here I began to speak openly at a small distance from the camp, just in the middle of the English army. We sung a hymn, which drew about two hundred soldiers together, and they all behaved decently. After I had prayed, I began to exhort them; and, though it rained, very few went away. Many acknowledged the truth; in particular a young man, John Greenwood, who has kept with me ever since, and whom God has lately been pleased to give me for a fellow laborer. Our society is now increased to upwards of two hundred, and the hearers are frequently more than a thousand; although many say I am mad, and others have endeavored to incense the field marshal against us. I have been sent for and examined several times. But blessed be God, he has always delivered me."

One of his hearers, who cried out to his comrades to " *come away*, and not hear that fool any longer," received an arrow to his heart, and "roared out in the bitterness of his soul," till God turned his heaviness into joy.

John Evans wrote of this same *divine:* "I believed myself a very good Christian till we came to winter quarters, where I met with John Haime. But I was soon sick of his company: for he robbed me of my treasure; he stole away my gods, telling me I and my works were going to hell together. This was strong doctrine to me. When the Lord had opened my eyes, and shown me that 'by grace we are saved through faith,' I began immediately to declare it to others, though I had not as yet experienced it myself. But Oct. 23d, as William Clements was at prayer, I felt on a sudden a great alteration in my soul. My eyes overflowed with tears of love. I knew I was through Christ reconciled to God; which inflamed my soul with fervent love to him, whom I now saw to be my complete Redeemer. O, the tender care of Almighty God in bringing up his children!"

But it must not be imagined that this growing cause was not opposed. The spirit that christened its early friends "*Methodists*" at Oxford, found sympathy in other places. The clergy generally threw themselves directly in the way, and exerted their influence against it. They had refused the preachers the use of their pulpits, and otherwise treated them as heretics and vagabonds. Mr. Wesley had been denied the privilege of preaching in the church of his native place, where his father had been rector many years, and therefore preached on his father's tombstone to such a congregation as Epworth had never seen. The members in many places, though correct in life and filled with the spirit, had been repelled from the sacrament, while infidels, and swearers, and almost every other kind of carnal and wicked men, had been admitted without objection. Sermons had been preached denouncing the whole fraternity as a pestilent concern, that ought not to be tolerated; and from the bishops down to their lowest clerical vassals, there was a hue and cry of hostility, not very dissimilar to that raised by the Scribes and Pharisees, under the ministrations of Jesus of Nazareth.

With such an example in the house of God, among the *priests* themselves, it was not difficult to predict a storm from without, which would have no limits, except such as God might be pleased to interpose. And so it came to pass. The new sect being every where spoken against by people of rank and religion, the tools by which they execute their nefarious and illegal will, — the rabble, — pursued them from place to place with sword in hand, and, but for the protection of Omnipotence, would have hurled them to oblivion.

In London, the society was often attacked with showers of stones; and once an attempt was made to unroof the Foundry where they were assembled; and for some time there seemed to be no redress. In the beginning of 1743 Mr. Wesley visited Wednesbury, where, in the course of three months, so powerful was the work of God, a society was formed, consisting of some three or four hundred members. But Satan came also among them. The minister of the place, with several *justices*, stirred up the baser sort of people to outrages of the grossest kind. "Mobs were summoned together by the sound of the horn; men, women, and children, were abused in the most shocking manner, being beaten, stoned, and covered with mud. Women in delicate circumstances were treated in a manner that cannot be mentioned. In the mean time, their houses were broken open by any that pleased, and their goods spoiled or carried away; some of the owners standing by, but not daring to oppose, as it would have been at the peril of their lives."

We have only room to narrate the circumstances of one

or two mobs, among the hundreds with which the church was infested in those times. But these sufficiently indicate the ferocity of the enemies, and the kind intervention of Divine Providence, to give some idea of what infant Methodism had to withstand, and the help she obtained. We give the account in Mr. Wesley's own words. The scene of the transactions was Wednesbury, where he preached in the open air, at 12 o'clock. He says: —

"I was writing at Francis Ward's in the afternoon, when the cry arose that 'the mob had beset the house.' We prayed that God would disperse them. And it was so; so that in half an hour not a man was left. I told our brethren, 'Now is the time for us to go;' but they pressed me exceedingly to stay. So, that I might not offend them, I sat down, though I foresaw what would follow. Before five, the mob surrounded the house again, in greater numbers than ever. The cry of one and all was, 'Bring out the minister; we *will* have the minister.' I desired one to take their captain by the hand and bring him into the house. After a few sentences interchanged between us, the lion was become a lamb. I desired him to go and bring one or two of the most angry of his companions. He brought in two who were ready to swallow the ground with rage; but in two minutes they were as calm as he. I then bade them make way, that I might go out among the people. As soon as I was in the midst of them I called for a chair, and, standing up, asked, 'What do any of you want with me?' Some said, 'We want you to go with us to the Justice.' I replied, 'That I will with all my heart!' I then spoke a few words, which God applied; so that they cried out with might and main, 'The gentleman is an honest gentleman, and we will spill our blood in his defence!' I asked, 'Shall we go to the Justice to-night, or in the morning?' Most of them cried, 'To-night! to-night!' On which, I went before, and two or three hundred followed.

"The night came before we had walked a mile, together with heavy rain. However, on we went to Bentley Hall, two miles from Wednesbury. One or two ran before, to tell Mr. Lane, 'they had brought Mr. Wesley before his worship.' Mr. Lane replied, 'What have I to do with Mr. Wesley? Go and carry him back again.' By this time the main body came up, and began knocking at the door. A servant told them, 'Mr. Lane was in bed.' His son followed, and asked, 'what was the matter?' One replied, 'Why, an't please you, they sing psalms all day; nay, and make folks rise at five in the morning. And what would your worship advise us to do?' 'To go home,' said Mr. Lane, 'and be quiet.'

"Here they were at a full stop, till one advised 'to go to Justice Persehouse, at Walsal.' All agreed to this. So we hastened on, and about seven came to his house. But Mr. Persehouse likewise sent word that 'he was in bed.' Now they were at a stand again; but at last they all thought it the wisest course to make the best of their way home. About fifty of them undertook to convoy me. But we had not gone a hundred yards when the mob of Walsal came pouring in like a flood. and bore down all before them. The Darlaston mob made what defence they could; but they were weary, as well as out-numbered. So that, in a short time, many being knocked down, the rest ran away, and left me in their hands.

"To attempt speaking was vain; for the noise on every side was like the roaring of the sea. So they dragged me along till we came to the town; where, seeing the door of a large house open, I attempted to go in; but a man, catching me by the hair, pulled me back into the middle of the mob. They made no more stop till they had carried me through the main street. I continued speaking all the time to those within hearing, feeling no pain or weariness. At the west end of the town, seeing a door half open, I made towards it, and would have gone in; but a gentleman in the shop would not suffer me, saying, 'they would pull the house down to the ground.' However, I stood at the door, and asked, 'Are you willing to hear me speak?' Many cried out, 'No, no! knock his brains out! down with him! kill him at once!' Others said, 'Nay; but we will hear him first!' I began asking, 'What evil have I done? Which of you all have I wronged in word or deed?' and continued speaking above a quarter of an hour, till my voice suddenly failed. Then the floods began to lift up their voice again; many crying out, 'Bring him away! Bring him away!'

"In the mean time, my strength and my voice returned, and I broke out aloud into prayer. And now the man who just before headed the mob, turned and said, 'Sir, I will spend my life for you. Follow me, and not one soul here shall touch a hair of your head.' Two or three of his fellows confirmed his words, and got close to me immediately. At the same time the gentleman in the shop cried out, 'For shame! For shame! Let him go!' An honest butcher, who was a little farther off, said 'it was a shame they should do thus;' and pulled back four or five, one after another, who were running on the most fiercely. The people then, as if it had been by common consent, fell back to the right and left; while those three or four men took me between them, and carried me through them all. But, on the bridge, the mob rallied again; we therefore went on one side, over the mill-dam, and thence through the meadows, till, a little before ten, God brought me safe to

Wednesbury; having lost only one flap of my waistcoat, and a little skin from one of my hands.

"I never saw such a chain of providences before; so many convincing proofs that the hand of God is on every person and thing, over-ruling as it seemeth him good.

"A poor woman in Darlaston, who had headed that mob, and sworn 'that none should touch me,' when she saw her fellows give way, ran into the thickest of the throng, and knocked down three or four men, one after another. But many assaulting her at once, she was soon overpowered, and had probably been killed in a few minutes, (three or four men keeping her down, and beating her with all their might,) had not a man called out to them, 'Hold, Tom, hold!' 'Who is there?' said Tom. 'What, honest Munchin? Nay, then, let her go.' So they held their hands, and let her get up and crawl home as well as she could.

"From the beginning to the end, I found the same presence of mind as if I had been sitting in my study. But I took no thought for one moment before another; only once it came into my mind, that if they should throw me into the river, it would spoil the papers that were in my pocket. For myself, I did not doubt but I should swim across, having but a thin coat, and a light pair of boots.

"By how gentle degrees does God prepare us for his will! Two years ago, a piece of brick grazed my shoulders. It was a year after that a stone struck me between the eyes. Last month, I received one blow; and this evening, two — one before we came into town, and one after we were gone out. But both were as nothing; for, though one man struck me on the breast with all his might, and the other on the mouth with such force that the blood gushed out imme diately, I felt no more pain from either of the blows than if they had touched me with a straw.

"It ought not to be forgotten that, when the rest of the society made all haste to escape for their lives, four only would not stir, — William Sitch, Edward Slater, John Griffiths, and Joan Parks. These kept with me, resolving to live or die together. And none of them received one blow but William Sitch, who held me by the arm from one end of the town to the other. He was then dragged away and knocked down; but he soon rose and got to me again. I afterwards asked him, 'what he expected when the mob came upon us?' He said, 'To die for him who had died for us;' and added, 'that he felt no hurry or fear, but calmly waited till God should require his soul of him.'"

At St. Ivers, Mr. Wesley was roughly handled, and the preaching house was pulled down to the ground; but we will only mention the particulars of his visit to Falmouth, which we find stated in his Journal.

"Thursday, July 4. — I rode to Falmouth. About three in the afternoon I went to see a gentlewoman who had been indisposed. Almost as soon as I sat down, the house was beset on all sides by an innumerable multitude of people. A louder or more confused noise could hardly be at the taking of a city by storm. At first, Mrs. B. and her daughter endeavored to quiet them; but it was labor lost. They might as well have attempted to still the raging of the sea, and were, therefore, soon glad to shift for themselves The rabble roared with all their throats, 'Bring out the *Canorum!* Where is the *Canorum?*' (an unmeaning word which the Cornish rabble then used instead of *Methodist.*) No answer being given, they quickly forced open the outer door, and filled the passage. Only a wainscot partition was between us, which was not likely to stand long. I immediately took down a large looking glass which hung against it, supposing the whole side would fall in at once. They began their work with abundance of bitter imprecations. A poor girl who was left in the house was utterly astonished, and cried out, 'O, sir, what must we do?' I said, 'We must pray.' Indeed, at that time, to all appearance, our lives were not worth an hour's purchase. She asked, 'But, sir, is it not better for you to hide yourself? To get into the closet?' I answered, 'No. It is best for me to stand just where I am.' Among those without were the crews of some privateers which were lately come into the harbor. Some of these, being angry at the slowness of the rest, thrust them away, and coming up all together, set their shoulders to the inner door, and cried out, 'Avast, lads, avast!' Away went all the hinges at once, and the door fell back into the room. I stepped forward into the midst of them, and said, 'Here I am. Which of you has any thing to say to me? To which of you have I done any wrong? To you? Or you? Or you?' I continued speaking till I came into the middle of the street, and then raising my voice, said, 'Neighbors, countrymen, do you desire to hear me speak?' They cried vehemently, 'Yes, yes! he shall speak. He shall. Nobody shall hinder him.' But having nothing to stand on, and no advantage of ground, I could be heard by a few only. However, I spoke without intermission; and, as far as the sound reached, the people were still, till one or two of their captains turned about and swore, 'Not a man shall touch him.' Mr. Thomas, a clergyman, then came up, and asked, 'Are you not ashamed to use a stranger thus?' He was soon seconded by two or three gentlemen of the town, and one of the Aldermen, with whom I walked down the town, speaking all the time, till I came to Mrs. Maddern's house. The gentlemen proposed sending for my horse to the door, and desired me to step in and rest the mean time. But, on second thoughts, they judged it not advisable to let me go out among the people again. So they chose to send my horse before me to Penryn, and to send me thither by water; the sea running close by the back door of the house in which we were.

"I never saw before, no, not at Walsal itself, the hand of God so plainly shown as here. *There* I had some companions, who were willing to die with me; *here*, not a friend, but one simple girl, who likewise was hurried away from me in an instant, as soon as ever she came out of Mrs. B.'s house. *There*, I received some blows, lost part of my clothes, and was covered over with dirt. *Here*, although the hands of perhaps some hundreds of people were lifted up to strike or throw, they were one and all stopped in the midway, so that not a man touched me with one of his fingers. Neither was any thing thrown from first to last, so that I had not even a speck of dirt on my clothes. Who can deny that God heareth the prayer? Or that he hath all power in heaven and earth?"

But mobs were among the least obstructions to the work. They usually beget a sympathy, which, though it may not have courage to repel them, will operate in other ways, and under other circumstances, with good effect. Popular derision presents a much more effective resistance to any cause. And this, accompanied with every other species of opposition which learning, wealth, prejudice, and power can give, formed the mighty current that the Wesleyan movement had to resist. Nevertheless, by the peculiar blessing of heaven, it advanced with accumulating energy, achieving reforms among the lower classes that had been regarded utterly impracticable.

CHAPTER III.

THE FIRST CONFERENCE, WITH THE TRIALS AND SUCCESS THAT FOLLOWED.

FOR several years the preachers travelled from place to place as circumstances seemed to require, and as Mr. Wesley directed, without any plan. But as they became more numerous, and the work more extensive and complicated, it became necessary to divide the country into circuits, to be supplied by the different preachers according to rules that might be adopted for that purpose. To effect so difficult a task in a way not to disturb the unity of the body, and at the same time secure the greatest possible success, Mr. Wesley invited a number of the preachers to meet him for consultation. The first meeting was held at the Foundry, in London, June 25th, 1744, and consisted of six persons. The preachers thus met, Mr. Wesley denominated "*The Conference*," a title that is now better understood, and of high significance, both in Europe and America. The meeting continued five days, and was occupied, first of all, in prayer to God, for his guidance and blessing; and then, in the consideration of the great doctrinal and practical questions particularly involved in their enterprise.

That they might come to right conclusions, it was desired that all should have a single eye, and be as little children, having every thing to learn; that every point should be examined to the foundation; that each should speak whatever was in his heart, till every question should be thoroughly debated and settled. This being premised, the design of the meeting was stated to be, to consider, 1. What to teach. 2. How to teach. And 3. What to do; i. e., how to regulate our doctrine, discipline and practice. Whereupon, they proceeded step by step in the form of conversation, beginning with the doctrine of *justification*, till they had agreed upon most of the great principles which constitute the framework and strength of our ecclesiastical fabric.

With an improved acquaintance with each other, and a better understanding of, and a stronger attachment to, the doctrines and discipline in which they were so happily agreed, they were now prepared to instruct and regulate the societies as they had never been before. And as the result of these deliberations, the work of God advanced with greater uniformity, and the different societies became moulded and fashioned after the same image, as was necessary to consolidate them into one grand confederacy.

This was the beginning of *Conferences*, and lies at the foundation of that series of annual meetings of the preachers which has been extended to the present day. The second Conference commenced Aug. 1, 1745, and consisted of *ten* persons, convened, as before, by Mr. Wesley's invitation. Some years after he gave a general permission to all the preachers to attend, but soon retracted it. At these Conferences the character of the preachers was examined, points of doctrine and discipline reviewed as occasion required, complaints considered, and difficulties settled. The minutes of the several conversations held, formed the discipline of the societies. The last revision of them, by himself, was made in 1789, two years before his death.

Arrangements now being more fully established, and the

preachers assigned to particular fields of labor for a time, Mr. Wesley took occasion to reason with the established clergy, to whose ignorance and prejudice he attributed most of the persecutions the societies were called to endure. And wishing to do it in a manner the least offensive, he drew up a short state of the case between the clergy and the Methodists, and sent it to a personal friend, to be used as he should see fit. This document so clearly indicates the principles, character, and condition of the societies at that time, we cannot deny our young friends the privilege of reading it in this connection. Who will say that its demands are unreasonable?

"About seven years since we began preaching inward present salvation as attainable by faith alone. For preaching this doctrine, we were forbidden to preach in most churches. We then preached in private houses; and when the houses could not contain the people, in the open air. For this, many of the clergy preached or printed against us, as both heretics and schismatics. Persons who were convinced of sin begged us to advise them more particularly how to flee from the wrath to come. We desired them, being many, to come at one time, and we would endeavor it. For this we were represented, both from the pulpit and the press, as introducing Popery, and raising sedition. Yea, all manner of evil was said, both of us and of those who used to assemble with us. Finding that some of these *did* walk disorderly, we desired them not to come to us any more. And some of the others we desired to overlook the rest, that we might know whether they walked worthy of the gospel. Several of the clergy now stirred up the people to treat us as outlaws or mad dogs. The people did so, both in Staffordshire, Cornwall, and many other places. And they do so still, wherever they are not restrained by fear of the magistrates.

"Now, what can *we* do, or what can *you*, or our brethren do, towards healing this breach? Desire of *us* any thing which we can do with a safe conscience, and we will do it immediately. Will *you* meet us here? Will you do what we desire of you, so far as you can with a safe conscience?

"1. Do you desire us, To preach another, or to desist from preaching this doctrine? We cannot do this with a safe conscience.

"2. Do you desire us, To desist from preaching in *private houses, or in the open air?* As things are now circumstanced, this would be the same as desiring us not to preach at all.

"3. Do you desire us, Not to advise those who meet together for that purpose? To dissolve our societies? We cannot do this with a safe conscience; for, we apprehend, many souls would be lost thereby.

"4. Do you desire us, To advise them one by one? This is impossible, because of their number.

"5. Do you desire us, To suffer those who walk disorderly still to mix with the rest? Neither can we do this with a safe conscience; for '*evil communications corrupt good manners.*'

"6. Do you desire us, To discharge those *leaders*, as we term them, who overlook the rest? This is, in effect, to suffer the disorderly walkers still to remain with the rest.

"Do you desire us, *lastly*, to behave with tenderness, both to the characters and persons of our brethren the clergy? By the grace of God we can and will do this; as, indeed, we have done to this day.

"If you ask, What we desire of you to do? we answer:

1. We do not desire any of you to let us preach in your church, either if you believe us to preach false doctrine, or if you have the least scruple. But we desire any who believes us to preach true doctrine, and has no scruple in the matter, not to be either publicly or privately discouraged from inviting us to preach in his church.

"2. We do not desire that any who thinks it his duty to preach or print against us should refrain therefrom. But we desire, that none will do this till he has calmly considered both sides of the question; and that he would not condemn us unheard, but first read what we say in our own defence.

"3. We do not desire any favor if either Popery, sedition, or immorality be proved against us. But we desire you would not credit, without proof, any of those senseless tales that pass current with the vulgar; that, if you do not credit them yourselves, you will not relate them to others; yea, that you will discountenance those who still retail them abroad.

"4. We do not desire any preferment, favor, or recommendation, from those that are in power, either in Church or State. But we desire: 1. That if any thing material be laid to our charge, we may be permitted to answer for ourselves. 2. That you would hinder your dependents from stirring up the rabble against us, who are certainly not the proper judges in these matters; and 3. That you would effectually suppress and discountenance all riots and popular insurrections, which evidently strike at the foundation of all government, whether of Church or State."

While thus reasoning with the clergy, and other opposers of his movements, he was not unmindful of the conduct of his friends His advice to them was equally pertinent and instructive. Nothing could more clearly certify the high moral purity of his purpose, or the wisdom of his plan. The following is sufficient to indicate the view he took of the enterprise in which he was engaged.

"The FIRST general ADVICE which one who loves your souls would earnestly recommend to every one of you, is, Consider, with deep and frequent attention, the peculiar circumstances wherein you stand. One of these is, that you are a new people. Your name is new, (at least as used in a religious sense,) not heard of, till a few years ago, either in our own or any other nation. Your principles are new, in this respect, that there is no other set of people among us, (and possibly not in the Christian world,) who hold them all in the same degree and connection; who so strenuously and continually insist on the absolute necessity of universal holiness both in heart and life,—of a peaceful, joyous love of God,—of a supernatural evidence of things not seen,—of an inward witness that we are the children of God,—and of the inspiration of the Holy Ghost, in order to any good thought, or word, or work. And perhaps there is no other set of people, (at least not visibly united together,) who lay so much, and yet no more, stress than you do, on rectitude of opinions, on outward modes of worship, and the use of those ordinances which you acknowledge to be of God; and yet do not condemn any man upon earth merely for thinking otherwise than you do—much less to imagine that God condemns him for this, if he be upright and sincere of heart.

"Your strictness of life, taking the whole of it together, may likewise be accounted new. I mean, your making it a rule to abstain from fashionable diversions; your plainness of dress; your manner of dealing in trade; your exactness in observing the Lord's day; your scrupulosity as to things that have not paid custom; your total abstinence from spirituous liquors (unless in cases of extreme necessity;) your rule 'not to mention the fault of an absent person, in particular of ministers, or of those in authority,' may justly be termed new. For we do not find any body of people who insist on all these rules together.

"Consider these peculiar circumstances wherein you stand, and you will see the propriety of a SECOND ADVICE I would recommend to you: Do not imagine you can avoid giving offence. Your very name renders this impossible. And as much offence as you give by your name, you will give still more by your principles. You will give offence to the bigots for opinions, modes of worship, and ordinances, by laying no more stress upon them; to the bigots against them, by laying so much; to men of form, by insisting so frequently and strongly on the inward power of religion; to moral men, (so called,) by declaring the absolute necessity of faith, in order to acceptance with God; to men of reason you will give offence, by talking of inspiration and receiving the Holy Ghost; to drunkards, Sabbath breakers, common swearers, and other open sinners, by refraining from their company, as well as by that disapprobation of their behavior which you will be often obliged to express. Either, therefore, you must consent to give up your principles, or your fond hope of pleasing men. What makes even your principles more offensive is, this uniting of yourselves together; union renders you more conspicuous, placing you more in the eye of men; and more dreadful to those of a fearful temper; and more odious to men of zeal, if their zeal be any other than fervent love to God and man."

During the year 1764 Mr. Wesley traversed the most distant parts of the kingdom, and revivals prevailed in many places. He usually preached two or three times every day, and regulated the societies wherever he came. His whole heart was in the work, and his fixed resolution surmounted every difficulty.

"At this period, the preachers were not skilled beyond the first principles of religion, and the practical consequences deducible from them: '*repentance towards God, faith towards our Lord Jesus Christ,*' and the fruits that follow, '*righteousness, and peace, and joy in the Holy Ghost.*' These were the subjects of their daily discourses, and these truths they knew *in power.* But such was the low state of religious knowledge among the people that it was absolutely necessary to enforce these *first principles*, and to give them a practical influence on the heart and life, before they were led any farther. In these circumstances, the limited knowledge of the preachers was so far from being an inconvenience, that it was an unspeakable advantage, as it necessarily confined them to those fundamental points of experimental and practical religion which were best adapted to the state of the people. Ministers of diversified knowledge, but of little experience in the work of the Spirit of God, seldom dwell sufficiently in their sermons on these important points; and hence the preachers were far more successful in awakening sinners to a sense of their dangerous state, and in bringing them to a saving knowledge of Christ. To enforce the necessity of repentance. and of seeking salvation by grace alone through a Redeemer, the preacher would often draw a picture of human nature in such strong and natural colors that every one who heard him saw his own likeness in it, and was ready to say, '*He hath shown me all that was in my heart!*' The effect was surprising. The people found themselves, under every discourse, emerging out of the thickest darkness into a region of light, the blaze of which, being suddenly poured in upon them, gave exquisite pain at first, but soon showed them the way to peace and consolation. Mr. Wesley foresaw that as knowledge was increased among the people it ought to be increased in the same, or even in a greater, proportion among the preachers, otherwise they would become less useful. He, therefore, began to think of a collection of such books in the English language as might forward their improvement in treating of the various branches of practical divinity." — *Moore's Life of Wesley.*

This foresight, for which Mr. Wesley was so peculiar, led him to consultation, particularly with Dr. Doddridge, in regard to the selection of a library. The Doctor treated the subject with great courtesy, and furnished the list of books desired, notwithstanding the printer was driving him hard for copy to complete the third volume of his "Family Expositor." It was about this time that it was inserted in the minutes, for the benefit of the ministry: "Read the most useful books, and that regularly and constantly. Steadily spend all the morning in this employ, or, at least, five hours in the four-and-twenty.

"'But I read only the Bible.' Then you ought to teach others to read only the Bible, and, by parity of reason, to *hear* only the Bible. But if so, you need preach no more. Just so said George Bell. And what is the fruit? Why, now he neither reads the Bible nor any thing else. This is rank enthusiasm. If you need no book but the Bible, you are got above St. Paul. He wanted others, too. 'Bring the books,' says he, 'but especially the parchments,' — those wrote on parchment. 'But I have no taste for reading.' Contract a taste for it by use, or return to your trade.

"'But I have no books.' I will give each of you, as fast as you will read them, books to the value of five pounds. And I desire that the assistants would take care that all the large societies provide our works, or, at least, the notes, for the use of the preachers."

It was at this period, also, that Mr. Wesley originated the Kingswood School for the complete education of the young, where their morals would be secure. He had succeeded in the establishment of one for the children of the colliers, several years before, and was now looking to the interests of others in higher life. This school has done immense good, and, for many years, has been wholly devoted to the sons of the itinerant preachers.

How Mr. Wesley obtained the means of carrying forward so many interests involving expense, is partly explained by the following fact in connection with the establishment of this school. "He was mentioning to a lady, with whom he was in company in the neighborhood of Bristol, his desire and design of erecting a Christian school, such as would not disgrace the apostolic age. The lady was so well pleased with his views that she immediately went to her scrutoire, and brought him five hundred pounds in bank notes, desiring him to accept of them, and to enter upon his plan immediately. He did so. Afterwards, being in company with the same lady, she inquired how the building went on; and whether he stood in need of farther assistance. He informed her that he had laid out all the money he had received, and that he was three hundred pounds in debt; at the same time apologizing, and entreating her not to consider it as a concern of hers. But she immediately retired, and brought him the sum he wanted."

What his unparalleled plan of finance did not secure in small sums among the poor, the Providence of God supplied in this way. But that plan! Who has fully estimated it? The rules for the government of its operators, the stewards, show that it was sanctified by prayer, like every other part of his system. He earned and begged money only for God and his cause, and he would have the business transacted in the spirit of vital piety, as much as preaching, or any other religious duty. Hence he drafted and gave to his stewards the following rules: —

"1. You are to be men full of the Holy Ghost and of wisdom: that you may do all things in a manner acceptable to God. 2. You are to be present every Tuesday and Thursday morning, in order to transact the temporal affairs of the society. 3. You are to begin and end every meeting with earnest prayer to God for a blessing on all your undertakings. 4. You are to produce your accounts the first Tuesday in every month, that they may be transcribed into the ledger. 5. You are to take it in turn, month by month, to be chairman. The chairman is to see that all the rules be punctually observed, and immediately to check him who breaks any of them. 6. You are to do nothing without the consent of the minister, either actually had or reasonably presumed. 7. You are to consider, whenever you meet, 'God is here.' Therefore be serious. Utter no trifling word. Speak as in his presence, and to the glory of his great name. 8. When any thing is debated, let one at once stand up and speak, the rest giving attention. And let him speak just loud enough to be heard, in love and in the spirit of meekness. 9. You are continually to pray and endeavor that a holy harmony of soul may in all things subsist among you: that in every step you may keep the unity of the spirit in the bond of peace. 10. In all debates you are to watch over your spirits, avoiding, as fire, all clamor and contention; being '*swift to hear, slow to speak;*' in honor, every man preferring another before himself. 11. If you cannot relieve, do not grieve the poor. Give them soft words, if nothing else. Abstain from either sour looks or harsh words. Let them be glad to come, even though they should go empty away. Put yourselves in the place of every poor man; and deal with him as you would God should deal with you."

In 1747 a Mr. Williams crossed the channel and began to preach the new doctrine in Ireland. Hearing of his success, Mr. Wesley was soon by his side, but returned after a few weeks, and was followed by his brother and others, from whom Ireland received the word of life. The itinerants were now moving in all directions, toiling hard, and suffering every inconvenience imaginable but that of a guilty conscience and the frown of God. Mr. C. Wesley, writing to his brother from Dublin about buying a preaching house, that would also accommodate the preachers, says: "I must go there or to some other lodgings, or take my flight; for here I can stay no longer. A family of squalling children, a landlady just ready to lie in, a maid who has no time to do the least thing for us, are some of our conveniences! Our two rooms for four people (six, when J. Healy and Haughton come) allow no opportunity for retirement. Charles and I groan for elbow-room in our press-bed; our diet answerable to our lodgings; no one to mend our clothes and stockings; no money to buy more. I marvel that we have stood our ground so long in these lamentable circumstances."

These inconveniences, accompanied by the most bitter persecution that Popery and carnality could devise, were enough to discourage ordinary minds; but these men were prepared for the emergency. To the personal enjoyment of true piety was added unparalleled success. Though ridiculed, and even mobbed in almost every place, souls were awakened and converted in great numbers, and new societies sprung up in various places.

Besides the difficulties which arose from poverty, unpopularity, mobs, &c., Mr. Wesley had others to surmount in carrying out his design, and what he understood to be the purpose of God, that must not be overlooked. He had no thought of leaving the Established Church, and did not leave it till he was removed to the church triumphant. The societies he formed were parts of the church, and aimed not at separation, but greater improvement in the knowledge and love of God. This circumstance exposed him to two classes of complainers, which made him much trouble; namely, those who thought he went too far,—that having got the people converted, he ought to leave them to the watch-care of their legal pastors, particularly where they were truly pious, and not organize them into societies; and, on the other hand, those who thought he did not go far enough—that he ought to secede, and form an independent church.

The arguments of both parties bore an aspect of plausibility, to say the least; but they were manfully answered. His reason for not leaving his followers to the regular clergy was, generally, that it would prove fatal to their piety. Most of the clergy would treat them with derision, while the better disposed, and even the most pious among them, were incompetent to train up spiritual children, with whom they never "travailed in birth." His reason for not forming an independency was, not that none could be saved out of the church, but that he could better spread Scriptural holiness over the land by remaining in it, than by seceding, which was probably true at that time. Hence he resisted every solicitation to closer adherence to the church, and a greater departure from it; and drew near or receded, as his object seemed to require.

But some of the most serious obstacles Methodism had to overcome were introduced by her own members. We have referred to Mr. Maxfield as the first lay preacher that appeared in the Wesleyan ranks, a young man of talent and usefulness. He was ordained by Bishop Barnard, on the recommendation of Mr. Wesley; the bishop saying, at the time, "Sir, I ordain you to assist that good man, that he may not work himself to death."

Mr. Maxfield met the bishop's design admirably at the time, but afterward fell out by the way. It is all the same with the enemies of religion, whether its friends betray the cause by inactivity or enthusiasm; and often, when the devil fails in producing the first, he will succeed in the second. This seems to have been the case in London, where Mr. Maxfield was preaching. A revival was in powerful progress, notwithstanding much resistance, when some became wise above what is written, and *dreams, visions,* and *revelations* took possession of several minds, and were regarded of paramount authority. Mr. Maxfield encouraged the delusion, which made it necessary to guard a little against his influence, and induced Mr. Wesley to write him quickly all that was in his heart. (*Wesley's Works, vol.* 4, *p.* 140.)

But it had no good effect. Mr. Maxfield was too far gone to be recovered. He was at the bottom of the mischief, the very life of the cause, and stirred up the people against Mr. Wesley and the other preachers, as too cold and blind to teach them the deep things of the Spirit, such as he himself revealed. At length the crisis came, and a considerable number of the society left, Mr. Maxfield among the rest. "And from that time," says Mr. Wesley, "he has spake all manner of evil of me, his father, his friend, his greatest earthly benefactor." Mr. Maxfield lived about twenty years after his separation; and Mr. Bell, another prominent character in the drama, lived much longer, but made no pretension to religion. When the last of February (the time for the world to come to an end, according to his prediction) arrived, and all things remained as they were, his spirit felt the rebuke, and veered to the opposite pole, where it sank into the icy depths of infidel indifference.

But the work of God still went on in London; and, though seventy-five persons left the society, several hundreds remained who were more united than ever. But the prediction that the world was coming to an end on the 28th of February created a great panic; and, taken in connection with the other errors of the separatists, and the transactions to which they gave origin, it was sadly injurious to the cause of religion.

CHAPTER IV

THE CALVINISTIC CONTROVERSY, THE DEED OF SETTLEMENT, AND MR. WESLEY'S STANDING IN THE COUNTRY.

THE next general conflict the societies experienced arose from a revival of *Antinomianism*, which was eating out the vitals of religion all over the kingdom. Though Methodism had excluded none from its fellowship on account of doctrinal errors, it nevertheless had a theory of its own, which was considered important, though not positively indispensable to regeneration. But it now became evident enough that some of those principles, which had been treated with great liberality, were working the *death* of practical piety. This was particularly the case with that system of error called Antinomianism, which assumes that, as the elect cannot fall from grace, nor forfeit the divine favor, the wicked actions they commit are not really sinful, nor violations of the divine law; and consequently they have no occasion either to confess their sins, or to break them off by repentance. Mr. Fletcher, vicar of Madeley, describes the state of religion in the popular walks of life in these words: —

"At this time we stand particularly in danger of splitting upon the Antinomian rock. Many smatterers in Christian experience talk of *finished salvation* in Christ, or boast of being in a state of justification and sanctification, while they know little of themselves, and less of Christ. Their whole behavior testifies that their heart is void of humble love, and full of carnal confidence. They cry, '*Lord, Lord!*' with as much assurance and as little right as the foolish virgins. They pass for sweet Christians, dear children of God, and good believers; but their secret reserves evidence them to be only such believers as Simon Magus, Ananias and Sapphira."

To prevent this terrible malaria from poisoning the young societies, which had now become pretty numerous, the Conference of 1770 called up the subject, and reaffirmed certain propositions directly opposed to the Antinomian theory. The *Minutes* of this Conference created great excitement. The Calvinists took the alarm, and the Honorable and Reverend Walter Shirley wrote a circular letter to all the serious clergy, and some others, inviting them to meet at Bristol on the sixth of the following August, the time and place of Mr. Wesley's next Conference, and go to the Conference in a body, and "insist on a formal *recantation* of the said Minutes," and in case of a refusal, "that they sign and publish their protest against them." What gave more influence to the letter, was the fact that the proposition originated with Lady Hundingdon, an old friend of Mr. Wesley and of the Wesleyan movement.

Mr. Fletcher, characterized as the "sainted Fletcher," because of his extraordinary piety, on receiving one of these circulars, communicated the contents to Mr. Wesley, proposing to stand by him and his doctrine to the last. He also wrote Mr. Shirley, entreating him to recall his circulars, and wrote other letters he thought necessary to counteract the influence of the plot. But all availed nothing. The opposition to the Minutes waxed warm, and a long controversy ensued, to which we are indebted for Fletcher's four volumes of Checks to Antinomianism; a work which has, indeed, agreeably to its talented author's promise, *stood by*

Mr. Wesley and his principles "to the last." Being written in a charming style, and with a power of argument which no sophistry can gainsay, and, withal, breathing the very spirit of heaven in every line, it has been a bulwark of defence to our theology, against which all the fiery darts of opponents have been hurled in vain. How much we owe, how much the truth of God owes, how much the universal church and the world owe to this work, we, of course, have no means of exact information; but in our opinion, there is not a work extant which has done more, under God, for the honor and perpetuity of Christian theology in its purity and power. Under its withering glance error has blushed and fled away, or assumed a new aspect, which, in its turn, has been rebuked, and retired. Its birth was a glorious era in Methodism. We commend the work to the careful examination of all who are in any way troubled with the Calvinistic delusion. They will find it a sovereign remedy against it as it was, or now is, when it is properly understood. And it is equally appropriate to those who would understand the doctrines of Methodism, and the grounds on which they rest for defence.

Tuesday, Aug. 6th, the Conference commenced its session, and Mr. Shirley and his friends appeared. The conversation that ensued lasted two hours, and was conducted with remarkable good temper; but there was no "*recantation*" or satisfaction; and the controversy ensued, to which we have referred; Mr. Fletcher managing the Arminian side of the question, and various gentlemen of distinction the Calvinistic; thus relieving Mr. Wesley from a task that in other controversies had devolved upon him, and leaving him at liberty to prosecute the great work of which he was the acknowledged leader.

Methodism had made a fair beginning in Scotland, also.

Many had been converted, and several societies formed. But in the midst of the work this question arose. The excellent Mr. Hervey, author of the "Meditations," and an old pupil of Mr. Wesley, had formerly been induced to write some letters, which being now published and scattered among the young believers did much harm.* "O," said one of the preachers then in Scotland, "the precious convictions which these letters have destroyed! Many, that have often declared the great profit they received under our ministry, were by these induced to leave us." "Though the preachers met with no mobs in Scotland to oppose their progress, they encountered prejudices that were more formidable." Says Dr. Whitehead: "They found the Scots strongly entrenched within the lines of religious opinions and modes of worship, which almost bade defiance to any mode of attack."

Mr. Wesley was now considerably advanced in life. But though his health and strength remained undiminished, he regarded his dissolution as near, and deliberately applied himself to provide for the government of the multitudes he had drawn around him. Who was to take his place and do his work, without his influence, (and no man could have it,) was a question which occupied, not his attention only, but that of the preachers, who already trembled for the unity of the body when Mr. Wesley should be called to his reward.

From reference already made to Mr. Fletcher, the reader would naturally infer that he occupied a high place in the affections of the whole body. This was the fact, in proof of which Mr. Wesley was frequently solicited to secure him for his successor. Accordingly, in January, 1773, he wrote Mr. Fletcher a very emphatic letter, urging him by high

* These letters were not published till after Mr. Hervey's death, and then against his dying prohibition; to serve two objects, viz.: the covetousness of one man, and the bigotry of another.

considerations to enter into the itinerant work, and be prepared to succeed him in office. Mr. Fletcher replied with his usual modesty, declining the overture, but promising such assistance as he might be able to afford in certain contingencies. This was construed into encouragement by some of the preachers, and Mr. Fletcher was addressed a second time; but to no purpose. He was a great man, an excellent scholar, and an eminent Christian; but he was not probably "born to command." He could not fancy the position offered him. "I am," said he facetiously to a friend, "like one of your casks of wine: I am good for nothing till I *settle*."

Methodism had found its way to America some time before. It now appeared in the Isle of Man, in Holland, and other places, and Mr. Wesley presided over the whole, travelling from country to country in his regular course with the same apparent ease and energy he had displayed in former years. But the question must be settled, "what is going to be done when Mr. Wesley dies?" Most of the trust deeds secured the right of appointing the preachers to the several chapels to him, some made no provision for their appointment after his demise, while many vested the right to appoint in the Conference. But who were the Conference? As before stated, it was composed of such preachers as Mr. Wesley called together to counsel with him, and none others. Here was a difficulty which many feared, and some hoped, would prove fatal to the union of the societies.

To avoid so great a calamity Mr. Wesley took legal advice, and prepared a "Deed of Declaration," constituting one hundred preachers, whom he named therein, the Conference of the people called Methodists — making provision for the filling of vacancies occasioned by death, superannuation, or excision; and defining their duties and powers so as to secure the occupancy of the meeting-houses, and other society property, to the Methodists, according to the original design; and preserve the itinerancy for ever unimpaired among them. This Deed being recorded in His Majesty's High Court of Chancery, in the year 1784, the question of authority and government was settled. The deed created some little uneasiness among certain preachers not named in it, particularly such as had left the work like Dr. Whitehead, and were hoping to obtain a settlement, as did Mr. Wesley's book-steward, in a Congregational Methodist Church. But in general it gave great satisfaction. Mr. Wesley's motives for this measure we find stated by himself in these words: —

"Without some authentic deed, fixing the meaning of the term, the moment I died the Conference had been nothing. Therefore, any of the proprietors of the land on which our preaching-houses were built might have seized them for their own use, and there would have been none to hinder them; for the Conference would have been nobody — a mere empty name.

"You see, then, in all the pains I have taken about this necessary deed, I have been laboring, not for myself, (I have no interest therein,) but for the whole body of Methodists, in order to fix them upon such a foundation as is likely to stand as long as the sun and moon endure. That is, if they continue to walk by faith, and show forth their faith by their works; otherwise, I pray God to root out the memorial of them from the earth."

The remarks of Mr. Moore on the importance of this "Deed" are full of sound sense. He says: —

"That men, (not a few of whom had departed from the society, and some had been expelled from it,) should, merely by virtue of their *legal* authority over the premises, appoint preachers to feed and guide the flock, exhibited a distressing prospect. Even where the Trustees continued members of the society, and attached to its interests, what could be expected, in a matter of such vital concern, from men so much engaged in worldly business? This has often been proved in religious communities. It was the chief cause of the decline of religion among the latter Puritans: their lay-elders assumed, after some time, the whole authority. From this proceeded that worldly spirit and political zeal which so greatly dishonored that work in its last days; and which had previously overthrown both church and state.

"The evil showed itself in prominent overt acts, previous to this period. Mr. Wesley, having striven to prevail on some Trustees in Yorkshire to settle their chapels, so that the people might continue to hear the same truths, and be under the same discipline as heretofore, was assailed with calumny, and with the most determined opposition, as though he intended to make the chapels his own! Another set of Trustees, in the same county, absolutely refused to settle a lately erected chapel; and, in the issue, engaged Mr. Wesley's book-steward in London, who had been an itinerant preacher, to come to them as their minister. This man, however, was '*wise in his generation*,' and insisted upon having an income of sixty pounds per annum, with the chapel-house to live in, settled upon him during his life, before he would relinquish his place under Mr. Wesley. What will not party spirit do! I was a witness, when, after Mr. Wesley's death, it was found that the preachers continued united and faithful in their calling, how deeply those men repented of their conduct in this instance. In vain they represented to the man of their unhappy choice how lamentably their congregations had declined, and how hardly they could sustain the expenses they had incurred. The answer was short: *They might employ other preachers if they should think it proper; but the dwelling-house and the stated income belonged to him!*

"We need not wonder that Dr. Whitehead should speak with such deep concern, and indulge such a spirit of calumny, concerning this important measure of settling the chapels. The Doctor, and many others who had departed from the work, had, through that wise measure, but little prospect of succeeding, like his friend the book-steward, to occupy chapels built for the people by Mr. Wesley's influence and the labor of the preachers. The favor of those Trustees who might be disposed to forget their sacred obligations, and incur such an awful responsibility, held out but little hope to such men, now that a legal definition was given to the phrase — The Conference: and, in fact, every appeal made to equity has fully succeeded, on this very ground.

"In that day of uncertainty and surmise, there were not wanting some, even among the itinerant preachers, who entertained fears respecting a settlement of this kind. One of those preachers, and of considerable eminence, attacked the Deed of Settlement, and declared that Mr. Wesley might as justly place all the dwelling-houses, barns, work-shops, &c., in which we had preached for so many years, under the authority of the Conference, as he had done the chapels; and that he thus assumed an authority that the Lord had not given him. This seemed far too strong to be generally received, and it was quickly answered. A preacher, in reply, observed, 'that, certainly, there was as much justice in the one case as the other, provided those dwelling-houses, barns, workshops, &c., had been built in consequence of the preaching, and by the subscriptions of the connection; and in order that those erections might continue to be used for the purposes for which they were thus built!' This closed the debate for that time."

To give this instrument a happier operation and more general acceptability, Mr. Wesley left the following letter to be read at the first session of the Conference after his decease: —

"TO THE METHODIST CONFERENCE.

"CHESTER, *April* 7, 1785.

"MY DEAR BRETHREN: — Some of our travelling preachers have expressed a fear that, after my decease, you would exclude them either from preaching in connection with you, or from some other privilege which they now enjoy. I know no other way to prevent any such inconvenience, than to leave these, my last words, with you.

"I beseech you, by the mercies of God, that you never avail yourselves of the 'Deed of Declaration' to assume any superiority over your brethren; but let all things go on among those itinerants who choose to remain together exactly in the same manner as when I was with you, so far as circumstances will permit.

"In particular, I beseech you, if you ever loved me, and if you now love God and your brethren, to have no respect of persons in stationing the preachers, in choosing children for the Kingswood school, in disposing of the yearly contribution and the preachers' fund, or any other public money. But do all things with a single eye, as I have done from the beginning. Go on thus; doing all things without prejudice or partiality, and God will be with you to the end.

"JOHN WESLEY."

This letter was read to the Conference, according to the writer's design, and responded to by resolutions pledging that body to entire acquiescence in its suggestions. But the effect was not all that was desired. Though it allayed the fears of individuals, it did not endear the government provided for in the "Deed" to all parties. Some had little fondness for the national church, and wished to have all connection sundered, that they might enter the lists against it. The heads of others were quite turned in favor of ecclesiastical democracy. They could away with no system that did not eschew all distinctions; while a considerable number of excellent men preferred something a little different from the existing plan. The matter was talked over privately, and a private convention or two was called, in which systems were suggested and discussed, and in which, too, strong preferences were expressed for our own. But the secret was soon out, and raised an excitement which alarmed the friends of the cause exceedingly. But the next Conference, by the timely aid of their "Deed," firmly resisted all attempts to effect a change in the constitution, in the face of great and good men whose names are still cherished with veneration.

Thus that instrument has ever proved itself the sheet anchor of Mr. Wesley's incomparable plan, and of the true interests of Methodism in every emergency. If the preachers have at any time inclined to diverge from it, it has restrained them; and it has compelled them to discountenance and suppress all tendencies to revolution; so that the designs of Mr. Wesley and his coadjutors have been steadily carried out. And, so far as we can now see, they must continue to be to the end of time, unless the Conference shall apostatize from God, and become indisposed to work the system; or the legislative or judiciary department of the country shall prove recreant to duty, and attempt to *mend* what it only ought to *protect*. But we think there is no immediate occasion of alarm. The experiments which have been made in vain at all these points, form ground of confidence in the integrity both of the Conference and the civil government.

Hence, instead of the societies being scattered at the death of Mr. Wesley, as was anticipated, they struck their roots still deeper, and extended their branches wider. Says Mr. Jackson: "Extensive revivals broke out in several places; new societies were formed, and older ones were quickened and augmented; and many chapels, of various sizes, were erected and enlarged. Within ten years after Mr. Wesley's death the societies were increased in Great Britain alone more than *forty thousand members*, and in twenty years they were increased upward of *one hundred thousand.*"

Mr. Wesley continued his labors and triumphs after this as before, without much interruption of health, till March 2, 1791, when he departed this life in glorious hope of a blissful immortality, in the *eighty-eighth* year of his age, and the sixty-fourth of his ministry; leaving numerous and flourishing societies throughout Great Britain and Ireland, the Isle of Wight, the Isle of Man, the United States, Canada, and Newfoundland, all cherishing the same faith, enjoying the same religion, and walking by the same rules. The societies in America were then divided in thirteen Conferences, and embraced 250 itinerant preachers, and more than 63,000 members.

The latter part of Mr. Wesley's career differed in one respect from the former. His early travels were constantly interrupted by mobs, and other persecutions, which not only embarrassed his work but often endangered his life. But God permitted him to live to command the respect and veneration of his greatest *enemies*. His old age was honored with all the attention that was safe for any man to receive. "The churches in London were generally closed against him in 1738; but now he had more applications to preach in those very churches, for the benefit of public charities, than he could possibly comply with. His visits to many places in the country created a sort of general festival. The people crowded around him as he passed along the streets; the windows were filled with eager gazers; the children waited 'to catch the good man's smile,' which the overflowing benignity of his heart rendered him ever willing to bestow. When he first went into Cornwall, accompanied by John Nelson, he plucked blackberries from the hedges to allay the cravings of hunger; and slept upon boards, having his saddle-bags for a pillow, till the bones cut through his skin. Now he was received, in that county especially, as an angel of God. On the 17th of August, 1789, on visiting Falmouth, he says, 'The last time I was here, above forty years ago, I was taken prisoner by an immense mob, gaping and roaring like lions. But how is the tide turned! High and low now lined the street from one end of the town to the other, out of stark love, gaping and staring as if the king were going by.'" — *Cent. of Methodism, p.* 143.

Thus, integrity to God is often honored even in this world. Whatever injustice, prejudice, and calumny, may heap upon our names for a time, if we take it patiently, and plod on in the way of well-doing, redemption will come, and Haman shall be compelled by his own convictions to honor the same Mordecai he would have hanged.

CHAPTER V.

DIFFICULTIES ABOUT THE SACRAMENTS, "PLAN OF PACIFICATION," AND MISSIONARY OPERATIONS.

THE tenacity with which Mr. Wesley adhered to the Established Church has already been mentioned. He required nothing as a condition of membership in his societies, nor indeed allowed any conduct among his adherents which was inconsistent with his relations to the church, or conformity to its lawful requisitions. He held no service in the chapels during the time of regular service in the church, but attended that service himself, and enjoined upon his followers to do the same. Nor would he allow the preachers to administer the sacraments, but required the members of the society to attend upon the sacrament in the church. His preaching places must not be called churches, but *chapels;* his helpers, not clergymen, but *lay preachers;* and the assemblies of his people, mere *societies.*

But he did not maintain this course without considerable difficulty, nor without strong apprehensions that something like a separation would ultimately take place. The repulsion of Methodists and Methodist preachers from the sacrament, and the infliction of cruel persecution from a domineering *priesthood,* created a general distrust of the piety of its incumbents, and a consequent disinclination to attend upon their ministry. Of course, there was a loud call for the sacraments in the chapels, which could not be fully answered without seeming to dissent from the establishment. Mr. Wesley's personal influence went far in moderating this demand, but was hardly sufficient. At all events, he found it necessary to administer the sacrament himself in some of the chapels, and to secure similar service from several others of the regular clergy who were interested in his objects.

This was the state of things at his death, when all eyes turned to the Conference for some accommodation. To prevent the administration of the sacraments to the people by their own preachers was impossible. The Conference had no power to do it, had it been disposed. "The question," says Mr. Watson, "stood on plain practical ground: 'Shall the societies be obliged, from their conscientious scruples, to neglect an ordinance of God? or shall we drive them to the dissenters, whose peculiar doctrines they do not believe? or shall we, under certain regulations, accede to their wishes?'"

The Conference was very unwilling at first to do any thing on the subject. They were delicately situated. They had always been taught to regard themselves as a *society* in the *church*, and not a church by themselves. With this understanding, many of their most wealthy and pious members had been induced to join, and were at that moment holding important offices of trust, who still regarded the church as their mother, and looked only to her for the valid administration of the ordinances. The Conference was aware how the change demanded would affect such people, and felt compelled to move cautiously. But their prudent tardiness and delay did not quiet the public mind. Discussion waxed warmer and warmer. The leading men in the Conference were on opposite sides, and the prospect for peace was dubious. A majority, however, agreed that the preachers might administer the ordinances where a majority in the society was in favor. This gave the high church party great offence, and created no little disturbance. They next, for peace's sake, retracted a little, and allowed the sacraments only where there was no objection. This only increased the difficulty, as it gave the power to a single churchman to bind all the rest of the society. The contention now became intolerable. *High church* trustees shut several of the chapels against *low church* preachers; con gregations were divided; many seceded from the society, and things looked threatening indeed. What could be done? The conference was as much divided as the people. Mr. Benson was high church, Mr. Moore, Mr. Wesley's biographer, was low church, and both had been in the same circuit, serving different parties to the controversy.

The opening of the Conference of 1795 was a critical period. Excitement had reached the culminating point. Argument was exhausted. All seemed to feel that the decisions of this session would decide the fate of the Wesleyan body; and yet it was obvious that no action, however wise, would please all, and prevent a separation of some from the connection. The alternation of hope and fear could be distinguished in every countenance. Many a pious heart trembled for the ark of God. Trustees and stewards from all parts of the kingdom were assembled in the lobby, to speak for themselves and their constituents, and by all lawful means to persuade the Conference to favor the preferences of their respective parties. Some would secede if the Conference should do thus and thus; and others would secede if it should not. The Conference heard all; and, fully impressed with the delicacy of their position, entered upon their work like men of God, determined to take no advantage that did not belong to them, and come to some decision that would end the controversy for ever, if possible.

It was first agreed to refer the whole matter to a "*committee of nine*," to be chosen by ballot. This was the fairest way to choose them, and yet it was to be feared that in this way they would all be on one side, as it was evident the conference was not equally balanced. But no; there was too much magnanimity in the body for this. All seemed to feel that both sides ought to be represented, and that minorities are to be respected. The ballotings resulted in the appointment of a mixed committee, consisting of Rev. Joseph Bradford, John Pawson, Alexander Mather, Thomas Coke, William Thompson, Samuel Bradburn, Joseph Benson, Henry Moore, and Adam Clarke. After sitting six evenings, three and a half hours each evening, in close deliberation, the committee presented a "Plan of Pacification," so accommodating all parties, and requiring concessions from all, that it was difficult to tell which party in the committee had prevailed. The truth was, (be it said to the praise of God, and to the credit of their hearts as well as their heads,) *both prevailed.* Their paramount interest was to *save the cause;* and the matter in dispute being rather a prudential arrangement than a positive duty, they acquiesced in a compromise that required concessions both ways, and still gave both sides their own way to an important extent. The Conference adopted the report with great unanimity, by slightly altering one article, after which it very harmoniously appended two or three more, and sent it forth among the societies. Few could say it was just what they wanted; but nearly all the real Methodists, embracing the trustees, stewards, and private members, acquiesced in it as a plan of peculiar wisdom, dropped their controversies, and united anew in the work of God. There was, however, a small secession about this time, to which we shall refer hereafter.

It is not necessary to state all the provisions of this plan. It is enough to say, that baptism and the Lord's supper, together with service in the chapels during the time of church service, were provided for on the condition that a majority of the stewards and leaders should approve of it. But it did not bind the conscience of any one. If a majority should favor the sacraments, &c., according to the "*plan*," it did not bind the minority to attend upon them. Members could go to church as before, and those who preferred it might receive baptism and the sacrament at chapel. Was not this kind? Was it not just? And was it not Wesleyan, too? We have not a doubt of it. Mr. Wesley loved the church, but he loved the souls of men better. He would not separate from her any further than he found it necessary to the work of God. The church was not his God. In a letter to Mr. Walker, he says, "Nor have we taken one step further than we were convinced was our bounden duty. It is from a full conviction of this, that we have, 1. Preached abroad. 2. Prayed extempore. 3. Formed societies; and, 4. Permitted preachers who were not episcopally ordained. And were we pushed on this side, were there no alternative allowed, we should judge it our bounden duty rather *wholly to separate from the church*, than to give up ANY ONE *of these points*. Therefore, if we cannot stop a separation without stopping lay preachers, the case is clear — we cannot stop it at all."

But the desire of the Conference to avoid all appearance of separation from the church, led them to qualify their preachers to administer the sacraments *without* the imposition of hands. This was not satisfactory to some, though they knew that the imposition of hands was a mere ceremony, which added nothing to the validity of the ministry. But custom had invested it with so much importance, they were sure many people would never regard them as regular ministers of the gospel unless they had been ordained in the usual way. Therefore they wished the Conference to avail itself of a venerable custom, which, while it would add nothing to their authority, nor subtract any thing from the authority of the Church, would give them an influence over some minds that could not be otherwise obtained. This measure, however, was delayed till 1836, when the Conference adopted it as a "standing rule."

From the year 1752 to the year previous to his death, Mr. Wesley held an annual Conference with the preachers in Ireland; and provided in his poll-deed for such gatherings as often as the British Conference should judge expedient The Irish Conference is now held annually under the presidency of some one appointed for the purpose. It embraces 97 circuits, 152 travelling preachers, and 0,740 members.

The missionary work was for many years carried on under the direction of Dr. Coke, who travelled through the kingdom and took collections for its support. His labors in this department were very extensive and successful. He was probably instrumental in sowing the seed in the West Indies, which has since brought forth so abundantly. The redeemed sons of Africa, in those islands, owe more to him than they will ever realize till they meet him in glory. He was a whole man, and gave himself entirely to the work.

"At the Conference of 1813, Dr. Coke, then in the sixty-seventh year of his age, expressed an earnest desire tc proceed to the East Indies, for the purpose of establishing a mission there. Eighteen times had he crossed the Atlantic for missionary objects; yet his godly ardor was unabated, and his conviction of the truth of Christianity and of its importance to mankind was increasingly strong and influential. Some of the brethren, recollecting his advanced age, the difficulties connected with the undertaking, and the serious inconvenience the missions already in existence would experience in consequence of his departure, attempted to dissuade him from the enterprise, desirable as they confessed it to be. He heard their reasonings and remonstrances, and then, bursting into tears, he exclaimed, in a manner which they could not resist, 'If you will not let me go, you will break my heart.' His brethren withdrew their opposition, and this honored patron and friend of missions, accompanied by seven others, embarked for the East, in December, 1813. On the third day of May following he was found dead in his cabin, having expired, it was believed, in a fit of apoplexy. Thus ended the life and labors of this estimable man, whose name will ever be remembered in honorable association with modern missions. Next to Mr. Wesley, no man was ever connected with the Methodist body who contributed more to extend the blessings of Christianity among mankind." — *Centenary of Methodism, p.* 162.

This calamity, however, did not frustrate the enterprise. The body of Dr. Coke was committed to the deep; but his associates continued their voyage, and laid the foundation of the mission at Ceylon, and on the continent of India, which has since attracted so much attention. And, strange as it may seem, the missionary spirit received a new impulse at home. The connection had been relying upon one man; but now that he was no more, all seemed to feel their responsibility, and rallied in support of the cause for which their venerated father and friend had given his fortune and his life. And here we find the opening of a new era in the history of Wesleyan missions. The necessities of the cause suggested to Rev. George Morley, superintendent of the

Leeds circuit, the idea of a missionary society in that town, by means of a public meeting. Rev. Richard Watson and James Buckley were appointed to preach, and Thomas Thompson, Esq., a member of Parliament, to preside. The meeting attracted general attention, and gave a powerful impulse to the cause. Similar meetings were now the order of the day, and followed each other in quick succession, "till the Methodist congregations, from the Land's End to the Tweed, caught the sacred flame. Collectors offered their services in all directions, the hearts of the people were every where impressed and opened by the state of the heathen, and the communication of authentic missionary intelligence; and money was, from year to year, poured into the sacred treasury beyond all precedent."

From that time the work has gone steadily on, commanding the affections of preachers and people, and having the superintendency of the greatest minds and noblest hearts that ever graced the world. While the society was yet mourning for Dr. Coke, and fearing that they should never see his like again, God not only suggested a new plan, by which to make up in a measure for the loss they had sustained, but raised up a man, peculiarly endowed in all respects, to operate that plan with wonderful effect. We refer to Rev. Richard Watson, than whom, perhaps, the cause of missions never had a warmer friend or an abler advocate. During his activity the missions flourished beyond what they had ever done before, and gave fresh encouragement to effort. This may be seen in the South Seas, "where the savage inhabitants of whole islands have abandoned the idols of their fathers, and where the people, by thousands, have become the spiritual worshippers of God. Civilization there walks hand in hand with Christianity; children and even old people are gathered together in schools; and persons of all ranks are successfully learning the useful arts. The change which has taken place in the spirit and habits of those savage tribes is so sudden, deep, and extensive — so obviously above all human power — that he is blind who cannot see in it the working of that Almighty Spirit by whose agency three thousand persons in Jerusalem were, in one day, converted from Jewish obstinacy and unbelief to the faith of Christ."

Other missionary fields have not been less fruitful. God has crowned the efforts of the Wesleyan Methodists with more than ordinary success. And they have deserved it for no people, in their circumstances, have contributed to the cause so liberally. The sun goes not down on their work. They have belted the earth with their missionary operations, and are waxing stronger and stronger every year. Their missionary society was formed in the year 1818, and has steadily advanced until it has become one of the mightiest engines for good in Christendom. Its collections the last year amounted to $503,375, a generous sum, indeed, especially when it is considered that they have first to support the regular church clergy, then their own, and are generally composed of the poorer classes of society.

Nor has God forsaken them at home. Though they have shared the common reproach of Methodists, they have exerted an increasingly powerful influence to the present moment. Said Mr. Watson, "It might almost be said of us, 'So the people shall dwell alone.' The high churchman has persecuted us because we are separatists; the high dissenter has often looked upon us with hostility, because we would not see that an establishment necessarily, and *in se*, involved a sin against the supremacy of Christ; the rigid Calvinist has disliked us, because we hold the redemption of all men; the palagianized Arminian, because we contend for salvation by grace ; the Antinomian, because we insist upon the perpetual obligation of the moral law; the moralist, because we exalt faith; the disaffected, because we hold that loyalty and religion are inseparable ; the political tory, because he cannot think that separatists from the church can be loyal to the throne; the philosopher, because he deems us fanatics; while some infidel liberals, generally exclude us from all share in their liberality, except it be in their liberality of abuse. In the meantime, we have occasionally been favored with a smile, though somewhat of a condescending one, from the lofty churchman, and often with a fraternal embrace from pious and liberal dissenters; and, if we act upon the principles left us by our great founder, we shall make a meek and lowly temper an essential part of our religion; and, after his example, move onward in the path of doing good, through 'honor and dishonor, through evil report and good report,' remembering that one fundamental principle of Wesleyan Methodism is anti-sectarianism and a catholic spirit."

Every weapon formed against them has most signally failed. An early application to Parliament for an alteration in the Toleration Act, that would have been ruinous to them had it been successful, resulted in an alteration in their favor. An appeal made to the Courts of Chancery, to break down Mr. Wesley's Deed of Declaration and subvert the Discipline, not only failed of its object, but established the Deed more firmly than ever, by procuring it the sanction of Mr. vice-chancellor Shadwell, and of lord chancellor Lyndhurst. And so of the movements of certain trustees and others, who have seemed desirous of tearing up the old Wesleyan track; they have only established it the more firmly, by attracting attention to its solidity and adaptation to its objects.

Nor have attacks upon their *doctrines* succeeded better. At no period have they lacked either men or means to vindicate themselves in this respect; and by circulating the well-selected sermons, biographies, and commentaries of their book-room broadcast over the land, they have been able to extend and establish the heart-stirring truths of Methodism, in spite of all the learning and sophistry that have been arrayed against them. The enemies' attacks, often made upon leading men, have been equally fruitless. Those men have uniformly survived the storm, and even shone the brighter for the shadow that was cast upon them. And we have no doubt this will be the experience of themselves and their successors in the future, while they strive to "*keep* our rules, and not to *mend* them."

In the progress of events they have been able to adopt measures for the full support of all their itinerant ministers, whether in effective service or superannuated; and years have elapsed since one had to fear the want of bread in entering their ministry. This has, no doubt, operated favorably on the cause. Men, good and true, have been secured to the work, who might have spent their energies in a less useful way, had the idea of becoming itinerants been identified with that of *starvation*, or suffering the want of the necessaries of life. To enter a ministry, even with a lucid conviction of a call to preach, in the certain prospect of poverty and dependence, and perhaps of great suffering therefrom, requires more grace than men generally enjoy. Where there is one who will do it, we apprehend there are many who, though constrained by conscience to preach the gospel, would impose some restrictions upon their preferences, and, as a matter of apparent necessity, enter the work in another branch of the church, where their supplies would be more liberal. We believe Methodism in this country has lost many noble men, whose influence would greatly have accelerated the growth of the church, — men of piety and talent, — merely by the paucity of the support she has afforded. She may have been saved, by this means, from the curse of a *hireling* ministry — a ministry that seeks the fleece and not the flock. But we have no doubt the losses have greatly exceeded the gains.

By providing amply for their ministers, not only while in effective service, but when disabled by sickness or old age, the Wesleyans have been enabled to *select* their men for the itinerant service. The supply of candidates is always abundant, though they only receive *single* men, unless their wives and children are provided for from other sources. They have also been enabled to hold them *rigidly* to the work when received, and make them feel that they *must* be *efficient*, or retire. And, besides, the people, paying the full amount required, are allowed to be more rigid in their claims than would be modest if they had but half fed their preachers. The advantages are, indeed, numerous, and the Wesleyans have been reaping them for many years.

CHAPTER VI.

WESLEYAN SCHOOLS AND FUNDS.

At the first Conference the question was asked, "Can we have a Seminary for laborers?" and answered, "If God spare us till another Conference." The next year it was inquired, "Can we have a Seminary for laborers, yet?" To which it was replied, "Not till God gives us a proper tutor." The matter did not sleep here, though the object was not soon gained.

A few years after Mr. Wesley's death a pamphlet was published by order of the Conference, showing the importance of a "plan of instruction" for preachers received on trial. In a letter written by Dr. Adam Clarke, in 1806, he says, "We want some kind of Seminary for educating such workmen as need not be ashamed. I introduced a conversation on the subject this morning; and the preachers were unanimously of the opinion that some strong efforts should be made without delay, to get such a place established. Every circuit cries out, '*send us acceptable preachers.*' How can we do this? We are obliged to take what offers. The time is coming, and now is, when illiterate piety can do no more for the interest and permanency of the work of God than lettered irreligion did formerly. Speak! O, speak speedily, to all our friends! Let us get a plan organized without delay."

In 1823, and from that time forward, the Conference

appointed a committee every year to consider the subject and report. In 1833 a committee, consisting of twenty preachers, was directed to meet in London, Oct. 23d, to settle upon a plan, which they completed after seven days' deliberation. The plan was adopted by the Conference, with some little revision, and the "Wesleyan Theological Institution for the improvement of the junior preachers" went into operation, at Haxton, London. In the year 1839, agreeably to a previous understanding, the Conference appointed a sub-committee, in the north of England, to find a suitable situation in that quarter for the establishment of another similar school, or a branch of the same, for the better accommodation of the whole work. This sub-committee reported in favor of a premises at Didsbury, near Manchester. The general committee reported in favor of a premises at Richmond, near London, for the southern branch, (having occupied hired rooms till then,) whereupon the Conference accepted the two reports, and provided for the erection of suitable buildings at the two localities, sufficient for the accommodation of one hundred students. The expense of these buildings was met by a part of the centenary fund, raised for the benefit of the schools.

To avoid men-made ministers, the Conference wisely determined, in the beginning, that none should be received into the institution but such as were evidently called of God to preach the gospel. And that there might be no mistake, candidates were required to pass the regular examinations preliminary to the ministry, obtain the consent of the Quarterly Meeting, the recommendation of the superintendent of the District Meeting, and be actually accepted by the Conference, and placed on the "*reserve list.*" Entering under these circumstances, they are put upon that course of training which their tutors think will best fit them for the field they are to occupy; always subject to the call of the Conference, and liable to remain three years. But if they remain this length of time the last year is counted as the second of the four years of their probation in the Conference.

This plan is peculiar, in that none are received till the people and the Conference are satisfied they are called of God to the ministry. Then, instead of teaching them theology only, or theology in connection with such other branches as are more intimately related to it, (for instance, moral science, the Greek and Hebrew languages, &c.,) and requiring them to remain a specified term of years, it teaches them just those things which they are ignorant of, and need to know, to fit them for their particular work; and when this is done, they send them forth into the field, whether they have been studying one month or three years. Thus they have saved themselves from the curse of a mere *literary* ministry, and the disgrace of ignorance, and have secured much *time* and *talent* to the cause of Christ that, under the regimen of other denominations, would have been squandered and lost.

Kingswood School was established by Mr. Wesley in 1748, for the special benefit of the colliers. But afterward it came to be devoted entirely to the sons of itinerant Methodist preachers. In this character Mr. Wesley urged it upon the support of the people as a noble charity. For several years this school was found insufficient for the accommodation of the preachers' sons who were entitled to its advantages. Hence, in 1811, a similar school was established at Woodhouse Grove, near Leeds, which, in honor of our founder, was denominated "The Wesleyan Academy at Woodhouse Grove."

Each travelling preacher sending a son to either of these

schools pays the sum of *five* guineas, and *two* guineas per annum afterward. Those preachers who receive *twelve pounds* annually for the education of a son at home, who cannot be admitted to the schools, subscribe *one guinea* per annum; while others subscribe only half a guinea. Preachers receive, also, an annual allowance for the education of their daughters.

Each of these schools is placed under the care of a travelling preacher, who is responsible for its internal arrangements and expenditures. He is called the "Governor," and may be continued or removed by the Conference, within certain limitations, at its discretion.

Sunday Schools were commenced in England by Mr. Robert Raikes, in 1784. When Mr. Wesley heard of the plan of this gentleman, he gave it his decided approval, and recommended its adoption to his societies, with this improvement, that the services of the teachers should be *gratuitous*. His advice was taken, and immediately large masses of the youth were brought under efficient Sabbath School instruction. But it was not till 1827 that the Conference adopted a complete code of rules for the government of these bodies. Since that time most of these schools have been conducted on the same general principles, and have achieved magnificent results.

The Wesleyans have long sustained various week-day schools, which have contributed very largely to the general intelligence of the people. Since the year 1833 the Conference has annually appointed a "Committee on Education," charged with the duties of collecting information and urging the people forward to higher attainments. In 1840 this committee reported a plan to the Conference for the promotion of religious education in immediate connection with that body. This plan was adopted, and affectionately recommended to all the societies, and has thus far met the highest expectations of its friends.

There is also a proprietary school in Sheffield, conducted strictly on Wesleyan principles, though not a Conference institution. It was established and is conducted as a private concern, but the deed secures it to the interests of Methodism. It has been in operation more than forty years, and furnishes facilities for pretty thorough classical and commercial education, combined with religious instruction.

The extent of these operations, with the nature and magnitude of various other institutions connected with the Conference, will be better understood by referring to the several *funds* under its special jurisdiction. But let not the reader be deceived. The term *fund*, with us, conveys the idea of large investments, as when it is asked, "Do you support your preacher by subscription or by a *fund?*" But there is nothing of this implied in the term among the Wesleyans. They mean little more by it than the aggregate of the collections and subscriptions taken in the several societies for the object in question, with, perhaps, the profits of the Book Concern, and the interest on some small legacies.

"THE CONTINGENT FUND" is one of the oldest and most excellent charities of the connection. It originated among the more liberal of the societies, for the purpose of liquidating debts on the preaching houses, making up deficiencies in the support of the preachers, and sustaining others in new fields of labor, in England, Scotland, Wales, and Ireland; and also to enable the preachers to meet the expenses of law-suits instituted in order to protect the societies against the outrages of cruel mobs. In 1756 the Conference ordered a collection to be taken in all the classes, and sent out an address on the subject, exhorting the people to liberality. So useful were these funds found to be in sustaining and extending the work, in the year 1815 the Conference ordered an annual public collection for the support and spread of the gospel at home, in all their congregations throughout the kingdom, in the early part of the month of July, the avails of which were to be paid to the Contingent Fund. To these gatherings is added a pretty large grant from the profits of the Book Concern annually. This fund is now principally applied in supplying the deficiencies of the poorer and smaller circuits in Great Britain and Ireland. The balance is applied to meet what are called "extraordinary deficiencies," such as arise from accidents, afflictions among the preachers, furniture for parsonages, &c.

The affairs of this fund are managed by a committee, consisting of the President and Secretary of the Conference, with *fifteen* other preachers, appointed annually by the Conference, and *fifteen* laymen, chosen by the stewards of different districts.

THE CHILDREN'S FUND was instituted in the year 1819, to relieve the embarrassment which had been long realized in working the itinerant machinery. Till then, the several circuits had to pay such an allowance for each of their preacher's children, as it is now with us. Hence, men with large families were often objected to purely on financial grounds, and were often embarrassed themselves at the thought of being burdensome to a kind but poor people. And not unfrequently these evils were rather aggravated by the fact that a rich neighboring circuit was enjoying the services of preachers who had less children, and perhaps none at all.

To remedy these difficulties, and equalize the expense of supporting the children of the preachers among the circuits, the District Meetings entered into an arrangement to require each circuit to pay the allowance of its proportion of all the children in the Conference, according to the numbers in society and their financial ability. This measure met with general favor, both among the preachers and the people. The operation of it is this: the rich circuits, having less children among them to support than is their equitable proportion, pay the claims of their preachers for such as they have, and pay over the balance to the treasurer of the "Children's Fund;" while the poor circuits, having more preacher's children to support than properly belongs to them, draw upon the "Children's Fund" for the amount of their claims.

Thus all the preacher's children are provided for; and that there may be no failure in the operation of the plan, each circuit is required to pay its annual apportionment to the Fund before it can receive any assistance, whatever its necessities.

"THE GENERAL CHAPEL FUND" was instituted in the year 1818. Owing to various causes, that can easily be imagined, many of the chapels were considerably involved in debt. The Conference had often been called upon by the trustees of different circuits for assistance, and had assigned them certain territory in which to solicit donations. But this measure was not equal to the demand. Therefore the Conference determined to establish this Fund, to be supported by private subscriptions, by public collections, by legacies, and by annual grants from the trust-funds of the chapels.

Accordingly, the preachers were required to apply to

their people for subscriptions in the month of February of each year, and close their efforts with a public collection. The trustees of every chapel in the connection were to be "respectfully and earnestly solicited to evidence their readiness to concur in the measure, by paying to the fund a sum not less than one guinea for each chapel, and more if they were able." These measures were urged upon those who would be most likely to neglect them; and the fund was guarded against becoming a source of vain confidence to poor societies by the adoption of the most salutary regulations. It is required of societies about to make application for assistance, that they first make an effort among themselves — that they shall have adopted the practice of anniversary sermons and collections, and of sending at least one guinea from the trust-estate to the treasurer — and shall not have solicited subscriptions for their relief beyond the limits of their own particular circuit. The wisdom of these arrangements must be recognized at a glance.

Another arrangement intimately related to this fund, is the appointment of a "chapel-building committee." Though this committee was actually appointed prior to the establishment of the chapel fund, and might have been very useful had no such fund been created, this fund gives it peculiar influence. The object of the committee is to prevent the contraction of unreasonable debts. Church building is a business with which few are acquainted. In new Methodist societies it is rarely the case that there is a man who is capable of preparing a suitable model of a house, or of arranging a practicable plan of paying for one. Nor is the preacher of a circuit always wise in this respect. Indeed, both he and the people, however intelligent, are in a most unfortunate condition to think closely and judge discreetly in the case. They are excited — they cannot look soberly and impartially into any plan. Hence, they often rush upon the most unwarrantable speculations. Men of the least experience in business become the agents of pecuniary transactions beyond their capacity, and, as might be anticipated, plunge the society into trouble.

Hence, Mr. Wesley exhorted "that all preaching houses should be built plain and decent, not more expensively than is absolutely unavoidable." In the year 1815 the Conference advised the societies to remember Mr. Wesley's advice, "Beware of building *expensive* chapels," and entreated them not to contract debts they could not manage without aid from other societies. Two years after, this committee was appointed, consisting of five brethren, to whom all plans of new chapels, with their locations, subscription lists, &c., &c., were to be submitted for consideration and deliberate judgment as to the propriety of the undertaking.* This committee has its regular times of meeting, and receives and considers proposals for building, altering, or selling, and approves or disapproves, as they judge proper. If any society chooses to go on with their project, notwithstanding the disapproval of the committee, they forfeit all claim upon the "chapel fund," and are left to bear their own burdens. This arrangement has, no doubt, saved the connection much mortification and financial embarrassment, and added greatly to its chapel accommodations.

THE PREACHERS' AUXILIARY FUND is designed to meet the necessities of supernumerary preachers, and the widows and children of deceased preachers. At the Conference of 1763 some of the preachers were found to be nearly worn out, and unable to travel any longer. This originated the

* The number has since been increased to *twenty-four*, thirteen of whom are laymen.

question, "How may provision be made for the old and worn out preachers?" and it was answered, "As to their employment, they may be supernumerary preachers in those circuits wherein there is most need. As to their subsistence, 1. Let every travelling preacher contribute ten shillings yearly at the Conference. 2. Let this be lodged in the hands of three stewards approved by the majority of the preachers. 3. Out of this, let what is needful be allowed yearly, 1. For the old and sickly preachers and their families; (if they have any.) 2. For the widows and children of those that are dead."

The fund thus formed was called "*The Preachers Fund;*" but it proved insufficient. In the year 1799 it was, therefore, superseded by what was called "*The Itinerant Methodist Preachers' Annuity.*" This aimed at the same objects, and was supplied by the preachers' subscriptions, by a portion of the profits of the book-room, and by occasional donations and bequests of special friends. The same year several leading members in London started "The Preachers' Friend Society," for the relief of itinerant preachers in great emergencies. It was well sustained, but met with serious difficulties, and ran down. After that, the contributions of the people went to form what was called the "*Methodist Preachers' Merciful Fund,*" which was distributed among the preachers according to their necessities. In the year 1813 these funds were denominated "*The Preachers' Auxiliary Fund,*" in reference to the "*Annuity*" before named; but it did not meet the demand and the pressing wants of the worn out preachers was a subject of painful consideration. In the year 1839 the Conference adopted the same plan for raising supplies they had previously devised for the children's fund, and determined upon a scale of general disbursement, graduating the appropriations according to the number of years the claimant had devoted to the ministry, varying from *ten* to *fifty* pounds sterling per annum. As, for example, a preacher who had travelled thirty-nine years and upwards was to receive *fifty pounds*, while one who had travelled under *twelve years* was to receive but *fifteen* pounds; and the widow of such an one but *ten* pounds. These are the two extremes of the scale, which divides the claimants into seven classes.

The plan of the Conference also provides for giving each preacher, on his becoming supernumerary, and each preacher's wife, on her becoming a widow, the sum of thirty pounds sterling to buy *furniture*, they having been supplied this necessity by the several circuits where they have labored up to that time. It provides, too, for the children of deceased preachers, for their education as well as their support, and for special emergencies either among the supernumeraries, the widows, or the fatherless. The means of meeting these several claims, the first year after the adoption of the plan, were chiefly obtained of the centenary committee, which, in accordance with the design of the donors, appropriated about *forty-five thousand dollars* of the centenary collections to this object.

The aggregate amount contributed to these funds the last year cannot be specifically stated, as these funds have been somewhat complicated with new ones for their better management, but it is safe to say it shows a liberal advance on previous collections. Add to this more than six hundred thousand dollars raised for missions, the salaries paid to the preachers, and various other regular and occasional collections, and the liberality of the Wesleyans will be seen to exceed that of any other church in Christendom.

A few remarks in relation to the various measures referred to in the foregoing pages will close the present chapter. The first is, that all these arrangements, particularly the funds, have been providentially demanded. Nothing has been devised before its time, and nothing really matured for many years after its first discussion. This circumstance ought to encourage the younger members of the Wesleyan family to "try again," and never to cease discussing important practical questions till they shall have hit upon the right plan, and seen it in successful operation.

Another thought, which might not occur to the reader from what has been said, is, that these several plans and measures, though providentially suggested, were the result of *profound study*. Not merely during the sessions of the Conference. The Conference seemed generally to be impressed that the necessary brevity of their sessions, and other circumstances, would not admit of the needful investigation. Therefore, when they found themselves approaching the crisis, when something must be done, they appointed large committees, embracing the wisdom of the ministry and the laity, and designated the time and place of their meeting. In these committees the matter was deliberately dissected limb by limb, every weakness and impracticability detected, and the whole consolidated and adapted to the Wesleyan system, so that, if approved by the Conference, it might become a part of that system, and seem indispensable to its healthful operation. But another advantage of this course was, the plan, when it came out, was as much the *people's* as the preachers', and was, in a great degree, to be managed by them. This gave it popularity, and secured its success.

To the reader of this sketch, these regulations may seem complicated. This is their first appearance to a stranger. But if one will examine them more closely, he will find them complicated, indeed, yet *simple;* and, taken together, the most finished and effective scheme of raising money extant. How else could such an interest be kept up, and such vast amounts of money be raised in a society embracing few of the wealthy, and composed chiefly of the poorer classes, many of whom are objects of charity themselves, and all of whom are exorbitantly taxed to support the extravagance of the Episcopal Church — taxed for every thing — not only for what they eat, and drink, and wear, but for the very light of heaven that shines upon them, and often oppressed in their wages, too, and compelled to work long and hard for what will scarcely procure them the coarsest fare? Should their children imitate the parent in this respect, Methodism would soon fill the whole earth.

CHAPTER VII.

SECESSIONS FROM THE WESLEYAN CONNECTION, THEIR PRINCIPLES, HISTORY, AND PRESENT CONDITION.

THE history of European Methodism is not complete, nor is a sketch of that history just, which does not refer to other sects taking rank under this general title. The Wesleyan Connection does not embrace all who revere the name of its founder. There are several minor bodies of Methodists which claim our attention.

I. THE CALVINISTIC METHODISTS. — This title comprehends two distinct denominations, one of which never had any connection with Wesley, and the other but little. We refer to the "*Welch Calvinistic Methodists*," and the "*Whitefield, or Lady Hundingdon Connection*." The first originated in Wales about the time the Wesleys began to attract attention in England. They have been a zealous people, and have succeeded in doing much good. In 1850 they reported 186 ministers, 241 local preachers, and 58,930 members. The *Whitefield, or Lady Hundingdon Connection*, was organized under the labors of Mr. Whitefield, patronized by the Countess of Hundingdon. The congregations connected with this sect are about *ninety* in number. In some of its chapels the service of the church is read. In others, the forms of the Independents are observed. A sort of itinerancy is also maintained, the respective congregations employing the same minister but a few weeks in succession. There is, however, little system or efficiency in it, and the congregations are fast relapsing into Independency.

This off-shoot from the parent Methodist stock, if it can properly be called such, is remarkable in one or two particulars. The first is, that it has the honor of being the only one that ever occurred on *doctrinal grounds;* a circumstance of great significance. The other, that it was conducted by persons of high rank and influence. Mr. Whitefield was a man of unbounded reputation as a Christian and pulpit orator; his theology was popular, and his leading supporters persons of wealth and distinction. But "the race is not to the swift, nor the battle to the strong."

II. The New Methodist Connection, sometimes called Kilhamites, after one Alexander Kilham, a leading man in its organization, was originally composed of seceders from the Wesleyan societies. There were individuals in the connection at the time of Mr. Wesley's death who were dissatisfied with his system, and hoped for a change. They did not fancy its peaceable policy toward the church, or its government. After much noisy discussion, several societies sent delegates to the Conference held at Leeds in the year 1797, who demanded a change in the government settled by Mr. Wesley's Deed. For important reasons, the Conference did not see fit fully to acquiesce in their wishes; whereupon they immediately assembled, and adopted a system of itinerancy and government according with their peculiar views, and went into operation under the title of "*The New Connection.*" Their treatment of the Conference was very severe, and threatened serious consequences; but it was too manifestly unjust to be successful.

A few disaffected ones in different places seceded and joined them, making an aggregate of some *five thousand.*

And they have done no better since. A correspondent, who has lived among them many years, writes: "They started under most favorable auspices, and they have been now nearly eighty years vigorously striving to extend themselves, and yet, up to 1874, they have not much exceeded 33,000 members and 240 ministers; while the parent body from which they separated has increased from 75,000 members to 550,473, notwithstanding several other secessions that have operated to thin its ranks and swell those of the *New Connection.*"

III. Primitive Methodist Connection. — This denomination originated in Staffordshire, under the united leadership of two brothers, local preachers, by the name of *Bourne.* Hearing from Lorenzo Dow about the work of God at our camp meetings, and being anxious to be more useful, in the year 1807 they began to hold field meetings, for which they were rebuked, and afterward *expelled.* They, however, continued their efforts, and were successful; but formed no distinct classes till 1810, when the organization of the Primitive Connection was effected, embracing the *expelled* members, and such others as agreed with them. They did not secede, had no war with the old church, did not leave it willingly, and have never had much controversy with it since. Though they have received such from the Wesleyans as desired admission to their ranks, they long since passed an act, that any member of their Conference being guilty of denouncing or criminating another branch of the Christian church, should by that act cease to be a member.

Thus, living at peace with all men, and adopting the most liberal and energetic measures, they have prospered exceedingly. They hold annual and quarterly meetings, maintain the itinerancy, and other Methodist peculiarities, and are a pious and devout people. They have faith in God, faith in the power of his word and in prayer, faith in sudden conversions, and, like the Wesleys, they go among the lowest and meanest of men and win them to Christ. At their Conference, June 3, 1874, they reported 3,826 chapels, 1,020 travelling and 14,838 local preachers, 9,961 class leaders, 164,660 church members, and 306,333 Sabbath School scholars. They have a few societies in the Canadas, which are also in a flourishing condition, but have not been able to do much in the States, because not needed. They are sometimes called Ranters, in reference to the freedom of their devotions.

IV. The Bible Christians, or Bryanites, seceded in 1815, under the leadership of one William O'Bryan, a local preacher. Having been rebuked for various extravagances in reference to preaching and supporting the ministry, he withdrew from the connection, and organized a new society under the imposing title of "Bible Christian Connection." There is a striking resemblance between this body and the Primitives. It admits lay delegates to its Conferences in equal proportion to its ministers, whereas the Primitives allow two to one. This connection reported, in 1874, 1,993 travelling and local preachers, and 26,878 members.

V. The Primitive Wesleyan Methodists. — This is the name of a party that seceded in Ireland in 1816, under the influence of Rev. Adam Averill, a clergyman of the Church of England, and a Methodist according to the custom of olden times. The British Conference had allowed the English to have preaching in "church hours," and to administer and receive the sacraments among themselves, some twenty years before. About 1810 the Irish Methodists began to petition the Conference to allow them the same privileges, and not require them to receive the sacraments of church clergymen, in whose piety they had no confidence. The petition was reasonable ; and after several year's delay the Conference yielded, and the Irish were permitted to exercise the liberties enjoyed by their brethren across the channel. This so offended the minority, who professed great reverence for Mr. Wesley's "Plan" and the mother church, that they seceded, with Mr. Averill at their head, and organized under the foregoing title, which answers well to their pretensions. But they did not prove to be quite as Wesleyan as their title would indicate ; for they first abandoned the legal obligations of Wesley's "Deed," and then altered the constitution of their Conference so as to admit lay delegates. Besides, they inserted a clause in their chapel deed, by which their houses are forfeited to the Crown the moment service is held therein during "canonical time," or the sacraments are administered by their own preachers, whom they regard as mere laymen.

The advancement of this society has not been very encouraging. At first, they had several preachers, and about 9,000 members, mostly located in the north of Ireland, where the outbreak occurred. Their servility to the church, lay representation, and hostility to the Wesleyans, have secured them many favorable glances from the world ; but still they drag on heavily, effecting little for themselves, and less for the cause of God, showing clearly that their secession has been more vexatious than profitable.

VI. The Independent, and Wesleyan Protestant Methodists. — These are two small bodies which separated from the British Conference in the year 1827, in consequence of not being allowed to dictate in important matters, contrary to Methodist usage. The Protestants thought the ministry had too much power. They also took offence at the introduction of an *organ* into the Brunswick chapel in Leeds; and would not countenance the use of the liturgy in the public services. Finding that the connection was against them, and that there was little hope of effecting a reform, they withdrew, and took a new name. But, strange as it may seem, we find in their "Rules," published three years afterwards, an express provision for the use of the liturgy in the London chapel, and the introduction of an organ into the Burley chapel.

The Independent Methodists are no better. They scarcely have any regular ministry, being served by local preachers. These two sects together number but very few members, and their history is a beautiful comment on those theories of church government which would subordinate clerical authority to the dictation of the people. The least we ought to learn from them is, that the *people* may be *popish* as well as the *priest;* and that they, having the *purse* of the church, cannot be invested with legislative power without some risk to their humility, and some danger to the rights of the clergy.

VII. The Wesleyan Association Methodists, or Warrenites. — The organization of this body occurred in 1834, under the direction of one Dr. Samuel Warren. Dr. Fisk, in writing from England, remarked, "It is thought Dr. Warren became disaffected from the same reason that Diotrephes opposed the apostles." To effect a change in the government, he began to agitate the subject, making clerical *domination* prominent in his bill of indictment. And finding certain leading men in his way, he attacked them with great violence, and would neither cease nor retract, whereupon he was brought before the Manchester district meeting, and suspended. This he took in high dudgeon, and, conspiring with his disaffected brethren, he "appealed to *Cæsar*," commencing suits in the court of chancery against the chairman of the district, Dr. Newton, and the Trustees of the Oldham street chapel, asking the court to reverse the decission of the district meeting and of the trustees, and restore him to the official duties and privileges from which he had been suspended. The case was argued, and all the weaknesses of the Wesleyan Platform exposed. But his honor, the vice-chancellor, understood the law differently, and decided in favor of the Conference and the trustees. But the doctor was not satisfied, and appealed to the "Lord High Chancellor," who, after giving the case a suitable hearing, confirmed the decision of the lower courts, leaving the doctor still in suspense, and establishing the legality of the old Wesleyan "Deed of Declaration," and the authority of the Conference.

This was more than the excited party could endure, and hence they seceded, and set up for themselves. The doctor stood by them for a time; but finding the laity inclined to exercise a little too much lordship over the ministry, or, at all events, the reform not working to his mind, he seceded again, and took refuge in the Church of England. The little band of adventurers which he led out from among the Wesleyans struggled bravely for the faith until 1857, when it combined with several other small secessions and formed what is now known as

THE UNITED METHODIST CHURCHES of England.—Its eighteenth Annual Conference was held July 29, 1874, and reported 358 travelling preachers, 3,374 local preachers, 71,427 members and probationers, 165,528 Sunday School scholars, and over $50,000 collected for missions.

It is to be hoped that they will now go on and do much good.

VIII. THE METHODIST EPISCOPAL CHURCH, in Canada, is not quite a secession from the Wesleyan connection, and yet it comes pretty near it. When the Canada Conference separated from the Methodist Episcopal Church, it was *episcopal*, and designed to remain so; but afterward changed its mind, and, constitutionally, "did away" with episcopacy, and united with the British Connection. A respectable minority were dissatisfied, and retained their old name and arrangements, adding thereto to meet the necessities of their unfortunate condition. They have *one* Annual Conference, two bishops, 236 travelling and 214 local preachers, and 22,641 church members. They publish a weekly paper, the "*Canada Christian Advocate;*" have a Book Concern, and are a pious and useful people.

IX. There was a secession projected in 1849, which seemed more alarming than any of its predecessors. It had been maturing several years. The main object of it evidently was to break down the Wesleyan Connection, and it was not altogether unsuccessful. More than sixty thousand members withdrew from that body in the course of a few months, and a very bitter controversy ensued, lasting several years and damaging all parties, and the cause of Christ particularly.

The disaffection arose from the rigidity and power of the Conference, or, more properly speaking, the position and influence of leading members of it. Such men are always an annoyance to ambitious aspirants, however kind and prudent. They have been particularly so in the British connection, and have excited the envy, jealousy, and, perhaps, the malignity of their inferiors. At all events, they have been pursued by them with great severity, for many years. They were finally attacked in certain "*Fly Sheets*," or tracts, and traduced in the most merciless manner; which elicited an inquisition for the detection of the writers, and resulted in the expulsion of Messrs. Everett, Dunn, and Griffith, who, no doubt, deserved the punishment they received.

As to the merits of the controversy, we may not be in a condition to judge discreetly. Yet, believing that many entertain mistaken notions, we can hardly forbear to say a few words upon the subject. We give it as our opinion, therefore, that both parties were at fault. Though the Conference has often yielded, we think it has always been too fastidious about *little things*, and has imprudently *crushed* both men and measures it should *kindly* have *managed* and turned to good account. *Intolerance* of individual opinions and movements has been its chief fault. It has attempted to *govern* too much, and that by dint of ecclesiastical *authority*, rather than *moral influence*, and has often aggravated the evil it would remedy. Had it adopted a written constitution many years ago, abolishing the distinction between the *platform* members and others, or, at least, making *platform* privileges equally eligible to all, and not dependent upon the *fancy* of the president and his favorites, it would have saved them much trouble. We think, too, that *open* Conferences would have been favorable to their interests; and have not a doubt that more frequent voting by *ballot*, rather than by hand vote, under the burning gaze of leading committee men, would have hindered those men from controlling every thing, and given better satisfaction. But we are afraid these venerable fathers have coveted more of the offices, honors, and emoluments of the connection than was proper. A few individuals long held all the offices of the Conference, notwithstanding others were equally qualified. Dr. Bunting, for instance, lived in London *eighteen* years out of forty-one, and Thomas Jackson *nineteen* years out of thirty-six; the former belonging to *twelve*, and the latter to *ten*, of the connectional committees most of the time. This concentration of influence in a *clique* of even the *best of men* is always offensive and impolitic.

But however faulty the Conference, it affords no justification of the reformers. If the "*Wesleyan Times*," their organ was a fair exponent of the spirit of the movement, it was evidently persecuting and wicked in the extreme. No Christian can countenance it for a moment, however he may dislike the Conference. We had reached this conclusion, when an Irish preacher, now of our church, wrote us as follows: —

"It is our deliberate conviction that the secession is more destitute of goodness than any that has occurred in Methodism Whether the Conference be right or wrong, the Secessionists are not right. The spirit they manifest and the means they employ have nothing of God in them, but bear the impress of the '*evil one*,' in envy, hatred, malice, and all uncharitableness. And it will be an evil day for Methodism, when it shall be administered by such men. We speak advisedly. We have no affinity for toryism, nor have we any sympathy for tyranny and oppression; but, having read most of the publications on both sides, (the *Fly sheets* not excepted,) having sat nearly three days in the British Conference listening to the trial of the expelled ministers, and having a personal knowledge of nearly all the parties connected with the controversy, it is our deliberate judgment that there is a great misunderstanding of the subject in this country, and that justice is not done to the Conference.

"The master spirit in the movement is John Harrison, formerly a local preacher, but now conductor of the '*Wes-*

leyan Times.' He is a man of limited prudence, great rashness, and entirely unfit to be the leading spirit of a *religious* movement. From first to last, the venerable Dr. Bunting has been the principal object at which has been aimed the envenomed arrows of this contest. We are not a blind and undiscriminating admirer of this great man. But when he has devoted his almost unequalled powers to our common Methodism, for fifty-two years, and stood by it in the hour of trial, when he has labored and sacrificed more for it than any other living man, we cannot approve of hiding behind a mask and blasting his fair fame, now that he is just upon the verge of the grave. The Methodist community will never consent, on anonymous charges, and without trial or conviction, to doom any man to degradation, much less Jabez Bunting. We see him now, as he stood up before the Conference, in 1849, on the examination of char acter. President Jackson, on reading his name, inquired, 'Is there any objection to Jabez Bunting?' and there was a pause. His enemies, who had striven to overthrow his character, and send him down to the grave in disgrace, under the charge of being a *lazy, selfish, and deceitful tyrant*, were there. The eyes of *six hundred* Methodist preachers turned alternately to them and to him. That was the time and place to accuse him; but all were silent! Although he arose, the question was asked again, '*Is there any objection to Jabez Bunting?*' and again there was a pause. But no accuser appeared. With a voice suppressed by emotion, which gave additional interest to his venerable appearance, never to be forgotten, Mr. Bunting addressed his brethren in a brief but noble speech, denying the various accusations published against him, and calling upon those who had known him for fifty years to judge between him and his acccusers. When he sat down, there was a burst of enthusiastic and repeated applause, in which every voice in the assembly was employed, except, perhaps, *three or four*.

"What could he have done more? And what could his brethren have done less than to expel a noisy faction, who would not prefer a charge in the disciplinary way, nor cease to pursue them and their worthy fathers with falsehood and abuse. If the venerable Bishop Hedding should be placed in such a situation, the hearts of American Methodists would burn with holy indignation, and they would drag his slanderers to the light, and require them to sustain their assertions or retract them. On receiving this communication we wrote as follows:

What will be the result of this agitation can only be inferred from the history of others which have gone before. Such movements seldom meet the expectations of their friends, especially where they are based upon a mere question of *order*, *or abstract right*. Most Christians care little about the technics of government, so long as they feel no undue restraint. There may be theoretical faults; but where *they* are not oppressed, especially where they enjoy peculiar privileges, and witness glorious practical results that do not appear in the working of other systems, they will be cautious in their attempts at reform, and will not abandon a certainty for an uncertainty, nor risk the life of the patient upon a darling experiment. Revolution seldom succeeds where there is no great moral grievance. Ambitious leaders may venture every thing on a less occasion; but honest Christians will not submit to ecclesiastical martyrdom for a doubtful hypothesis. Nor can they conscientiously lay waste the fair fields of Zion for certain *notions* of government, however they may desire to see them adopted We predict, therefore, that the storm will blow over with less numerical loss to the connection, and vastly less of union and strength in the new organization, than is anticipated. Yet it is a moral pestilence, the disastrous consequences of which will reach to the latest generation, and affect the destinies of eternity.

This prediction has been more than fulfilled. The seceders contended among themselves, struggled with their difficulties, and, finally, combined with the Warrenites and others, in 1857, to form the UNITED METHODIST CHURCHES before mentioned.

We have referred to these painful divisions for the purpose of erecting a beacon of warning to those who may come after. They speak to all concerned, in a language that cannot be misunderstood. The great and the strong should learn not to despise the weak and foolish, but to cherish them as a mother her children. If they pray, hear them *patiently*, and treat them *kindly*. Never stand for technicalities, where the peace of the church, and the welfare of souls, is at stake. If they "compel you to go a mile, go with them *twain*," if you can do so with a good conscience. It is magnanimous to be conciliatory. If you cannot comply with their wishes, *respect* them, however unreasonable. This may influence them to love you, though they may still think you in error.

The disaffected should also learn to be modest in their demands, and patient under defeat. The fact that they are in the minority is presumptive evidence that their views are erroneous. Their brethren are as likely to be wise and good as themselves. If they are not, which is possible, they are in no condition to be hurried, much less *driven*. Besides, measures carried in a bad spirit, and by artifice, will not prosper.

CHAPTER VIII.

ORIGIN OF METHODISM IN AMERICA.

How little we know of the ultimate results of our endeavors! In crossing the Atlantic, to trace the history of Methodism in the new world, we are first of all met with the interesting fact that the handful of seed scattered in Ireland by Mr. Wesley and his helpers germinated a Christian family in America, that, in little more than half a century, was unequalled in numbers and moral influence by any other in the catalogue of evangelical denominations.

The first Methodist society in this country was organized in the city of New York, in the year 1766. It was composed of emigrants from Ireland, who had been converted at home and joined the Wesleyans. Coming among strangers, when vital piety was at a low ebb, and sinful pleasure the idol of all classes of the community, they turned away from the simplicity of the cross, drank into the spirit of the world, and commenced to run after its vanities. But another family arrived, in which there was a "mother in Israel," whose heart was grieved at the recreancy of her fellow pilgrims. Learning at a time that they were engaged in vain amusements, and feeling that their course demanded a rebuke, trusting in their respect for her age, and in God for the success of the measure, she rushed into the room where they were assembled, seized the cards with which they were playing, and threw them into the fire. She new exhorted them to desist from their backsliding, and return unto the Lord. To Mr. Philip Embury, one of the party, but formerly a preacher, she said, "And *you* must preach to us, or we shall all go to hell together, and God will require our blood at your hands!" When he objected that he had neither house nor congregation, she replied, in the true spirit of Christian enterprise, "Preach in your own house first, and to our own company." The duty was too obvious and important to be resisted, and he yielded to importunity and preached the first Methodist sermon ever delivered in the country, "*in his own hired house*," and to a congregation of *five persons*.

This opened the way for other meetings, in which the little band exhorted each other to faith and good works, and revealed to the few who condescended to notice them the spirit of vital religion. However, they did not attract much attention, or attain any great achievements, though they gradually increased, and found it necessary to obtain a larger room. Here they assembled regularly, and Mr. Embury led their devotions. But not being a man of much talent, and having to follow his secular calling for a livelihood, he did not make a great impression. Something a little startling was necessary to call the people out. And this, Divine Providence was about to introduce.

In the year 1765 an officer in the English army was awakened and converted under the ministry of Mr. Wesley, at Bristol. Such was the grace of God in him that he felt constrained to declare what the Lord had done for his soul, and to warn his fellow soldiers to flee from the wrath to come. About this time he was constituted barrack-master at Albany, New York. Hearing, on his arrival, of the little society in the city, he soon appeared in the midst of them, in his official costume, and awakened no little interest. A converted soldier was a novelty, but not quite so great as a minister of Christ preaching the gospel in regimentals. But Capt. Webb had other charms ; he spake the word with power and with the Holy Ghost.

Thus the new room was soon overflowed, and the society was obliged to seek other accommodations. This led to the hiring of a rigging-loft in Williams street, which, however, did not answer the purpose long. There was too much of novelty, and too much evidence that God was in the movement, to allow the matter to pass unnoticed! The people would come to hear for themselves, though the established ministry warned them against it; and many became alarmed about their souls, turned to the Lord and joined the society, so that the loft became too strait for them. This suggested a meeting-house, which, after much prayer, planning and begging, resulted in the erection of the old John Street Church, the modest picture of which so often appears in our books and papers. This was the first Methodist meeting-house in America, and it was dedicated to God Oct. 30, 1768, about thirty years after the birth of Methodism in England, and two years after its appearance in this country. The services were performed by Mr. Embury.

This interesting event was too good to conceal; and as one supply usually creates another necessity, so it did in this case. Mr. Wesley would rejoice to hear of what was doing, and another preacher was necessary to occupy the new house. Mr. Wesley was, therefore, addressed upon the subject, and immediately acquiesced in the wishes of the society so far as to send them *fifty* pounds sterling toward their debt, and two missionaries, Richard Boardman and Joseph Pillmore. They arrived in Philadelphia, Oct. 24, 1769, when Mr. Boardman repaired immediately to New

York, and commenced his labors in the city and the surrounding country.

But while the society was reaching this advanced point, there were influences at work in other parts. Capt. Webb had been reconnoitering Long Island, and other places, even as far as Philadelphia, and had succeeded in laying the foundation of a good work. In the meantime, Robert Strawbridge, another local preacher from Ireland, arrived in Maryland, and commenced preaching in his own house, and other places, in " demonstration of the Spirit," raised up a society, and built a log church. Mr. Pillmore entered at once into the labors of the former, finding about one hundred in society at Philadelphia, and visited and strengthened the latter in the work that filled his heart. He also went into Virginia and North Carolina.

The ministry was soon strengthened by the arrival of Messrs. Robert Williams and John King, local preachers from England. October, 1771, Messrs. Francis Asbury and Richard Wright arrived, as missionaries sent out by Mr. Wesley. They found about six hundred members in society, and entered into the harvest in good cheer, and with a single eye. Mr. Asbury labored in New York and its vicinity during the winter, and displayed itinerant enterprise by penetrating all parts of the country. In the summer of 1773 two other missionaries arrived, Messrs. Thomas Rankin and George Shadford. The former, having travelled considerable longer than Mr. Asbury, was made general Assistant, or Superintendent, in his place.

Up to this period no regular Conference had been holden, and little conventional business had been done. The preachers were scattered about in different States, and were appropriating their labors as circumstances seemed to require. But now, Mr. Rankin, having received authority from Mr. Wesley, summoned a Conference of the preachers in Philadelphia, to commence on the fourth of July. Here it was agreed that Mr. Wesley ought to exercise the same authority over the preachers and societies in this country he did in England, and that the doctrine and discipline contained in the *Minutes* should be the rule of their action. It was further agreed that the ministers should not administer the ordinances, and the people should be encouraged to receive them at the Episcopal Church. The societies embraced *ten* itinerant preachers and *eleven hundred and sixty* members. The appointments of the preachers made at this Conference may be of some interest. They were as follows: —

New York — Thomas Rankin. } To change in four
Philadelphia — George Shadford. } months.
New Jersey — John King, William Waters.
Baltimore — Francis Asbury, Robert Strawbridge, Abraham Whitworth, Joseph Yearbry.
Norfolk — Richard Wright.
Petersburg — Robert Williams.

William Waters was the first native that joined the itinerancy, and he continued in it till he entered into his Master's joy.

From this period to the Conference of 1784, when the society was organized into a separate and distinct church, it was subjected to various conflicts, which at times threatened its existence. One class of these arose from the revolutionary struggle, which commenced in 1776 and continued to 1783. War, in any circumstances, is disastrous to religion and virtue in the community at large. Where armies are marching and counter-marching through the country, and husbands, and sons, and brothers, of every neighborhood, are in the battle-field, amidst carnage and death, it is impossible to fix the public mind on any other subject, even where there is the utmost harmony in relation to the cause and objects of the war. But one unfortunate feature of this war was, that the community were divided about it, a part contending earnestly for independence and the other part for continued subordination to the mother country. On this question the father was often found arrayed against the son, and the son against the father; the husband against the wife, and the wife against the husband, for the women were nearly as strong politicians as the men. So that, had the ministers of the sanctuary been angels, they would have been exposed to the cruel jealousy of both parties, and, therefore, unlikely to convert either to the Lord. But they must have been more than angels to have gained great spiritual victories amid so much excitement, even in the absence of all jealousy.

But it was unfortunate for Methodism that most of our preachers were Englishmen. This exposed them to peculiar suspicion. It was still more unfortunate that some of them allowed their patriotism to betray them into imprudencies, which justly exposed them, not only to suspicion, but to other evils; and finally compelled them to leave the country The difficulty was greatly augmented by a pamphlet published by Mr. Wesley, and addressed to Americans, condemning their conduct, and taking sides with the English Cabinet. In the existing state of the public mind, these intimations of denominational toryism were of no doubtful character. But, as if to leave no room to doubt, a backslider must needs set himself to enlist three hundred men for the British standard, which cost him his life, and his old Methodist friends considerable trouble, as they were supposed to be parties to the plot.

The excitement arose to such a pitch that the preachers were greatly interrupted. Most of the missionaries returned to England; Mr. Asbury concealed himself at Judge White's, in Delaware, for almost one year. Mr. Garrettson and others, who ventured to continue in the field, were severely mobbed, persecuted, and imprisoned.

The question of the sacraments was another source of difficulty that came near destroying the unity of the body. The missionaries, and many others, were intent upon cleaving to Mr. Wesley and the church, and would not countenance the administration of the sacraments on any account; while some believed that Methodists had as good a right to the sacraments as churchmen, and repudiated the practice of depending upon the English clergy, who were generally irreligious, if not immoral and profane. They, therefore, broke away from the old custom, and administered the sacraments as the people desired. Hence the action had at the first Conference. After this the subject was called up and discussed from time to time, till 1779, when the war had driven most of the clergy out of the country, changed our relations to England, and had thus created a new argument for the sacraments in the society. The Southerners could stand it no longer, and, therefore, as they were in the minority, and could not get a vote in the Conference to carry out their wishes, they called the preachers together at Fluvanna, Va., on the 18th of May, 1779, where, in spite of many entreaties, they set up their standard, and appointed a committee to ordain ministers. The committee first ordained each other, and then they ordained their brethren, whereupon they all went forth preaching the gospel of the kingdom, and administering the sacraments. Mr. Asbury labored hard to reclaim them, but in vain, till the Conference of 1780, when he persuaded them to suspend their new order for one year. This suspension was continued till Mr. Wesley provided for the necessities of the society in a way that gave general satisfaction.

It was during this period, too, that Methodism commenced its conflict with slavery, and received its first onset from slaveholders. It dared then to say, in Baltimore, that "slavery is contrary to the laws of God, man, and nature, and hurtful to society; contrary to the dictates of conscience and pure religion, and doing that which we would not that others should do to us and ours." It spake out, also, against distilling liquor, and warned the people against these evils, as too wicked to be tolerated. But in the midst of all their perplexities they prospered. God wrought mightily upon the public heart, and many were born of the spirit. Mr. Rankin's account of what he saw and felt gives a pretty clear view of what was rather common in those times. He says: —

"At four in the afternoon I preached again, from 'I set before thee an open door, and none can shut it.' I had gone through about two-thirds of my discourse, and was bringing the words home to the present *now*, when such power descended that hundreds fell to the ground, and the house seemed to shake with the presence of God. The chapel was full of white and black, and many were without that could not get in. Look wherever we would, we saw nothing but streaming eyes, and faces bathed in tears; and heard nothing but the groans and prayers of the congregation. I then sat down in the pulpit; and both Mr. S. and I were so filled with the divine presence that we could only say, 'This is none other than the house of God! this is the gate of heaven!' Husbands were inviting their wives to go to heaven, wives their husbands, parents their children, and children their parents, brothers their sisters, and sisters their brothers. In short, those who were happy in God, themselves, were for bringing all their friends to him in their arms. This mighty effusion of the spirit continued for above an hour; in which many were awakened, some found peace with God, and others his pure love. We attempted to speak or sing again and again, but we had no sooner begun than our voices were drowned.

"Sunday, 7. I preached at W.'s Chapel. I intended to preach near the house, under the shade of some large trees. But the rain made it impracticable. The house was very greatly crowded; four or five hundred stood at the doors and windows, and listened with unabated attention. I preached from Ezekiel's vision of dry bones: 'And there was a great shaking.' I was obliged to stop again and again, and beg of the people to compose themselves. But they could not; some on their knees, and some on their faces, were crying mightily to God all the time I was preaching. Hundreds of negroes were among them, with the tears streaming down their faces."

Thus, by the divine blessing, the society stemmed the current, and gained a little every year, so that, in 1784, it numbered *eighty-three* travelling preachers, and 14,986 members.

The question that now seemed to command particular attention was that of ordinances, before mentioned. It was plain that something must be done, or there would be a division in the body. Mr. Wesley had watched the progress of the controversy, and was prepared for the crisis. Accordingly, by the aid of Dr. Coke and Rev. Mr. Creighton, presbyters of the Church of England, he ordained Richard Whatcoat and Thomas Vasey presbyters for America; after which, he ordained Dr. Coke a superintendent, and sent them out with all proper testimonials of orders and of office.

These good men arrived in New York on the 3d of November, 1784. After consultation with Mr. Asbury, and others, it was agreed to call a Conference of all the preachers, to convene in Baltimore the ensuing Christmas. The time arrived, and *sixty* of the *eighty-three* travelling preachers then in the connection, appeared. Dr. Coke presided, assisted by Mr. Asbury, whom Mr. Wesley had appointed joint superintendent. The first act of the Conference was to elect Dr. Coke and Francis Asbury superintendents. This was done to accommodate the scruples of Mr. Asbury, who declined acting on the appointment of Mr. Wesley, without such an election; not that he doubted the authority of Mr. Wesley, but he wished to know that his appointment was approved by the body over which he was to preside. He was then first ordained deacon, afterwards elder, and finally consecrated, by Dr. Coke and others, to the office of superintendent, all according to Mr. Wesley's directions. The Conference then elected twelve others to the order of elder, who were duly consecrated by the imposition of hands.

It was at this Conference that our present articles of religion, and the general system of discipline by which the church has since been governed, were adopted. The prudential arrangements of the church have, of course, experienced various modifications, and prudence will dictate others; but the main features of the discipline agreed upon at that time have been sacredly maintained to the present.

This is a brief outline of the organization of the Methodist Episcopal Church in the United States of America. Till now, like her maternal ancestor on the other side of the Atlantic, she had only been a *society*, and her members stood connected with the various churches in the country, to suit their respective tastes. The measure gave general satisfaction, both to the ministry and membership, and is susceptible of the strongest defence; but defence is not necessary.

CHAPTER IX.

THE FIRST GENERAL CONFERENCE, WITH NUMEROUS HISTORICAL EVENTS WHICH OCCURRED PREVIOUS TO 1820.

PASSING along to the year 1792, we are attracted by another important event in our history, viz.: the *first* session of the General Conference. But we must not dismiss this interval of eight years without noting a few particulars. Dr. Coke was in England a part of the time, but always popular and useful. Bishop Asbury traversed the country from end to end, preaching, attending Conferences, and overseeing the work, amid dangers and deaths that few men, and especially men of his office, would have brooked. But he construed his official distinction into a divine call to be more abundant in labors and sufferings for Christ's sake; and to set an example to the flock, especially to the preachers. Therefore he forded rivers, and traversed mountains and swamps, sleeping in the forests, and on miserable beds and floors, that made him sigh for "a clean *plank*." O, how much is the church indebted to this noble man for his unexampled activity and willing sacrifice for the cause of God at that time! Had an aristocratic, dronish, worldly-minded man happened to have been in that sacred place, American Methodism would have been a different thing from what it is.

These men had only entered upon the duties of their new office, before they projected a literary institution for the education of the preachers' sons, and others, which its friends were pleased to call "*Cokesbury College.*" This was located in Abingdon, Maryland; but had been in operation less than ten years, when the nice brick buildings, which cost the bishops immense labor, were burnt to the ground. Dr. Coke now rallied, and having a liberal offer in Baltimore, re-opened the college in a large building in that town, purchased for the purpose. This was also consumed soon after, which led some to believe that God was not pleased with the enterprise.

As we have designated the superintendents by the term *bishops*, it may be proper to say that the *Conference* adopted this title in 1787. But they did not change the nature or powers of their office. Dr. Coke was still just the officer that Mr. Wesley ordained him to be when he set him apart to the superintendency. Mr. Wesley knew that his proper title was *bishop*, but he was aware if he called him by that title he would offend the church. Therefore, he preferred the harmless name of superintendent. But the Conference stood in a different relation to the church from what Mr. Wesley did, and saw no good reason why they should not call its officers by their proper titles. Whether it has injured the superintendents, or benefited the Conference, we are unable to determine. Croakers have made much noise about the matter, but to very little purpose.

The year 1789, in particular, was a memorable year. The itinerant work had become so extended the bishops held eleven Conferences. This multiplication of Conferences brought up another difficulty. No one of them was authorized to make rules binding upon the whole. This suggested the idea of a *council*, to be composed of the bishops and the presiding elders of all the Conferences. (And, by the way, this is the year that the title of presiding elder was first used in the Minutes, though the office was created four years before.) The suggestion was adopted, and the council went into operation; but only met twice before it was repudiated, and gave way to a General Conference. Here, also, we find the first mention of a *book-steward*, John Dickens, whose first work was to print "A. Kempis."

But the matter of principal interest during the whole eight years was the triumphs of divine grace over the sins and prejudices of the people. Revivals were powerful and extensive. The Lord seemed to attend the word with peculiar energy, so that at the Conference in 1792 there were *two hundred and sixty-six* travelling preachers in the connection, and *sixty-five thousand nine hundred and eighty* members, scattered over an immense territory, embracing Nova Scotia and Upper Canada, on the north and east, and the extremes of the settled portions of the south and west.

This General Conference, properly enough called the *first*, was held in Baltimore, November, 1792. Here the whole economy of the church was reviewed, and such alterations made as the experience of previous years suggested. But one man especially had it in his heart to produce a radical change in the government. We refer to the Rev. James O'Kelley, a very popular preacher, and an old presiding elder, from Virginia. His plan provided that, after the reading of the appointments of the preachers by the bishop, if any one thought himself injured, he might appeal to the Conference, and state his objections, when, if the Conference thought them sufficient, the bishop should change his appointment. It was discussed about three days with great interest, and then rejected by a large majority. This gave Mr. Kelley great offence, and the next morning he resigned his seat. Every thing was done by the Conference to appease him, except to adopt his plan, but to no purpose. He withdrew from the church, and formed a separate party, raising a hue and cry against the church he had left, and denouncing the ministers, and especially Bishop Asbury. The good bishop simply replied: "I bid all such adieu, and appeal to the bar of God. I have no time to contend, having better work to do. If we lose some children, God will give us more. Ah! this is the mercy, the justice of some, who, under God, owe their all to me and my *tyrants*, so called. The Lord judge between them and me."

The excitement was great, and many seceded and joined the new party. To make some gain of the political fever which raged in those times, they took the name of "*Republican Methodists*." This brought the spirit of the world to their aid, and many of the people, some whole societies in Virginia, withdrew, and took their meeting-houses with them, while others were imbittered, divided, and destroyed. In the course of the four years immediately succeeding this outbreak, the church decreased in her membership more than twelve thousand. But, after all, the enterprise did not succeed. The travelling preachers found there was more popery in the new concern than in the old, notwithstanding its title and pretensions, and all but *one* returned to the church, bringing large numbers of the people with them. Those who remained, struggled on, but with little encouragement. In 1801 they sought to help a sinking cause by a new name, and came out under the imposing cognomen of "*The Christian Church*." The exclusiveness of this title operated against them, and, falling into a contention among themselves, they divided, and sub-divided, till not a vestige of their ecclesiastical edifice remained. Mr. O'Kelley sunk away into obscurity, and died a pitiful specimen of human weakness, and a beacon of warning to his successors, not to sacrifice the unity and prosperity of the church, or their own integrity and usefulness, upon hypothetical notions of reform, and especially upon slight occasions.

But the effects of this movement did not soon disappear. Some who seceded lost their religion and their souls, we fear; others, who retained some regard for the cause, became too much disaffected to be at home and useful in any church; while a prejudice was excited against Methodism, and religion itself, in the community, that was not easily obliterated. But it settled the question of appeal from the appointment of the bishops for sometime. We hear no more of it till the year 1800, when Dr. Coke introduced it, and finally recommended that the new bishop (not making it to apply at all to Bishop Asbury) be assisted in making the appointments by a committee of three or four preachers to be chosen by the Conference. This was rejected by the Conference, with several propositions of like effect. The next we hear about restricting the appointing power, is in the year 1808, when it was proposed so to alter the Discipline as to allow the Conferences to elect the presiding elders. This proposition was ably discussed, and rejected by a vote of *seventy-three* to *fifty-two*. In 1812 the same question was again introduced, and, after a thorough discussion, the proposition was rejected only by a majority of three. Four years later it met the same fate, though it was presented in a modified form. In 1820 it was again discussed, and disposed of as before. But there being considerable feeling on the subject, it was called up again in the spirit of compromise, and referred to a committee composed of an equal number of brethren of different views, to confer with the bishops, and strike out some course that might conciliate all parties. Their report recommended that, on the occurrence of vacancies in the presiding eldership, the presiding bishop should nominate three times the number wanted, out of which the Conference should elect the necessary number by ballot; and the presiding elders, thus elected, should be an advisory council to the bishops in appointing the preachers. The report was adopted by a vote of *sixty-one* in favor, to *twenty-five* against it, and it was supposed this would put the question to rest, perhaps for ever.

But this was not the case. Bishop Soule, who had been elected to the episcopal office a few days previous, signified to the Conference that he thought the measure unconstitutional, and he should not conform to it. Bishop M'Kendree, in a feeble state of health, urged that it was unconstitutional, and subversive of the superintendency, and also of the itinerancy. The former tendered his resignation, which was accepted, and the Conference adhered to its position. But considering the age of Bishop M'Kendree, the decision of Bishop Soule, and the anxiety of many others, it was voted to suspend the new rule for four years. The next General Conference continued the suspension; but in 1828 the rule was rescinded; since which time little has been said on the subject, except in periodicals and lectures in resistance of ultra reformers. The presumption is, that these men, and their severe measures, operated against the very thing they sought, and delayed the consummation they wished to hasten.

The first General Conference was composed of all the travelling preachers who pleased to attend. In the year 1800 it was limited to those who had travelled four years In 1808 it was agreed that it should be composed in future of one delegate for every five members of each Annual Conference. The ratio of representation has since been altered as the ministry has increased in number. It is now *one* delegate to every *forty-five* members, and the Conference assembles once in four years, and is governed by a constitution, limiting its powers, adopted also in 1808. This constitution is popularly known as the "*Restrictive Rules*," and may be seen in the Discipline, in the section which defines the duties and powers of the General Conference.

Taking our leave of the General Conference of 1792, and the secession which occurred about that time under the leadership of Mr. O'Kelley, we move pleasantly along amid labors and triumphs for many years. The men on whom it devolved to command, in those days, were extraordinary characters. Dr. Coke, Bishop Asbury, Jesse Lee, George Roberts, Freeborn Garrettson, Ezekiel Cooper, Benjamin Abbott, and others, acted a chivalrous part, and left their successors an example of prudent legislation and of heroic effort, that can never be forgotten. New England was about the hardest soil they found to cultivate; but even this yielded to their perseverance, and many societies were formed.

The theology of this section of country had always been Calvinistic, and *Congregationalism* was sustained by law in two of the States at least; so that Methodists were obliged to pay their parish taxes, have their property attached, or go to jail. Men are now living who submitted to imprisonment, because they could not conscientiously pay taxes to support a system they believed to be false and dangerous: the parish thinking a little "prison discipline" would have a better effect in subduing their obstinacy than the loss of a few articles of property which it might have taken. Others have a distinct recollection of their property being attached to meet parish claims, when it was known they were Methodists, and supported Methodist preaching. But this state of things could not long endure. The right of petition had not then been trampled down, and Methodists, and others who were not so wedded to popular views as to be blind to the claims of justice, prayed the honorable court of legislation to allow them to worship God according to the dictates of their own consciences. They were only ridiculed at first, but afterward they succeeded in throwing off the yoke, and securing the right of thinking for them selves, and sustaining such views and modes of worship as they considered Scriptural. How much the various classes of dissenters in Massachusetts and Connecticut owe to the Methodists for the liberties they have long enjoyed in this particular, they cannot now realize.

Another reason why Methodism found it so difficult to get a foothold in this country, was its theology. It discarded principles that had been long cherished as the very marrow of the gospel, and vindicated others that were held to be dangerously heretical. It broke over parish lines, too, that had been drawn by law with great precision, and planted itself wherever sinners could be induced to repent and believe the gospel. And its ministry, instead of taking any particular location, ransacked the whole country, and excited the people to think about their souls. All these things, and many others, created a prejudice, and brought out the clergy in violent resistance of the new measures. The pulpit rang with denunciations of Methodism. Its real views were misrepresented; its errors were magnified; its ministers decried as the false prophets and deceivers that should come in the last days; and its assemblies persecuted and scattered. But, nevertheless, the Lord converted some, and the cause lived, not to be loved, we fear, by the dominant sects, but to be more patiently endured, if not respected. And not only so, but it lived to regenerate the body that at first repelled it with the greatest virulence and force. Not that it was entirely subdued to the new faith or modes of operation, but that it became so essentially modified in its creed, public instructions, and various movements for the conversion of souls, as to look very unlike its former self. This, we trust, will not be denied. It has been recognized on both sides of the house. Methodists have rejoiced to see their theology and ecclesiastical regimen transforming and imbuing other systems, and the rigid Calvinist has mourned over the defection of his people, and longed for the good old days, now, alas! for ever gone.

In other States and territories Methodism had less of this kind of opposition to resist. In no section had the people become so settled and united in theological error, and in hostility to Arminian views. Much of the country was new, and Methodists were permitted to take an even start with other sects. The result was, in many places they commanded the faith and affections of the people, and have been the leading denomination ever since, proving the superior adaptation of their system to convert men to God, where it can have an "open field and fair play," by exceeding all its competitors in rapid growth.

Dr. Bangs speaks of its early conflicts in these words: —

"For sometime the number of Methodists in this country was so inconsiderable that other denominations affected to treat them with silent contempt; and if, occasionally, they condescended to notice them at all, it was more in the way of caricature and misrepresentation than by sober argument or an attempt at a fair and direct refutation of their doctrin and usages. The high churchman would sneer at our ordination, and, wrapping himself in the cloak of apostolical succession, with an air of assumed dignity, prate about 'John Wesley's lay bishops,' as though these jokes were sufficient to put us out of countenance. Others, panoplied in the stern decrees of Calvin, and priding themselves in their exclusive

10

orthodoxy, would tantalize us 'with salvation by the *merit of good works*, the omnipotency of *free-will*, and the unsoundness of our doctrine of justification;' while some would smile at '*baby baptism*,' as an affront offered to the Deity, and an innovation upon apostolic usage."

In respect to church legislation in the early times of which we are speaking, it need only be said it was moderate; consisting in those slight changes which the progress of the cause seemed to demand. The General Conference of 1796 contemplated the numerous locations that had annually occurred with deep regret. And yet, while the labor was so excessively hard, the fare so poor, and the liability of premature old age, with poverty and want, was so great, there was little room to complain. To relieve these difficulties, and, if possible, check the tendency to location, the Conference established what is now known as the "Chartered Fund," and provided for an address to the people to meet the emergency, by contributing of their substance. Though this measure did not make up the deficiences of the preachers' claims, it did something toward it, and has since afforded partial relief; but whether it has not been the occasion of more withholding on the part of the people, is a question.

The year 1799 was distinguished for the origination of "*camp meetings*." This wonderful means of grace was providential in its conception. Two brothers by the name of *M'Gee*, one a Presbyterian minister, and the other a Methodist, went to attend a sacramental occasion with Rev. Mr. *M'Gready*, a Presbyterian minister in West Tennessee. The Methodist preached first, and was followed by the Presbyterian and the Rev. Mr. Hoge, whose preaching produced a powerful effect. One woman became so deeply impressed she shouted aloud for joy, and there were other demonstrations of an extraordinary character. Messrs. M'Gready, Hoge, and Rankins, all Presbyterian ministers, left the house; but the *M'Gees* remained to see the salvation of God. Great was the power that rested upon them. John was expected to preach, but he told the people that his feelings were such he could not, and sat down amid sobs and cries from every quarter. This brought the people out to see what these things might mean. Many came a great distance with horses, and waggons, and provisions, and so numerous was the crowd the church would not contain them. This drove them into the forest; and the distance of many from home, and the impossibility of obtaining accommodations among the people, made it necessary for them to camp out, which they did, worshipping God day and night.

This was something new, and attracted great attention. And it was no less effective. The different denominations, seeing that God was in the measure, gave it their countenance; but one after another withdrew, until it was left almost exclusively to the Methodists. Since that time they have employed it to good purpose, notwithstanding its old friends have said many hard things against it. In the early days of Methodism, when meeting-houses were few and preachers scarce, camp meetings were peculiarly useful. Hundreds were converted through their instrumentality. In the course of the eight years following their introduction, the net increase to the church was *eighty-two thousand six hundred and sixty-four members*, and a corresponding increase of preachers.

March 31, 1816, closed the career of that great and good man, and pioneer of Methodism in this country, Bishop Asbury. When he came to New York, *forty-five years* before, the Methodist connection numbered about *six hun dred* members. After battling with the winds and storms of near half a century, he bade a peaceful adieu to the church he had loved and cherished as a mother her children, embracing *six hundred and ninety-five travelling preachers, and two hundred fourteen thousand, two hundred and thirty-five members.* But these statistics convey only a faint idea of what was accomplished during the period named. To estimate this properly, we must consider how many were converted and taken to Abraham's bosom; how many joined other churches; how many more were improved and made happier and better in various respects; and how much was accomplished in extending the itinerant plan through the States and territories, and in the British Provinces; and in placing ministers at different points, among the various classes and tribes of men, to watch the indications of Providence, and preach the gospel in every place, whether palace or wigwam, that might be opened to receive it. A foundation was laid upon which others have built so nobly since, and without which they must have labored with less effect.

In looking over the history of the four years following the decease of this patriarch of Methodism, it is delightful to observe that, though the Lord took away the "master builder," he did not suffer the work to cease. Indeed, death was not permitted to touch him till others had been raised up with hearts and heads to take the cause where he left it, and bear it on toward its grand destination. The net increase during this time was *forty-five thousand, six hundred and fifty-five* members, and *two hundred and one* travelling preachers.

This period was distinguished, also, by certain prudential arrangements, which contributed greatly to the strength and influence of the body, and the extension of the work. The "Tract Society" of the Methodist Church was formed by a few individuals in 1817, with a view to supplying the poor with suitable religious reading. This furnished an easy and cheap method of reaching many people the church had never addressed, and answered as well for defence, as attack on the sins and prejudices of unbelievers. It was an old measure of Mr. Wesley's, and had been very useful. Its influence since that time is well understood.

The year following, the Methodist Magazine was issued, under the editorship of Rev. Joshua Soule. This was an advance step. It opened a medium of communication with the people that had long been needed. Not less than ten thousand subscribers were obtained the first year; and the doctrines and institutions of the gospel became better understood, and the people of God more established in the unity of the faith.

About this time, too, another effort was made to promote the cause of education in the church. The "Cokesbury College" had been twice burned, an attempt to establish district schools had failed, and the people were quite discouraged. But in 1817 Dr. Samuel K. Jennings and some others opened a literary institution in Baltimore, which they called "Asbury College." This, however, appeared but for a little time, and then, to the mortification of many, it vanished away. The same year an academy was established in Newmarket, N. H., under the patronage of the New England Conference; and two years after, another, in the city of New York, under the patronage of the New York Conference. These were approved by the next General Conference, and other Conferences were advised to establish similar institutions. The bishops were also authorized to appoint presidents, principals, or teachers, to all such establishments. But this was not effected without some opposition. Though the church owed so much to the learning of its founders, some did not realize the importance of education.

This period was also marked by the revival of camp meetings in Kentucky, where they had been quite suspended on account of various irregularities. The first one held in that quarter about this time was visited by many young men, with bottles of whiskey in their pockets, whose intention was to disturb and break up the meeting. But the church trusted in the Lord, and moved forward. Toward the close of the meeting the power of God fell upon the encampment. The young men referred to became alarmed, and some, dashing away their bottles, humbled themselves in prayer, while others fled to the woods, wailing with bitter anguish, and crying earnestly for mercy. Thus a great revival of religion commenced, which resulted in the conversion of hundreds.

"The Missionary and Bible Society of the Methodist Episcopal Church" was organized in the city of New York, April 5, 1819. A Missionary Society was formed within the bounds of the Philadelphia Conference about the same time. The next General Conference approved of both organizations; but considering the Book Room was in New York, and for some other reasons, it adopted the constitution of the society located there, bating that part which related to the publication of Bibles, and made its head quarters at the Book Room. To this central organization were soon added numerous auxiliaries, and the missionary spirit has continued to increase till the present moment, though not in proportion, we think, to the increase of our numbers and wealth.

During the last war with Great Britain, which was declared June 18, 1812, the relations of certain societies in the Canadas, with the Methodist E. Church, became considerably disturbed; and they applied to the British Conference for preachers, which were immediately supplied. This laid the foundation of much correspondence and negotiation between the two bodies. It was, however, conducted in an excellent spirit, all parties seeming determined not to contend, nor suffer their feelings to be agitated, or their friendly relations to be broken up. In the year 1820 the General Conference appointed Mr. John Emory a delegate to the British Conference, and adopted an address to that body, proposing a division of territory as the best method of bringing the question of difference to a settlement. The proposition was duly considered, and acceded to, by which Lower Canada became connected with the English Conference, and Upper Canada retained its former connection with us; each body withdrawing all its preachers from the other's ground, and agreeing in no way to interfere therewith; an example of urbanity and prudent management seldom if ever set before by two great denominations of Christians We mention this to show how our church became disconnected with a portion of territory upon which she bestowed early attention, and in which she achieved magnificent results; and will only add, that there has been no revival of the difficulty since.

CHAPTER X

IMPROVEMENTS, DEFECTIONS, AND SUCCESSES IN THE METHODIST EPISCOPAL CHURCH, PRIOR TO 1840.

As our Hymn Book has undergone several thorough revisions, it may be interesting to the reader to refer to its former history. The first collection in use in this country was prepared and printed by Mr. Wesley, and was entitled, "A collection of Psalms and Hymns for the Lord's day." It was printed in 1784. We are not informed whether it underwent any essential change till the time of which we are speaking, but presume it did not, as there was little enterprise in the Book Concern in those days. But the General Conference of 1820 adopted a revision made by the Book Committee, and ordered it to be printed. That edition was afterwards altered by affixing the names of the tunes to the hymns, and in 1836 a supplement was added. Thus it remained till superseded by another revision, ordered by the General Conference of 1848.

The General Conference of 1820 also provided for the publication of a tune book adapted to our wants. This continued in use till 1832, when it was revised and republished. Four years after, arrangements were made for an improved edition, which was in use for several years, when others were issued, of which we need not speak.

Up to this time, most of our houses of worship were free. The difficulty of erecting churches on this principle, however, had become quite obvious to many minds, and some had adopted the pew system. This gave considerable alarm, and the General Conference took decided ground on the subject. But its action had little effect. The *people* in certain sections found free houses utterly impracticable without encumbering themselves with unmanageable debts, and, therefore, took the responsibility of erecting pewed houses, as their English brethren did before Mr. Wesley's death, and have ever done since. [See *Dr. Dixon's remarks before the General Conference of* 1848.] This has always been a little afflictive to the South and West, but they have endured it as a less evil than no churches at all, which was the other alternative in many places. Had there been no restriction of this kind, it is believed we should have had more and better churches, with less debts, than we now enjoy; but perhaps not. So far as our free churches are concerned, we doubt if they can be legally altered without permission from the courts, however desirable, and we think it should not be attempted to make a division among brethren. But if enough desire a pewed house, in any portion of the country, to build one and maintain public worship therein in a peaceable and brotherly way, we think that they will be treated in a kind and conciliatory spirit by any Conference in the connection, however strongly biased in favor of free churches. In essential things, Methodists go for *unity;* in *non*-essentials for *liberty;* and in all things for *charity*. If some are Methodists in every thing except in relation to free houses, they should not abandon us, though denied the blessing of a good pew; but if they are willing to pay for such a pew, and will go with us in every thing else, we should not abandon them. The matter is too unimportant to contend about, and cannot separate brethren of different views without disgracing all parties. The truth is, in our circumstances we need both pewed and free houses, and must have them if we will not miss our aim.

There was some complaint about this time among the local preachers, because they were amenable to the Quarterly Conferences They claimed the right of being tried by their peers. To quiet any uneasiness from this source, the General Conference provided for "*District Conferences*," to be composed of all the local preachers in any one Presiding Elder's district who had been licensed two years. The Elder of the district was to preside, or, in his absence, the Conference might elect one of its own body to take his place. This new judicatory was empowered to grant and renew licenses to preach, to recommend candidates to the Annual Conferences for admission on trial, and for orders; and to try, suspend, expel, or acquit, such local preachers as might be accused; but they could license no one to preach unless he was recommended for that office by the Quarterly Conference of his circuit. But this innovation upon Methodist usage did not work as was hoped. Many of the most useful of the local preachers disapproved of it, and would not take the trouble to attend the Conferences; while those who needed restraint, rather than more liberty, made these meetings the occasion of considerable mischief. The result was, their powers were restricted from time to time, and restored to the Quarterly Conference; and in 1836 the District Conferences were disbanded; since which the Quarterly Conferences have exercised their former prerogatives.

During the four years following the General Conference of 1820 there was much peace and prosperity. In some parts revivals were numerous and powerful. The net increase to the church was *sixty-eight thousand, six hundred and thirty-three* members, and *three hundred and seventy six* travelling preachers; making the total membership of the church *three hundred and twenty-nine thousand, seven hundred and ninety-five.*

The General Conference of 1824 was distinguished in several respects. It was honored with the presence of Rev. Richard Reece, as a representative from the British Conference, and Rev. John Hannah, as his travelling companion. This was the first time the church had received the Christian salutations of that body by an official representative, and this occurred in reciprocation of the regard the Conference manifested for our honored matron four years before, in sending Mr. Emory representative to her annual assembly. The intercourse was both pleasant and profitable, and has since been kept up, to the credit of all parties and Methodist unity. Our church has since been represented among them by Wm. Capers, Bishop Soule, Dr. Fisk, Dr. Olin, Bishops Simpson and Ames; and theirs has been represented in our General Conference by Rev. W. Lord, Drs. Newton, Dixon, Hannah, Thornton, and Wiseman. We hope the day is far distant when any thing shall occur to disturb the fraternity of these grand divisions of the Wesleyan family. The difference between us is not essential; nothing, indeed, but what either of us could cheerfully adopt in an exchange of position. If the question should be started as to which is the most thoroughly Wesleyan, we, of course, would contend earnestly. In regard to free seats, organs, and some other minor matters, neither will be likely to covet investigation but we can plead against the charge of innovation, even here, that our rules remain as they were, and that these innovations are the work of *individuals*, whereas their rule-making body has sanctioned them. As to our episcopacy and ordinations, we are just what Mr. Wesley meant we should be, all but the *name bishop.* That, for prudential reasons, he did not fancy But their ordinations are not Wesleyan in this sense. Mr. Wesley did not authorize them, though we have no doubt, if he were on earth, they would have his approval. Nor are we less defensible on other points; but it is not necessary to refer to them. We have made these allusions for the exclusive benefit of croakers, who sometimes complain that we have departed from Wesley, while our brethren over the water adhere to him with remarkable fidelity.

It was at this session that the mission to Liberia was suggested — that the section in the discipline on slavery received its present form — that Bishops Soule and Hedding were elected and consecrated to their responsible offices — and that the superintendents were requested so to lay out the itinerant work as to allow more time for pastoral labor, which was probably a leading step toward the restriction of circuits, now so frequently matter of lamentation.

Running hastily over the history of the church from this point, we find it every where marked with revivals and the extension and confirmation of the church. The missionary spirit was gradually advancing, and more interest was being felt in education. But the mortification of the church in relation to education was not complete, though it was very great. In 1826 the Pittsburgh Conference started another literary institution under flattering circumstances. It was denominated "Madison College," and was under the presidency of the late Rev. Henry B. Bascom; but it soon passed away, for the want of funds. The academy, however, established at Wilbraham, the same year, under the charge of Dr. Fisk, has run a glorious race of usefulness, and done the church incalculable service.

On the ninth day of September, 1826, the Christian Advocate made its first appearance. There were two papers published in the church at that time; one in Boston, the Zion's Herald, and the other in Charleston, S. C. But it was thought desirable to have one issued at the Book Room in New York. Its subscription list soon numbered *thirty thousand.* It has since been much larger, and exceeds that number now, though our periodicals have greatly multiplied. The publication of this sheet met a demand of the church that had long been felt, and it is wonderful that it had not been commenced before.

An institution, established the year following, contemplated another necessity which it aimed to meet. We refer to the "Sunday School Union of the Methodist Episcopal Church." The church commenced Sabbath School operations as early as 1790, but had often been embarrassed for the want of Bibles and other books. Measures had been adopted, several years before, with reference to these necessities, but they had not proved sufficient to their supply. The design of this institution was to afford some little pecuniary aid to poor societies, and, by the establishment of auxiliaries and other means, to wake up an interest, and extend this efficient instrumentality of renovating the world. The society is now doing a good work in exercising a particular watch-care over this department of effort throughout the connection, and in raising funds and making donations to new and poor societies in the regular work, and among our missionary stations. A small collection from each of our churches will enable the managers to do immense good, without injury to any one.

The year 1829 brought out another prudential measure, which for a time exerted a powerful influence for good; we refer to "*four-days'*" or "*protracted*" meetings. This was not the first time that religious meetings had been ex tended beyond a single day. Under particular circumstances they had been continued to great lengths, and were justified only by the great religious interest that pervaded the community. But these "*four-days'*" meetings were instituted where there was no interest, for the purpose of promoting a revival. They were introduced by the Rev. John Lord, of the New England Conference, in the month of September, 1827, and were attended with the divine blessing. Such were their good effects they soon spread abroad in every direction, and were holden by most of the evangelical denominations with good success. But at length they seemed to lose their power, and are now held with less frequency. We trust, however, their day is not past. We have no doubt they may now be employed in many places, and, under certain circumstances, to great advantage. It will be a sad day for the world when all our public religious efforts shall be confined to the Sabbath and an evening or two in each week. This can never be the case, we think, till the ministry and the church become generally backslidden from God. While they feel concerned for the ark of God, they will see the necessity of holding extra meetings, and calling in their brethren to help them preach and pray, and arouse the people to a proper state of concern about their souls. And it is to be hoped they will not want the necessary courage to hold them, though some may mock, and accuse them of "*getting up revivals.*" The truth is, those who do right will be censured, and especially if they infringe upon secular time by their religious movements. Many people will never brook such "extravagance." But there are some who will rejoice in it. They may be a small minority, but nevertheless they are the hope of the church. God has gained more conquests by these little bands of earnest, burning Christians, than by whole kingdoms of professors, who have had a name to live while they were dead.

We will now pass on to the celebration of the centenary of Methodism, which occurred, as before stated, in 1839. Though it was but about seventy years since the first Methodist meeting was holden on the continent, the organization of the first society in London, in the year 1739, was thought to be too important an event to the church on this side of the water to be passed over in silence. But it was impossible to bring our people to the same concert of feeling and action that was displayed among the Wesleyans, scattered as they were over so vast a territory, and pressed with so many different objects, often requiring more than they were able to perform. But a general plan of religious exercise and benevolence was adopted, and carried out with as much uniformity as was to be expected. The services were salutary in their influence. They contributed to a better understanding of the history, principles, unity, aims and successes of Methodists, and gave a new impulse to the general body. The amount contributed for different objects is estimated at *six hundred thousand dollars;* but it is exceedingly doubtful whether so much was realized by the various treasuries for which it was contributed.

"It was, indeed, a sublime spectacle to contemplate the assemblage of more than *one million* of people, joined by, perhaps, three times that number of friends, uniting to offer up thanksgiving to God for his boundless mercy to a lost world, manifested in the gift of his Son! And as one of many rivulets, which flow from that exhaustless fountain of eternal love, ran through the channel opened by Wesley, it seemed right and proper for his numerous sons in the gospel to commemorate the day which gave the first impetus to this flowing stream of grace and mercy. Some, indeed, affected to call it a species of idolatry. But why is it any more an act of idolatry to praise God for raising up and blessing the world with such men as John Wesley, than it is to praise him for any other blessings, whether temporal or spiritual. It is, indeed, marvellous that many, whose tender consciences will not permit them to render honor to whom honor is due, do not scruple to defame the character of those men who, like John Wesley, have rendered the most important services to mankind, merely because they have dissented from them in opinion on some important points." — *Bangs' History, vol.* 4, p. 296.

The church numbered at this time *seven hundred and forty-nine thousand, two hundred and sixteen* members; *three thousand five hundred and fifty-seven* travelling preachers; and *five thousand eight hundred and fifty-six* local preachers.

We have already referred to the origin of our Book Concern in 1789. It was during that year that the first volume of the "Arminian Magazine" was published; also the Hymn Book, Primitive Physic, and "Saints' Rest." The Concern was then located in Philadelphia, and was under the agency of John Dickens. It began with about *six hundred dollars* capital, borrowed of the agent, and advanced slowly but surely, till the death of Mr. Dickens, in 1798, when it fortunately fell under the superintendency of Rev. Ezekiel Cooper. In 1804 it was removed to New York, where it was conducted four years by Mr. Cooper, assisted by John Wilson. In 1808 Mr. Cooper resigned his office, leaving a capital in the Concern of *forty-five thousand dollars.* Up to this period the Book Agent had received a regular appointment to a station, but, as the business had become considerably extended, he was now released from pastoral duties, and John Wilson appointed to the office, with Daniel Hitt for an assistant. Two years from that time, Mr. Wilson was taken to his great reward, and was succeeded by Mr. Hitt, assisted by Thomas Ware. Since then, the Concern has been managed by the following agents:

When Elected.		*When Elected.*	
1812.	D. Hitt & T. Ware.	1844.	G. Lane & C. B. Tippett.
1816.	J. Soule & T. Mason.	1848.	G. Lane & L. Scott.
1820.	N. Bangs & T. Mason.	1852.	T. Carlton & Z. Phillips.
1824.	N. Bangs & J. Emory.	1856.	T. Carlton & J. Porter.
1828.	J. Emory & B. Waugh.	1860.	T. Carlton & J. Porter.
1832.	B. Waugh & T. Mason.	1864.	T. Carlton & J. Porter.
1836.	T. Mason & G. Lane.	1868.	T. Carlton & J. Lanahan.
1840.	T. Mason & G. Lane.	1872.	R. Nelson & J. M. Phillips.

The Cincinnati branch house was established in 1820, and has been managed by the following agents:

1820.	Martin Ruter.	1848.	L. Swormstedt & J. Power.
1824.	Martin Ruter.	1852.	L. Swormstedt & A. Poe.
1828.	Charles Halliday.	1856.	L. Swormstedt & A. Poe.
1832.	C. Halliday & J. F. Wright.	1860.	A. Poe & L. Hitchcock.
1836.	J. F. Wright & L. Swormstedt.	1864.	L. Hitchcock & J. M. Walden.
1840.	J. F. Wright & L. Swormstedt.	1868.	L. Hitchcock & J. M. Walden.
1844.	L. Swormstedt & J.T. Mitchell.	1872.	L. Hitchcock & J. M. Walden.

But the Concern has not been entirely exempt from misfortunes. Based on benevolence, it has been governed, perhaps, by a too liberal policy for its financial interests. Its losses, by bad debts, have been considerable; but its greatest loss was occasioned by fire, in the month of February, 1836, when the new buildings in Mulberry street, and nearly all the property, were consumed, amounting to *two hundred and fifty thousand dollars*, at least. This created a powerful sensation throughout the church, and many contributed to rebuild and put the establishment again in operation. About *ninety thousand dollars* were realized in donations for this object, which, with some *twenty-five thousand dollars* that was insured upon it, enabled the agents to start anew with encouraging prospects. Since then, the Concern has been scattering its various and interesting publications broadcast, though with less profit than formerly.

But still, the capital stock has been gradually increasing, and the profits have met liabilities that could not have been discharged by subscription without considerable difficulty. Its capital stock at New York is estimated at $ 867,599,01, and at Cincinnati, Ohio, $484,948,11, and its facilities for usefulness, in the diffusion of books, tracts and periodicals, are much greater, therefore, than formerly. No friend of the church can but rejoice in the improvement that has been made in the several departments of the Concern within a few years past. Yet in all these years, and in all this complication of business, the Concern has been managed with unwavering integrity. An opposite opinion obtaining, to some extent, in the year 1868, led to a most searching investigation, which the General Conference of 1872 concluded by affirming the integrity of the Agents, and an entire absence of fraud save in the bindery, implicating the foreman who had at that time already been dismissed. So far as we know, this verdict is generally accepted, and the administration approved.

To obtain the results indicated by the foregoing references has required an immense sacrifice. But the cause has been more embarrassed by internal differences than from all outward hindrances together. Whether they have been overruled for good, is a question we are unable to decide. They have generally exerted an unhappy influence for a time, but still may have provoked some to love and good works, who would have done little under other circumstances. We will refer to a few of them.

In the year 1813, one Pliny Brett, whose reception into the Conference had been delayed a year beyond the ordinary time, withdrew from the church, and placed himself at the head of a party pretending to peculiar attainments in holiness, and went about to infect others with the disease of his own heart, and rally for a new organization. The project was successful. Several local preachers, and others, soon displayed unmistakable symptoms of disaffection, and united with Mr. Brett to form a "bran-new" church, under the name of "*Reformed Methodists*." With this specious title they went forth, berating their old friends as backsliders and formalists, and calling upon all who loved the *power* of religion to come to the new standard. Ranters, and others who were impatient of discipline, and particularly such as saw more in the *name* than they afterwards realized, heeded the call. Several societies on Cape Cod and in Vermont were greatly agitated, and some of the younger and smaller ones broken up, by which means the church lost several worthy members; but were amply indemnified for the loss by being relieved of a much larger number which had been borne with as a burden.

The new party being thus organized, and having spent their first love in scattering the old church, a project in which they were particularly united, found that they had gathered of "every kind," and some that were not so easily managed. Later experience taught them that it is easier to make divisions than to maintain peace, and to tear down than to build up and consolidate. The highest number of members we recollect of their reporting was about *two thousand;* and the most of those who remained in 1843 united with the church organized about that time under the leadership of Rev. Orange Scott, since which we have heard little of the Reformers, except in connection with the "Wesleyans," whose history will be sketched hereafter.

The "African Methodist Episcopal Church" was organized in the year 1816. Richard Allen, of Philadelphia, a local elder, and a man of good character, and considerable wealth and influence, separated himself from the church in consequence of some local difficulties between the two races. A considerable number of others followed his example, and united to form an independent church under the above title. They made no change in doctrine, nor even in discipline, farther than to accommodate their new circumstances. The object of the movement was to govern themselves, and not be subject to a government in which they had no part, on account of their color. At their first Conference Allen was elected bishop, and ordained by the imposition of hands, since which others have been inducted into the same office. They hold Annual and General Conferences, and maintain a system of itinerancy with considerable success.

These transactions created some excitement among the colored people in the city of New York, and they declared for independence. But not having all confidence in Allen, or his new scheme, they struck out a little different plan, and organized another "African Methodist Episcopal Church," to be governed by elders of their own choosing, one of whom was to be annually elected to superintend, but not to be set apart by the usual forms of ordination. They now claim to number about 694 ministers and 164,000 church members in the United States and Canada. But they are much divided and scattered. The truth is, they lack acknowledged leaders. There is too much of a disposition to *rule* among them, and too little capacity to do it with discretion. While we can hardly blame them for coveting a separate existence on account of public prejudice against color, we doubt the policy of trying to maintain it, especially in those places where they are not numerous. Their object can be better gained by association with their white brethren.

The year following, New York experienced another slight explosion. In rebuilding John street church the Trustees and other members fell into some differences. A part, per haps, wished to have the finishing a little nicer than the others fancied, or could conscientiously approve. One thing led to another, till the contest became very sharp, and resulted in the secession of William M. Stillwell, a travelling preacher, three Trustees, and about three hundred members of the church. The disaffection was communicated to several local preachers and others in the vicinity, and *Stillwellites* multiplied for a time with considerable rapidity. But a second sober thought turned the tables again, and most of the seceders returned from whence they went out, more than ever convinced that it is easier to destroy a good church than to establish a better one. Those who remained soon laid aside all pretensions to itinerancy, and settled down on the congregational plan, with the father of the movement for their pastor; since which little has been heard of them.

We mention this case to show how easy it is to make a division in the church of God, and how little it avails, compared with the expectations of its promoters. It was, no doubt, believed in this case, that the secession would shake the church to its foundations, and bring about a glorious state of things, in which the seceders would be eminently popular, if not *canonized*. But how disappointed! It was only as a pebble falling into the ocean. You hear the sound thereof, and mark a circular ripple upon the wave, and pass along as though nothing had happened. The Methodist Church is not to be overturned so easily. But such beacons of warning are of little use, after all. Adventurers will not learn by the experience of others. *They are wiser*, or their idol scheme has some advantage that ensures it success. So on they go to the same oblivion that covers their predecessors, the wreck of whose darling visions should have deterred them from such presumption. Still, it is our duty to admonish them of their danger.

We have already referred to a difficulty in relation to Canada, which was amicably settled with the Wesleyan connection by a division of territory. By that arrangement, Upper Canada fell under the jurisdiction of the Methodist Episcopal Church. But the preachers being chiefly from the United States, the civil authorities were jealous of them, and denied them certain rights enjoyed by natives, and by those who were from England, particularly in reference to the rites of matrimony. The Canada Conference, therefore, applied to the General Conference to be released from their responsibilities to that body. After careful deliberation, the General Conference of 1828 passed the most friendly resolutions anticipatory of their voluntary withdrawal on their *own* responsibility, and providing so far as practicable to secure them an equitable share of the Book Concern property. (See *Journal*, pp. 338, 354. *Great Secession*, pp. 709, 710. *Christian Advocate, Nov.* 22, 1849. They also advised the Canada Conference to adopt their form of government, with such modifications as their particular relations should render necessary, and requested the bishops to ordain such persons to superintend the new organization as said Conference should elect.

These measures, and all others relating to the subject were adopted with the best of feelings, and with the purest motives. The Canada Conference, however, maintained its independence but a short period, and then, instead of adopting the Episcopal form of government, under which they were raised, became connected with the Wesleyans of England, which connection was peaceably maintained until September, 1874, when it combined with the Wesleyan Methodist Church of Eastern British America and the Conference of the Methodist New Connection Church of Canada, and formed THE METHODIST CHURCH OF CANADA, retaining the old Wesleyan doctrines and most of its general usages. The new organization is divided into six Annual Conferences, which are to meet in General Conference by lay and clerical delegates once in four years, and exercise governmental control of the Connection. They number 1,004 travelling and 1,027 local preachers, and 102,887 members. It is to be hoped that the other Methodists of Canada will join them, and thus form one grand family of Canadian Methodists.

Another attempt at reform remained to be executed. It first appeared in private circles. The subject of lay representation in the Conferences was the main topic, and it was argued that such representation was both right and expedient, and should be allowed. Some became very sanguine, and sat upon bringing about the desirable change.

But private talk was not alone sufficient, and public discussion was impracticable, since few had courage enough to come out openly and vindicate their new conceptions ; and, besides, there was little opportunity. For the interest was so limited, the discussion would not be tolerated in ordinary religious meetings, and special meetings could not be sustained. To give greater publicity to the discussion, the leading spirits in the movement started a paper at Trenton, New Jersey, called the "Wesleyan Repository." This occurred in 1820, and afforded a fine opportunity for the malcontents to vent their spleen against the church, and paint the beauties of their imaginary systems before the eyes of all people, without being detected. To secure more efficiency by a concentration of influence, the friends of the cause in Baltimore formed what they called a "*Union Society*," and called upon the friends of reform to do the same throughout the country — to which call many responded.

To harmonize the contending elements, the male members

of Baltimore were called together in 1824, and united in a compromise memorial to the General Conference, then about to meet, asking for certain modifications of the government. This, however, did not please the more zealous of the "reformers," and they formed themselves into a separate society, and *demanded* lay representation in the General Conference *as a natural and social right.* But the General Conference did not see cause to acquiesce in their wishes. That body knew full well that there was general satisfaction with the government as it was, and that while the alterations proposed might please the memorialists, they would give offence to ten times their number, and cripple the operations of the church, which were advancing with wonderful success.

The failure of these memorials, got up with so much labor and care, and speaking with so much emphasis, and even authority, as one of them did, was quite intolerable. The Conference was denounced in the most unsparing manner, and the war raged with increasing clamor. To give the more certainty to their movements, another paper was started in Baltimore, under the fascinating title of "*Mutual Rights.*" This at once became the vehicle of all the reasoning and wrath of the party. Men who were unwilling to take the open field, would hide here behind a fictitious name, and complain bitterly. Indeed, it was an abusive concern, and it became obvious enough that no person was fit to belong to the church who would patronize it. The Baltimore Conference, therefore, in 1827, called Rev. D. Dorsey, a member of their body, and yet one of the "Reformers," to an account, and left him without an appointment. A little after, eleven local preachers of Baltimore city, who were chief actors in the drama, and twenty-five lay members of the more belligerent and daring kind, were cited to trial, and either expelled or suspended.

But these steps were not taken till the revolutionists had been long borne with, and earnestly entreated to desist from their ruinous course. Others were expelled afterwards, and some withdrew; but the great mass, who sympathized with the movement at first, saw the folly of carrying it to such lengths, and preferred the church without reform to the hazards of *revolution*, which they saw approaching. So that, on the whole, the loss to the church was comparatively small.

A similar operation was experienced in other places, though on a smaller scale, and it seemed that the church would be destroyed at a stroke. But when the crisis came, there was too much sectarianism, or religion, or something else, to admit of it. The more considerate retraced their steps. They could not sell their religious privileges and the enjoyments of church fellowship for a mere *abstraction*. *They* had never been oppressed, nor did they know of a member of the church who had been. Why, therefore, be alarmed? Besides, they knew our government had worked to admiration, that it had accomplished all the ends of government, had been the means of more good than any other in the world; and they knew not what the new system would be, or what it would effect.

The two principal writers on the side of the "Reformers" were Rev. Nicholas Snethen and Rev. Alexander M'Caine, both formerly influential travelling preachers. To the surprise of many, Dr. Thomas E. Bond, a local preacher of Baltimore, and since editor of the "Christian Advocate and Journal," took the first in hand, and presented to the public one of the clearest and most convincing defences of our government ever written; and it took effect. Meeting all the various objections and prejudices in the community, and placing the subject in its proper aspect before the mind, it essentially enfeebled the spirit of secession, and restrained many who had not already gone too far to be forgiven. Dr. Emory, afterward bishop, reviewed Mr. M'Caine's "History and Mystery of Methodist Episcopacy," and produced "The Defence of the Fathers," a work of singular strength of argument, that can never be answered. The student who makes himself fully acquainted with the writings of these two defenders of our government, will need to look no further. He will be satisfied, and will be able to satisfy others, that it is not only Scriptural, but emphatically *Wesleyan*, and wisely adapted to the regeneration of the human family.

The new system having been arranged and put in operation, and both sides of the controversy fully canvassed, the subject lost its interest, and the agitation subsided. Since then we have heard an occasional gun from the enemy's barracks, but have suffered no damage worth remembering. They have taken some prizes from the world, and, perhaps, some from other sources; and if they continue to hold fast the form of sound words, that is, stand fast in the doctrines and earnest measures of Methodists, they may become a great people, notwithstanding they have no bishops and presiding elders to watch over them, and have admitted the laity into their councils. But we fear for them. They lack energy in their government — a *head*. Responsibility is too diffused, and there is too much tinkering of the system, and too little hard work and personal sacrifice. They have modified their economy in various ways, but not with entire unanimity, or with any thing like the success anticipated. Well, let them experiment; but let us learn by their misfortunes not to precipitate ourselves into the whirlpool of speculation in the hope of originating a better system. We will see them prosper before we abandon the old Wesleyan economy; but, in the mean time, will wish them well, and rejoice in their multiplication, if it be done fairly. The least they can do for us is to provoke us to good works; and the more stimulants we have in this direction, the better. Some thousands, probably, withdrew from the church and turned Protestants. The number, however, could not have been very great, or else the church was peculiarly favored, for we observe by the minutes, that our increase in 1829 was about *thirty thousand* members, and one hundred and seventy-five preachers, notwithstanding the loss of eight or nine thousand by the separation of the Canada Conference. The next year it was nearly the same.

The Protestants now report 423 travelling preachers, 250 local, and 65,000 church members. Whether they are more happy or useful under their new system is a question. It is, however, certain their expectations have not been realized; nor can they be, while the old church displays the piety, good sense and conciliation which have characterized her past history.

CHAPTER XI.

GREAT REVIVAL OF RELIGION — ANTI-SLAVERY DISCUSSIONS —AND THE GENERAL CONFERENCES OF 1840 AND 1844.

FROM the year 1840 to the year 1844, a general revival of religion prevailed throughout the country. This has been attributed to various causes. The real exciting cause was, doubtless, the out-pouring of the Spirit of God upon the public heart, directing attention to the subject. While we believe that the Spirit operates more or less at all times, and upon all minds, and that all good thoughts, purposes, and emotions, are attributable to its influence, we cannot doubt that it is occasionally shed forth in peculiar copiousness and power, arousing Christians to an unusual degree of spiritual interest, and begetting tenderness on the minds of others. This seems to have been the case at the time referred to; one evidence of which was, that numerous little prayer meetings were instituted, to pray especially for a revival of religion and the conversion of sinners. There was a pretty general conviction among evangelical Christians that it was time for God to work, and they were so anxious to see a revival they exerted themselves with a degree of earnestness, appropriateness, and energy, scarcely ever witnessed among some of them since the days of Whitefield.

While, therefore, we attribute the work to God, as its

efficient author, we recognize peculiar Christian exertion as its means. If it originated in a remarkable out-pouring of the Spirit, it was encouraged and carried forward instrumentally by a remarkable effort. Measures which had been repudiated as repugnant to the true philosophy of revivals, were now introduced and pushed with much fervor. The laity were called into action, foreign aid was invoked, evangelists were flying from field to field, and the work of saving souls was made the all-absorbing object.

Another circumstance probably had considerable effect. We refer to the emphatic inculcation of the doctrine of Christ's second coming and the transactions which are to follow. Various ministers of different denominations heralded these truths all over the land with great pathos and power. The errors with which they were associated did not lessen their influence, but rather rendered them more impressive. Taken together, the presentation was an alarming affair. Some of the sermons delivered on different occasions were almost enough to frighten "the very *elect*," and it would not have been wonderful if many had plunged into hopeless despair. For the argument was so nicely drawn that few could see its fallacy; the honesty and devotion of many of the speakers so manifest, they could not well be questioned; and the sentiments inculcated so exciting in their tendency, that none but very good or very bad people could hear them proclaimed without trembling for their own safety. Hence, while few believed the doctrine that Christ would come in 1843, many *feared* it; and having full confidence in the divine reality and importance of religion, they were impelled to seek it then, whereas, under other circumstances, they might have remained impenitent. But still they were really converted. Though it was a mistake which stimulated them to action, the process they pursued was right, and the result pure. The mistake had no other influence in this regard, than to prompt them to seek religion *then;* which done, they found peace in believing. But it afterwards became identified with so many other heresies it poisoned all who came under its influence, and interposed one of the greatest obstacles to the progress of religion that has ever been contrived. This we believe to be a just view of the subject, in general. There were, doubtless, instances in which religion and Millerism were so combined, that, when the error of the latter was demonstrated, all confidence in the former was abandoned.

Under all these circumstances, it is not improbable that some improper measures were employed, or that others were carried to extremes, and operated to produce more chaff than wheat. But, notwithstanding, there was much wheat gathered. It is true many fell away, but not a larger proportion, we think, than is usual. When it is said that the Methodist Episcopal Church suffered a net decrease of more than *fifty thousand* members, between the years 1844 and 1847, it should be remembered that in 1843 her net *increase* was 154,634; and the year following, 102,831; making a net *increase* in two years of 257,465 members; thus exceeding all precedent by tens of thousands. The ordinary ratio of apostasies, therefore, accounts for an appalling decrease, without disparaging the character of the work in the least.

But other items come into this account that are important to the calculation. During this time, there was a vigorous effort made by come-outers of different classes to break down the churches, and scatter them to the four winds. While the revival was in progress, their influence was partly counteracted; but as the excitement abated they became more successful. This, taken in connection with the fact that there was scarcely a revival in the country, and that thousands of church members die annually, goes far to explain the decrease conceded, and leaves little to charge to the mismanagement of the revival under consideration; and especially if it be remembered that many of the converts were treated by certain ministers and laymen more as dupes or hypocrites, than as the lambs of Christ's flock.

But some, we are aware, take other views of the subject, and, we fear, have so far fallen out with God's method of converting sinners that they will do little good at present. It is certain they will never make many genuine converts by preaching against *excitement* and ridiculing revival measures. But still there is hope for them. Some have already run so low, their churches become so sleepy and cold, and their congregations so thin, they are about willing to let the Lord work in any way, and by whomsoever he will. And others will have to come to the same point, and abandon their *freezing operations*, or they will find themselves forsaken of both God and man, as is really best they should, unless they change their course.

Another question intimately connected with the history of the church in those times was that of *slavery*. Mr. Wesley having early taken a bold stand against this evil, and published a tract condemning it and its abettors, in the most sweeping terms, his followers emigrating to the country, or coming as missionaries, were in no mood to treat it with the moderation the popular sentiment required. The first Conference, which was held in 1780, came down upon it with a vengeance, declaring it to be "*contrary to the laws of God, man, and nature*, contrary to the dictates of conscience and pure religion, and doing that which we would not that others should do to us." Here the war began, which continued with more or less severity until the year 1824, when the Discipline received its present form. But slavery waxed stronger and stronger, and its advocates were greatly multiplied. Indeed, the righteousness of slaveholding was hardly questioned. If it was not just right in the abstract, it was unavoidable, and therefore not to be condemned; and, as the poor proscribed race were doomed to be slaves, it was the duty of good men to hold them, and keep them out of wicked hands. Thus, slaveholding members of the church were tolerated, notwithstanding the known sentiments of Mr. Wesley and the early Conferences.

But there was to be a revival of the question. The public mind, in the providence of God, was beginning to show signs of *moral life*. Temperance had been under discussion for several years, and the better sort of people had become convinced that the use of ardent spirits as a beverage was wrong. How strange that they had never thought of this before! But such is our blindness. This suggested that other popular practices might not be right, and they, too, were agitated, found to be wanting, and corrected. About the year 1830, the colonization scheme, an enterprise of unbounded popularity, was called in question; and with it the subject of slavery, some of whose more stirring aspects were developed in an alarming manner. Several of the New England preachers felt it their duty to discuss it in the pulpit and papers; which they did, with powerful effect. But many demurred. "They feared the consequences. They could not un-Christianize good brethren of the South. They were true men, and Methodists, — often more to be pitied than blamed, — had some show, at least, of divine authority for their course; but, though they were all sinners, abolition *measures* were too severe, too exciting, and must not be countenanced." The contest was sharp and alarming. The officiaries of the church, anxious to save the trembling ark of Methodism, interposed to stay the desolating tide, when lo! their *authority* was called in question, and a tedious discussion of "*Conference and Bishops' rights*" followed.

That both sides committed some serious errors is not to be doubted, nor that both were correct in important particulars. Neither party would probably think the writer an impartial judge of the questions at issue. It will be conceded, however, that the discussion had the good effect to elicit a more thorough knowledge of slavery and of the discipline of the church. The General Conference of 1836, thinking, no doubt, to allay the excitement, and restore peace, declared that they "were decidedly opposed to modern abolitionism, and wholly disclaimed any right, wish, or intention, to interfere with the civil and political relation between master and slave, as it exists in the slaveholding States of this Union." But this measure failed to satisfy either party. It went too far for the North, and not far enough for the South. The latter considered it of doubtful import, as to the main question, while slavery was condemned by the discipline, and was a bar to the episcopal office; and the former regarded it as an unwarrantable rebuke of their principles and measures. Hence the excitement continued; the rabid slaveholder threatening to secede if a slaveholder should not be elected to the episcopacy at the next session; and the rabid abolitionist significantly intimating a similar result in the North, if his rights should not be conceded, and slavery treated more in conformity with the views of Mr. Wesley and the example of the fathers.

During the four succeeding years the action of the Annual Conferences was *diverse*, and not very satisfactory. Some said one thing and some another, according to their respective opinions, while many thought it prudent to say nothing. The excitement in certain quarters ran very high.

and ministers of different views were called in their turn to endure trials they little anticipated. The secessions which had been predicted seemed increasingly probable, and the real friends of the church contemplated the event with profound concern.

The General Conference of 1840 was more satisfactory to the North than the last preceding. A committee was appointed on slavery, to which numerous petitions were referred with all due respect. Petitions for a moderate episcopacy, having reference to certain exercise of authority on the part of some of the bishops, were also received. The decision of the Missouri Conference, finding Silas Comfort guilty of mal-administration, in admitting the testimony of colored persons against white persons in a church trial, was reversed; all of which was very pleasing. But these circumstances were seriously modified by the Conference sustaining the appeal of a brother whose administration as Presiding Elder had been condemned by his Conference; the passage of a resolution offered by Ignatius A. Few against the admission of the testimony of colored persons in church trials; the adoption of the report on the Westmoreland petitions against the Baltimore Conference, for refusing to ordain certain local preachers because they were slave-holders; by a remonstrance from New York against an anti-slavery petition before presented, and by several other less important particulars. Abolitionists were not satisfied. Some became despondent, and began to think more seriously of secession; but the larger part thought they saw indications of improvement, and were quite willing to toil on, and trust the issue to an all-wise Providence.

This gave a new aspect to the controversy. Till near this time, the question of an anti-slavery secession had not been openly debated. An intention to secede had been charged upon the party, but had been unequivocally denied, except, perhaps, by a few, who spake with less apparent concern about an event of that nature. "They could not tell what would take place, but they had not determined on ny such step as yet." Now they began to teach the sin- ulness of maintaining church relations with a denomination which countenanced slavery; that there was no hope of eforming the church; and to give other unmistakable inti nations of alienation and radical intentions. But here they were met. Those who had been with them in the heat of he battle, loved the church, notwithstanding her tardiness, nd would not cherish the thought of dissolving their con- nection with her. Nor would they allow the party they had coöperated with in good faith for the extinction of slavery, o run off in a tangent, or bring in divisional questions, without resistance.

Thus the anti-slavery ranks became much divided on hese and collateral questions, into loyal and radical parties, oth of which contended earnestly for their respective views nd modes of operation. But the wheels of the radicals ragged heavily. The new issue, which they were endeav- ing to make, and the project they had evidently under- ken, depreciated their influence among their anti-slavery iends, and left them little hope of regaining their former anding in the Conference; whereupon the leading spirits emed to adjust themselves to their unfortunate condition, d watch the developments of time. Little was heard om them for several months, except now and then a mur- ur of despondency and complaint; and it was a question of uch interest, among their old friends, whether they would ake the desperate plunge, or let the excitement blow over, d become the able and efficient laborers they had been in rmer days. But the stillness of that hopeful hour was at fast broken, (in 1842,) by the proclamation that Rev. Orange Scott had seceded, and was calling for volunteers to join his standard.

We speak of these circumstances with painful recollections. These men were our friends and elder brethren. We stood with them in the very heat of the conflict, and loved them as our own life. They were good men and strong; they meant right, and they did right in many particulars. But they thought themselves injured, and it grieved them to the heart — perhaps enraged them — and they could not endure it. That others would have done better in their situation is not certain. The movement was, to some extent, successful. Several preachers, with a considerable number of lay members, withdrew, and united in the formation of a new church, which they were pleased to christen "The Wesleyan Methodist Church." The loss of numbers and influence to us, though considerable, was not the greatest evil connected with the affair. The bitter discussions, and the division of young and feeble societies, unavoidably connected with the outbreak, were most to be deprecated. However, the contest was carried on with as little asperity, and with as few evil consequences, as could have been expected, every thing considered. The lines of demarcation were soon drawn, and the controversy passed away to swell the history of human infirmities.

The Wesleyans take high ground against slavery — eschew all bishops and presiding elders, supplying their places by presidents of Conferences, stationing committees, and chairmen of districts. In doctrine, and in most other respects, they have adhered pretty closely to their old principles. They have a Book Concern in Syracuse, a missionary society, and the other *etcetera* usually connected with such establishments. Many who left the church, at first, have re turned, not having succeeded in the new enterprise as they anticipated. It is their opinion that the old church is the least objectionable; but some are of a different opinion. They are now called the American Wesleyan Church, and claim about 250 preachers and 20,000 members.

The doings of the General Conference of 1840 were not less offensive to the South than to the abolitionists. They evidently saw that the tide was turning — that anti-slavery views were more deeply rooted among northern and middle men than in 1836. This was plain enough to be seen in the discussion of the colored testimony question, which was long and able, and in other discussions having more or less reference to the subject of slavery. But this was not the only ground of offence. They had felt implicated and dishonored in the fact that no *slaveholder* had ever been elected to the episcopacy. William A. Smith had appealed to the South, inquiring whether they would submit to such proscription, and declaring, if the General Conference did not recede, he would seek to establish a *Southern* General Conference. But the Conference, it seems, did not recede, nor did it exactly continue on its former course. There was difficulty. To come square up to the question, and elect non-slaveholders to the office, would have given unpardonable offence to the South. To elect slaveholders, they could not consistently with their principles, nor with the peace of the church at large; for it was well understood that such promotion of slaveholders would not be tolerated in the free States. But Dr. Fisk having declined ordination it was necessary to supply his place, and it was proposed to strengthen the episcopacy by the addition of one or two others. But so critical were the circumstances, it was deemed inexpedient, by a majority of the Conference, to elect any more. This the South regarded as dodging the question, and an evasion of their rights.

Four years more rolled away, and still the subject was not at rest. Abolitionists were making less ado, perhaps, than formerly, but others were waxing more and more decided. Besides, slaveholders were determined to have the question brought to an issue. At the opening of the General Conference of 1844, it was learned, to the regret of many, that there were two cases that must come before the Conference, involving the very gist of the matter, and that *must* be decided. One was the appeal of Rev. F. A. Harding from the decision of the Baltimore Conference, by which he was suspended from his ministerial standing for refusing to manumit certain slaves which came into his possession by marriage; and the other was the fact that Bishop Andrew had married a woman having slaves, by which he had become a slaveholder.

The appeal was argued *pro* and *con* with singular ability; Rev. John A. Collins, of Baltimore, speaking for his Conference, and Rev. William A. Smith, of Virginia, for the appellant. The trial occupied several days. It was regarded by many as the great question of the session. But the decision came, at last, sustaining the action of the Baltimore Conference by a vote of *one hundred and seventeen* to *fifty-six*. This was a heavy blow, though just and right according to Methodist discipline, and it gave high offence.

The other question was not long delayed. A resolution was adopted, stating the rumor about one of the bishops, and calling upon the committee on episcopacy to make inquiry and report the next morning. The report fully sustained the rumor, and brought out all the circumstances over Bishop Andrew's own signature. What ought to be done?

was now the all-absorbing question. Those who knew the bishop best, whispered that he would resign; and had he studied his own feelings, he probably would have done so. But there was another spirit abroad. His brethren said, "No; southern rights and interests require you to stand your ground. It is time to have this vexed question settled." Hence he left the Conference to take such action as it deemed advisable. The subject was discussed in all its aspects, chiefly by middle and southern men. Abolitionists, who had been in collision with both before, had little to do but to watch the contest. At length the crisis was reached, and it was modestly declared, as "the sense of the Conference, that Bishop Andrew desist from the exercise of his office, so long as this impediment remains;" that is, till he should cease to hold slaves.

This, together with the Harding case, indicated that the discipline on slavery was not "a dead letter," and blasted all hope of electing a slaveholder to the office of bishop. The object now seems to have been to retreat as handsomely and with as much advantage as possible, though it was not then distinctly understood. The plan was laid, and Dr. Capers appeared before the Conference with a long string of resolutions providing for a division of the church into two distinct General Conferences. The unconstitutionality of this measure was too obvious. The paper was, however, referred to a committee, which did not fail to see at a glance that the thing was impracticable.

Next appeared a "declaration," signed by the southern delegates, representing that the agitation of the subject of slavery, and the frequent action of the General Conference, and especially the action had in Bishop Andrew's case, must produce a state of things in the South which rendered the continued jurisdiction of the General Conference over

Southern Conferences *inconsistent with the success of the ministry in the slaveholding states.* This was immediately referred to a committee of NINE, with instructions, if they could not devise a plan for the amicable adjustment of the difficulties on the subject of slavery, to devise, if possible, a constitutional plan for a mutual and friendly division of the church. But the latter could not be done. "But," said the South, "we cannot live under these circumstances,— we shall be driven from our fields, and the souls committed to our care will perish. What shall we do? Suppose, on getting home, we should find it *indispensable* to separate, how will the General Conference view us? How shall we be treated? Shall there be friendly relations, and an amicable settlement of the property question; or shall we be viewed as enemies?" Middle men were anxious to accommodate, and Eastern men were fearful of the consequences of not doing so; for it was already under contemplation to reconsider Bishop Andrew's case, and lay it over four years, agreeably to the recommendation of the board of bishops, unless something conciliatory should be done. It was an exciting moment, and great men were at their wits' end to know what to do.

Finally, the committee agreed upon a plan to meet the anticipated *emergency*, and reported it to the Conference. It was not all they could wish, but it was the best they could devise, and it was favorably received. Southern delegates were greatly relieved, and submitted to the rescinding of Few's colored testimony resolution, passed four years before, with remarkable composure; and the Conference was permitted to leave New York without the honor of being mobbed, as it was tremblingly feared they would be, and without *un*doing the work it had unexpectedly wrought, in the several particulars before mentioned.

Whether the Conference acted the prudent part in this measure is seriously questioned. Some, who were foremost in getting the plan through, have deeply regretted it since. Northern men, generally, who favored it, did so *purely* to avoid what they regarded a greater and insupportable evil. To have left Bishop Andrew in the full exercise of episcopal powers at that time, would have scattered our churches to the winds; and *that*, it was believed *on good authority*, would have been the result of preventing the adoption of this or some similar plan of conciliation. Indeed, we only escaped, as it was; a circumstance which should never be forgotten in treating of the action of New England men in the premises. Our choice was between having a slaveholding bishop, the transfer of our churches to Wesleyanism, so called, or a *general New England secession*, on the one hand; and acquiescence in a plan, some features of which we did not approve, but could not get altered, either in the committee, or in the Conference, on the other. We preferred the latter. It seemed to us better to be *the* Methodist Episcopal Church, united and at peace, than to be a distracted limb of it, or separate, however harmoniously, and let the South hold the old title, and the perquisites connected therewith. And if they who had caused so much trouble by their connection with slavery, had a mind to take the responsibility of seceding, we were not disposed to demur, to treat them discourteously, or to withhold from them any thing that they could lawfully claim, and the church lawfully bestow. Hence, we concurred in the plan, though not satisfied with it, and the South has taken all the advantage of it possible to become an independent body, and adjust themselves to what *they* regarded the *necessities* of their situation. For one, the writer has never regretted the action of the General Conference or the organization of the South into an independent church. They were both momentous events, pregnant with unutterable evils, but with greater good; and were necessary, in God's inscrutable providence, to deliver the country, North and South, from the "*great evil*" of American slavery.

The Methodist Episcopal Church, South, now embraces *eight bishops, three thousand eight hundred and seventy-one travelling, and five thousand three hundred and forty-four local preachers; and six hundred and sixty-seven thousand eight hundred and eighty-five members.* They have a Book Concern, Missionary Society, and nearly all the paraphernalia of the old church. They publish seven weekly papers, besides a Sunday School Advocate, Ladies' Companion, and Quarterly Review. And, so far as we can learn, they are doing a good business in all these departments, and feel quite happy in their new relations.

CHAPTER XII.

OTHER IMPORTANT MOVEMENTS, AND THE PRESENT STATUS OF THE METHODIST EPISCOPAL CHURCH.

The separation of the South did not terminate the controversy on slavery. We had some slave territory left, and not a few ministers and others who retained their old prejudice against abolition. The subject created a temporary excitement at the General Conference in 1852; but in 1856, abolitionists being in the majority, it received the first thorough investigation it had obtained at any General Conference in many years. This was repeated in 1860; and in 1864 the Discipline received its final touch forbidding slaveholding, and placing the church on its original platform.

The history of the church since 1844 is marked by many startling questions, which, at the moment of their greatest prominence, portended serious results. In reviewing the petitions, resolutions, motions, remonstrances, protests, appeals, committees, and reports which appeared in the *seven* successive General Conferences, of which the writer was a member, it is surprising to see how *few* changes were made in our economy, and yet how soon the troubled waters over any question subsided. Of these changes some were inoperative from the beginning; others had better have been so, while the majority have been useful. We can only glance at a few of them.

As before noticed, our Wesleyan brethren long since established a "Chapel Fund" to aid poor societies in the erection of churches. This, together with the necessities growing out of our advancing work, brought the subject of some similar arrangement to many leading minds. Difficulties appeared in the way, but after long delay the discussion culminated in the organization of a "Church Extension Society" by the General Conference in 1864, much after the style of our other connectional societies, to have its headquarters at Philadelphia. Its affairs are conducted by a Board of Managers and a Corresponding Secretary appointed by the General Conference. It has been a very useful appliance, and is likely to be more so as it shall become better known. Its collections in 1874 amounted to $83,347 50, all of which, over and above expenses, have gone to aid needy societies to build new churches, or liquidate embarrassing debts resting on old ones.

When our Book Concern was removed from Crosby to Mulberry-street in 1833, the church was more than satisfied. The addition of new buildings from time to time was a high source of many congratulations. But in the progress of events the place became rather too strait for the business, and a better location was urged with much emphasis. Having, however, to incur a heavy debt in the division of the property with the Church South, the desirable change was impracticable. Working over this embarrassment, and nothing of the kind having been effected, the General Conference of 1868 appointed a Lay and Clerical Committee to purchase land, and erect buildings thereon for the purpose, the cost not to exceed *one million* of dollars. This committee proceeded accordingly, and purchased the building now occupied by the Book

Concern and our connectional societies, No. 805 Broadway, New York. *Three-fourths* of this property belong to the Book Concern, and cost $717,904 13; and the other *fourth* to the Missionary Society, and cost $232,452 49 when ready for use; total, $950,356 62.

The reader of the preceding pages must have noticed traces of disturbance arising from the question of lay delegation, particularly in 1828. The claim of Episcopal prerogatives before mentioned revived the subject among certain abolitionists, who, with others, petitioned the General Conference with some emphasis, but without making the slightest impression, The General Conference, as late as 1852, and even in 1856, declared it *in*expedient to provide for it. But it was believed by many that great changes had occurred in the times, and in the circumstances of the church, which rendered the co-operation of laymen in the General Conference highly desirable; and after a pretty full discussion of the subject, it was finally carried by a constitutional vote, and laymen appeared in the General Conference of 1872 for the first time, *two* from each Annual Conference entitled to two or more clerical delegates, and *one* from each Conference having but one clerical delegate. We are frank to confess that we did nothing intentionally to favor the measure. If it shall prove as great a blessing to the church as was promised by its friends, its opponents will rejoice, though they can claim no credit for its adoption.

The General Conference of 1872 was distinguished also by establishing "District Conferences," to go into effect when and where the Quarterly Conferences of any district should request it by a vote of the majority. The plan constitutes the travelling and local preachers, exhorters, district stewards, and the first Sunday-school superintendent of each charge members, requires them to convene *twice* a year, and do a large part of the business heretofore done by the Quarterly Conferences. (See *Discipline*, pp. 60–63.) Some of the districts have approved of it, and the plan is now in process of experiment. It is evidently favored from different considerations. Many think it will be useful in keeping out of the ministry a class of men who found their way into it too easily through the Quarterly Conferences. Others hope that the balance of the business of the Quarterly Conferences will be transferred to the District Conferences, and pastors appointed to preside over them, and thus supersede the presiding eldership in such districts as may feel that they have little need of them. But still others favor the measure, believing that it will dignify the presiding eldership, and render it more useful and acceptable to all concerned. The Methodist Episcopal Church, South, which originated the scheme, speaks favorably of the District Conference meetings, yet *ominously* suggests that if they shall operate to depreciate the Quarterly-meeting Conferences, they will prove injurious rather than helpful. The plan will evidently need considerable modification to become generally popular.

There is another late improvement in our economy worthy of notice. For many years we lost valuable legacies for the want of corporate existence under the law. Therefore, the General Conference of 1864 provided for and appointed a General Board of Trustees, to receive and hold in trust, for the benefit of the Methodist Episcopal Church, any and all donations, bequests, grants, etc., made to said church, "not especially designated or directed." This board is now in charge of certain properties to be appropriated for the promotion of specific and general objects. We have no means of determining their value

In 1866 the Methodist Episcopal Church completed its first hundred years, and took occasion to celebrate the event by public religious services and benevolent contributions. By this means two funds were created, called "The Children's Fund," and "The General Education Fund," which seemed to find no appropriate custody in any of our then existing Boards. The General Conference, therefore, in 1868, established a Board of Education for the whole Methodist Episcopal Church, and confided these funds to its charge and management. A charter was duly obtained, and the new corporation reported to the General Conference of 1872, that "The Children's Fund" had reached the sum of $83,785 66, and "The General Education Fund" $15,727 78; total, $99,543 44, the interest of which is to aid our poor but pious aspirants after education. It is not likely that all its arrangements are perfect, as this never occurs in the beginning of human enterprises, but they are open to such improvements as experience shall show to be desirable. The expenditure of every dollar in meeting *immediate* necessities where the law will allow of it is thought by some to be advisable, but others have preferred to invest the principal and only expend the interest, which it is their right to do. All can be accommodated, and it is to be hoped that this fund will share in their benefactions.

The war of the rebellion having liberated more than four millions of slaves, January 1, 1863, measures were immediately adopted for their education. Among others, "The Freedmen's Aid Society" of the Methodist Episcopal Church was organised. This was presented to many of the Annual Conferences, and approved. It was also recognized by the General Conference of 1864, and recommended to the sympathy and patronage of the whole church. Four years after it was adopted, and placed side by side with our older connectional societies. It has done, and is still doing, a grand work for our redeemed brethren of the South. Its collections and disbursements amounted, in 1874, to $37,028 29.

We must not omit to mention another important auxiliary to our work. Our foreign missionaries found great difficulty in getting access to mothers and daughters, who, by the customs of society, were kept concealed at home. This suggested the "Woman's Foreign Missionary Society," which was organized in 1869. It has 1,839 auxiliaries; 54,160 members; publishes "The Heathen Woman's Friend;" supports 19 missionaries, 100 schools, 108 Bible women and teachers, 150 orphans; and raised, in 1874, $55,406 26. It has done a noble work, and is destined to be a powerful agency in Christianizing the heathen world. And we are happy to add that it works in harmony with our general Missionary board.

Other changes of more or less magnitude have been made in our Discipline during the last twenty years, but we have not room here even to name them. Considering, however, that nearly five hundred and fifty resolutions were offered in the last General Conference, with nearly as many memorials and petitions proposing numerous modifications, our legislation has been remarkably moderate. For a few years during the rebellion we suffered considerable loss in members, but that being over, we soon repaired the loss and more, showing, during the years 1866 and 1867, a net gain of 215,822 members.

The Methodist Episcopal Church is now (January 1, 1875) divided into *eighty* Annual Conferences, located in the United States and Territories, the colony of Liberia, Germany and Switzerland, and India. It embraces 12 bishops, 10,854 travelling preachers, 12,581 local preachers, and 1,563,521 members; showing an increase since 1847, when the tide of separation had about ceased to flow South, of 7,212 travelling preachers, 7,668 local preachers, and 931,963 members.

Our Missionary, Sunday School, and other benevolent contributions keep pace with our numerical increase, but not with our marvellous investments for home accommodations. While we raised but $667,360 80 for missions last year, the value of our churches increased $3,956,235, and our parsonages $1,061,656.

Our Sunday School interests are justly entitled to special attention. Last year's reports show 18,628 schools, 200,492 officers and teachers, and 1,363,876 scholars, giving an increase in one year of 597 schools, 3,312 officers and teachers, and 45,273 scholars.

Thus, with 12 bishops, 80 Annual Conferences, several hundred presiding elders, 10,854 travelling preachers, assisted by 12,581 local preachers, with more than a million and a half of members, the Methodist Episcopal Church stands before the world to-day, *not finished*, but in good condition to move forward in her noble work of spreading scriptural holiness over the world. At her birth, a little more than a hundred years ago, she had not one minister, or member, or church, or friend—not one dollar. At the bidding of a pious woman she sprang forth into being, and sang her first song.

Now she is numerous and strong. Besides all we have enumerated, she has 27 universities and colleges, training 5,000 students, and 65 seminaries, teaching more than 14,000 students, involving a net capital of about *seven millions of dollars*. To these may be added *five* theological institutions, whose business is to train our young ministers for their work. The Book Concern, which is capable of producing all necessary books, tracts, and requisites for the use of the Church and the Sunday Schools—the Tract Society, whose business it is to purchase and circulate tracts at home and abroad—and the Sabbath School Union, whose special object is to supply new and poor schools with the necessary outfit for carrying on their work with efficiency. Properly appreciating these appliances, together with those offered by our Missionary, Church Extension, and other societies, it will be difficult to find so complete an organism for the spread of Christianity in the world. Yet it will all amount to little without work, —hard, persistent, self-sacrificing work. We have outgrown in many places the necessity of travelling on horseback, swimming rivers, and sleeping in log-cabins, but not the necessity of cross-bearing, personal sacrifice, and untiring exertion. Maintaining these in the spirit and enterprise of our heroic fathers, with our present capital of men and means, another century will plant the gospel in every nation and tribe under the whole heavens. But, laying them aside, we have no power to resist the waste of death for half that time.

Well may it be said, "what hath God wrought!" It is certain that such a work has never been accomplished in so short a time. And it is not less certain, that no system of religious operations has ever had so much opposition to endure and overcome. Yet it has gone steadily on in weal and woe, converting its *worst enemies*, and succeeding often in its greatest defeats. Its prosperity has been universal and unceasing; its adversity, only local and temporary; and its progress was never greater, or its prospects brighter, than at present.

With the Church of England, and other national establishments, we, of course, can institute no comparisons, because they swallow up all sects and parties that come within their bounds, whether good, bad, or indifferent. Nor is it fair to compare Methodists, and other evangelical churches, with those sects which pander to the popular taste, and receive persons of all descriptions to their fellowship, without regard to their religious character. Rich and popular societies, which say little of our obligations, beyond the observance of mere church rites, may draw around them an accumulation of chaff in which there will be little wheat. The comparison, to be just and fair, should relate only to those whose circumstances are equal in other respects, and who require the same change of heart and life as the condition of their fellowship. But we will not be particular. A few facts will be sufficient for our purpose.

The *Independents*, of England, arose about the year 1600. They dissented from the establishment under the leadership of Rev. John Robinson, adopted Calvinistic views, and the model government of Congregationalism in New England. The Baptists appeared soon after, adopting similar views and modes of operation, but differing from the Independents in relation to the subjects of baptism and the manner in which it should be administered. They were afterward divided; a part becoming Arminians. The Presbyterians had commenced their career half a century before. But with this advantage as to time, and with other advantages we need not enumerate, the aggregate numbers and influence of all these denominations in England is not equal to that of the Methodists.

Methodism has not been less successful in America. The Congregationalists have occupied this field ever since the landing of the May Flower in 1620. They first settled the country, particularly New England, and for many years managed matters, both civil and religious, much in their own way, and excluded all dissenters from their territory. They now number 3,233 ministers, 323,679 church members. The Baptists have had nearly the same time to multiply, their first church having been formed by Roger Williams in 1638. The regular Calvinistic Baptists now number 12,598 ministers, and 1,633,939 members. The first presbytery in the country was organized in 1705, about eighty years before the organization of our church; and, in common with the other leading denominations, the Presbyterians have done a great and good work. The Old and New Schools together embrace 6,241 ministers, and 675,042 members. The Protestant Episcopal Church has been less successful, though it commenced its operations in the very infancy of the colonies, and had much to favor it till after the Revolution. It at present numbers 3,095 ministers, and 254,857 members. Other denominations have done well, and have contributed greatly to the religious influence of the country, but are less numerous.

Now, when it is considered that the first Methodist missionary to this country arrived in 1769, and that the church was not organized until 1784, and has since had to contend with poverty and prejudices incident to no other Christian body that has attained to any considerable importance in the community, and that Methodism now numbers in its several divisions 19,156 ministers, and 3,031,988 members, it must be conceded that it has been wonderfully favored.

Another view of the subject will indicate this truth with equal distinctness. In 1795 the different Methodist Churches numbered 60,604 members, which was about one to every sixty of the whole population of the country. They now embrace about one in every six of the present population —showing a proportionate increase, exceeding that of the rapid increase of the population of the country, as three to one. Now, with all respect to sister denominations, and we certainly entertain a high regard for them, we affirm that the like advancement is not to be seen in the progress of any one above mentioned. Indeed, several of them have lost nearly in the proportion that we have gained, and no one of them has increased in the same ratio by a very large per centum, notwithstanding *tens of thousands* who have been converted among us have united with them.

What has given us this peculiar distinction, is a question that wise men have solved differently. Some say one thing and some another; but all, who trace it to any single circumstance abstract from others, evidently err, not fully comprehending the system in all its parts.

It cannot be attributed to our doctrines, merely, for others have preached the same. Nor to our literary attainments, for in this respect we are frank to acknowledge ourselves behind some other denominations. Though many of our preachers are literary men, and have astonished the world by their productions, the mass lay no claim to this character. They have, however, been grossly misrepresented by certain clerical pretenders, who have not distinguished themselves for modesty and good breeding, however profound their learning. But some of these have had their reward in the mortification of seeing their enlightened hearers forsake them to attend upon the more tangible and effective ministrations of their itinerating neighbors. They may yet learn that ministerial education does not consist in mere sheepskin diplomas, and that it is not policy to ridicule whom God and his people "delight to honor."

Had Methodists been *rich* in this world's goods, their success might have been attributed to this cause; but, like the Saviour and his early disciples, they have generally been poor. They could not appeal to the pride and vanity of the world, by erecting splendid churches, and otherwise making a great display, if they were disposed. They have had to preach in private dwellings, school-houses, barns, and in the open air, till they could erect churches. And many of these, for the want of means, have had to be small, and often out of place, and uninviting. And the world has looked on and mocked, and professors of religion have not unfrequently joined in the sport. This same cause has been an occasion of reproach to preachers, who have often had to live in a style directly calculated to lessen the respect of community for them, and also for their enterprise.

We cannot trace this prosperity to any one instrumental cause, and say, that is it; for it is evidently attributable to many causes. Our *doctrines*, our *style* of presenting them, our *itinerancy*, and other prudential regulations, have all had an influence. No one item in our economy has been without effect in pushing forward this grand consummation; and we think some of the least prominent of our measures have been most effective. God has seemed to approve the whole movement, and crown every honest and faithful endeavor with his blessing. To him we ascribe all the glory. He has gone before his people, and led them as a shepherd his flock, into green pastures and beside the still waters. He has attended them in dangers, and made a way for their escape. In difficulties he has been their helper, suggesting measures, suppressing prejudices, converting foes to friends, and begetting interest and liberality where there was enmity and covetousness.

Numerous instances have occurred where the influential, supported by the rabble, as usual, have determined the Methodists should not make a stand among them, and united to prevent it; and not unfrequently the minister of the place has taken a leading part in the conspiracy. But, notwithstanding their vigilance and power, Methodism has taken root, and become established; and would have been alike successful in more places of the kind, had its friends been true to their principles.

From this hasty sketch it must appear to every reader, who is not blinded by prejudice, that Methodism has been peculiarly successful. A little more than one hundred years ago, it had no organized existence upon the face of the earth. Some *eight* or *ten* persons then came to Mr. Wesley, who appeared to be deeply convinced of sin, and earnestly groaning for redemption. Here was the nucleus around which we now behold this mighty array. Has not the "little one," indeed, "become a thousand?" This movement occurred in the city of London, and, for aught that was known to the contrary, was to be limited to that great metropolis. No mortal could then foretell that it would be reënacted in any other place. It was a mere *trifle*, a circumstance that might have occurred a hundred times without public notice, and indicated nothing remarkable. But, like the "grain of mustard seed (which is the least of all seeds") that became the "greatest among herbs," this germ has shot forth its branches over the four quarters of the globe, and innumerable birds lodge therein.

What its destiny is, we are unable to foretell. But if, with such means, against such fearful odds, and under so many discouraging circumstances, it has achieved such results, what may we not anticipate if we walk by the same rules and mind the same things? The gospel is no less efficacious now than formerly, and people are, probably, about as susceptible of being affected by it. Only let the church maintain the simplicity and faith of the fathers, and employ her improving facilities for doing good as she ought, and what has been, will be only as the first fruits of a mighty harvest. But if she shall prove recreant to her high trusts, her sun will go down in shame and everlasting contempt.

We close our sketch of its fortunes with the following statistical table for 1874 :—

TABULAR VIEW OF METHODISTS.

	Itinerant Ministers.	Local Preachers.	Lay Members.
I. EPISCOPAL METHODIST—			
Methodist Episcopal	10,845	12,706	1,563,521
Methodist Episcopal, South	3,371	5,344	667,885
Colored Methodist Episcopal	635	683	67,888
African Methodist Episcopal	600	1,300	200,000
African Methodist Episcopal, Zion	694	1,416	164,000
Evangelical Association	737	476	90,249
United Brethren	967	742	120,445
Total Episcopal Methodists	17,749	22,667	2,873,988
II. NON-EPISCOPAL METHODIST—			
The Methodist Church	624	300	65,000
Methodist Protestant	423	250	65,000
American Wesleyan	250	190	20,000
Free Methodist	90	80	6,000
Primitive Methodist	20	25	2,000
Total Non-Episcopal Methodists	1,407	1,845	158,000
Grand Total Methodists in United States.	19,156	24,512	3,031,988
British Wesleyans in Great Britain	1,715	13,720	376,439
Irish Wesleyan Churches	152	760	20,740
French Wesleyan Churches	28	96	2,012
Australian Wesleyan Churches	848	1,438	66,686
Primitive Methodist Church	1,020	14,838	164,660
Methodist New Connection Church	240	1,270	33,563
United Methodist Free Church	358	3,361	66,909
Bible Christian Churches	244	1,747	26,878
British Wesleyan Reform Union	365	148	8,109
Methodist Church of Canada	1,004	1,027	102,887
Methodist Episcopal Church in Canada	286	214	22,641
Grand Total	24,866	63,181	3,923,512

PART SECOND.

DOCTRINAL VIEWS OF METHODISTS, AS DISTINGUISHED FROM THOSE OF OTHER DENOMINATIONS.

CHAPTER I.

POINTS OF AGREEMENT.

MOST of the controversies that have agitated the church in all ages, have related to points of doctrine. The unity of the Methodists in this particular is remarkable. Though divided into several branches, in common with other leading denominations, they have maintained the strictest integrity in theology. But they differ from various influential bodies of Christians on important points, and are as often condemned for this as for other peculiarities. The object of this part of our work is to unfold these points, and the arguments upon which they rest for support, in as brief and explicit a manner as possible. But in accordance with the advice of a wise man, who would unite all denominations in one, we shall, in the first place, consider the points wherein we *agree* with Christians in general, that we may be able to determine whether, after all, we do not agree more than we disagree.

Following this arrangement, the first particular that naturally claims attention is the authority of the Holy

Scriptures. Have they the sanction of Almighty God, or are they the mere utterances of erring men? This is a great question, and it takes precedence of every other. Nearly all we know of divine things we owe to these writings. If they are from God they *must* be true; if from man they *may* be false.

Christians of all denominations, Methodists among others, regard them as the oracles of God. They agree that "holy men of God spake as they were moved by the Holy Ghost," or, to adopt the language of St. Paul, that "God, who, at sundry times, and in divers manners, spake in time past unto the fathers by the prophets, hath in these last days spoken unto us by his Son," in such a way that "all Scripture is given by inspiration of God, and is profitable for doctrine, for reproof, for correction, for instruction in righteousness," and is "able to make [us] wise unto salvation, through faith which is in Christ Jesus."

They, therefore, hold them as the *standard* of religious truth, to which all moral questions are referable, and by which they are to be settled; and admit nothing to be true that is inconsistent with their teachings, and nothing to be false which can be clearly proved thereby. And, further, that they teach all things necessary to salvation. Hence, they look upon those who esteem them only as the opinions and precepts of men, — containing a mixture of truth and falsehood, to be sifted by the reader, and received or rejected at discretion, together with those who assume that they are *insufficient*, and may be improved by additions and subtractions, as the world advances in the arts and sciences, — as *infidels*, and enemies to vital godliness. And in this judgment they are sustained by reference to the incontestable evidence of their *fruits*.

It is not our intention to discuss the divine inspiration and authenticity of these Scriptures, farther than what is necessary in a brief statement of the grounds of our faith. That man *needed* some definite instruction in relation to his Maker, his own duty and destiny, is but too obvious from his whole history. However *we* may see traces of an infinite and eternal spirit in the wonderful exhibitions of nature, having Him first revealed to us in the Holy Scriptures, no such discoveries ever cheered the investigations of the most acute philosopher who had not obtained some intimations, directly or indirectly, from the same source. The boasted discoveries of philosophy, so far as they are founded in truth, are none other than those of revelation, borrowed from tradition, or stolen from the sanctuary. But even with these helps, the infidel philosopher has furnished the world with meagre proof of his competency to understand and effectively to teach all necessary truth. His clumsy account of the great problems of revelation, but too clearly indicates that his theory is the creature of fancy, stimulated by self-conceit and enmity against God. The whole history of Pagan mythology is a standing demonstration that man, by wisdom, cannot find out God or himself. Hence, it is reasonable to *presume* that a revelation has been made, and, if so, that the Scriptures contain that revelation; since it is generally conceded that they are incomparably superior to any and all other writings which claim divine authority.

But we place little reliance on such reasoning, however correct; and the Creator does not require it. He knew what was in man, and that something more tangible and demonstrative would be necessary to command his confidence. *That* something he furnished in various ways. *First,* he endowed his messengers to perform certain feats of power, in attestation of the *authority* with which they spake, and the *truth* of what they said, that could not be imitated, or reasonably attributed to any other than himself. Thus, he qualified Moses and the prophets, Jesus and the apostles, so that, wherever they came, the blind received sight, the sick were healed by a word or a touch, the mouths of lions were shut, the violence of fire quenched, the sea hushed its rage or stood back for them to pass, and even the dead were restored to life. The readers of the Bible are familiar with the account of all these transactions. Had Moses, or Jesus or the apostles, never done the works described and published in their writings, their enemies would have contradicted them; for they were not done in a corner. The most of them were performed in public, in the presence of their enemies. But we hear no such contradiction from witnesses who were in a condition to know to the contrary. The enemies of Christ did, indeed, deny that he arose from the dead; but, in attempting to account for his absence from the tomb, entangled themselves in the meshes of the net they were spreading for others, where they remain to this day.

To the performance of peculiar works, works entirely above human energy, these men added prophecies not less unaccountable on any other hypothesis than that they spake as they were moved by the Holy Ghost. They related future events with great precision, giving the time, place, and circumstances of their transaction, and events, too, so distant, and improbable to human apprehension and belief, that no one could credit them for a moment, who did not regard the speakers as divinely imbued to reveal the deep things of eternity. Some of the events thus described were hundreds of years distant, others came within a few days of the prediction; as, for example, the death, burial and resurrection of Jesus. How could he have known when he should die, who should betray him, or that he would be betrayed at all, and that he would rise after three days, had he not been possessed of the wisdom of God? It was impossible. By what power did Isaiah discover the coming, character, and history of Christ seven hundred years prior to his advent? His predictions look quite like history, and entitle him to the honor he has long enjoyed of being "the evangelical prophet." How came Daniel to know the secrets of the future which brought him into notice? He claimed to be instructed from on high, and his enemies were forced to concede that he was not deceived.

Now, with these facts before us, established beyond all reasonable doubt, to believe what these prophets and workers of miracles taught, seems almost unavoidable, At least, it requires no undue amount of credulity to do so. We believe, and act, upon less evidence on every other subject. Many renounce all religion on that which bears no comparison with it. How many have shown their willingness to discard the whole Bible, because it seems not to recognize what are called the modern discoveries of science! The infidel astronomer finds that the sun stands comparatively still, and does not rise and set as was formerly supposed. He, therefore, is ready to conclude that the Scriptures are not the word of God, because they speak after the *manner of men*, and not scientifically. Geologists have often come to the same conclusion, because the Scriptures do not seem to allow time enough since the creation, to make out the various formations of their half-fledged theories.

And a herd of mesmeric wizards are not less credulous. The secret of miracles and prophecy, they say, is all out. Daniel mesmerized the lions. Shadrach, Meshach, and Abednego were made fire-proof by somnambulic influence; and the Apostles healed diseases and cast out devils by a similar agency, and no mistake. And yet, believing all this folly, they ask for a "sign," that they may believe that God speaks in the Scriptures!

But the tricks of such pretenders must not be allowed to unsettle our confidence. While we would not encourage people to believe every honest fancy of good men, nor be easily led away by every fresh "wind of doctrine" that may arise, we think when men come among us in the name of God, teaching sentiments of good moral tendency, and, in confirmation of their authority, heal our sick by a look or a touch, give sight to our blind without medical or surgical means — turn our rivers backward — hush our tempests to peace — raise our dead, and perform other similar phenomena — and foretell what shall be in the future, with certainty, and we see it occur without the failure of a single circumstance — we say, when men do this, it is unsafe not to have credulity enough to believe them divinely commissioned, and submit to their teachings as to the command of God. And such men were the teachers developed in the Bible, and such was the tendency of their doctrine and the character of their acts and predictions.

To these grounds of evidence we add another of the highest importance. Physical science is often demonstrable by experiment. The chemist informs us that the combination of given substances in specific proportions, and by a given process, will form a compound of a certain character, which, employed in a particular way, will effect certain results. To deny it outright is folly, however improbable it may appear. Reason suggests that we try the experiment, recognizing this as the proper test of all such theories. If, on collecting the materials, and combining them as prescribed, we find the exact results enumerated, we are prompt to say the theory is correct.

Now, though the subject in question is strictly of a moral

nature, and may not, therefore, be demonstrated to the senses in this manner precisely, it is, nevertheless, susceptible of demonstration not less satisfactory. The Bible is committed to the production of certain moral phenomena For example, it is pledged for the weary and heavy laden who come to Christ, that they shall find *rest to their souls*,— to the ungodly, who " believeth," that he shall be *justified*,— to him that seeks the Lord while he may be found, and calls upon him while he is near, that he *shall obtain mercy and abundant pardon*. And it marks the state to which faith, seeking the Lord, — mourning, repenting, &c.,— introduces the sinner, by so many distinguishing characteristics that it need not be mistaken. It describes it as a *new creation*, in which old things, old affections, prejudices, enjoyments, and pursuits, are done away, and all things are become new,— as " righteousness, peace, and joy in the Holy Ghost." The mental process by which these results are attained, and the evidences by which they are distinguished, are not less clearly defined. So that if one wishes to test the truth of Scripture in reference to these vital questions, he has only to follow their prescriptions, under the influences of the Holy Spirit, which are given to every man to profit withal.

Many have adopted this course, even with serious doubts and prejudices in the outset, and with strong tendencies to unbelief, and have obtained the most satisfactory results. Indeed, they have realized a salvation from themselves, their passions and propensities, they little anticipated, and experienced a fulness of spiritual delight of which they had no previous conception. We have known some to succeed thus who entered upon a religious life more as an experiment than from a pungent conviction of sin. God, in his mercy, led them along, step by step, according to their several necessites, till he brought them to the promised state, and enabled them to rejoice in the full assurance of hope, that proved like an anchor to the soul. And we have not the least doubt that all persons, in a rational state of mind, would obtain like "precious faith," would they only "bring all the tithes into the storehouse," and prove the Lord agreeably to his command.

Evidence of the divine authority of the Bible, obtained in this way, is of the most substantial and interesting character. That which is obtained by a mere logical process is good, and cannot be overthrown, yet, in the perversity of the carnal heart, it may be accompanied with many doubts and with great indifference. But this evidence, not only appealing to the intellect, but being written on the heart by the Holy Spirit, producing a profound, holy and joyous experience, seems to be incorporated into our being; in other words, to become a part of ourselves, and, therefore, not easily eradicated. Truths we ascertain by reasoning, we *believe;* those we demonstrate by experience, we *know.*

To these arguments in favor of the divine origin of the Scriptures, we may add their general tendency. This may be seen by a comparison of those communities where they are read by the people, with those where they are little known. In the former, every thing wears an aspect of life, enterprise and comfort; in the latter, an aspect of stagnation and wretchedness. Where have art, and science, and literature, and commerce, and agriculture, and useful invention, and morality, and religion, reached their richest growth during the last half century? In what country do we see railroads, and steam engines, and telegraphic wires, starting up in the greatest numbers, and effecting the best results? Nay, where do we find any improvement of the kind, save in the domain of the unshackled word of God? Other countries remain as they were, and plod along as did their great grandfathers, in ignorance, ill-bred vice, and hardship.

For these Scriptures Methodists cherish the highest regard. Their founder declared himself a "*Bible bigot.*" Not that he despised the writings of the good and the wise, for no man read them more carefully than he; or had no confidence in the traditions of the fathers; but he esteemed the Scriptures as the only reliable source of divine knowledge, and an all-sufficient rule of faith and practice. He would, therefore, have the Bible, and nothing but the Bible, as the ground and support of all he taught or believed.

In relation to the perfections of God, we generally harmonize with Christians of other denominations. The knowledge of God, together with his sovereignty, we hold in a little different light from that which appears in the writings of Calvinists. *We* consider his knowledge of the future as a natural *attribute* of the divine mind, rather than an *acquisition* resulting from his decree; and we understand the Divine *sovereignty* in such a way as to make it agree with man's free-agency. We also differ a little with the same class of theologians in relation to the extent of God's love to mankind, and several other collateral points, all of which will be considered in connection with our peculiar doctrines.

On the great question relative to the personal character of Christ, which has divided the Christian world into Trinitarians and Unitarians, we have uniformly maintained what is called Orthodox ground. We are not Sabellians, holding a mere nominal Trinity, nor are we Arians, giving Christ a high character, and talking well of the atonement, but denying his godship. Neither are we Socinians, or Humanitarians, but we strictly adhere to the ancient doctrine of the

Trinity, attributing to Christ personality and all the attributes of the godhead, mysteriously blended with those of manhood, and to the Holy Spirit the attributes that belong to the Father. And we do this not because we see the philosophy of such a Trinity in the divine unity, but because the Scriptures attribute the proper titles, attributes, and works of God, to the Son and the Spirit, as well as to the Father. We see the philosophy of very few things which we know to exist. Of God we know little, except what is revealed in his word. The philosophy of his existence, and even of our own, is still an impenetrable mystery. Those who insist on holding the Bible subordinate to their own reason, or to philosophy, will find, if they are true to their principles, that their theology is very limited and superficial. If they do not get into a wrangle with their own senses, it will be for the want of courage to carry out their theory to its legitimate consequences.

The fall of man in Adam, and the consequent depravity of the race, we hold as a great fact lying at the foundation of the whole gospel scheme, not only revealed in the Bible, but substantiated by the unequivocal evidence of observation and experience. Men are as conscious of aversion to God and religion, and of love to sin, as they are of personal identity. The very first developments of the heart of infancy indicate evil passions, and suggest to the parents the duty of repressing these germs, and creating dispositions of a better character. The whole system of domestic government seems to recognize this evil principle. If the hearts of infants were pure and holy, they would be as averse to sin as they now are to good, and much of our present discipline would be unnecessary. If they were *indifferent*, that is, without predisposition to either good or evil, like a sheet of white paper, as susceptible of one impression as another, it would be reasonable to expect that some would receive the right impression, and grow up in holiness. But they have "all gone out of the way." They "are estranged from the womb, they go astray as soon as they be born, speaking lies," and God has, therefore, reckoned them all "*under sin*," that he might have mercy upon all.

Thus, we say that "original sin standeth not in the following of Adam, (as the Pelagians do vainly talk,) but it is the corruption of the nature of every man, that naturally is engendered of the offspring of Adam, whereby man is very far gone from original righteousness, and is of his own nature inclined to evil, and that continually." — (*Discipline.*) *How* this principle of evil is *transmitted*, we do not undertake to explain. This is as inscrutable to us as the transmission of complexion, form, and features, which we every where see and acknowledge. But our ignorance in this respect does not destroy the *fact*. We are as sure that children possess this evil nature, as that they are white, or black, or that they belong to the human, and not to the brute race, because it develops itself with the greatest distinctness and uniformity.

We are, therefore, prepared to recognize the mission of Christ in its proper character. Man, having sinned and incurred the penalty of the law, must have been cut off, but for the institution of an atonement, by which God could be just, and yet the justifier of the ungodly. One object of Christ's mission was, therefore, to suffer in man's stead, that he might magnify the law, and make it honorable, by so far enduring its penalty as to preserve the race, and assure man that the law is not to be broken with impunity. Another object was, to endow him with grace and strength to over come his propensities, and obey God, and finally to bring him to everlasting life in heaven.

To have pardoned him without the formality of such an atonement would not justly have represented God's abhorrence of sin, or his regard for his law. Nor would it have impressed men with suitable notions of the divine government, of their own obligations to avoid sin, or the danger of committing it. Hence, we consider our lives, our privileges, our hopes, and our enjoyments, among the benefits of the atonement, and look to God through Christ for all that we desire.

We are also prepared to appreciate that great *moral* change in the human heart, called the *new birth.* Those who believe the natural heart to be pure, see no necessity for such a change. Education will do all that is required. But, if the "carnal mind is enmity against God," if the leprosy of sin "lies deep within," and "the whole head is sick, and the whole heart faint," *training* will not suffice; there must be *revolution* — a radical overturn of the whole moral system, and a new foundation laid in "righteousness, and peace, and joy in the Holy Ghost." We, therefore, fully believe, that, "except a man be *born again*, he cannot see the kingdom of God." And this new birth "is not of blood, nor of the will of the flesh, nor of the will of man, but of God." It is an inward spiritual change, obtained in the exercise of repentance toward God, and faith in our Lord Jesus Christ, and is evidenced to the soul of the believer by the witness and fruits of the Spirit, and to others by the manifestation of new affections and habits.

We also hold to the organization of Christians into churches; to the ordinances of baptism, and the Lord's supper; to the religious observance of the holy Sabbath; to the resurrection of the dead; the doctrine of a general judgment, in which every man shall be judged according to the deeds done in the body, to be followed by everlasting rewards and punishments. And all these we hold in the language of Scripture, taken in its most natural and obvious sense, and in common with all evangelical Christians. We believe them, *first*, because they are taught in the word of God; and, *secondly*, because we have demonstrated some of them by the most satisfactory experiments. We believe them sincerely and devoutly, and rest all our hopes of salvation upon their truth. We have proved them a thousand times in our writings, and preaching, and keep them always before the people as our settled faith. And yet, it is not uncommon for us to be published as Socinians, or Palagians, and deceivers of the people, holding the doctrine of devils. But we submit the question, whether, with the sentiments herein avowed, we are not entitled to a better name?

CHAPTER II.

THE CHARACTER AND HISTORY OF CERTAIN SENTIMENTS WITH WHICH METHODISTS HAVE BEEN MOST IN COLLISION.

METHODISTS were more distinguished, at first, for their piety and zeal, than for any peculiarity of sentiment. Indeed, they adopted no new principle or theory, except what was necessarily connected with personal experience. Their object seemed to be the revival of pure religion on an old basis, the general soundness of which was conceded. They avowed no creed, nor required subscription to any from those who came among them. A desire to flee from the wrath to come, was the only condition of membership. But this was to be manifested by strict conformity to the requirements of God. They were to abstain from evil of every kind, and do good in every possible way, and thus work out their "salvation with fear and trembling."

Herein the origin of the Methodist Church differs from that of most other denominations. *They* commenced with a mere opinion, as their respective names import. For example, the Baptists became a distinct people on the ground of holding to immersion as the *only* mode of baptism; the Congregationalists and Presbyterians derived their existence from certain notions of church government; and the Unitarians from particular views of Christ and the atonement

Methodists received their denominational name from their enemies, and in ridicule ; not on account of any opinion they held, but because of their *methodical* manner of living, and of their singular *devotion*. They instituted no new system of divinity, or form of government, and labored for nothing but to live correctly themselves, and persuade others to be reconciled to God.

But in reproving sin, exhorting others to duty, and particularly in relating their Christian experience, they came in collision with sentiments to which they could show no indulgence, without doing violence to their solemn convictions, and hindering the work they would promote and extend. These sentiments were various, but none were urged with more earnestness and perseverance than those taught by John Calvin. Though it would seem that Calvinists should be the last to feel concerned about any thing, believing, as they profess to do, that God fore-ordained whatsoever comes to pass, and that the number of the elect is so definite that it can neither be increased or diminished, they were among the first to attack Methodism on doctrinal grounds, and they did it with a zeal indicative of fear, lest it should deceive the "very elect." The ideas of free and full salvation for every sinner, by Jesus Christ ; and of free will, by the grace of God, in every one, so that all may come to Christ and be saved ; and particularly the liability of believers becoming "cast-aways," at last, through their own unfaithfulness, — sentiments which the little band believed with all their hearts, and proclaimed with great pathos and power, not controversially, but persuasively, gave particular offence. And they attacked them in high places, and pursued them into every street and lane, with a recklessness in relation to the spiritual results of such procedure befitting their system. And from that day to the present, and in all countries, Methodism has experienced more opposition from this quarter than from any other. In New England, especially, every step of her progress has been resisted. Her ministers have been openly attacked in their own congregations, they have been preached against, and published in papers and pamphlets as heretics, and "wolves in sheep's clothing," and many have been so deceived and prejudiced in relation to them, they would almost as soon hear or harbor a *demon*, as a Methodist preacher. The doctrines, therefore, by which we have been particularly distinguished from other Protestant sects, are those wherein we differ from the Calvinists. And we differ from them only on those points which constitute them *Calvinists*, and not on many others we both hold in common with Christians in general. The doctrine of the atonement by Christ, and the new birth, are *not* Calvinism, though John Calvin believed and taught them, and his followers do the same. Calvinism embraces those particulars in which Calvin differed from others, and wherein his system was new and peculiar. A few extracts from his writings will exhibit it to the reader in its original character.

"Predestination," he says, "we call the eternal decree of God, by which he hath determined in himself what he would have to become of every individual of mankind. For they are not all created with similar destiny; but eternal life is fore-ordained for some, and eternal damnation for others. Every man, therefore, being created for one or other of these ends, we say he is predestinated either to life or to death." And he adds, "Though it is sufficiently clear that God, in his secret counsel, freely chooses whom he will, and rejects others, his gratuitous election is but half displayed till we come to particular individuals, to whom God not only offers salvation, but *assigns* it in such a manner that the certainty of the effect is liable to no suspense or doubt. * * *

In conformity, therefore, to the clear doctrine of Scripture, we assert, that, by an eternal and immutable counsel, God hath once for all determined both whom he would admit to salvation, and whom he would condemn to destruction. This counsel, so far as it concerns the elect, is founded on his gratuitous mercy, totally irrespective of human merit; but that to those whom he devotes to condemnation, the gate of life is closed by a just and irreprehensible, but incomprehensible, judgment."

That he might not be misunderstood, he explains, by saying, "It is a notion commonly entertained that God, foreseeing what would be the respective merits of every individual, makes a correspondent distinction between different persons; that he adopts as his children such as he foreknows will be deserving of his grace; and devotes to the damnation of death others whose dispositions he sees will be inclined to wickedness and impiety. Thus, they not only obscure election by covering it with the veil of foreknowledge, but pretend that it originates in another cause. God hath mercy on whom he will have mercy, and whom he will he hardeneth. If, therefore, we can assign no reason why he grants mercy to his people, but because such is his pleasure, neither shall we find any other cause but his will for the reprobation of others. Many, indeed, as if they wished to avert odium from God, admit election in such a way as to deny that any one is reprobated. But this is puerile and absurd; because election itself could not exist, without being opposed to reprobation; whom God passes by, he, therefore, reprobates, and from no other cause than his determination to exclude them from the inheritance which he predestinates for his children."

Attempting to smooth this "*horrible decree*," by referring to the natural corruption of man, as a good reason for their reprobation, the inquiry of opponents — "were they not predestinated to that very corruption, also?" stood directly in his way. In answering it, he says: — "I confess, indeed, that all the descendants of Adam fell, *by the divine will*, into that miserable condition in which they are now involved; and this is what I asserted from the beginning, that we must always return, at last, to the *sovereign determination of God's will*, the cause of which is hidden in himself. But it follows not, therefore, that God is liable to this reproach; for we will answer them in the language of Paul: 'O, man, who art thou that repliest against God? Shall the thing formed say to him that formed it, Why hast thou made me thus?'"

The sophism of more modern times, that "God saw that all were lost, and determined that he would save some, and therefore elected them to glory, passing by others," found no favor with this honest man. "For," says he, "since God foresees future events only in consequence of his decree that they shall happen, it is useless to contend about foreknowledge, while it is evident that all things come to pass rather by ordination and decree." "It is a *horrible decree*, I confess; but no one can deny that God foreknew the future fate of man, and that he did foreknow it, because it was appointed by his own decree."

Yet, strange enough, he denies that God is the author of sin. But how he could will and decree that it should happen, and appoint all the circumstances connected therewith, and not be the author of it, is an insolvable question. What God decrees, he *does*, and is the author of, and the responsibility of his act rests with himself and upon no other. All attempts, therefore, to find a justifiable cause of man's destruction in his corruption, after having attributed that corruption, with its various consequences, to God's will and decree, seems to us an insult to common sense. If man has done only as God decreed he should do, and is only as he was ordained to be, he is *right;* or, if not, he is not to blame, and cannot in justice be punished for it.

The writings of Calvin, evolving these, and correlative views, new and startling, elicited much controversy. His friends, enamored with his dogmas, refined them, and educed (legitimately, we think) some of the most shocking sentiments ever uttered. These were afterwards collected and published in a pamphlet, entitled "A Correct Copy of some Notes concerning God's Decrees," embracing *ten* extracts from popular Calvinistic works, "to prove that there are men of no small name, who have told the world that all the evil of sin which is in man proceedeth from God only as the author, and from man only as the instrument." The nature of Calvinism, and the state of the controversy, may be inferred from the following: "A wicked man, *by the just impulse of God*, doeth that which is not lawful for him to do." "When God makes an angel or a man a transgressor, he himself doth not transgress, because he doth not break a law. The very same sin, namely, adultery or murder, inasmuch as it is the work of God, the author, mover, and compeller, is not a crime; but, inasmuch as it is of man, it is a wickedness. God can will that man shall not fall by his will, which is called *voluntas signi;* and in the meantime he can ordain that the same man shall infallibly and efficaciously fall by his will, which is called *voluntas beneplaciti.* The former will of God is improperly called his will, for it only signifieth what man ought to do by right; but the latter is properly called a will, because by that he *decreed* what should inevitably come to pass." "God's will doth pass, not only into the permission of the sin, but into the sin itself which is permitted."

If any should incline to question the authority of these statements, he will do well to remember that the first is from Calvin himself, who certainly understood his own system; the second is from Zuinglius; and the third from Dr. Twisse. But they were not alone. In the same tone and spirit Zanchius wrote: "Reprobates are compelled with a necessity of sinning, and so of perishing by this ordination of God; and so compelled that they cannot choose but sin and perish." "God works all things in all men, not only in the godly, but also in the ungodly." And, says Piscator, "Judas could not but betray Christ, seeing that God's decrees are immutable; and whether a man bless or curse, he always doth it necessarily in respect of God's Providence; and, in so doing, he doeth always according to the will of God." "It doth, or, at least, may, appear from the word of God, that we neither can do more good than we do, nor omit more evil than we omit; because God, from eternity, hath precisely decreed that both should be so done. It is fatally constituted when, and how, and how much every one of us ought to study and love piety, or not to love it."

Such views could but find opponents in any age. They were early resisted and refuted, but not destroyed. Various corrections and modifications were invented to make them more palatable, when, to set the matter at rest as to what Calvin did teach, and what his followers believed, the Synod of Dort took up the subject, and resolved the whole into five articles, which constitute the standard of what is called "strict Calvinism," and embrace the points of difference between Calvinists and Arminians. These were very shrewdly drawn, with a view, no doubt, to making them satisfactory to all parties. But they form a perfect snarl of conflicting doctrines, unless we construe them strictly in the light of the clear writings of Calvin himself, and pass over those parts which savor of better sentiments, as a slight sprinkling of honey intermixed with the poison to catch Arminian flies. Then all is plain and unmistakable. Taking this view of them, these articles are in substance as follows:

1. *Predestination*, embracing the election of some to eternal life, and the reprobation of others to eternal death. 2. *The Atonement* made by Christ, limiting it to "those who were from *eternity* chosen to salvation, and given to him by the Father, that he should confer on them the gift of faith." 3. *Depravity*, assuming it to be so deep and thorough that none are able or willing to return to God, without the regenerating grace of the Holy Ghost; thus placing *regeneration* before *repentance* in the order of time, and making it indispensable thereto. 4. *Free Grace and Free Will*, restricting both to the elect; the grace consisting in spiritually quickening, healing, correcting, and sweetly and powerfully inclining the will of the elect to obedience; and the *freedom* of the *will* consisting in the disposition thus begotten *to* obey. 5. *Perseverance of the Saints*, assuming, in strict accordance with the preceding views, that the elect, thus called, regenerated and inclined to obey God, "will never *totally fall* from faith and grace, nor *finally continue* in their falls, and *perish*."

The early discussion of these doctrines was not without some good effect. Horror-stricken at their logical consequences, multitudes deserted the Calvinian standard, and went completely over to the ranks of Arminians, or halted midway under the command of Baxter. From that time to the middle of the eighteenth century, ultra-Calvinism, otherwise called Antinomianism, received little support. But the success of the Wesleys in preaching more Scriptural sentiments, aroused the cry of heresy, and brought out a class of men, who, under the delusion that nothing could be evan gelical that was not Calvinistic, adopted the Antinomian theory, and stoutly defended it. And we fear there are some, even now, who hold it as the only pure doctrine of *grace*, though the verdict of the Christian world is against it.

Many, however, as Baxter and his coadjutors, while they have taken rank under the general cognomen of Calvinists, have holden the dogmas of their leader with considerable modification. Hence, they are called "*moderate* Calvinists." The points to which they chiefly except are, *reprobation*, and the limitation of the atonement to the elect. Yet they mend the matter more in *appearance* than in *fact*, since, after all their admissions in favor of Arminian views, there is something lacking in their systems, which is as *fatal* to the sinner's interest, if he is not one of the elect, as the most positive decree of reprobation could be. It has been truly said, that "The main characteristic of all these theories, from the first to the last, from the highest to the lowest, is, that a part of mankind are shut out from the mercies of God, on some ground irrespective of their refusal of a sincere offer of salvation through Christ, made with a communicated power of embracing it. Some power they allow to the reprobate, as '*natural power*,' and degrees of superadded moral power; but, in no case, the power to believe unto salvation; and thus, as one well observes, 'when they have cast some fair trenches, as if they would bring the water of life unto the dwellings of the reprobate, on a sudden they open a sluice which carries it off again.' The whole labor of these theories is to *find out* some plausible reason for the infliction of punishment on them that perish, independent of the only cause assigned by the word of God — their rejection of a mercy free for all and attainable by all." — *Watson.*

Calvinism was imported into America by the first settlers, and became the established theology of the churches. But it was not formed into a creed, and made binding, till the year 1648, when the Synod met at Cambridge, and adopted the "Cambridge platform." In the preface to this formulary, the Synod avow their concurrence in the "Confession of Faith" adopted by the assembly of divines which met at Westminster, England, long before. Those who have examined the Westminster Catechism cannot, therefore, misapprehend the peculiar type of Calvinism under which our churches were nursed. But this measure was not altogether satisfactory; and the Synod which met at Boston, in 1780, with Rev. Increase Mather in the chair, adopted the "Savoy Confession," the distinctive features of which are stated in these words: —

"I. OF GOD'S ETERNAL DECREES.

"God, from all eternity, did, by the most wise and holy counsel of his own will, freely and unchangeably ordain whatsoever comes to pass; yet so as thereby neither is God the author of sin, nor is violence offered to the *will* of the creature, nor is the liberty or contingency of second causes taken away, but rather established.

"Although God knows whatsoever may or can come to pass upon all supposed conditions; yet hath he not decreed any thing, because he foresaw it as futnre, or that which would come to pass, upon such conditions.

"By the decree of God, for the manifestation of his glory, some men and angels are predestinated unto everlasting life, and others fore-ordained for everlasting death.

"These angels and men, thus predestinated and fore-ordained, are particularly and unchangeably designated, and their number is so definite that it cannot be either increased or diminished.

"Those of mankind that are predestinated unto life, God, before the foundation of the world was laid, according to his eternal and immutable purpose, and the secret counsel and good pleasure of his will, hath chosen in Christ unto everlasting glory, out of his mere free grace and love, without any foresight of faith or good works, or perseverance in either of them, or any other thing in the creature, as conditions or causes nerving him thereto, and all to the praise of his glorious grace.

"As God hath appointed the elect unto glory, so hath he, by the eternal and most free purpose of his will, foreordained all the means thereunto. Wherefore, they who are elected, being fallen in Adam, are redeemed by Christ, are effectually called unto faith in Christ by his Spirit working in due season, are justified, adopted, sanctified, and kept by his power, through faith unto salvation. Neither are any others redeemed by Christ, or effectually called, justified, adopted, sanctified, and saved, but the elect only.

"The rest of mankind God was pleased, according to the unsearchable counsel of his own will, whereby he extendeth or withholdeth mercy as he pleaseth, for the glory of his sovereign power over his creatures, to pass by, and to ordain them to dishonor and wrath for their sins, to the praise of his glorious justice.

"The doctrine of this high mystery of predestination is to be handled with special prudence and care, that men attending the will of God revealed in his word, and yielding obedience thereunto, may, from the certainty of their effectual vocation, be assured of their eternal election. So shall this doctrine afford matter of praise, reverence, and admiration of God, and of humility, diligence, and abundant consolation to all that sincerely obey the gospel.

"II. OF THE FALL OF MAN, OF SIN, AND OF THE PUNISHMENT THEREOF.

"By this sin they, and we in them, fell from original righteousness and communion with God, and so became dead in sin, and wholly defiled in all the faculties and parts of the body.

"They being the root, and by God's appointment standing in the room and stead of all mankind, the guilt of this sin was infected, and corrupted nature conveyed, to all their posterity, descending from them by ordinary generation.

"From this original corruption, whereby we are utterly indisposed, disabled, and made opposite to all good, and wholly inclined to all evil, do proceed all actual transgressions.

"III. OF FREE WILL.

"God hath endued the will of man with that natural liberty and power of acting upon choice, that it is neither forced, nor by any absolute necessity of nature determined, to do good or evil.

"Man, in his state of innocency, had freedom and power to will and do that which was good and well pleasing to God; but yet mutably, so that he might fall from it.

"Man, by his fall into a state of sin, hath wholly lost all ability of will to any spiritual good accompanying salvation, so as a natural man being altogether averse from that good, and dead in sin, is not able by his own strength to convert himself, or to prepare himself thereunto.

"When God converts a sinner, and translates him into a state of grace, he freeth him from his natural bondage under sin, and by his grace alone enables him freely to will and to do that which is spiritually good; yet so as by reason of his remaining corruption, he doth not perfectly nor only will that which is good, but doth also will that which is evil

"IV. OF EFFECTUAL CALLING.

"All those whom God hath predestinated unto life, and those only, he is pleased in his appointed and accepted time effectually to call by his word and spirit out of that state of sin and death in which they are by nature, to grace and salvation by Jesus Christ, enlightening their minds spiritually and savingly to understand the things of God, taking away their heart of stone, and giving unto them a heart of flesh. Renewing their wills, and by his almighty power determining them to do that which is good, and by effectually drawing them to Jesus Christ, yet so as they come most freely, being made willing by his grace.

"V. OF THE PERSEVERANCE OF THE SAINTS.

"They whom God hath accepted in his beloved, effectually called and sanctified by his Spirit, can neither totally nor finally fall away from a state of grace, but shall certainly persevere therein to the end, and be eternally saved.

"This perseverance of the saints depends *not upon their own free will*, but upon the *immutability of the decree of election;* upon the free and unchangeable love of God, the Father; upon the efficacy of the merit and intercession of Jesus Christ, and union with him; the oath of God, the abiding of his Spirit, and the seed of God within them, and the nature of the covenant of grace; from all which ariseth the certainty and infallibility thereof."

This creed, with the form of discipline adopted at Cambridge, was presented to the general court the same month, and printed by that body for the benefit of the churches in Massachusetts and Plymouth colonies. The churches of Connecticut had been subject to the Cambridge platform, also, which they helped to adopt; but, following in the steps of Massachusetts, they sighed for a change, which was effected by the synod that met at Saybrook, in May, 1708, and formed the "Saybrook platform." This body agreed to the Boston Confession, and recommended it to the General Assembly for their adoption. Thus, Massachusetts and Connecticut were united on the foregoing basis, and thus they remain to this day, having never repealed or altered, to our knowledge, a single particular of their published faith. Individuals, however, have seen the difficulties of the system, and attempted various modifications not known to the original framers; but, tenaciously holding to its essential features, have been like one beating the air. No modification of a falsehood can convert it into a truth; nor is it possible for any explanation, however sagaciously contrived, to justify what is radically and inherently wrong. Dr. Edwards' ingenious discovery of governing men by motives, relieves the system only in appearance. It attributes the damning power to irresistible motives, and thus only removes the immediate cause one step further from the primary and efficient cause, which Calvinists recognize to be God himself. Yet his learned and logical reasoning, on a false premise, had the effect to quiet many who were unable to detect its fallacy, and keep them along in the profession of doctrines they could not prove, and did not believe.

The same may be said of the system of Dr. Samuel Hopkins, of Newport, R. I. It came, indeed, in fearful conflict with the Boston Confession in several particulars;

but it maintained the offensive points of that Confession on other grounds. Of what avail is it to the sinner that the atonement of Christ is universal, if there are no promises of grace to the unregenerate, or if none have moral power to repent, and God will give that power to none but the elect? Yet his theory was highly serviceable to the cause of truth in one respect. Coming from a strong Calvinist, and declaring in several particulars what the Confession positively denied, it suggested the thought that *neither* might be true, and aroused investigation, where all before was settled. Many embraced the new system, and many denounced it as an innovation not to be tolerated. The pulpit and the press were taxed to their utmost capacity on both sides. The old party avowed that God is not the author of sin; the new, that he is. The Confessionists claim that the atonement was limited to the elect; the others, that it was made for all. While the clergy were trying their strength on these and kindred topics, the people took the liberty to think for themselves, and had the courage to renounce the Calvinian system, under all its modifications; some to adopt a system more agreeable to the Scriptures and universal conviction; and others to plunge into the errors of Socinians and Universalists.

Another improvement was subsequently attempted by Dr. Taylor of New Haven, who prepared a sort of *hash* of the different theories before mentioned, and seasoned it with various borrowed errors, adapted to suit the popular taste. The denial of natural depravity, as commonly held, and the assumption of *natural ability* in man to serve God, and even convert himself, figured largely in his system. Still he held fast to many of his old opinions, which seemed, after all, to be paramount. And thus it has ever been, as before hinted. The object has seemed to be, not to reform their creed, but to conceal its offensive features, or contrive some apology for them. Calvinism is still the peculiar element of all the modifications named. They are only new editions of the same thing, under different titles and in different styles of binding. Like opium, in certain medical practice, it is an essential ingredient in most compounds, however labelled. The lamented Dr. Fisk classifies Calvinists as follows: —

"The present advocates of predestination and particular election may be divided into four classes. 1. The Old School Calvinists. 2. Hopkinsians. 3. Reformed Hopkinsians. 4. Advocates of New Divinity. By Reformed Hopkinsians, I mean those who have left out of their creed Dr. Hopkins' doctrine of disinterested benevolence, divine efficiency in producing sin, &c., yet hold to a general atonement, natural ability, &c. These, doubtless, constitute the largest division of the class in New England. Next, as to numbers, the New School; then Hopkinsians; and last, the Old School."

The Calvinistic Baptists throughout the country, with some minor sects of Baptists, rank with moderate Calvinists, though many take stronger ground. The Presbyterians of the south and west, of the different schools, are much more rigid. They assert election and reprobation, with other associate sentiments, in the strongest manner, in their confession of faith, and, at times, in their public discourses. But, in common with all other sects of Calvinists, they have found it necessary to exhibit their peculiarities with great caution. The people do not generally believe them; and had they continued to speak out as they spake formerly, on the subjects of election, reprobation, the damnation of infants, and some other points, it is probable that they would have existed now only in history.

This whole family of errors we uniformly and most heartily

reject, as a dangerous and miserable combination, suggested by Augustine, but systematized and embodied into a form of theology by John Calvin, in the sixteenth century. And we rejoice that, though some still cleave to these views theoretically, they have so far varied their policy, as to pass them in silence, or conceal them under Arminian phraseology. It is to this circumstance that Calvinistic denominations owe their success. The very sentiments they disown in theory, are their life. If they must retain their heretical fancies, we admire their wisdom in letting them sleep in the Boston Confession, and other formularies, or in clothing them in the Scriptural drapery of Arminianism. We think it better, however, to renounce them *toto cœlo*, — to erase them from all the old formularies, creeds, and covenants, and come back to the simplicity of Christ.

CHAPTER III.

PREDESTINATION.

OUR objections to the Calvinistic view of predestination are numerous, a few of which we will enumerate.

1. It renders all preaching vain. The elect do not need it, their salvation being secured on other grounds. It is useless to the reprobate, for he cannot possibly be saved. So that, in reference to both, our preaching is vain, and their hearing is also vain.

2. It directly tends to destroy all religion. We do not say none who hold it are religious. Many of them are better than their creeds would indicate. But, assuming that every man is elected or reprobated, from eternity, and cannot alter his destiny, it wholly takes away those first motives to follow after it so frequently proposed in the Scriptures, — the hope of future reward and fear of punishment, the hope of heaven and the fear of hell. That these "shall go away into everlasting punishment," and these "into life eternal," is no motive to him to struggle for life, who believes his lot is cast already. His destiny is fixed, and he cannot alter it; why, therefore, should he try? "But he don't know what it is!" True; but that alters not the case; he believes it is unalterably determined, and "what is the use?"

3. It naturally *begets a feeling of asperity towards those*

who need the largest sympathy. All sincere worshippers philosophically become assimilated to the character of the being they worship. To contemplate a God who, out of his own will, and merely because it was his own good pleasure to do so, has created myriads of human beings for the express purpose of tormenting them eternally, and who will give no other explanation of his conduct, but silences all inquiry by exclaiming, "Who art thou that repliest against God? shall the thing formed say to him that formed it, why hast thou made me thus?" can but produce the most unlovely tempers toward those we regard to be the objects of his wrath. The historian who seeks to account for the fate of Servetus, and the severity often experienced by the Arminians, and other reputed or real heretics, at the hand of ultra-Calvinists, need look no farther. One who regards himself as the favorite of such a Being, may infer, without logical extravagance, that he is doing him commendable service in torturing those he supposes Him to have hated from everlasting. Many Calvinists have never suffered themselves to fall into this delusion; but this does not invalidate our objection. The tendency of the doctrine is, nevertheless, just what we have asserted, but has been counteracted by other and better principles.

4. It is also calculated to *engender enmity toward the Creator.* "The carnal mind," we know, "is enmity against God," independent of any such consideration; but it sees, and often feels, the injustice of it under correct views of his benignity toward his creatures. In the belief of this sentiment, one who considers himself a reprobate, not only feels the enmity naturally arising from his unlikeness to God, but all the *revenge* incident to unmerited and unmitigated injury and injustice, and feels that it is *deserved.* Nor does it admit of the best of feelings in the *elect.* Im-

partial justice disallows of our esteeming a benefactor whom we know to be unkind and cruel to others. It would seem, therefore, that none but the most conceited and selfish of beings could *enjoy election*, associated, as it necessarily is, with the idea that a vast majority of mankind were made vessels of wrath, and doomed to perdition by mere sovereign caprice.

5. This doctrine directly tends to destroy our *zeal for good works*. *First*, as it naturally destroys our love for those whom God hates without reason; and, *secondly*, as it extinguishes all hope of saving them. Is it said, "we do not know who the reprobates are," we reply, but if you believe that every one's doom is fixed, why trouble yourself about them?

6. It also tends to *destroy the Christian revelation*. The enemies of religion claim that revelation is not necessary; and are they not right on this hypothesis? God's decree is sufficient to save the elect without it, and to damn the reprobate in spite of it.

It tends to *overthrow revelation*, also, by making it contradict itself. For it makes parts of it plainly to contradict other parts, and even its whole scope and design. God says in his word, as if to vindicate himself against this aspersion, "I have no pleasure in the death of him that dieth," that "He is not willing that *any* should perish," but that "*all* should come to repentance." This Calvinists deny, and avow that of his own good pleasure he created some men for everlasting death. Thus they make the decree of predestination the cause of the sinner's ruin, whereas the Bible attributes it to himself, in rejecting the counsel of God, and refusing to come to Christ. "*Because* I have called, and ye *refused*, [saith the Lord;] I have stretched out my hand,

and no man *regarded;* I also will laugh at your calamity, I will mock when your fear cometh?"

7. It *contradicts the counsels of God* in reference to the atonement. The Scriptures teach us that "God sent his Son into the world, that the *world* through him might believe;" that Jesus "gave himself a ransom for all;" that "God so *loved the world* that he gave his only begotten Son, that whosoever believeth on him might not perish, but have everlasting life." But this doctrine teaches us that it is not so; God *never* loved the world, that he gave his Son to die *only* for the elect, and that he did not come to save any other.

8. It *discards the judgment,* or, what is still worse, represents it as a *solemn farce.* The doctrine of the Bible is, that God will "judge the world in *righteousness,*" that then "every one shall receive according to the deeds *done in the body.*" We are premonished that the Judge will say to the wicked, "Depart, ye cursed; for I was an hungered, and ye gave me no meat; I was thirsty, and ye gave me no drink; a stranger, and ye took me not in; I was naked, and ye clothed me not; sick, and in prison, and ye visited me not." Thus attributing the rejection of the poor wretches to their *own fault;* whereas, according to Calvinism, it is attributable solely to a decree of reprobation, lying back of their existence, even, determining not only their destiny, but the very circumstances to which it is to be falsely charged. Now, if this be so, why will they be *speechless?* For no other reason, certainly, than that they are deceived, in being made to *feel* themselves *guilty* for answering the exact ends of their creation, and fulfilling the decree of their Maker.

The deception, it would seem, is to be carried out on

the other side, also. For the elect are to be rewarded, whereas they will be no more entitled to reward than the wicked are deserving of punishment. This doctrine, therefore, represents the Bible as a *complicated lie*, and the divine government as a system of fraud and legerdemain For there can be no *reward* or *punishment*, as there can be no virtue or vice, properly speaking, where there is no moral freedom. And there can be no moral freedom where every thing is bound by an almighty decree.

9. It impeaches the *goodness* of God. Revelation teaches us that he is love — that his love reaches even to the "evil and the unthankful," — "to *every man*,— and his mercy is over *all his works*."

But how can it be said that he is good to reprobates, the victims of his eternal hatred, whom he "passes by," and leaves in blindness and corruption, that they may be damned? Does he give them food? It is but to fatten them for the slaughter. Are they endowed with personal excellencies? It is to heap coals of fire upon their heads. Is it said, he gives them grace, too? We ask, what grace? Not *saving* grace. That is only for the elect. Not grace to convert them, but merely to convince; not to deprive them of *sin*, but of *excuse;* not to make them feel happy, but *guilty*, not to remove an evil conscience, but to increase its power of tormenting. Is it not *damning grace?* What else can it be? It never has saved a soul, and we are told it never will save one. And yet, it is made the basis of guilt and punishment.

10. But this is not its worst feature; it is *full of blasphemy*. We say it with profound regret; but the truth demands it. It represents "Jesus Christ, the righteous," as a hypocrite, a deceiver of the people. For it cannot be denied, that he every where spoke as if he were willing that

all men should be saved. But this doctrine represents him as not *willing* that they should be saved — as mocking the helpless victims of eternal wrath, by offering them what he never intended to bestow. It represents him as saying one thing and meaning another, as pretending to love which he had not, and weeping "crocodile's tears" over Jerusalem. under pretence of grief at their impenitence, when he had determined that they should be just so impenitent, and be damned, before they were born, and raised them up for that very purpose.

And as it honors the Son, so it honors the Father. It destroys all his attributes at once; it overturns his justice, mercy, and truth, at a stroke. Yea, it represents the most holy God as worse than the devil, as more false, more cruel, and unjust. More *false*, because the devil, liar as he is, hath never said "he willeth all men to be saved;" more cruel and *unjust*, because the devil cannot, if he would, be guilty of creating millions of souls for everlasting fire, or dooming them to its flames for not exercising powers they never possessed, and that he will not bestow.

But it may be said there are certain passages of Scripture that indicate this doctrine, and cannot be explained without admitting it. This we deny. But if it were so, it would be better to say that they have no meaning, than that they mean this. They cannot mean that the God of truth is a *liar*, or that he is unjust, or that he is not love, or that his mercy is not over all his works. To say of different passages, we do not know what they mean, is safe; but to construe them so as to contradict many other passages which are plain and easy to be understood, and thus array the Bible against itself, and implicate its divine author in purposes he unequivocally disclaims, is impious.

We object to this doctrine, finally, that God has decreed a

very different thing, even this: "I will set before the sons of men life and death, blessing and cursing. He that believeth shall be saved, but he that believeth not shall be damned." This decree stands fast as the moon, and as the faithful witnesses in heaven. And it affords high encouragement to effort. It is worthy of God. It is consistent with every attribute of his nature; it corresponds with the whole scope of revelation, as well as with all its parts, with the dictates of conscience and the Spirit of God. Thus Moses, in the name of God, cried: "I call heaven and earth to record against you this day, that I have set before you life and death, blessing and cursing; therefore choose life, that thou and thy seed may live." And Jesus said, "If *any man* thirst, let him come unto me and drink." And St. Paul, "God commandeth *all men* every where to repent." St. James wrote, "If any of you lack wisdom, let him ask of God, who giveth to all men liberally, and upbraideth not; and it shall be given him." St. Peter avers, "The Lord is not willing that any should perish, but that all should come to repentance." Is not this enough? What could he have said or done more? He denies the charge Calvinism prefers. "As I live, saith the Lord God, I have no pleasure in the death of the wicked. Turn ye, turn ye from your evil ways, for why will ye die, O, house of Israel?" "Turn yourselves and live." "Repent and turn from all your transgressions; so iniquity shall not be your ruin." — See *Wesley on Predestination.*

But some will ask, "Did not God foreknow who would reject the gospel, and be lost?" We presume he did. "But how could he know it, if he had not decreed they should do so?" We answer, just as he is wise without study or learning, — good, without *reform. We* depend, for our knowledge of what shall occur in the future, upon our *pur-*

poses, and the *calculation of the chances;* but knowledge with God is an attribute, no more dependent upon his decree than is his holiness. His foreknowledge, therefore, can have no more influence in causing the sinner's impenitence and ruin than our after knowledge. Those who suppose *fore*knowledge and decree imply the same thing, greatly err. *Knowledge* with God is an *attribute* by which he sees future events; his *decree* is an *act*, by which he determines certain events shall occur. To assume that his knowledge is derived from his decree, implies that there was a period when he was ignorant; for a decree being an act, cannot have existed from all eternity; but must have been put forth at some definite time, previous to which, on this assumption, God must have been ignorant of the thing he decreed.

To foresee an event does not cause it to take place. I foresee, for example, that a certain ship will run upon the breakers and be lost, because I observe her position and understand the deception that pervades her commander's mind; but my knowing it, has no influence upon the winds and tides, nor does it cause the deception of the commander, or the wreck to which it leads. As God foreknows the sinner's conduct, and destiny, so he foreknew it was unnecessary. He knew that the same being who rejected the offers of mercy and perished, might have made himself a different destiny. He had the same beneficent God, the same Jesus, the same atonement, the same Holy Spirit, the same divine call; but he rejected them and ran the terrible risk of losing his soul. This doctrine finds no apology in foreknowledge. Seeing what course men would choose, and what end they would make, one thousand or ten thousand years before they were born, no more caused them to take that course than seeing the same things ten thousand years afterward.

To evade these objections some claim to hold *election only*. They say God saw that all had fallen and become polluted, and determined that he "would have a seed to serve him," and, therefore, elected some, only *passing by others*. But this does not help the case. For God to pass by one of the fallen sons of Adam, and withhold from him his enlightening, softening, and subduing Spirit and grace, is tantamount to the most positive decree of damnation. Let a mother pass by her nursing child for a week, and she will destroy it as effectually as if she were to cast it into the deep. To give men existence, with their natural tendencies, and then pass them by, withholding the grace necessary to their salvation, amounts to the same as dooming them by an irreversible decree.

To escape this consequence, certain divines have invented what they are pleased to call "*natural ability*." Under the old system, man has *no ability* whatever to repent and obey God, until he is converted. He cannot repent, even with "common grace." But the new system teaches us that he can do so of his own natural strength, without grace, and deserves to perish if he neglects it. It is assumed that he can convert himself, wake himself up, and love God with a pure heart fervently. Thus error plunges from one extreme to another in quick succession. But these same divines concede that no one ever did thus repent, and they have no hope that one ever will do it. So that, after all, natural ability amounts to just *nothing* to the purpose, and is, therefore, no ground of justification to the God of all grace in passing men by. Still, it is often repeated, "men might repent *if they would*," — "all may come if they will," &c. But this does not relieve the case, so long as the sinner cannot *will* to come without special grace, which the elect only receive.

It is also reiterated, in justification of the doctrine, "God might justly have passed by all men." But where is that written? We do not find it in the sacred records; nor is it true. We admit, with Mr. Fletcher, "that after Adam fell, and his posterity in him, God might justly have passed them all by, without sending his Son to be a Saviour for *any one*." "God might justly have sent them, and us *in their loins*, into the pit of destruction." But "the great flaw consists in confounding our *seminal state* with our *personal state;* and in concluding that what would have been *just* when we were in our *seminal state*, in the loins of Adam, must also be just in our *personal state*, now we are out of his loins." "Is it not contrary to all equity to punish a sin *seminally* and *unknowingly* committed, with an eternal punishment, *personally* and *knowingly endured?* For illustration: I have committed a horrible murder; I am condemned to be burned alive for it; my sentence is just; having personally and consciously sinned without necessity, I deserve to be personally and consciously tormented. The judge may, then, without cruelty, condemn every part of me to the flames; and the unbegotten posterity in my loins may justly burn with me and in me; for with me and in me it has sinned as a part of myself. Nor is it a great misfortune for my posterity to be thus punished; because it has as little knowledge and feeling of my punishment as of my crime. But suppose the judge, after reprieving me, divided and multiplied me into ten thousand parts; suppose, again, that each of these parts necessarily grew up into a man or woman, would it be reasonable in him to say to seven or eight hundred of those men and women, 'You are all *seminally* guilty of the murder committed by the man whom I reprieved, and from whose loins I have extracted you, and therefore my mercy *passes you by*, and my justice absolutely reprobates your *persons*, [and leaves you without grace, so that you will personally and unavoidably commit murder, as did the being from whom you sprung, for which I shall punish you as he deserved?'] Who does not see the injustice and cruelty of such treatment? But if the persons, whom I suppose extracted from me, are reprieved as well as myself, — if we are all put together in remediable circumstances, where sin indeed abounds, but where grace abounds much more, — who does not see that upon the personal commission of avoidable, voluntary murder, [and much more upon the personal refusal of a pardon sincerely offered upon reasonable conditions,] my posterity may be condemned to the flames as justly as myself?" Upon these grounds, we admit, God might have given us up long ago, because we have had and abused the grace that reprobates are said never to receive.

But this supposition of what God might justly have done, implies that his justice may be separated from his other attributes, particularly his mercy. This, however, never was done; nor can it be. His attributes are inseparably joined; they cannot be divided without destroying the Godhead. To say, therefore, that he might have passed by all men, is to say that he might not have been God. It belongs to the same class of unmeaning assertions with that just now considered in regard to sinners, viz., they might repent if they would, that is, if they were not sinners, or were altogether different characters from what they really are.

CHAPTER IV.

FREE GRACE AND FREE WILL.

THE term *grace* is employed in the Scriptures to mark different objects. We use it here to designate all those dispositions, acts, and influences, of the Creator, which were necessary to endow, and place our first parents after their fall, and all their progeny, in a condition so far to believe and obey God as to obtain everlasting life. This, of course, embraces a power to *will*, no less than to perceive and do. We speak of this grace as *free*, to indicate that it is not purchased by man, but bestowed by the mere goodness of God; *and that, upon all the sons and daughters of Adam*, in opposition to Pelagianism on the one hand, and Calvinism on the other. That it is free, in the first sense, is obvious from the fact that the constitution under which the human family was organized, made no provision for pardon in case of transgression, nor for any thing else but death. "In the day thou eatest thereof thou shalt surely die." As a transgressor, therefore, man had no just claim upon his Maker for aught but death. Nor was it in his power to *create* any other claim. Hence, all man receives better than this is by mere grace or favor.

That it is free in the other sense — free for the whole race — is clearly proved from our remarks on predestination in the last chapter. We shall, therefore, treat the subject here with great brevity, referring only to a few particulars not before mentioned.

We argue that this grace is equally free for all, from the divine character. God is *good.* But this is not a sufficient reason why he should not punish the *guilty*, because he is *just* as well as good. But is it not an *infinite* reason why he should not punish the *innocent?* Why he should *not* make sentient beings, and place them in circumstances necessitating them to sin, and then punish them with everlasting destruction *for their* sins? Why, if in his wisdom he determined to suspend the penalty of the violated law, and suffer the first pair to propagate their species, he should furnish them the needful help to work out their salvation?

It is agreed by predestinarians that his goodness did provide for a part of mankind, and that grace is so richly bestowed on them, they cannot avoid being saved — they will be "made *willing*," and "brought in." Can any mortal give a good reason why that same goodness did not provide for the others, also? Were they any worse than the chosen ones? There was no difference. Why, then, should God love and endow them so richly, and do nothing effectively for others? Is it said that it was to display his *justice?* That was to be displayed in the atonement; and besides, it is not a display of justice, but of the most horrid *injustice* the human mind ever conceived. Hence, to believe in such limitation of divine grace, we must believe that God's goodness is *not* "over all his works," that he is a capricious "*respecter of persons*," or was incapable of doing for all what was necessary to place them in a salvable condition.

The freeness of this grace is equally obvious from the *Scriptures* in regard to it. The first promise of redemption, "the seed of the woman shall bruise the serpent's head," conveys no intimation of restriction. Nor, indeed, does any other announcement of revelation. Christ was given to the "*world*" — "appeared to put away *sin* by the sacrifice of himself" — "died, the just for *the unjust*" — "is the propitiation for the sins of the *whole world*" — invites all to come to him, sends forth his ministers to "preach the gospel to *every creature*" — justifies the "*ungodly*" — and is the "Saviour of *all men*, especially of those who believe." Is it possible that only a small part of mankind are embraced in these provisions? The gospel, then, is a *lie*, and its ministers teachers of falsehood, and the Spirit a *deceiver and tormenter of reprobates* by false encouragements and alarms "before the time." But this is not the case. Let God be true, whatever becomes of human theories. "God is love." He loved all mankind, and provided for their salvation. All *may* come, whether they will or not. The way is open; the Spirit is gone forth; the light that has come into the world "lighteth *every man;*" and there is nothing in God, nothing in his election or reprobation, nothing in the sinner's infirmities of intellect, heart, or will, to make it impossible for him to come to Christ and be saved. No, *nothing* For, "the grace of God that bringeth salvation, hath appeared unto *all men*, teaching us that, denying ungodliness and worldly lusts, we should live soberly, righteously, and godly, in this present world."

One of the first and unconditional results of this grace was the endowment of man with *free will*, that is, to refuse the wrong and choose the right. That Adam possessed this in his primeval state, is evident from the provisions of the government under which he was placed. Without it he would not have been a proper subject of moral government. But the effect of his disobedience divested him of it, and left him free to evil only, that is, a *slave* to the devil

Hence, we say with the Church of England, in our eighth article: "The condition of man after the fall of Adam is such that he cannot turn and prepare himself, by his own natural strength and works, to faith, and calling upon God; wherefore, we have no power to do good works, pleasant and acceptable to God, without the grace of God by Christ preventing us, that we may have a good will, and working with us when we have that good will." It is when we speak of him as destitute of this grace that we say he is *totally depraved*, "very far gone from original righteousness, and of his [fallen] nature inclined to evil, and that continually." But by the light that "lighteth *every man*," and the "*grace of God* which hath *appeared* unto *all men*," he is redeemed from this low estate, and invested with such a measure of *moral power* as to be able to resist his evil propensities, "forsake his way, and return unto the Lord who will have mercy on him." This is *freedom* in the only proper sense. It is that attribute in man, which constitutes him a fit subject of rewards and punishments. It is that, too, which invests the commands, expostulations, promises, and other appliances of the gospel, with interest and solemnity. That which lies at the foundation of all our hopes and fears — the grand stimulants of effort; and without which the human family would be completely *unmanned*.

Thus, "*Free Grace and Free Will*" constitute the two grand pillars of Wesleyan theology. The first enables us to draw near to God "in the full assurance of *hope*," believing that with him "all things are ready, that there is nothing wanting on his part to save *every man;*" the last encourages us to "preach the word; be instant in season, out of season, reprove, rebuke, exhort, with all long-suffering and doctrine," believing that man, by the grace of God, is able to choose "that *good part*" which shall never be taken from him. The one guards us against the Pharisaic notion of salvation *by works*, the other against the Calvinian heresy of salvation *without works*. Together they explain and justify " the ways of God with man," and convict the condemned sinner of destroying himself.

Those who assert that these principles detract from the *glory* of God, must have strange views of the nature of that glory. God's intrinsic glory is infinite and unchangeable. His declarative glory, or the honor he receives among men, is most promoted when his character and government are most correctly represented. Whether *partial* grace and reprobating *hatred*, are more honorable to him than *free grace and free will*, every one must judge for himself. We think there is greater honor in making a *free* agent, and endowing him with self-determining power, than in making a mere *machine*, which acts only as impelled by a foreign force. And can any one doubt that, since God made men capable of the highest pleasure, there is more glory in giving them all an opportunity to enjoy it, than in dooming a part to sin and everlasting pain? According to our theory, God is *good*, and gives every man his Spirit, and an opportunity to work out his salvation; is grieved when he will not do so; and casts him off as the last resort. According to the *partial grace and bound will* notion, he cast off many before they were born; indeed, *made* them for this very purpose. However such conduct may glorify God, any thing analagous to it in an earthly monarch would expose him to universal execration.

The doctrines of *free grace and free will* are equally consistent with the *sovereignty* of God. Our Calvinistic friends talk about sovereignty as though it were the same as *fatality*, and entirely independent of the divine attributes; whereas it results from these attributes, and is strictly governed in its operations by them. Because God is a great king, it does not follow that he has not made all men free agents, and made it possible for them to be saved. It was his sovereignty that enabled him to do this very thing. He had an undoubted right to make men free agents, and endow them with grace to serve him, and with power to disobey him, and expose themselves to everlasting banishment. And, so far as we can see, this was perfectly consistent with his goodness. To suppose that he would take any measure in regard to the eternal states of men, merely because he is *almighty*, irrespective of his moral attributes, is as absurd as to suppose that he will save all free agents, irrespective of their conduct, merely because he is *merciful.*

Mr. Wesley remarks, "Whenever God, as a governor, acts as a rewarder or punisher, he no longer acts as a mere sovereign, by his own sole will and pleasure; but as an impartial judge, guided in all things by invariable justice. Yet it is true that in some cases mercy rejoices over justice; although *severity* never does. God may *reward* more, but he will never *punish* more, than strict justice requires. It will be allowed that God acts as a sovereign in convincing some souls of sin; arresting them in their mad career by his resistless power. There may likewise be many irresistible touches during the course of our Christian warfare. But still, as St. Paul might have been obedient or 'disobedient to the heavenly vision,' so every individual may, after all that God has done, either improve his grace, or make it of no effect.

"Whatever, therefore, it hath pleased God to do, of his sovereign pleasure, as Creator of heaven and earth, and whatever his mercy may do on particular occasions, the general rule stands firm as the pillars of heaven. 'The Judge of all the earth will *do right.*' He will punish no man for doing any thing which he could not possibly avoid; neither for omitting any thing which he could not possibly do. Every punishment supposes the offender might have avoided the offence for which he is punished; otherwise, to punish him would be palpably unjust and inconsistent with the character of God our governor."

These are eternal truths, which commend themselves to every man's judgment and conscience, and form the basis of all equitable government. So far from their impeaching the divine sovereignty, they defend and hold it in harmony with all the other attributes which belong to the Deity. They honor the author of all good, exalt man to his proper rank in the scale of being, reconcile the Scriptures with themselves, and at the same time avoid the errors of Calvinists and Universalists on the one hand, and of Pelagians on the other.

Says Mr. Fletcher, in his able discussion with the Antinomians, "Impartially read any one book in the Bible, and you will find that it establishes the truth of the two following propositions: —

"'1. God hath *freely* done great things for man; and the still greater things which he *freely* does for believers, and the mercy with which he daily crowns them, justly entitle him to all the honor of their salvation; so far as that honor is worthy of the Primitive Parent of good, and first cause of all our blessings.

"'2. He wisely looks for some returns *from* man; and the little things which obstinate unbelievers refuse to do, and which God's preventing grace gives them ability to perform, justly entitle them to all the shame of their damnation. Therefore, although their *temporal* misery is *originally* from Adam; yet their *eternal* ruin is *originally* from *themselves*.'

"The first of these propositions extols God's *mercy*, and

the second clears his *justice;* while both together display his *truth* and *holiness*. According to the doctrine of *free grace*, Christ is a *compassionate Saviour;* according to that of *free will*, he is a righteous Judge. By the *first*, his rewards are *gracious;* by the *second*, his punishments are *just*. By the *first*, the mouths of the blessed in heaven are opened to sing *deserved* hallelujahs to God and the Lamb; and by the *second*, the mouths of the damned in hell are kept from uttering *deserved* blasphemies against God and his Christ. According to the *first*, God remains the genuine Parent of *good;* and according to the *second*, devils and apostate men are still the genuine authors of evil. If you explode the first of these propositions, you admit Pharisaic dotages, and self-exalting pride; if you reject the *second*, you set up Antinomian delusions, and voluntary humility. But if you receive them both, you consistently hold the Scriptural doctrines of faith and works, free grace and free will, divine mercy and divine justice, the sinner's impotence and a saint's faithfulness." — *Checks to Antinomianism, vol.* 3, *p.* 33.

Hence, those who accuse us of denying the grace of God, and holding to salvation by the *merit* of works, greatly err. We teach that man is "*totally depraved*" by the fall, and owes all he is now better than that to enlightening and preventing grace. If we assure men that they can repent, and turn to God, that God will accept and save them upon their doing so, it is because we believe them already possessed of a measure of *grace* sufficient for the undertaking. We have no idea that they have any "*natural ability*" to choose, or to do their duty in any proper sense; but we *do* believe that "where sin abounded, grace did much more abound," "that grace might reign through righteousness unto eternal life by Jesus Christ our Lord." Therefore, they can attend to the word, break off from their sins, and believe unto the saving of their souls. And this is what the apostle means by working out our "salvation with fear and trembling." But still, he is not chargeable with Pelagianism, so long as he holds that God worketh in us the power both to "will and to do of his own good pleasure."

The state of the case, then, is this: the *power* to act is of God's free grace, and it is sooner or later given to every man; the *exercise* of that power is of man. Bestowing this, God commands, "choose life that ye may live," "seek the Lord while he may be found;" but man so "rejects the counsel of God against himself" as to deserve to be cast off for ever. Can any thing be more reasonable? If the Scriptures teach any thing different from this, we have been deceived, and are entirely ignorant, both of their import and their object. This view of the subject explodes the idea of *universal election*, based upon the general doctrine of Predestination; the "horrible decree" of Calvinian reprobation, the Pharisaic notion of salvation by the merit of works, and the fancy that all will be finally pardoned and saved. And yet, like other simple Scriptural truths, many overlook it altogether, or attempt to patch it up with their own dogmas, to suit the popular taste. But it will stand fast till heaven and earth pass away.

CHAPTER V.

THE NEW BIRTH, WITH ITS MEANS AND MANIFESTATIONS.

IN tracing the work of grace upon the heart, no one can fail to observe that its operations vary under different circumstances. Where it is least perceptible, close investigation will detect its presence, and where most obvious, *free will* may be observed with equal distinctness. In general, however, its first impulses prove ineffectual in bringing sinners to repentance. Though often painful in its convictions, it only elicits a resolve to reform, accompanied, it may be, by an occasional prayer and transient improvement. So that, instead of resulting in conversion, it hardens, and creates the necessity for more powerful appeals. It is astonishing to see into what a state of moral insensibility the sinner plunges, and how entirely dependent he is on the Spirit of God for that sensitiveness which is necessary to repentance.

According to the Scriptures, people in this condition are "dead in trespasses and sins," in the "bondage of corruption," "under the law of sin and death." They perceive neither the divine claims nor their own deficiencies. They often fancy themselves "rich, and increased with goods, and in need of nothing; and know not that they are wretched, and miserable, and poor, and blind, and naked." Not unfrequently do they congratulate themselves on their morality and even piety, and thank God they are not "like other men;" and dream of obtaining heaven by the merit of works. Or, sinking into vice, too palpable and flagrant to admit of so gross a deception, they talk of the mercy of God as sufficient security for eternal life, and vainly hope to be saved, till aroused to see themselves in their true character.

The means by which people are awakened are various. In a thousand cases, no two, perhaps, would be found exactly alike; and yet in all important points they might not be distinguished. In one, a word of pious conversation was effectual; in another, a powerful sermon, or prayer, or the reading of a good book, or some alarming providence. But whatever the occasion, the mind is drawn toward God, to contemplate religious things, and to use more or less means to obtain the pardon of sin, and the renewing of the Holy Spirit.

"By some awful providence," says Mr. Wesley, "or by his word applied with the demonstration of the Spirit, God touches the heart of him that lay asleep in darkness, and in the shadow of death. He is terribly shaken out of his sleep, and awakes into a consciousness of his danger. Perhaps in a moment, perhaps by degrees, the eyes of his understanding are opened, and now first (the veil being in part removed) discern the real state he is in. Horrid light breaks in upon his soul; such light as may be conceived to glow from the bottomless pit. He at last sees the loving, the merciful God, is also a 'consuming fire;' that he is a just God and a terrible, rendering to every man according to his works, entering into judgment with the ungodly for every idle word, yea, and for the imaginations of the heart. * * *

"The inward, spiritual meaning of the law now begins to glare upon him. He perceives 'the commandment is exceeding broad,' and there is 'nothing hid from the light thereof.' He is convinced that every part of it relates, not barely to outward sin or obedience, but to what passes in the secret recesses of the soul, which no eye but God's can penetrate. If he now hears, 'Thou shalt not kill,' God speaks in thunder, 'He that hateth his brother is a murderer.' And thus in every point he feels the word of God 'quick and powerful, sharper than a two edged sword.' It 'pierces even to the dividing asunder of soul and spirit, the joints and marrow.' And so much the more, because he is conscious to himself of having neglected so great salvation; of having 'trodden under foot the Son of God,' who would have saved him from his sins.

"He now sees himself naked, stripped of all the fig leaves which he had sewed together, of all his poor pretences to religion or virtue, and his wretched excuses for sinning against God. His heart is bare, and he sees it is all sin, deceitful above all things, desperately wicked. He feels that he deserves to be cast into hell. Here ends his pleasing dream, his delusive rest, his false peace, his vain security. His joy now vanishes as a cloud; pleasures once loved delight no more. With St. Paul he can say: 'I was alive without the law once;' I had much life, wisdom, strength, and virtue, so I thought; 'but when the commandment came, sin revived, and I died;' the commandment which was ordained to life, I found to be unto death. 'For sin, taking occasion by the commandment, deceived me, and by it slew me;' it came upon me unawares, slew all my hopes, and plainly showed that in the midst of life I was in death. Wherefore the law is holy, and the commandment holy, and just, and good; I no longer lay the blame on this, but on the corruption of my own heart. I acknowledge that 'the law is spiritual; but I am carnal, sold under sin.'"

This is, no doubt, a true picture of the condition of

awakened sinners in general; yet many never see themselves precisely in this light, ncr feel the misery here indicated. They know they are sinners, and are concerned about their souls, but have not that deep sense of sin they desire. They are unhappy to think that they feel no more, and strive to obtain more pungent convictions. But they cannot excite the emotion they covet, and often, therefore, tremble, lest they shall never obtain the blessing they seek; though they are willing to bear every cross, and perform every known duty.

Persons who have reached this point are in an interesting state. David was here when in the horrible pit and miry clay. Saul of Tarsus was here, too, when smitten to the ground by the power of God, and heard those convincing words, "Saul, Saul, why persecutest thou me." O, how subdued! How willing to have salvation on any terms! He objects to nothing; he is ready to sit at the feet of Annanias, the poor disciple he was commissioned to arrest. Yes, to be led along the way, to be accounted a fool, to have his honored name aspersed. What an achievement! So it was with the Philippian jailor. Terrified by the interposition of Almighty God in defence of his servants, trembling, he fell down before them and said, "SIRS, what must I do to be saved?" indicating his readiness to do any thing, to follow their instructions, however crossing and difficult; willing to obey God, at the loss of all things.

Now, however convictions may differ, they must possess this element to be successful. All must be brought, not to the same degree of *emotion*, but to entire *submission* to the will of God — to the terms of salvation, and the consequences that may follow. But not willing to be damned, as Hopkinsians assume. This is absurd and impracticable. No mortal ever came to this, unless it was some one who had outlived the day of grace, and preferred the companionship of devils and damned spirits to that of God and his holy angels. There must be no reservation, no partial acquiescence, no unfaithfulness, no compromise. The sinner must come fully up to God's terms, though, in doing so, he has to forsake father, and mother, and houses, and lands, and honor, and wealth, and even life itself. He must lay all at the feet of Christ, and confess that his only dependence is on him; that he has nothing to offer but sin, and nothing to expect in justice but wrath. He must give up trying to make himself any better, trying to atone for the past, either by good works, or tears, or bad feelings, or long prayers and sighing. The sin he has committed cannot be mitigated; the blessing he needs cannot be purchased. It must be sought as a mere *favor*, that can be bestowed only by *infinite condescension*. Here he must stand, not discouraged by darkness or doubts; by littleness of faith or feeling; but holding fast, reading, hearing, praying, bearing the cross, confessing his need of Christ, and his desire for religion. This is *conviction*.

This brings us to the consideration of another element in religious experience, not very distinctly understood, viz.: *Faith*. This term is used to indicate different states of mind, varying from an unsettled historical *belief* of the truth of divine revelation, to implicit *trust* in God, that he does now, for the sake of Christ, pardon all my sins, accept, and save me, and love me; that I am now a child of God, and an heir of heaven.

According to this definition, our faith begins when we begin to believe the Bible and regard its instructions. Some very daring sinners believe it without a doubt, others believe it with less confidence, while some, who have been unfortunately educated, or have abused a good education, only believe it with slight confidence. Some degree of faith is necessary to the first honest religious effort. With no more faith in the Bible than we have in the Koran, not one of us would feel the least obligation to obey its precepts, or experience the first twinge of guilt for neglecting them. Of course, we should treat them as we now do the various precepts of Mahometanism. How little faith will suffice for the first movement is a difficult question. In worldly matters we often act at considerable sacrifice, where the evil we aim to avoid is only *possible*. For example, we get our property insured, when we know it is only possible that it will be burned. The evil is so great, we think it better to be secure against the possibility of its occurrence, even at great inconvenience. Where the evidence that a great calamity will befall us amounts to *probability*, we act with still more energy, and make greater sacrifices. For instance, in guarding against epidemics, what expensive precautions do men use, though there is not one chance in many that the malaria will effect them in the least! Where an evil is certain to occur, without specific measures to prevent it, we do not hesitate, nor do we think pleasantly of those who have the temerity to delay one moment.

Why may we not act on similar faith in the word of God? The least degree of which any one can boast, does not exclude the *possibility* of a judgment to come, of heaven and hell. Most wicked men believe the cardinal truths of revelation; not without hope, indeed, that they may prove false, but with the same confidence that they believe in the existence of a God. Others believe without a doubt. They believe that salvation is possible; that if they will repent and come to Christ, the Lord will have mercy on them. They have no doubt of it. And this ought to stimulate every one to address himself to the work with all his strength, and never rest till he has demonstrated what he believes, and experienced its full import in his own heart.

But there is a difficulty. When those whose faith com passes all these things in the cool deliberation of carnal security, while they see little of the malignity of sin, and feel little of its guilt, come to view themselves in their true character, and see the depth of their ingratitude and unworthiness, doubts often rush upon them like an armed man, and they tremble with fear that the day of grace is past. We scarce ever knew one to be deeply humbled, without faltering on this point. And sometimes under false counsel, they have gone down into deep despair, not daring to venture their souls on the mercy of God, and believe unto salvation.

But to go back to the penitent we have described, all subdued and anxious, we remark, nothing remains for him to do now, except to *believe*. But what is he to believe? This is an important question. Is it that, *perhaps*, he shall obtain mercy if he seeks aright? He believed this when he commenced. We think any doubt here savors more of unbelief than of faith, and dishonors God, whose promise is unequivocal. Yet the instructions given to penitents by many good, but mistaken, people of the Calvinistic school, are calculated to create doubt on this very point. "It *may be* God will have mercy," say they; "he is under no obligation;" whereas, he has pledged himself to save to the uttermost all who come to him, weary and heavy laden; and has given strong evidence of his readiness to do so, by calling up their attention to the subject, and stimulating them to seek him.

The penitent is to believe, therefore, not only that God is, but that he is the *rewarder* of *all* who diligently seek him. That there can be no failure on his part. And, having examined himself thoroughly, and taken counsel of God and his people, and being in the way of duty according to his best understanding, and determined to continue therein, he is to believe that God *now* approves of him, and will shine forth upon his heart in attestation of his acceptance. That is, he must trust in God to save him; to save him just as he is. He renounces his sins, and tries to act the part of the Christian, but finds no light. Darkness reigns. All hope of saving himself vanishes. His heart seems to grow harder and harder, and his case more and more alarming. What can he do? One thing only — *trust in God*, that he will save, save *now* — ***saves***. Here is a nice point. The sinner abandons all his old grounds of hope in despair, throws away his idols, and cleaves to the mere *mercy of God in Christ Jesus*, as his last and only resort, and rests all upon it, to "live or die, survive or perish." Laying himself down thus, in *despair* of relief from any other source, and resigning all upon the sufficiency of this to meet the exigency of his case, scarcely does his mind make the *surrender*, before he feels himself encompassed in the everlasting arms, and a warming throb of confiding, assuring joy, come sweetly over his soul, powerfully convincing him that he is born again. *Faith* is that act by which he withdraws all trust in every other object, and ventures on Christ.

Its several stages may be marked by a single illustration. The patient at first declines the aid of a physician; but growing worse and worse, and finding his own prescriptions ineffectual, consents that one be called; but will only follow his advice so far as he deems it expedient. He is not entirely wanting in faith, but has less in the physician than in himself. At length a prescription is made at which he demurs. He will not follow it. But finding that his situation is growing more critical every day, and his own skill is ineffective, and that something must be done or he shall soon pay the sad debt of nature, and that others in a similar situation have resorted to the remedies proposed, with the best results, he yields, and is restored. The act by which he throws himself entirely into the hands of his physician, *renouncing* his own wisdom, and *doing* in all things according to direction, is the final, the *restoring act of faith*, and it is much stronger than that which sent for the physician, or adopted his simpler remedies.

This is the faith to which the sinner must come. He may attend to his own prescriptions for a time, if he will, but they will make him none the better. He may then adopt some of those proposed by the Physician of souls, but they will prove no more effective than the others. It is only when he *entirely surrenders* himself to Christ, to *do and be as he wills*, that he reaches the culminating point, and finds the boon for which he sighs; and this is *faith.*

The gracious result of such a surrender of one's self is the CONVERSION of his soul to God. This implies two things. 1. That his sins are all forgiven; and, 2. That his heart is renewed by the "washing of regeneration." The first changes his relation to the law from that of a condemned sinner exposed to its penalty, to that of a pardoned sinner exempted *from* that penalty. The last changes his *heart*, conforming him to the *image of God*, and producing in him the fruits of the Spirit, such as "love, joy, peace, long-suffering, gentleness, meekness," &c. The first saves him from *condemnation*, and unfits him for hell; the last fills him with all *goodness*, and fits him for heaven. The one is "a work done *for* him, the other a work wrought *in* him." One justifies; the other "crucifies the flesh, with the affections and lusts," and thus makes him a new creature in Christ Jesus.

And this is usually accomplished in a moment. Pardon,

being an *act* of God by which he absolves the sinner from punishment, is *instantaneous*, by the necessity of its nature. Regeneration may be gradual, and probably is so, in some cases; but it is often effected as quick as Christ could say, "I will, be thou clean." This is according to the indications of both Scripture and experience. Many have passed from extreme fear and anguish, to the brightest hopes, and the most thrilling raptures, in a moment. Shouts of victory have taken the place of groans and lamentations, as quick as thought; and smiles of joy have been seen springing from the face of melancholy, amid a profusion of tears. And it was no deception. The subjects feared, perhaps, that it was too good to be lasting, and scarcely dared to sleep, lest they should lose it; but found it more than the meteor's glare — an abiding sun; and their subsequent lives attested that the work was divine.

Sometimes, however, the evidence of this change is less sudden, and less satisfactory. Perhaps the *convictions* were less painful. But in every case of real conversion, it will be manifested by increased interest in prayer, in reading the Scriptures and other good books, unusual affection for Christians, and love for the means of grace, accompanied with great power over old habits and passions, and pleasure in the discharge of duty. Thus, in the first impulses of persuasion that he is born again, the Christian will have the "witness of *the* Spirit;" and in the *fruits which follow*, the witness of his own spirit, agreeably to Rom. viii. 16: "*The* Spirit *itself* beareth witness with *our spirit*, that we are the children of God." By the former we mean "an inward impression on the soul, whereby the Spirit of God directly witnesses to my spirit, that I am a child of God; that Jesus Christ hath loved me, and given himself for me; and that all my sins are blotted out, and I, even I, am reconciled to

God." This, in the nature of things, must be antecedent to the testimony of our own spirit. Pardon is an act of the divine mind, and is a secret, until God is pleased to reveal it. Moreover, "we love him because he first loved us," and we never love his word or people till we are conscious that we love him; and, of course, never bring forth the fruits of conversion till we know that we are converted.

This knowledge is communicated by the Spirit, not audibly, nor by apparitions, but by the removal of guilt and fear, which it has impressed upon the mind, and by producing therein a joyous persuasion that God loves me, and has forgiven all my sins; a persuasion, generally, that leaves no more doubt of *acceptance* with God, than there was of *guilt and condemnation before*. As there was *no doubt* then, so neither is there any doubt of pardon and acceptance now.

Thus we see the progress of grace in the human heart, from the fall to the full accomplishment of the new birth. Reader, have you been born again? O, remember that in this respect your righteousness must exceed the "righteousness of the Scribes and Pharisees, or you can never see the kingdom of God!"

CHAPTER VI.

CHRISTIAN PERFECTION.

There is no doctrinal peculiarity by which Methodists have been more distinguished than that of *Christian perfection.* Nor is there one for which they have been more generally condemned. This may be attributed to various causes. One is, no doubt, that the doctrine has been misunderstood. It has generally been taken to mean more than was intended, owing, perhaps, to the term itself, which we are accustomed to apply to the Deity, and which, least of all, designates the character displayed by the mass of professing Christians. To this we may add the novelty of the doctrine. Not that it originated with us. God commanded Abraham and Moses to be perfect; and he commands us, by his Son, "Be ye perfect, even as your Father which is in heaven is perfect." But as an article of faith and experience, Methodists have given it a prominence others do not. For, though many pray for it, few believe in its attainability, and most contend earnestly for imperfection until death. They bound Christian duties and privileges by the seventh chapter of Romans, while we insist on those portrayed in the eighth.

The abuse which the doctrine has experienced from its reputed friends, has probably contributed its full share to its unpopularity. Some, in their zeal, have overdrawn it, so as to make it utterly impracticable; others have taken the opposite extreme, and made it less than we claim for justification — indeed, rather a license to sin than deliverance from it. This is particularly the case with a class of Antinomian Perfectionists, which appeared in another denomination a few years since. Some have given it such a peculiarly sour and unsociable cast as to make it offensive to most Christians; while others have associated it with so many extravagances of expression and deportment, so many religious *antics* and visionary notions, that prudent men have been afraid to approach it.

But all these excrescences do not alter the nature of the thing itself, though they may conceal its loveliness. The doctrine is still true, and has claims to consideration. Our limits will only admit of some explanation of our views, and a bare reference to the grounds upon which they rest. We say, then,

1. That by Christian perfection we do not mean the perfection of *angels*. Those glorious beings, which left not their "first estate," occupy a higher rank in the scale of being, are exempt from ignorance and enticement to evil, and endowed with such attachments to duty and holiness as hardly to admit of the least defection.

2. Nor do we mean the perfection which was enjoyed by our first parents previous to their fall. They were probably as pure as the angels, though less in capacity. They were liable to sin, but still possessed no inward tendency to it. Nor were they surrounded, as most men now are, with excitants to sin, or with worldly cares, which engross most of our time.

3. Much less do we mean perfection in knowledge. We are ignorant, at best. How little do we know of God, of his word or works, of ourselves, even, or of the plainest matters of daily occurrence! Every advance step we take in this

direction but reveals our deficiencies; and the more we learn, the less confident we become that we really know any thing. How little we know of our brethren and neighbors, — of the claims of justice or mercy, — of our rights, duties, and privileges, — of our duties to others, or of their obligations to us. Hence, therefore,

4. It does not exclude *error in practice.* Every honest man will act in the light of his intelligence. If that light be darkness, he will err, of course. The fond mother, acting with all tenderness and care, by mistake administers a poison to her child, and destroys it. Attempting a kindness to a brother, through ignorance of some circumstances, we do him great injustice. And in thousands of other cases, we may commit wrong acts when the intention is pure, merely for want of knowledge. And for this there is no remedy. This arises from *intellectual* imperfection, and should teach us modesty; but we may be perfect in a *moral* point of view, nevertheless; that is, our *purposes* may be entirely religious and benevolent, and we may maintain a conscience void of offence toward God and toward man.

This distinction between errors of *judgment* and of *intention* is not always considered in judging of Christians, especially in judging of those who claim to be perfect in love Hence, the doctrine and its friends are sometimes reproached, when they are entitled to full credit. Mr. Wesley saw this, and remarked, "Those who are now really perfect in love, may be still an occasion of temptation to you; for they are still encompassed with infirmities. They may be dull of apprehension; they may have a natural heedlessness, or a treacherous memory; they may have too lively an imagination; and any of these may cause little improprieties, either in speech or behaviour, which, though not sinful in themselves, may try all the grace you have; especially if you impute to perverseness of will (as it is very natural to do) what is really owing to defect of memory or weakness of understanding; if those appear to you to be voluntary mistakes which are really involuntary. So proper was the answer which a saint of God (now in Abraham's bosom) gave me, some years ago, when I said, 'Jenny, surely now your mistress and you can neither of you be a trial to the other, as God hath saved you both from sin.' 'O, sir,' said she, 'if we are saved from sin, we still have infirmities enough to try all the grace God has given us.'"

5. Nor does it imply a uniform brilliancy of mind and engagedness of heart in the worship of God. The most brilliant and devotional have bodies like other men, and may find them weary and dull just at the time they would be zealous and animated in their religious duties. The perfect man will lament this; but he cannot avoid it. It is rather a physical than a moral evil; and if it is known to operate similarly in other cases, where the business is of a different nature, it is no argument against a perfect state of heart before God, though it must be a source of temptation both to the subject of it and his observing brethren. Our animal spirits sometimes flag, and become bad *conductors* of grace, making the good man appear sluggish and wanting in interest. At other times they flow in excess, and display full as much grace and religious zeal as he enjoys. A well informed judgment and a settled purpose, are equally necessary in both cases; in the first, to keep him from becoming despondent and inactive; and in the second, to restrain him from extravagance.

6. Nor yet does Christian Perfection imply such a degree of faith and knowledge as to exclude an increase of either, or any other Christian virtue. It rather relates to *purity*, than to the *extent* of our *powers*, and indicates exemption

from sin, more than maturity in the graces of the Spirit One may, therefore, be perfect in our sense of the term,—that is, entirely sanctified, and possess nothing in his heart but good, — and still be limited in knowledge and in general faith. But it is undeniable, that, where there is purity, there is usually a respectable development of the Christian graces.

We would also remark, that the Perfection we teach relates rather to the essential elements of piety than to their results — to faith and love rather than to joy and peace, though the latter ordinarily accompany it. One may possess perfect faith, and love God and his neighbor perfectly, whose joy and peace, owing to physical causes, will, at times, be quite inconsiderable and unsatisfactory. The fond mother, who loves her child perfectly, does not always enjoy it in the same degree. When we speak of the perfect Christian, therefore, we do not mean one who is in perpetual raptures, since perfection does not imply this, though raptures are its frequent accompaniment. We think our views on this point have been misapprehended by some of our best friends, who, in seeking the blessing under consideration, have looked more to be *happy* than to be *holy*.

To be perfect, is,

1. To love God *supremely* — that is, more than we love any other being or thing; to love him with "all the heart, and with all the soul, and with all the strength, and with all the mind." But the anxious reader will ask, "What is love?" We answer: "It is a sovereign preference given to *one* above others; a *concentration* of the thoughts and desires in a single object, which we prefer to others." Should he ask, "What is it to love God, whom we have not seen?" we reply; "It is to approve, admire, prize, affectionately contemplate, cleave to, and be satisfied with him, in the charac-

ter he ascribes to himself; pleased to acknowledge him as our Creator, Redeemer, Governor, and Judge, and happy in the hope of seeing him as he is, and being like him, and with him for ever. The sinner contemplates his character with the conviction that it is *right* and *good*, but not with *affection*. It does not please him; much less is he gratified with the idea of seeing God or being judged by him. But the Christian loves him, rejoices that he is just such a God as he is, and is delighted in being permitted to regard him as his friend, and in obediently resting his soul in his everlasting embrace.

To love God, therefore, with all the heart, is to love him to the extent of our capacity, " with all the *strength;* " to prize him above every thing else, and cleave to him in our affections, and in filial endeavors to obey and please him, at the sacrifice, if necessary, of every other good. It is, in a word, to make him *our God;* and every other love, and interest, and pursuit, subordinate to him. So that we love nothing, desire nothing, and seek nothing, knowingly, but what is pleasing to him; and commune with him in meditation, prayer, and all the means of grace, with a confidence and fervor of affection equal to our present susceptibility.

Those who suppose that it excludes the love of relatives, and friends, or a proper regard for worldly interests and pursuits, are deceived. The divine claims upon us are consistent with each other. We have bodies, and dependents, to be cared for; we hold relations which involve duties that would be a burden and a tax in the absence of peculiar affection. This doctrine recognizes these facts, tempers and purifies this care, and these affections, investing them with a religious character, and thus making them more interesting and profitable; but always subjecting them to supreme love to God.

2. It implies, therefore, some degree of intelligence, by which the character of God and the instructions of his word are apprehended; and that faith, by which they are pronounced *just* and *true*, — adopted, relied on, and brought home to the soul as divine realities, — realized and enjoyed above all other views and possessions. Love is not blind in this case, however it may be in others. It lavishes not its fondness upon indifferent objects, upon an "*unknown* God." It, at least, has some glimpses of the divine character by faith, which invests it, in the view of the renewed heart, with infinite loveliness. Turning from God to his works in the heavens above, and in the earth beneath and around, its view becomes enlarged. Especially when it considers the plan of salvation, and contemplates the wisdom and goodness of God therein displayed, does it burn and throb with peculiar ardor. But whatever its attainments in these respects, they can never reach a point, either here or hereafter, beyond which there will not be much to learn, and, of course, ample room for love to warm and strengthen.

3. Christian Perfection implies, also, the loving our "*neighbor as ourselves*," which is the second great commandment. That is, regarding and treating all men with equity, charity, benevolence, and affection; otherwise, doing to them as we would that they should do unto us in a reverse of circumstances. By this rule we are required to forgive their sins against us, bear with their weaknesses and errors, rejoice in their prosperity, lament their adversity, and in all possible ways contribute to their improvement and happiness, to the extent of our knowledge and ability, and in consonance with our obligations to God and ourselves. It therefore excludes *envy*, for this regrets another's talents, excellence, success, or popularity, and involves more or less malignity and evil desire, if not a positive effort to eclipse and

injure. *Covetousness*, for this inordinately desires the possessions of others, and retains its own with a tenacity inconsistent with our duty to the destitute and the cause of Christ. *Jealousy*, for this is a peculiar uneasiness, arising from the fear that another will obtain some good which we desire for ourselves. *Emulation*, for this would hinder the progress of others, to secure us the profit or honor of exceeding them. *Wrath*, for this is an evil and turbulent passion, which leads to broils and contentions. It also excludes every other passion which tends to wrong action, and implies all those kind and heavenly tempers which sweeten and perfect the happiness of fraternal intercourse. Consequently, it excludes all misrepresentation of another's views, plans, or feelings; all tale-bearing, tattling, and slanderous insinuations; every kind and degree of reference to others, which shall detract from their respectability, influence, or pleasure; indeed, all expressions, actions, and surmises, that we would dislike to have arrayed against ourselves.

But this is "*faint praise.*" Silence is sometimes the worst kind of injustice. Negative goodness is often positive evil. We are to regard our neighbors with *affection* and *charity*. To speak well of them when defamed, or, at all events, to give them the benefit of what we know in their favor. To hear one injured in his absence, and make no apology for him, is to be accessory to the slander. We wink at the outrage, unless we suggest that there may be a mistake in what has been said, or that it is only a *part* of the truth, and ought not to be circulated. Perfect love thinketh no evil, and is loath to believe evil of others. It will defend them just so far as the truth will admit, and hope for them when it can say no more. But this is not the extent of its solicitude. It will strive to improve them, to increase their influence for good, their happiness, and usefulness, and will rejoice in their promotion. This is a great attainment, but still, by the grace of God, it is practicable. *Selfishness* is among the last of Satan's strongholds to yield. When we get so far purged from it as to love God and his cause supremely, and to be willing to occupy any place in his vineyard, even the least conspicuous and important, if God please, and see others rising above us in talents and influence, and rejoice in, and contribute to it, with all our hearts, we may be assured grace has done a great work for us.

4. *Meekness* is another prominent trait and evidence of Christian Perfection. By this, we mean mildness, "patience in tribulation; suffering severe provocation without feeling anger, or revenge; entire self-control." So that, "being reviled, we bless; being persecuted, we suffer it; being defamed, we entreat; and are made the filth of the earth, and the off-scouring of all things," without the least disposition to retaliate.

It embraces *patience*, too, under afflictions, disappointments, and grievances; excluding all murmuring, fretfulness, and complaint. Not that we would have no choice, if the matter were left to us; for we should, of course, prefer ease to pain, prosperity to adversity, friendship to hatred, &c., other circumstances being equal. Those who represent the perfect Christian as without choice, do the cause injustice. Piety does not destroy his natural appetites; I mean those which are not sinful in themselves. Bitter is still bitter, and sweet is sweet; and if he were left to choose, he would take the latter now as ever. But if God chooses the bitter for him he prefers it, as best, and enjoys it, often, as though it were sweet, and possibly even better. So he prefers health to sickness, prosperity to adversity; but if the latter fall to his lot, he is reconciled, knowing that they are wisely appointed, and shall be graciously overruled for his good.

5. We add, it implies *purity of motives.* But by this we certainly do not mean motives which have no reference to ourselves. The idea of "*disinterested benevolence*" we regard as a mere fiction of imagination. It is utterly impracticable, and if it were not, it would be *fatal.* God has endowed every man with a degree of self-love which is essential to his being, and to which all the motives of the gospel appeal. It is difficult to act without some reference to it. To study our *interest* only, or chiefly, is selfishness ; to seek the good of others to the neglect of ourselves, is recklessness. There is a happy medium lying between these two extremes, where the claims of all are properly balanced and respected. Here the perfect man plants himself, and acts at once so as to please and glorify his Maker and Saviour, to benefit his fellow men, and promote his own spiritual and eternal interests. He makes every thing earthly bow to these objects, and lays himself out in such efforts as may seem right and expedient.

6. It also implies *rigid obedience* to all the divine commands, so far as they are known. "He that committeth sin [knowingly] is of the devil ;" and "Whosoever is born of God doth *not* commit sin." The perfect Christian strives to do every duty, however crossing. The language of his heart is, "Speak, Lord, for thy servant heareth." And when duty appears, he goes straight forward in it, whatever the difficulties or the cost. If he is in doubt, he seeks all the light the circumstances will permit, and then follows it ; endeavoring, if he errs at all, to err in favor of Christ and his cause, and against the claims of the flesh. So that he can say, when he retires at night, and that from an enlightened conscience, and a critical review of his conduct, "I have lived in all good conscience before God this day ;" and lay him down in the full and joyous assurance

that "to die is gain." And this obedience is not the drudgery of an unwilling heart, extorted by a solemn conviction of duty, and of the painful consequences of neglecting it. O, no! it is the outgushing of a mind strongly disposed to it, not by resolution merely, but by a free and cheerful impulse. "This is the love of God, that we keep his commandments; and his commandments are *not grievous.*"

7. Finally, it is a state of *conscious union with God*, and of delightful correspondence with him. Free from *guilt*, for all his sins are pardoned, and he has the "witness of the Spirit with his spirit, that he is a child of God;" free from the *power* of sin, for sin no longer has dominion over him; free from *the love* of sin, being *cleansed* from the *filthiness of the flesh and spirit*," he is free from all inward impulses thereto, though not free from the temptations of the devil. He walks in the light, rejoicing evermore, praying without ceasing, having his heart, thoughts, and conversation, as it were, in heaven, and feeling the glorious presence of an all-surrounding Deity. And this, not for a day, or during the calm of congenial circumstances, or the occasional visitations of revival influence, but for days and weeks, and years, even, of diversified life, embracing the most embarrassing duties, and the most painful sufferings.

But this is not a different religion from that which every one experiences in being truly converted, or born again. That is, not different in its *nature*. It is rather the same work carried on to perfection. If that sanctifies partially, this completes the work; if that extracts many roots of bitterness, this extracts the whole; if that is a great achievement, this is the greatest of all. The resemblance between the two is so striking, many have regarded them as one and the same work. This was the doctrine of Count

Zinzendorf's followers, and it is no doubt believed by some now with considerable confidence. Mr. Wesley so far conceded it, as to admit that one might be entirely sanctified in the moment of conversion, but denied that this was the order of divine grace, or that it often occurs. His sermon, entitled "Sin in Believers," was designed to demonstrate his views. Our church has followed him in this particular, and holds entire sanctification, or Christian perfection, as a distinct work, usually effected sometime subsequent to conversion. Yet we do allow, that, where the penitent is properly impressed with a sense, not only of his guilt, but of the corruption of his nature, and embraces the atonement by faith as an all-sufficient remedy for both, he may be entirely sanctified at the same instant he is pardoned.

This view, we believe, is in strict accordance with the sentiments of the universal church throughout the world, and in all ages, except the few cases above named. However, there need be no strife on this subject. If we are saved from all our sins *now*, if we feel no emotions, and perform no actions, contradictory of this, and have the joyous attestation of the Spirit to our hearts, it is a matter of little consequence whether we experienced it at the time of our conversion or subsequently. If we are not thus saved, it is time we were crying to God for help, and seeking him with all our hearts. Facts must take precedence of theories. It is of no more advantage to us that we were sanctified in our conversion, than that we were not until a year or two after, or never were, if we are destitute of the blessing *now ;* nor is it any good reason why we should not seek it now. Nor does the doctrine of sanctification as a second and distinct work, afford any encouragement to unsanctified professors to regard themselves *justified* Christians, while they are living in any known sin, either of omission or commission; since no one is justified in remaining in an unholy condition a single minute after he discovers the fact that such is his condition, without striving to escape from it. To retain sinful tempers, and indulge in practices we know to be wrong, and still flatter ourselves that we are *justified*, is a *delusion*. We are not justified, but con demned. Yet we may be justified, and feel certain lusts and evil desires, or thoughts, if we strive against them, and come to Christ to have them cast out. There is, therefore, no justification, and, of course, no security, but in the positive enjoyment of the blessing under consideration, or in earnestly seeking it. One who knows he is not sanctified, who feels wicked tempers, indulges in loose and uncharitable conversation, and does not strive against sin, and sincerely seek to be purged from all the corruptions of "flesh and spirit," gives good evidence that he is not a Christian, that he is under condemnation, and cannot enter heaven without repentance; though he may be a minister, a leader, or steward, and be prompt in the outward observance of all the ordinances of the gospel. Who, then, is prepared to die and meet the Judge? Reader, let us examine the grounds of our hope, and see if, after all, we are not building on the sand.

The great objection to our views on this subject comes from another quarter. Other denominations generally assume that complete deliverance can be expected only at the moment of our demise, and that then it will be accomplished in all believers. This is the main point of difference All agree that the Bible requires us to be holy, that we should constantly aim to become so, that we can become very much better than we are at present, that no line can be drawn this side of entire holiness, beyond which it is not possible to go, and that we must be holy, or never enter heaven. But here we part.

The possibility of attaining this blessing is argued from various considerations, a few of which only will be noticed. 1. It is the will of God that we should be holy. God cannot look with pleasure upon sin in any degree, or in any place. 2. He has, therefore, enjoined holiness upon his creatures. "Be ye, therefore, perfect, even as your Father in heaven is perfect." 3. He has provided for this in the atonement "For what the law could not do in that it was weak through the flesh, God, sending his own Son, in the likeness of sinful flesh, and for sin, condemned sin in the flesh; that the *righteousness of the law might be fulfilled in us*, who walk not after the flesh, but after the Spirit." The object of Christ's mission was to save his people *from* their sins, to "*destroy* the works of the devil," "that we, being dead to sins, might live unto righteousness." There are, therefore, "given unto us exceeding great and precious promises, that by these ye might be partakers of the divine nature, having escaped the corruption that is in the world through lust." 4. The Spirit, and its associate gifts, were bestowed upon the church for this very object. "He gave some, apostles; and some, prophets; and some, evangelists; and some, pastors and teachers; for the *perfecting* of the saints, for the work of the ministry, for the edifying of the body of Christ; till we all come in the unity of the faith, and of the knowledge of the Son of God, unto a *perfect man*, unto the measure of the stature of the *fulness* of Christ; that we henceforth be no more children, tossed to and fro, and carried about with every wind of doctrine, by the sleight of men, and cunning craftiness, whereby they lie in wait to deceive." Again: "For this cause I bow my knees unto the Father of our Lord Jesus Christ, that he would grant you, according to the riches of his glory, to be strengthened with might by his Spirit in the inner man; that Christ may dwell in your hearts by faith; that ye, being rooted and grounded in love, may be able to comprehend with all saints, what is the breadth, and length, and depth, and height; and to know the love of Christ, which passeth knowledge, that ye might be *filled* with all the *fulness of God.*"

5. The prayers dictated by Christ aim at the same result. "Thy will be done in earth as it is in heaven." "Neither pray I for these alone, but for them also which shall believe on me through thy word; that they all may be one in us. And the glory which thou gavest me I have given them; that they may be one, even as we are one; *I in them*, and thou in me; that they may be made *perfect in one;* and that the world may know that thou hast sent me, and hast loved them as thou hast loved me." If the will of God should be done, if Christ should dwell in believers as the Father dwells in him, agreeably to this prayer, would they not be perfect in love?

6. The attainability of this blessing is evident, also, from the prayers of inspired men. "Epaphras, who is one of you, a servant of Christ, saluteth you, always laboring fervently for you in prayers, that ye may stand *perfect in all the will of God.*" "Now the God of peace, that great Shepherd of the sheep, through the blood of the everlasting covenant, make you *perfect* in every good work, to do his will, working in you that which is well pleasing in his sight, through Jesus Christ."

7. Some of old did attain the blessing. St. Paul says of himself: "I am crucified with Christ; nevertheless, I live; yet *not I*, but *Christ liveth in me;* and the life which

I now live in the flesh, I live by faith on the Son of God." "Ye are our witnesses, and God also, how holily, and justly, and *unblamably*, we behaved ourselves among you that believe." St. John, the loving disciple, was evidently an example of Christian perfection. Speaking from experience, no doubt, he declared: "Herein is our love made *perfect*, that we may have boldness in the day of judgment; because as he is, so are we in this world." "There is no fear in love; but perfect love casteth out fear."

If this doctrine has created some prejudices against us, if it has occasioned some of our members at times to be extravagant in word or deed, and thus brought upon us undeserved trials and reproach, it has, on the whole, been an infinite blessing. The church has enjoyed more religion than she would have done under different views, though, in common with others, she has fallen far below her own standard. There has never been a time when we have been without witnesses to this glorious truth; and these witnesses, where they are consistent and reputable, are the moral strength of the church. They have sustained our prayer, class, and other meetings; have spoken when others were silent, believed when they doubted, and have held on when their brethren were discouraged and gave up in despair. Long may such characters grace our assemblies, and exemplify the truth as it is in Jesus.

CHAPTER VII.

PERSEVERANCE OF THE SAINTS.

Error, like some fruit, grows in clusters. Ignorance is contented to stand alone, with her back to the truth; but error is more active, and stumbles on in the direction she looks. Thus Calvin, having embraced the doctrine of particular election, found it necessary, to be consistent, to assume that of the *infallible perseverance of the saints;* that is, that those whom God has elected, called, and renewed, cannot so far fall from grace as to perish everlastingly. This is regarded by Calvinists as a very precious doctrine, and held with the greatest tenacity.

But Methodists have ever viewed it as a deduction from false premises, without Scripture authority, and, therefore, not to be countenanced. We do not deny that every converted soul may and ought to persevere to the end, but rather that every one does so. In our opinion, the argument is against it; for,

1. Thus saith the Lord, "When the righteous turneth away from his righteousness, and committeth iniquity, in his trespass that he hath trespassed, and in his sin that he hath sinned, in them shall he die." He immediately adds, to show that the death named is *eternal*, and not temporal: "When the righteous man turneth away from his righteousness, and committeth iniquity, and *dieth* in them, [tempo-

rally,] for his iniquity that he hath done, he shall die," [eternally.] The whole scope of the chapter seems to aim at the same point, viz., to prove that "the soul that sinneth, it shall die," and this does not mean the body, certainly, for that will die whether we sin or not.

"When I shall say to the righteous that he shall surely live; if he trust in his own righteousness and commit iniquity, all his righteousness shall not be remembered; but for the iniquity that he hath committed, shall he die." — Ezek. xxxiii. 13. What could be more explicit? And how strange does such language sound in connection with that which avers, that one who has been made truly righteous, can no more die in his sins than God's word can fail.

2. The testimony of Christ is to the same effect. "He that *endureth to the end* shall be saved." "Verily, verily, I say unto you, if a man keep my saying, he shall never see death." — John viii. 51. "I am the true vine, and my Father is the husbandman. Every branch in me that beareth not fruit, he taketh it away." "If a man abide not in me, he is cast forth as a branch and is withered; and men gather them and cast them into the fire, and they are burned." — John xv. 1, 6. Do these announcements indicate nothing? Does Christ mean to be understood, after all, that his disciples can never prove fruitless or neglect his sayings, so as to be taken away, and cast into the fire?

3. The apostles testify to the same thing. St. Paul had no doubt of Timothy's piety, and yet he exhorted him: "War a good warfare, holding faith and a good conscience, which some *having put away* concerning faith *have made shipwreck:* of whom is Hymeneus and Alexander, whom I have *delivered unto Satan*, that they may learn not to blaspheme." — 1 Tim. i. 18, 19. Of Alexander he afterwards says, "he did me much evil. The Lord *shall reward*

him according to his works." — 2 Tim. iv. 14. He exhorts the Romans, "Be not high-minded, but fear; if God spared not the natural branches, take heed lest he spare not thee. Behold the goodness and severity of God! On them which fell, severity; but toward thee, goodness, if *thou continue in his goodness; otherwise thou shalt be cut off.*" — *Chapter* x. 20, 22.

Another apostle says: "If, after they have *escaped the pollutions of the world*, through the knowledge of the Lord and Saviour Jesus Christ, they are again entangled therein and overcome, [a contingency which all admit to be possible,] the latter end is worse with them than the beginning. For it had been better for them not to have known the way of righteousness, than, after they have known it, to turn from the holy commandment delivered unto them." — 2 Peter, ii. 20, 21.

In the epistle to the Hebrews we read, "It is impossible for those who were once enlightened, and have tasted of the heavenly gift, and were made partakers of the Holy Ghost, if they fall away, to renew them again to repentance, seeing they crucify to themselves the Son of God afresh, and put him to an open shame." — vi. 4, 6. And, "the just shall live by faith; but if any man draw back, my soul shall have no pleasure in him." — x. 38.

We make no comments upon these Scriptures, because they need none. They speak for themselves; and any man, not blinded by a creed he is anxious to support, need not err therein. Nor can the most acute reasoner so explain them as to destroy their testimony against the dogma of *infallible* "*perseverance.*" And yet they are but a small part of the passages of similar import that might be adduced.

In perfect agreement with these announcements, is the argument to be derived from *free agency*. If men are free agents at all, they are not less so, as Christians, than they were before their conversion. As the grace of God did not and would not compel them to repent and believe the gospel, as sinners, so it will not compel them to be faithful as Christians, much less *infallibly* "*renew* them again to repentance," in case they should "draw back." This is entirely contrary to the divine economy, both in relation to *free grace* and *free will*, and equally so to the declaration of God, that he will "have no pleasure" in those that "draw back." If a Christian be a free agent, surrounded as he is by temptations and worldly allurements, and perhaps not entirely cleansed from the corruptions of flesh and spirit, he is *liable* to fall into sin. This is admitted on all sides. He is liable also to continue in it, despite the remonstrances of conscience and of God, and to die in his sins, agreeably to the testimony of the Lord by Ezekiel. Hence he is liable to lose his soul for ever.

We might argue the possibility of final apostasy from frequent examples, were it not for the courage of our opponents in meeting all such cases. If we refer to one who gave unequivocal evidence of piety, but is now deeply sunk in vice and corruption, they reply, either that he never was converted, or that he will be "brought in." If such an one dies without being restored, they avow he never was a Christian, and read us a lecture on the danger of being deceived. If the thought of dying wakes him up, and he seems to repent and be restored, they construe it into a lively proof of the truth of their doctrine, and lecture us on the faithfulness of God. So that, like a heathen priest consulting his oracle, they make these circumstances to testify just as they please, and always to favor their own fancies, however strong the probabilities against them.

Nevertheless, we cannot altogether lose the benefit of this

class of evidence. Their mere statement weighs nothing. In all these assumptions, as, for instance, that a backslider dying impenitent, never was, therefore, a Christian, they beg the question, and merely assert what they ought to prove. What is the evidence that he was not a Christian? Simply that he was not revived and renewed again before his death. We might just as reasonably say the man never lived, because he died. But this will not do. For one to die impenitent no more proves that he never was converted, than that he never was born. To test this point we must look at the evidences of conversion, and see whether he possessed them in sufficient clearness, — how long they continued, &c., — was he truly awakened and humbled, — did he take up his cross and come out from the world, and follow Christ, — did he faithfully abstain from every known sin, and perform every known duty, — did he claim to experience a change of mind from sorrow to joy, from enmity to love, love to God, and his people, his word and worship, — did this change appear in his life, spirit, conversation, associations, business, and other deportment, — did he lead a life of prayer and devotion, so that the more experienced Christians thought him, indeed, a "bright and shining light," and rejoiced to take him to their fellowship? If so, with what face can any one claim he was not a converted man? The Master says, "By their fruits ye shall know them." Not by the doubtful indications of the last flicker of life, but by their spirit and conduct in their more deliberate moments.

Now, many have been known to give just this evidence — all that any one could reasonably ask for himself or his brethren — and after a term of years, by a change of circumstances, they have been led astray, one step after another, until they not only lost the spirit, but the form, of religion, and became its deadly enemies, and died relentless. They bore the first fruits of piety in public and private — they enjoyed the assurance in themselves, that they were born again, and clearly evidenced the same to others ; and even after their decline, looking back upon their experience, they believed and confessed that they were converted. Is this all to pass for nothing? Why so? The only objection to its genuineness is, they fell away from God, as did our first parents, and died without repentance. But this cannot be allowed. Such kind of reasoning is a burlesque. We must pay some deference to the evidence of experience and observation, or reasoning is out of the question. These men gave as good evidence of being Christians, as they did of being sinners, before or afterwards.

But what is still more unreasonable in these asserters of perseverance, they apply the same assumptions to Scripture characters, irrespective of consequences. For example, it is said Judas was never a Christian, though called to the apostleship, and sent forth as a "sheep among wolves," and entrusted with high responsibility in regard to the great interests of religion, because, in an hour of temptation, he betrayed his master, and died, so far as we know, without pardon. But Peter, though he *lied* out-right, *cursed and swore*, publicly *denying his master*, was a Christian, even in the midst of his crimes, because he afterwards repented. Other cases are disposed of in the same way.

But this seems to be charging a little too much to the Son of God; and it denies the only infallible test of character which he has given us, viz., its *fruits*. To believe that Christ called a *devil* to the apostleship, and flattered him with so many endearing titles, and other intimations of his entire confidence, as he did, exeeeds our credulity. If he was a hypocrite, the Saviour knew it at the time he called him. But he treated him as a real friend, promoted and caressed him as a disciple indeed. Thus, in trying to sustain this dangerous notion, Calvinists implicate the honesty of him in whom there was no guile; and holding Peter a Christian, while he displayed such incontestible marks of a sinner, they leave us in utter confusion as to who are Christians, and who are not. For aught we can tell, if this assumption be well founded, the man who raves in falsehood and profanity before us, may be a *saint*, while his apparently humble and pious neighbor is a *hypocrite* and a *devil*. A system which leads to such consequences needs the very strongest proof to command our confidence.

In view of the facts that Judas was appointed to the highest office in the Church, and clothed with power "against unclean spirits, to cast them out, and to heal all manner of sickness and all manner of disease," and sent forth to preach the kingdom of heaven, raise the dead, and cast out devils, and to be hated of all men, with the promise if he should "endure to the end" he should be saved, and the encouragement that the hairs of his "head were all numbered," and treated in other respects by the Saviour as his "own familiar friend," till just before the betrayal—I say, in view of these facts, we are constrained to believe that Judas was at first, and for most of the time, a sincere Christian. There was no encouragement to be a hypocrite at that age. It cost too much. Those who would be Christians were required to take up their cross and follow Christ, forsaking father and mother, and all else. None were received on any other terms.

To suppose that he was sincere, but *deceived*, is unreasonable; for, if this were the case, Jesus would have pointed out his error. Besides, it is intimated that the matter of betrayal was a sudden thing, and originated not in the malice and forethought of a murderer, but in the devil. Says St.

John, "supper being ended, the *devil having now put it into the heart* of Judas to betray him," &c. — *Chapter* xiii. 2. And, in the twenty-seventh verse, he says, "*after the sop, Satan* entered into him." It was not a thing he had been planning; nor is it more marvellous that he was tempted and overcome, than that Peter should conduct as he did. Some claim for him that he was looking after the money, and did not intend that his Master should be crucified, but supposed he would exercise his almighty power, and escape out of their hands. Hence they account for his agony when Christ was condemned. If this were so, it modifies his conduct a little; but, viewing it in its worst aspect, it is not inconsistent with the idea that he was previously the *real* FRIEND of Christ.

Hymeneus and Alexander furnish other examples of apostasy, and the latter evidently died without mercy, however it might have been with the other. They had "*faith* and a *good conscience*," which they "*put away*," and thus made "shipwreck." St. Paul saw and mourned their fall. He knew his own liability, and feared that he might commit the same fatal error. "I keep under my body," says he, "and bring it into subjection; lest that by any means, when I have preached to others, I myself should be a *castaway*." But why fear becoming a castaway. He knew he had "passed from death unto life." He had not seen Jesus, and been caught up to the third heaven, to no purpose. He as well knew that he was converted, as that he was formerly a persecutor. Why fear, then? The truth is, the apostle had never heard of the Genevan theology. He had only been taught from *above*, and felt, as he preached and wrote, that there was danger of falling fatally out of the way.

Yes, say Calvinists, there is danger of falling, but we shall be brought back. This is the very thing to be proved. "God will not suffer his *dear children* to perish." We admit it; but when they turn from him, they are not his "dear children," but children of the devil, whose works they do. "But the real Christian will not entirely forsake him." Let us see. Adam was made in the *image* of God, yet he fell; and certain angels, which "kept not their first estate," "are reserved in everlasting chains, unto the judgment of the great day." Why, then, may not Christians fall? God loved these angels, and our progenitors, as much as he loves us, and had as much power to uphold them.

But does not God say, "My *loving kindness* will I not utterly take from him, nor suffer my truth to fail. My covenant will I not break, nor alter the thing that has gone out of my mouth. I have sworn in my wrath that I will not fail David?" Verily, but what does it prove? Simply that God is *true*, and will never fail to fulfil his engagements. Yet he did fail David. He did "alter the thing that had gone out of his lips." He "*abhorred* and cast off his anointed." He did "break the covenant of his servant, and cast his crown to the ground;" clearly showing that the covenant was conditional, and the fulfilment on the part of God depended on David's fidelity. But David proving recreant to duty, God was "wroth," and cursed his anointed, instead of blessing him; but at the same time blessed the church, notwithstanding the infidelity and overthrow of its political head.

This suggests two mistakes Calvinists are rather under the necessity of making, in construing the Scriptures in reference to this particular, as well as several others. *First*, they have to apply promises made to the church, and statements made of her in her *organized* capacity, to *individuals;* and, *secondly*, to construe those which do not distinctly express a condition, as *unconditional and certain* as the decree of God can make them; whereas, what may be true of the church, *as such*, may be utterly false of an *individual;* and what is so often expressed in the Scriptures as the *condition* of salvation, should always be considered as implied in the few places where it is not expressed. The promise of God to the Jews, his ancient church, that he would bring them to the land he had described, was fulfilled, yet many individuals perished by the way. What Jonah preached was also true of impenitent Ninevah; but it implied such conditions, though none were expressed, that when the people "believed God," and repented of their sins, they were spared.

Some suppose that the *unchangeability* of God is an argument for the perseverance of the saints. But not so. The failure of any to persevere does not imply a change in Him. He purposed to save none except such as should "hold out to the end." But is he not *faithful?* Certainly he is, and will redeem all his promises when their conditions are performed. He is prompt in helping us to work out our salvation, and will be equally so in rewarding all whom he can address as "*good and faithful* servants," and in punishing those who will not have him to reign over them. Thus far his promises are "yea and amen," and can never fail to those who embrace them by faith, and comply with their conditions.

Was St. Paul "persuaded that neither death nor life, nor height nor depth, nor any other creature, should be able to separate him from the love of God, which is Christ Jesus our Lord?" It was because he knew as his day so his strength would be, and he *intended* to be faithful. Others may have had the same "full assurance;" not because they believed it impossible for them to backslide so as to perish, but because they knew God would never leave nor forsake them while they lived as they were then doing, and as they designed to live to the end. Paul also said, "We are not of them who draw back unto perdition;" but this, so far from proving that no Christian can thus draw back, plainly implies that some do so.

That it is the will of the Father that all he has given to Christ should be saved, is most certain; but it by no means follows that they will be saved. The Father's will is not done in many cases. He wills that sinners should repent and live, that believers should cleanse themselves from "all the filthiness of the flesh and Spirit;" but they do not. He willed, also, that Christ should keep all he gave him; but one escaped, and was lost, notwithstanding the tears, prayers, and watch-care of his Master and his brethren.

"What! a child of God go to hell?" Never! But if one who is such now, "trust in his own righteousness, and commit iniquity, all his righteousness shall not be remembered, but in the iniquity he hath committed shall he die." The judgment will decide the destiny of men according to the character they bear when arrested. To plead that we were once Christians, will rather condemn than justify us; for the greater the light abused, the greater will be our guilt.

"Then Christ is dead in vain." Not altogether. Many will continue to the end, and be saved, though others "trample the blood of the covenant under their feet, as an unholy thing." "My comfort is then all gone." Poor soul! If your comfort rests on this imaginary ground, the sooner it is gone the better. This leaning upon the doctrine of decrees for religious comfort, is miserable business. Those who hope God has predestinated *all* to salvation, those who limit his election, with all who are hoping to be brought in at some future day, are in a dangerous position. The only safety is in being *saved now;* in having "the witness in ourselves" that we are "new creatures in Christ Jesus," that we are "born of the Spirit." This gives us "peace in believing and joy in the Holy Ghost." We know that we are the children of God, because we love God, and keep his commandments, "and his commandments are *not grievous.*" No old hope will suffice. Confidence that we shall be restored and die well, is presumptive. Trusting in predestination is to lean upon a fragile reed, that will pierce us through with many sorrows. There is no safety but in coming to Christ, and "abiding in him, as the branch abides in the vine."

We have spoken thus frankly, because we believe this doctrine of certain perseverance is of very dangerous tendency. Its influence on believers is similar to that of Universalism on its votaries. Both declare, "*Thou shalt not die;*" and the difference is, one addresses itself to all mankind, and the other to a part. We know it is said, the Christian serves God from disinterested motives; but that is contrary to all experience, and the whole tenor of Scripture. Others suggest that the *delights* of religion are sufficient to command our devotion to its claims, without the additional motive of escaping perdition; but observation does not confirm it. Such are the influences in operation to lull us to sleep in sin, we need all the motives of the gospel to keep us from plunging into the world, and destroying our souls.

CHAPTER VIII.

THE SACRAMENTS.

We refer to this subject more to define our position as a people than with the design of discussing the various topics it suggests. And this is necessary, because there is such a diversity in the opinions of good men, and such tenacity on the part of many, in reference to matters of the least importance.

The word *sacrament* is derived from the word *sacramentum*, which signifies an oath. It was adopted by the Latin church to designate the ordinances of the gospel to be observed by Christians, by which they solemnly pledged themselves to obedience. Romanists maintain that there are *seven* sacraments enjoined, viz.: baptism, the Lord's Supper, confirmation, penance, extreme unction, ordination, and marriage. They insist, too, that there is virtue communicated in them when administered by a *priest* with good intention, if not opposed by a mortal sin in the recipient, though they be received without faith, or any purpose of amendment. Thus they make their benefits to depend on the nature of the ordinance, and the will of the administrator, and *not on the subject*, any farther than that he be not guilty of *mortal sin.*

Socinians, to keep the farthest possible distance from these absurdities, take the ground that the sacraments are in no wise different from any other religious ceremonies ; that they are merely symbols of spiritual grace ; but appealing to the senses in a way to revive the recollection of past events, and excite pious sentiments, are of great utility. They also consider them important as *badges*, by which to distinguish Christians from other men, and as furnishing an expressive method of publicly professing their faith in Christ.

This, we believe to be correct, so far as it goes ; but it comes short of the whole truth. Protestants generally agree that the sacraments of baptism and the Lord's Supper (for they reject all others as Romish inventions) are not only signs of inward purposes and grace, and pledges of obedience, but *seals* of God's covenant with us, and *standing memorials* of his promise to communicate grace to all who remember and seek him in all the appointed means. We hold them, therefore, as express institutions of God for specific purposes, the right observance of which he stands pledged to crown with his blessing. And herein they differ from a mere ceremony, which may or may not be employed with success, and which may be exchanged for something else, or be abandoned, at pleasure.

I. OF BAPTISM.

Upon this subject we remark :

1. That the *obligation* of baptism arises from the example and command of Christ and his apostles. The commission given to his first ministers is explicit: "Go and teach all nations, *baptizing* them in the name of the Father, and of the Son, and of the Holy Ghost." Not *with* the Holy Ghost, as the Quaker would say, but with *water*. Thus the apostles understood it, and thus they practised. Hence Peter exhorted the anxious multitude on the day of Pente

cost, "Repent, and be baptized, every one of you, in the name of Jesus Christ, for the remission of sins, and ye shall receive the gift of the Holy Ghost;" showing that baptism and receiving the Holy Ghost are two different things. While he spake to Cornelius the Spirit descended; whereupon he said, "Can any man forbid *water*, that these should not be baptized which have received the Holy Ghost, as well as we? And he commanded them to be baptized in the name of the Lord." John declared, "I baptize you with *water;*" and the eunuch said to Philip, "See, here is *water*, what doth hinder me to be baptized?" Indeed, the Scriptures abound in allusions of this nature, which indicate the apostolic practice, and our duty to be baptized, beyond reasonable doubt.

2. *The nature of baptism* is to be ascertained from the same source. Taking the place of circumcision, as is easily proved, it is an outward sign of our covenant relations to God. *First*, it indicates that we are in a state of acceptance and reconciliation with him; and, *secondly*, it marks and ratifies the mutual pledges subsisting between him and his people; he, to be their faithful God, and they, to be his loving and obedient children. Instituted by him, it is a visible assurance of his faithfulness to his covenant engagements; and submitted to by us, it is that act by which we become parties to the covenant, and solemnly bind ourselves to live according to its stipulations. Thus, in baptism, we die unto sin, cease from all fellowship with, and affection for it, and live unto Christ, reclining upon him, expecting to realize the fulfilment of all his gracious promises.

The *personal benefits* of baptism to adults, therefore, depends not so much upon who administers it, as upon the honesty and faith of the recipient. If he understands the nature of the transaction, and submits himself fully to the claims of the covenant to be ratified, not doubting the faithfulness of God, it will bring life and peace to his soul. But if he is wanting in these particulars, it will profit him little or nothing, whatever the character or faith of the administrator.

3. *Its subjects.* In respect to the proper subjects of baptism, we pretend to have made no improvement. Adult Christians who have not been baptized, are universally acknowledged to be eligible. We believe, also, with the general church in all ages, that *infants* are proper subjects; a position which most Baptists discard. But why not? Are they not in the very state indicated by the ordinance — in a state of justification by the mercy of God, who lays not the sins of their parents to their charge, nor holds them guilty for their evil tendencies? Who can doubt it? If, then, they have the thing *signified* — if they are the Lord's, belong to his spiritual family, and are candidates for his kingdom — why not give them the *sign;* put the Lord's mark upon them, and let them afterwards know that they were consecrated to him from the birth?

Besides, God is the same, and his main design has been the same, under all dispensations. The Abrahamic and Christian covenants are one, in their nature and object. Under the first, children were brought into covenant with God by *circumcision*, the baptism of that dispensation, and the Lord strongly indicated displeasure if it was neglected. Why should they be left out under the second? As baptism is the covenant sign under the Christian, as circumcision was under the Jewish dispensation, we can but administer it to our children, indicating the divine promises to us in relation to them, our own interest in their spiritual welfare, and our *faith* that they legitimately belong to the family of the redeemed, and are entitled to all the benefits of the new covenant. And we are encouraged in this practice, by the fact that Christ manifested such deep interest in children, and blessed them,—that the apostles baptized *whole households*, embracing, no doubt, a considerable number of them,—that for the first three hundred years the *practice was general* in the church, and from the year 400 to 1150 no society of men pretended to say that it was unlawful,—and, finally, from the fact that the earliest Christian fathers, whose writings have come down to us, declare that they *received the practice from the apostles.*

The objection that there is no express command for it, is of no weight. There is no such command for immersion or sprinkling,—none for women receiving the sacrament, and many other duties; but we hold them obligatory, and observe them on account of *circumstances* which enforce them upon us with all the authority of an express command. Nor is the objection that it does *no good* of any importance. It certainly does as much good as circumcision did to Jewish children. Besides, our not *perceiving* the good that is to accrue from the observance of a divine ordinance, is not a sufficient excuse for neglecting it.

But does not the New Testament say, "he that believeth and is baptized shall be saved?" Verily, but it does not say that *none shall be saved* or baptized, who are *incapable* of believing. This was spoken of adults, none of whom, at that time, had been baptized; as Christian baptism had never till then been instituted; and we think it requires faith in all such to constitute them proper subjects of baptism. But this does not touch the question. Infants are not required to *believe*,—are not capable of it; and yet they are objects of God's love, and are proper subjects of his salvation, and ought to be distinguished by the mark he puts upon his flock.

4. *Of the mode of baptism.* This ordinance being designed to indicate an inward grace, by which the subject is in a state of acceptance with God, no one mode can be claimed as being more expressive of its design than another Baptists speak without authority, when they assume that it was instituted to symbolize the burial and resurrection of Christ. We have no such intimation in the Scriptures. This is a controversial *invention* to furnish some reason for exclusive immersion; but, wanting authority for its premises, it avails nothing.

The commission given by Christ to the apostles, "Go ye into all the world," &c., by which Christian baptism was instituted, indicates that baptism consists in the religious application of water to the candidate, "in the name of the Father, and of the Son, and of the Holy Ghost." It does not specify the amount of water necessary, nor the manner of its application, because these were matters of little moment; but the *name* in which it is to be applied is given at full length. We say, therefore, that baptism consists not in any one mode, but in the application of water *in the proper name.* And this is amply supported by the meaning of the original term *baptizo* and its derivatives, which, according to the best authorities, is restricted to no mode, but admits of *sprinkling*, *pouring*, *immersion*, &c. This was the reason why our excellent translators chose to *anglicize* the word, rather than to translate it. There was no word in our language that admitted of the same latitude of meaning, and to have employed one of less compass, as the Baptists have done in their late translation, would have been to misrepresent the teachings of the Holy Ghost.

In this view of the subject, Methodists concur in the prevailing sentiment of the church, and leave candidates to make their own selection in regard to the *mode;* gratifying them therein, by plunging them into the water, pouring or sprinkling it on them, as they may prefer. Hence, some go down into the water and are immersed, others go down into it and are sprinkled, or poured, and all come "up straightway out of the water" together, having answered a good conscience and followed the Scriptures. Others, believing that the baptisms which occurred at Jordan and elsewhere, in the open air, were rather accidental as to the place, it not having been sought for this purpose more than the jail was sought for the baptism of the jailer and his household, and having no intimation in the Bible that Jesus or his apostles ever left the place where they were assembled, to find conveniences for immersion, they receive the ordinance in the house of God where they hear the word and believe.

Thus we preach and practise. Those who insist on immersion or nothing, and some who allow immersion to be Scriptural, but will baptize only by sprinkling, complain that we have no principles; but they mistake us. Our principles are fixed and definite, and by following them we avoid the extremes of our opponents — exclusive immersion on the one hand, and exclusive sprinkling on the other — and unite those in the bonds of Christian union who would be immersed themselves, but have no disposition to require it of others; and those who would not be immersed, but are willing that others should be, if they prefer it.

The arguments on this point are before the public in so many different forms, it is unnecessary to refer to them here.

5. *Baptism is not a pre-requisite to the Lord's supper.* The idea that Christians are not eligible to receive the emblems of the body and blood of Christ, however pious, till they have been baptized, is a device of Close Communion

Baptists, that has no foundation in Scripture. We have no evidence that the first partakers of this sacrament had themselves been baptized. Indeed, Christian baptism was not instituted till afterward. Nor have we the slightest intimation, among the numerous allusions made to it, that it was a necessary qualification for the other sacrament.

That baptism was usually administered soon after believing, and previous to the eucharist, is probable. So it preceded many other duties, as it does now; but that it was a *necessary qualification* for the eucharist is another thing. There is not the slightest evidence of it, any more than that it was a pre-requisite for the other duties it preceded. Hence, we regard young Christians, who have had no opportunity to be baptized, but who purpose to be, as soon as practicable, as suitable candidates for the Lord's supper as any other. Because they have not attended to one ordinance, for the want of opportunity, we do not feel authorized to exclude them from another. And yet the general practice of the church, to baptize converts soon after they believe, and prior to their going to the Lord's table, we have no doubt, is a prudent arrangement. But it affords no justification of Close Communicants, in excluding all Christians from their table who will not consent to be *plunged* by their own ministers.

Those who wish to examine this question critically, will find all needful assistance in the writings of Robert Hall, who, though a Baptist, repudiated Close Communion as unworthy of a place in the Christian Church.

II. OF THE LORD'S SUPPER.

On this subject we need say but little. Our views are entirely Protestant, and do not essentially differ from those of other evangelical denominations. We generally receive the elements on our knees, because we think it more appropriate; but if any prefer to receive them sitting or standing, they can do so. The ordinance is usually administered in our regular stations the first Sabbath in each month, and it is desired that all our members, and other Christians who may be present, should partake. Those only who have experience on this subject can appreciate the high spiritual advantages the ordinance is calculated to secure.

PART THIRD.

OF GOVERNMENT, PARTICULARLY THAT OF THE METHODIST EPISCOPAL CHURCH

CHAPTER I.

A GENERAL EXHIBIT OF DIFFERENT SYSTEMS.

WE use the term government here to indicate that form of rules and principles, by which the affairs of our church are conducted. The fact that most of the divisions in the Wesleyan family, owe their origin to questions of this nature, is a sufficient reason of itself for a pretty thorough investigation of the subject. So many outbreaks indicate that all is not right. If our principles are correct, our administration is erroneous, or else there is fault on the other side. It is not impossible that the seceders have been too ambitious of power, or of ease ; of profit, or of honor ; or they may have fallen into a pet, and struck for division out of revenge, and raised objections to our government only to cover their retreat and punish their old friends. This can be best judged of when all the facts are known.

But others complain. Some say we are too *episcopal*, and they cannot like us ; while another class avow that we have no legitimate episcopacy among us. Thus we are berated, first on one side and then on the other ; and it is a little wonderful, considering the talent that has been arrayed against us, that we have not been quite destroyed. But we have had friends, and able defenders. Nevertheless, we are not out of danger. Other separations will occur in their time, and new opponents will rise up to accomplish what their predecessors attempted in vain. The more ignorant of our system they find the community, the more successful will be their endeavors. It seems desirable, therefore, that we fortify ourselves and our friends by a thorough knowledge of our plan, and its philosophy, that we may be able to withstand the fiery darts of any future enemy that may appear. To contribute to this result is our present object.

The importance of some definite form of government cannot be too highly appreciated. Those churches which have undertaken to manage their affairs under the general directions of the New Testament, each member interpreting for himself, have experienced difficulties to which others are strangers. They have almost universally fallen into indifference, or disagreements, and perished without remedy. *Discipline* is as necessary as instruction. To live together profitably in church fellowship, Christians need to agree as to the import of Scripture, both as to doctrine and practice, in respect to each other, as well as to Him whom they serve. Otherwise, no one will understand his duties or privileges, and all will be in danger of serious mistakes and punishments.

But what form of government a church should adopt, is not so easily determined. It is generally conceded that the Scriptures do not impose any one form in particular, but leave it to the church to adopt such as circumstances may require. This is the testimony of the most eminent divines of all ages. Says Mr. Watson, adopting the language of Bishop Tomline: "As it has not pleased our almighty

Father to prescribe any particular form of civil government for the security of temporal comforts to his rational creatures, so neither has he prescribed any particular form of ecclesiastical polity as absolutely necessary to the attainment of eternal happiness. Thus, the gospel only lays down general principles, and leaves the application of them to men as free agents."

In agreement with this view, Mr. Wesley says: "As to my own judgment, I still believe the episcopal form of church government to be Scriptural and apostolical. I mean, well agreeing with the practice and writings of the apostles. But that it is *prescribed* in the Scriptures, I do not believe. This opinion, which I once zealously espoused, I have been heartily ashamed of ever since I read Bishop Stillingfleet's *Irenicum*. I think he has unanswerably proved that neither Christ nor his apostles prescribe any particular form of church government, and that the plea of the divine right of the episcopacy was never heard of in the primitive church."

"No certain form of church government," says Dr. Law, "is prescribed in the word; only general rules laid down for it." Says Neander: "Neither Christ nor his apostles have given any unchangeable law on the subject. Where two or three are gathered together in my name, says Christ, there am I in the midst of them. This coming together in his name, he assures us, alone renders the assembly well pleasing in his sight, whatever be the different forms of government under which his people meet." Indeed, this is the concurrent testimony of all sects and parties, if we except Romanists and high churchmen, whose shameless pretensions meet with deserved rebuke. We say, therefore, in our Discipline, in the language of an article of the Protestant Episcopal Church: "It is not necessary that rites and ceremonies should in all places be the same, or exactly alike; for they have been always different, and may be changed according to the diversity of countries, times, and men's manners, so that nothing be ordained against God's word."

The early Christians were not in a condition to settle upon any definite and unchangeable form. They were in a state of great embarrassment, and governed themselves as circumstances required. When persecution had somewhat ceased, and they found it practicable to be more systematic, they adopted the form with which they were most familiar, viz.: that of the Jewish synagogue, from which they derived the two orders of the ministry, presbyter, or bishop, and deacon. The appointment of presbyters to the episcopal superintendency of cities, and larger districts, was an after consideration, introduced as circumstances seemed to require, and not by divine command. Christians, therefore, of different ages and countries, having the same book for their guide, have considered themselves at liberty to adopt such a system of government as in their judgment was best suited to the ends of the gospel scheme.

Civil governments are divisable into *three* kinds, *monarchical, aristocratical, and republican.* Some are pure, and others mixed. Where supreme power is vested in a *king*, there is a pure monarchy. Where it is vested in a few of the principal men, there is pure aristocracy. Where it is vested in the people, there is a pure democracy. A mixed government is one in which these different forms are more or less blended, so as to constitute a government embracing parts of each.

To be more explicit, the king makes a monarchy; the House of Lords, an aristocracy; the House of Commons, a democracy. The king and House of Lords make a limited monarchy. The king, House of Lords, and House of Commons, make a still more limited monarchy; or a government somewhere midway between a pure monarchy and a pure democracy.

Ecclesiastical governments may also be divided into three kinds, *Episcopal*, *Presbyterian*, and *Independent*. The Episcopal form is that which recognizes bishops as having authority beyond the limits of a single congregation. The Presbyterian is that which governs any number of congregations by presbyteries, synods, and general conventions; or by other legislative and judicial bodies, by whatever name distinguished, which exercise jurisdiction over several congregations. The Independent form is that which lives, and moves, and has its being, in and by a single *congregation*.

The Episcopal form, under one modification or another, extends over the Roman Catholic, Greek, Moravian, Arminian, Lutheran, English and American Episcopal, and Methodist Episcopal Churches; the Presbyterian, over the Scotch and American Presbyterian Churches, with some smaller sects; the Independent, over all others, embracing Congregationalists, Baptists, Unitarians, Universalists, Swedenborgians, &c.

The government of the Roman Catholics is unquestionably a pure *despotism*. The Pope of Rome is its supreme head. In him is vested all power, legislative, judicial, and executive. Hence, he is called "God," "the most holy father," "God's vicegerent," &c. From his decision there is no appeal. To resist him is to resist God, and is punishable to any extent he may please, where the civil authority interposes no obstacle. He may act by person or by deputy. The former being impossible in regard to most of his subjects, he acts by primates, patriarchs, archbishops, bishops, and priests, and thus makes his power felt wheresoever his claims are admitted. In spiritual matters, he *impudently* assumes what the devil assumed to Christ in temporal, viz.: universal jurisdiction.

The powers exercised by his subordinates are thus defined in the Encyclopedia of Religious Knowledge: "An archbishop has jurisdiction over all the bishops of his province, who are his suffragans; summons them every third year to a provincial synod, and the constitution formed by it affects all the churches in the province. In like manner primates and patriarchs have a jurisdiction over all the archbishops, and other bishops, in the kingdoms or nations where they hold their dignified rank. The constitutions of the national councils, convoked by the primate, bind all the churches in that nation; and the constitutions of the patriarchal council, bind all the patriarchate." Thus all Roman Catholics obey their bishops, the bishops the archbishops, the archbishops the primates and patriarchs, and all of them their head, the *Pope*.

The Moravians derive their origin from the Greek Church, which is strictly Episcopal. They, however, allow their bishops much less authority than is exercised by the bishops of the mother Church. They govern themselves by councils, composed of deputies from the congregations, and by inferior bodies, called Conferences. Their councils meet once in seven years, and make laws for the whole church, decide questions of doctrine and discipline, elect bishops, appoint a kind of executive board, called "the Elders' Conference of the Unity," to exercise a general supervision over the whole work, during the interim of the councils. This Conference superintends the missions, watches over the doctrine, moral conduct, and temporal concerns, of the congregations sees that discipline is every where maintained, removes and appoints servants of the unity, and authorizes the bishops to ordain presbyters and deacons, and to consecrate other bishops.

There is another Conference belonging to each congregation, which directs its affairs, and to which bishops and all other ministers, and laymen, are amenable. It is called "the Elders' Conference of the Congregations," and is composed of the minister, who is president, the warden, a *married pair*, who have the spiritual oversight of the married people, a *single* clergyman, who looks after the young men, and a committee of women, whose business it is to care for the interests of their sex. This body is answerable for its proceedings to the Conference of the Unity.

The government of the Lutheran Church is a little singular. In Denmark and Sweden it is strictly *Episcopal*. In Hamburg, Frankfort, and the United States, the ministers together form a body for the purpose of governing the church and examining and ordaining ministers. In the United States the ministers are under the inspection of ecclesiastical overseers, called seniors, or presidents, whose business it is to admonish, to examine applicants for the ministry, grant licenses, *ad interim*, and make reports to the Synods. They are regarded as *primus in paribus* — first among their equals. They have three judicatories in this country, viz.: the vestry of the congregations, the special Conference, and the General Synod. The Conference meets once a year, and is composed exclusively of ministers. Its province is to regulate the spiritual and doctrinal affairs of the church, while the Synod, being composed of an equal number of clerical and lay members, takes a wider range, and admits of no appeal from its decisions. Though this church has no bishops in name, it is, nevertheless, *Episcopal*. Names do not alter the nature of things. Its seniors, or presidents, though not authorized to perform all the offices usually assigned to bishops, give it too high an Episcopal tincture to allow of its receiving any other classification.

The orders of ministers recognized by the American Protestant Episcopal Church are *three* — bishops, priests, and deacons. They hold a triennial convention, in which each diocese is represented by lay and clerical delegates, each having one vote, and the concurrence of both being necessary to an act of the Convention. The bishops of the church form a separate house, having authority to originate measures for the approval of the house of delegates, and having a negative on all acts passed by the said delegates. The canons ordained by this assembly, constitute the laws of the church. It is the highest legislative and judicial tribunal of the denomination, from whose decisions there is no appeal.

Passing the Methodist Episcopal church for more particular consideration hereafter, the *Presbyterians* come next in order. The officers of this denomination are pastors, ruling elders, and deacons. The pastors preach the word, administer the ordinances, and have the general oversight of the church. The *ruling elders* exercise government and discipline in conjunction with the pastors. The *deacons* take care of the poor, and distribute among them such moneys as are raised for that purpose. They also manage other secular matters.

The judicatories of this branch of the general church are *three* — Congregational, Presbyterial, and Synodical. The first, called Church Session, is composed of the minister, or ministers, and ruling elders, of a particular congregation. It is the duty of this body to admonish, try, suspend, and exclude, offenders from the church, as in their judgment the case may require, and appoint delegates to the higher courts.

The Presbyterial Assembly consists of all the ministers, and one ruling elder from each congregation, within a certain district. This body exercises a general supervision over all the churches within its bounds. It has power to receive and try appeals from the Sessions; examine and license candidates for the ministry; decide questions of doctrine and discipline; ordain, settle, and unsettle ministers; divide or unite congregations, at the request of the people; and order whatever pertains to the spiritual concerns of the churches under its care.

The *Synodical* Assembly consists of all the ministers, and one ruling elder from each congregation, within the bounds of several Presbyteries. The Synod receives and tries appeals from the Presbyteries, corrects whatever has been done contrary to order, and adopts such regulations as it judges best for the Presbyteries under its jurisdiction.

There is yet another tribunal above all these, called the "*General Assembly*." It consists of an equal delegation of ministers and elders from each Presbytery; that is, one minister and one elder to every six ministers. To this body belongs the power of consulting, reasoning, and judging in controversies respecting *doctrine* and *discipline*, of putting a stop to schismatical contentions and disputations, and of establishing new Synods where it is deemed necessary. Its decisions are final.

The *Independents* derive their name from this sentiment, to wit: *that every particular congregation of Christians has full power of ecclesiastical jurisdiction over its members, independent of the authority of bishops, presbyteries, or any other ecclesiastical assemblies.* This sentiment being held in common by Congregationalists, Baptists, Universalists, and various other sects, entitles them equally to a place in this general category, though they differ considerably in their *particular* arrangements, and no one of them embraces every principle of the *original* Independents.

Congregationalists denominate themselves "a class of Protestants, who hold that each congregation of Christians, meeting in one place, and united by a solemn covenant, is a complete church, with Christ for its only head, and deriving from him the right of choosing its own officers, to observe the sacraments, to have public worship, and to discipline its own members." Yet they disclaim the name of Independents, because they are pleased to associate in Conferences for mutual counsel, and refer questions of difficulty to each other for advice. But this, it will be perceived, does not alter the nature of their government, since neither these Conferences or councils have any authority, but to advise. Most Independent Churches, however, have no such provision. They attend to their own business, and leave others to do the same.

As it respects the *particular* governments of Independent Churches, little is known beyond their own limits. They all claim to be purely democratic, and in theory they may be so. But nothing is plainer than that in practice they are strongly *aristocratic*. A few individuals control every thing. We do not mention this as an *evil* of itself. As a general thing, matters are much better managed than they would be by the mass. The truth is, there are but few in any church that have interest enough to attend to these things. The number who possess this, in connection with other necessary qualities, is still less. So that the real business is generally done by *the few* in Independent Churches, as well as in Episcopal and Presbyterian, and done better and more efficiently than it would be by a larger number. Hence, they gain, in *spite* of their system, some advantages other systems provide for; but there are others they cannot have under their advisory arrangements, valuable as we acknowledge them to be. These will be enumerated in another chapter.

Now, of all this variety, none claim to be positively and unmistakably Scriptural and right in such a sense that the others are wrong, except the Romanists, and a Romish class of Protestant Episcopalians. Yet these denominations embrace men of piety, talent, and learning, of the highest order, who have every possible means of knowing the truth, and have canvassed the whole subject with profound interest. Their united conviction is, that no definite order of church government is laid down in the Scriptures; and, therefore, though they have a preference for one form instead of another, (perhaps on Scriptural grounds,) they cannot deny the validity of the others. They, therefore, allow their brethren the same indulgence they claim for themselves, viz.: to exercise their own judgment, and adopt such arrangements as they deem best suited to the nature and objects of the gospel, believing it to be practically true, that "the government which is *best administered, is best.*"

CHAPTER II.

THE GOVERNMENT OF THE METHODIST EPISCOPAL CHURCH. ITS OFFICERS AND JUDICATORIES.

THE system of polity recognized by this branch of the Christian church, is peculiar. It differs from every other form of the general class to which it belongs. Originating as it did, it could not well have been otherwise. How far it is sustained by Scripture and reason, will be considered hereafter. Our first object is to exhibit its several parts in their proper character and connection.

Of orders in the ministry, strictly speaking, we recognize two, — *elder* and *deacon*. Our elders are constituted by an election in the Annual Conference, and the laying on of the hands of a bishop and some of the elders. They are authorized to administer baptism and the Lord's supper, perform the office of matrimony, and all parts of divine worship. They may belong to an Annual Conference, and be subject to the appointment of the bishops, if they prefer it, and the Conference deem them suitable; or they may be *local*, and exercise their authority as they have opportunity

Deacons are constituted in the same way, except the imposition of the elders' hands. They are authorized to baptize, and perform the office of matrimony in the absence of the elder, and assist the elder in administering the Lord's supper. What was said of the elders belonging to an An nual Conference, is equally true of deacons. Four years' exercise of the functions of this order in the local ranks, or two as travelling preachers, are indispensable to advancement to the order of elder, except in the case of missionaries, who may be ordained, at the discretion of an Annual Conference, without serving out the regular probation.

Though this delay may sometimes seem unnecessary, considering the sacredness of the ministerial work, and that our ministers are not required to pursue a thorough literary and theological course of study before entering upon their public duties, it is evidently a wise arrangement. Many first served as class leaders, then as exhorters, and afterward as local preachers, before they were graduated to deacon's orders, and two or four years more before they were ordained elders. By this gradual advancement in office, they have steadily matured in knowledge and grace, and are in little danger of falling out with our system, or making many dangerous mistakes in its administration. The two years' probation, preparatory to admission into an Annual Conference, is also a salutary arrangement. It gives the Conference an opportunity to become acquainted with the candidates and their qualifications, and the candidates get a better idea of the work, and can judge more correctly as to the propriety of undertaking it. Two years often satisfies them, or the Conference, or both, that they have missed their calling, and hence they abandon it for something more congenial with their adaptations. If some brethren might be admitted with less delay, experience has demonstrated that two years' probation is none too long, as a general rule.

The regular officers of the church are bishops, presiding elders, preachers in charge, preachers, exhorters, class leaders, stewards, trustees, book-agents, editors, and various secretaries. These are all provided for, and their sphere of action defined in our Book of Discipline. The last three have been added since the organization, to strengthen and extend the departments of labor indicated by their respective titles. In the same spirit, and in obedience to the same prudent policy, others will, no doubt, be originated when the necessity for their services shall be developed.

Our bishops, at the present, are five in number. They are constituted by the election of the General Conference, and the laying on of the hands of three bishops, or, at least, of one bishop and two elders.

Their duties are: 1. To preside in the Conferences, both General and Annual. 2. Fix the appointments of the travelling preachers, under certain limitations and restrictions. 3. Travel through the connection at large. 4. Change, receive, and suspend preachers during the intervals of the Conferences. 5. Oversee the spiritual and temporal business of the whole Church. 6. Ordain bishops, elected and presented to them for the purpose by the General Conference, and elders and deacons elected and presented by the Annual Conferences. And, 7. To decide all proper questions of discipline in the Annual Conferences, subject to an appeal to the General Conference. Hence, to borrow the language of the State, their duties are chiefly executive, but partially judicial. Their business is not to *make law*, but to *keep* and *enforce* it upon others; not to originate new plans, but to carry those into successful effect which have already been adopted. And to these duties they are firmly bound, and for the neglect of any one of them they may be disfranchised by the body which elected them, and to which they are amenable. Indeed, if they cease to travel and attend to their work, without the consent of the General Conference, their episcopal authority is at an end.

This may sound very odd to Episcopalians, who do not understand our views; but it is, nevertheless, true. The doctrine that a man, "once a bishop, is always a bishop," forms no part of our creed; nor that a bishop is a higher order in the ministry than an elder, and, therefore, to be tried only by bishops. In this respect, our bishops stand on a par with the elders. Their distinction is that of *office*, not of *order*. They are regarded as first among their equals, — constituted and endowed by them for convenience sake, to perform important duties.

A *presiding elder* is a sort of *sub-bishop*, more of the diocesan character, as he only travels through a given territory, which he can compass several times a year. He is appointed by a bishop, and required by the discipline to hold Quarterly Conferences in the several societies in his district, — in the absence of a bishop, to preside in the Annual Conferences, — take the charge of all the elders, deacons, preachers, and exhorters within his territory, — and change, receive, and suspend preachers, during the intervals of the Conference, according to our rules. He is to oversee the spiritual and temporal business of the church — promote the cause of missions, Sunday Schools, Bible and tract distribution; decide all questions of law in his Quarterly Conferences, subject to an appeal to the president of the next Annual Conference — take care that every part of the discipline is enforced, and report the state of his district to the bishops.

He may occupy the same field four successive years, and, after an absence of six years, he may return to it if the bishops see cause; or, if they find him unsuited to the work, they may remove him at pleasure. Each Annual Conference is divided into several districts, according to the extent of its territory and the number of its societies, in each of which there is a presiding elder. But these officers, though appointed by the bishops, and are their "helpers" in the superintendency, are strictly responsible for their conduct to the Conference of which they are members.

A *preacher in charge* is one having jurisdiction of a circuit or station. In the absence of the presiding elder he is chairman of the Quarterly Meeting Conference; has the oversight of all the preachers and members, as well as of the spiritual and temporal business connected with his society; appoints and changes the class leaders; receives, tries, and expels members, according to the discipline, and attends to all other matters necessary to the prosperity of the cause, as specified or implied in the catalogue of duties printed for his guidance. He is required to report quarterly to his presiding elder.

The term *preacher* indicates, in our dialect, one who has a license to preach. Elders and deacons are necessarily preachers, but all preachers are not elders or deacons. We have many preachers, both travelling and local, who are not ordained, and, of course, not represented by the term elder, or deacon. They are sometimes placed in charge, as are deacons; but more experience, and fuller ministerial endowments, are desirable. They receive their license from a Quarterly Conference, and are amenable to it for their conduct, as are all local preachers, but have the right of an appeal to the Annual Conference. Travelling preachers, in full connection, whether elders or deacons, are amenable to the Annual Conference to which they belong. But a superannuated preacher, living out of the bounds of his own Conference, being accused, may be held to trial in the Conference within whose bounds he resides, and be acquitted, located, suspended, or expelled, in the same manner as if he were a member of said Conference. But in all cases of condemnation, he may appeal to the General Conference.

An *exhorter* is one who, in consideration of his possessing gifts and graces adapting him to the work, is licensed to hold meetings, as he may have opportunity, and exhort the people. Where there is a scarcity of ministers, or a call for more meetings than the ministry can attend, this office is very useful. Many who are not qualified to preach, and who, were they to attempt it, would make a lamentable failure, may do important service to the cause in this way. The office designates them, as, in the judgment of the church, the most suitable to take the lead of conference meetings, in prayer and exhortation; and it often gives them confidence to do what they would not dare to undertake without it, if, indeed, it would be proper. It has been a very useful office, furnishing a sort of probation to the ministry, and preparing the way for the more efficient discharge of its functions. But we fear it is not now as useful as it might be made. The gift of exhortation should be encouraged in the church as well as the gift of prayer, and is hardly less important to success. The warm out-speaking of the heart, in fervent expostulation and warning, is often more profitable than explanatory preaching. The license is first given by a preacher in charge, on the recommendation of the class to which the candidate belongs, or the leaders' meeting, but is renewed annually by the vote of the Quarterly Conference.

Class leaders are church officers of the highest importance. As we divide the whole country into Conferences, and the Conferences into districts, and the districts into circuits and stations, so we divide the circuits and stations into classes, and place them under the supervision of men we denominate *leaders*, whose duty it is to see each member of his class weekly, and, by religious counsel and advice, help them to fight the good fight of faith. All the members of the church being thus classified, if the leaders are true to their obligations, they will be useful, and always ready to see the preacher, and give him a strict account of each one. Thus, by the aid of these functionaries, whom Southey compares to non-commissioned officers in the army, the preacher is enabled to learn the condition of his church at once, though a stranger, and exercise pastoral care that would be utterly impracticable without them. They are often, as this same writer humorously remarks, "tax-gatherers," and take weekly collections, and pay them to the stewards; in view of which he represents our "spiritual policy" as "perfect." This sounds better coming from an enemy than from a friend. However, the classes usually consist of from twelve to thirty persons, located contiguously to each other and to the place of meeting, if practicable, and assemble once a week, either in a class-room prepared for the purpose, or in private houses, and the presence or absence of each is noted in a book. If any are sick, or fail to attend for other cause, the leader is expected to visit them, and advise, admonish, encourage and pray with them, as their circumstances require. Bishops Coke and Asbury give the office its proper character. They say: "The revival of the work of God does, perhaps, depend as much upon *the whole body of the leaders as it does upon the whole body of the preachers.* We have almost constantly observed, that when a leader is dull, or careless, or inactive, the class is, in general, languid; but, on the contrary, when the leader is much alive to God, and faithful in his office, the class is also, in general, lively and spiritual. Every leader is, in *some degree*, a gospel minister. Our leaders, under God, are the sinews of our society, and our revivals will ever, in a great measure, rise or fall with them."

With this view of the office, who can fail to see its admirable adaptation to our itinerant system? It is an indispensable *adjunct*, without which the system would be essentially defective. And, exercised with fidelity, it furnishes a complete refutation of some of the strongest objections urged against our itinerancy; for, after all, though our ministry is itinerant, we have a *settled pastorate.*

But leaders should be men of *sound, fervent, and enlightened piety.* Without this sacred endowment, they cannot properly appreciate their high responsibilities, or discharge them successfully. They may, indeed, go through with the form, but, alas! it will be a spiritless operation. They must feel the "blessedness," before they can speak of it with becoming interest and power. And, besides, they are to be *examples* to their flock, — not only to teach and exhort, but to furnish the model in their own experience and practice, both in religious meetings and before the world. We have been mortified and afflicted many times by the bad example of class leaders in our prayer meetings and love feasts; and, indeed, on other occasions. If *these* functionaries neglect their duty, what may we expect of their class members. Piety, profound, burning piety, is indispensable to their efficiency.

Stewards are another class of officers connected with each circuit and station, whose principal business is to provide the elements for the Lord's Supper, and attend to the finances of the church, particularly the current expenses, and contributions for the poor. But, as they are supposed to be men of solid piety and sound judgment, and as their pecuniary duties require them to be considerably acquainted in the society, they are a sort of advisory committee to the preachers, to inform them of cases of sickness and disorderly conduct, to suggest what they think wrong in them, and counsel them when asked in reference to various questions of administration. They are nominated by the preacher in charge, and elected by the Quarterly Conference, to which body they are accountable for the faithful performance of their duties. The number connected with each charge varies from three to seven, according to the difficulties of the business, and the supply of suitable candidates.

Trustees are a useful class of local officers, to whom is entrusted our church property, particularly our meeting-houses and parsonages. They generally number from *five* to *nine*, and are incorporated with full powers to hold a certain amount of property for the use of the church to which they belong, according to our discipline and usages. They are responsible to the Quarterly Conference, and are required to make an annual report of their doings. They are bound, also, by the laws of the State where they live, to hold whatever property is committed to them, agreeably to the stipulations of the trust. One of these is, and always ought to be, that our meeting-houses and parsonages shall be for ever open to the ministers of our church duly appointed to occupy them. Otherwise, a board of trustees might dismiss their preachers, and appropriate the property to the support of opposing doctrines and measures, leaving the donors to seek accommodation elsewhere. This will not do. The founder of Methodism had sagacity enough to see, that to invest trustees with discretionary control of our meeting-houses, would break down the itinerancy at once. And he provided against so fatal a contingency by restricting their power, and requiring them to hold our pulpits open to the men and for the purposes for which they were made. Hence, if our deeds are properly drawn, and trustees undertake to divert our property to other uses, the civil courts will soon set them right on a general principle of law recognized in all civilized countries, viz., that *trust property must be holden for the purposes, and to the uses, for which it was given.* The experiments of recreant trustees, and the action of the courts, both in Europe and America, have placed this matter in its true light, and given us entire confidence in the inalienableness of our pulpits, so long as the church wishes to occupy them according to the design of their construction.

This arrangement has occasioned us some little trouble. Our opponents, who have never lacked a disposition to complain of us, have made it the occasion of saying and writing many foolish things to our disadvantage. For instance, they have published, for the thousandth time, probably, that the bishops *own all our meeting-houses*, and can do with them as they please. There are tens of thousands in New England who believe this, and will, probably, carry the belief with them to their graves. They have read it in their religious papers, and heard it from the pulpit and in private, and "it *must* be true." They look upon our bishops as enormous *church-mongers*, having and holding any quantity of meeting-houses, for which they never paid a cent, and which they may sell at pleasure. Our denial of it has only given fresh occasion for a re-publication of the old falsehood, and, therefore, of fuller assurance of its truth, and we see no way to correct the evil. However, the influence of it is not so injurious as formerly. New England ministers and churches have learnt something by experience. When they had every thing their own way, and Church and State were nearly allied, their mode of settling meeting-houses did well enough. But when the absurdities of their theology came under investigation, and drove some into Unitarianism, and others into Universalism; and their societies were divided, and they lost several hundreds of their meeting-houses, and many of their parsonages and parish funds, they began to wake up to the idea that people sometimes change their opinions, and that property holden subject to their will, may be used for a very different purpose to-morrow than what is contemplated to-day. The result was the adoption of a principle similar to our own; since which much less complaint has been heard. They now build meeting-houses for a church or society, properly described and recognized, and define the *use and purposes* to which they are to be applied, as they should do, and find it the more peaceable and economical way.

With slight variations to accommodate it to State laws, our disciplinary deed is a very safe instrument. In building free houses, for which it was drawn, it will need very little alteration in any place. In building proprietors' houses, brethren sometimes make a different provision for the appointment of trustees, but seldom in securing the use of the pulpit to the church. This is indispensable. If those who propose to build will not so frame their deeds as to make this matter sure, our better course is to stand aloof, and have nothing to do with it. Though it may commence in peace, it will end in war, and in the subversion of the cause it is intended to promote. The few instances in which societies have attempted to *mend* Methodism in this respect, ought to be a sufficient warning to all who come after, that such attempts are disastrous, both to the owners of the pews and those who occupy them. Every meeting-house should be secured to one object or another. If it be designed for the *Baptists*, let it be so stated in the deed. Their proper title, as it is known in law, should be given. If it is for our church in any particular place, let it be so stated, and that it is to be held for ever for the worship of God, according to the discipline and usages of the Methodist *Episcopal* Church. Then there will be no chance for misunderstanding; and if trustees should attempt to divert it, it will not be difficult to restrain them.

But let it be observed, this does not imply *ownership* in the bishops or Conferences. Neither can *sell* the house, or *let* it for any other purpose, nor indeed for this; but they can claim to *use* it according to our rules. If the house be free, the ownership lies with the church which erected it; but still, only as a *house of worship*. They cannot *sell it* any more than the trustees. They have entered into legal covenant with each other, to appropriate so much money to build a house for this purpose. If any get tired of it he can adopt another mode, but he cannot appropriate the house to its maintenance. Where individuals have covenanted to erect a house, and take the amount of their subscription in a pew or in pews, the case is a little different. But the *fee* of the house is no more in the pewholders than it is in the contributors where the house is free. They cannot sell it, or pervert it to any other purpose. But they may *occupy the pews* of which they have deeds, or they may *rent*, or *sell* them, or make them *free;* but they can do neither or any thing else, only in subordination to the objects agreed upon in the outset, and incorporated into the deed. This arrangement protects minorities against the perversion of their money to uses they never would agree to, prevents them and their ministers from being turned out of doors, and obviates contention, by withholding from disaffected and apostate individuals all ground of hope, that, by any stratagem, they can alienate the property and employ it to suit their new, and perhaps impious ends. If this is not both right and expedient we greatly mistake. But, as before stated, other sects have come to do the same thing

Our Book Agents are four in number; two at New York, and two at Cincinnati, Ohio, having equal authority, all appointed by the General Conference. They have our denominational book business in charge, embracing the publication of Sabbath School, and general books and tracts, and our various periodicals. They are, of course, responsible to the body from which they received their appointment; which body is represented, during the intervals of its sessions, by a large and respectable Book Committee, who supervise their doings, and decide all questions necessary to the security and success of the concern.

The *Editors* of our books and periodicals are also appointed by the General Conference, and are responsible to that body for their official conduct. They, too, come under the supervision of the Book Committee, who have power to suspend them, as well as the agents, if they judge it necessary for the interests of the church and the concern.

Besides these officers, we have three Corresponding Secretaries connected with our Missionary operations, who give their whole time to raising funds, etc., under the direction of the Missionary Board. Our Church Extension Society has also a Corresponding Secretary and an Assistant, who look after its operations in connection with its Managers. The Freedman's Aid Society, too, which aims to assist and elevate the millions of our colored people who have lately emerged from slavery, has a Corresponding Secretary looking after its operations. These officers are all elected by the General Conference, as are the Boards of the first two societies named, embracing an equal number of ministers and laymen. They are to their respective interests what the Editor of our Sabbath School Department is to the Sabbath School interests; with this difference, he is *less confined*, and may render important service in extending the kingdom of Christ in the earth.

Thus our church is marshalled: the secretary looking after the heathen, — the Sabbath School editor after the children, — the agents, and other editors, after both, in connection with the general intelligence, defence, and purity of the whole church, — the trustees taking care of our churches and parsonages, — the stewards attending to our current expenses, — the leaders to the spiritual welfare of their classes, — the preachers watching over their flocks, — the presiding elders superintending both preachers and people in their districts, with all the other interests of the cause,— and the bishops overseeing the whole.

But the reader will have an imperfect view of our government, however closely he may study this picture, unless he looks also at our *judicatories*. There are two points to be considered in criticizing a system of government, viz., its *safety* and *efficiency*. A government may be so safe,— that is, so guarded, — as not to be efficient; or it may be so efficient and powerful, as not to be safe. The best system is that in which the safety and efficiency are about equally balanced. Power too diffused is useless; too condensed it is dangerous. It is therefore that communities, having the right of self-government, clothe an individual, or a small number of individuals, with all their own executive and judicial power. This renders the authority of the whole community available to meet every emergency, and hence promotes security. But lest the individual, or individuals, thus endowed should prove recreant, and oppress their constituents, they limit their authority, and hold certain checks upon them for their own safety. Thus the Crown of England is limited by the Houses of Lords and Commons, and the President of the United States by the Constitution and Congress.

From what has been said, it will be perceived that the offices recognized in the Methodist Episcopal Church involve considerable authority. A brief reference to our judicatories will show, in part, how that authority is guarded.

The highest is that of the General Conference. This body meets once in four years, and is composed of one delegate for every forty-five members of each Annual Conference. Though it is presided over by the bishops, it is *above* them, and makes and unmakes them, under the provisions of its own constitution, which is not easily altered. It is the only rule-making, or legislative body, of the church, and ordains such alterations in our discipline, from time to time, as experience shows to be necessary. But it is not without limit. 1. It cannot revoke or alter any of our articles of religion, or establish any new standard of doctrine; nor is there any power in the church to do it. 2. It cannot allow of more than one representative to every fourteen members of each Annual Conference, nor less than one to every thirty, except in case of a fraction of two-thirds of the number fixed as the ratio of representation, when the Conferences shall be entitled to an additional delegate, and except, too, that no Conference, however small, shall be deprived of the privilege of one delegate. 3. It cannot destroy our episcopacy, nor the plan of its general superintendency. 4. Nor can it revoke or change our general rules. 5. Nor do away the privileges of our ministers or preachers of trial by a committee, and of an appeal; or the privileges of our members of trial before the society, or by a committee, and of an appeal. 6 It is also limited in the appropriation of the produce of the Book Concern and Chartered Fund; But any of these restrictions, *except the first*, may be modified by a vote of two-thirds of the General Conference, provided it be recommended or concurred in by three-fourths of all the members of the several Annual Conferences, who shall be present when the subject is considered in their respective Conferences, and vote.

This is also a *judicial* body. It takes original cognizance of the bishops, and is authorized to expel them for improper conduct, and receives and settles appeals from their decision on law questions, and from the action of the Annual Conferences, in the trial and conviction of any of their members. Besides, it reviews the records of the said Conferences, and proscribes any action it shall deem unconstitutional.

It is, indeed, the great wheel of the connection, and gives motion, direction and stability to all the others. Considering that it appoints and controls the bishops, and our other general functionaries, it may be said to possess important executive powers also. But its powers are none too extended to be effective, or too loosely guarded to be safe.

Our Annual Conferences come next in order. These assemble, as their title indicates, every year, and are composed of all the travelling preachers who are in full connection within certain geographical limits. The number of these bodies is, at present, eighty, and in rights, privileges, and duties they all stand on a par, and are subject to the same regulations, and to the superintendency of the same bishops. They have no legislative authority whatever. Their official work is judicial and executive. It is indicated by the following inquiries, which are introduced by the president as here recorded. 1. What preachers are admitted on trial? 2. Who remain on trial? Upon this question being asked, the list of those who have been on trial one year or more (for sometimes they are kept on trial three or four years) is called, and their character and prospects are reported by their presiding elder, and others; and if they are succeeding, they are continued; if not, they are dropped. 3. Who are admitted into full connection? 4. Who are the deacons? 5. Who have been elected and ordained elders this year? 6. Who have located this year? Every travelling preacher can locate, and thus leave the Conference when he pleases. 7. Who are the supernumeraries? That is, who are so far worn out in the itinerant work, as to be unable to do full service? 8. Who are the superannuated preachers? or, the preachers who are so infirm as to be unable to preach at all. 9. Who have been expelled from the connection this year? 10. Are all the preachers blameless in life and conversation? To answer this intelligently, a thorough examination of each member is had in the presence of the Conference. 11. Who have died this year? 12. What numbers are in society? This brings out a numerical report from all the preachers in charge, which answers the question. 13. What amounts are necessary for the support of superannuated preachers, and the widows and orphans of preachers, and to make up the deficiencies of those who have not obtained their regular allowance on the circuits? This involves the report of our estimated salaries, and the amount paid on them. 14. What has been collected on the foregoing amounts, and how has it been applied? This brings out our stewards' reports, and the amount of our collections in each society for these objects. 15. What has been contributed for the support of missions, &c., &c.? This secures a report of all our benevolent operations. 16. Where are the preachers stationed this year? This is answered by the bishop, after all the other business is done. 17. Where and when shall our next Conference be held?

The place is settled by the Conference, — the time by the president.

To these items of regular business the Conferences frequently add others, by mutual consent. Thus, they discuss temperance, peace, moral reform, slavery, and other great questions, and send forth their manifestos to the world, as they judge right and expedient.

In their judicial capacity, they receive and try complaints preferred against any of their members, and reprove, suspend, and expel them, as the nature of the case requires. They also try appeals, made by local preachers, from the decision of Quarterly Conferences by which they have been impeached. And it is proper to observe that the members of the Conference are liable to arraignment, not only on moral and religious grounds, but on account of their administration of discipline; and that, too, by any member who may be aggrieved with their conduct.

Quarterly Conferences are holden quarterly by the presiding elders in each circuit or station in their respective districts. They are composed of all the travelling and local preachers, exhorters, stewards, and leaders of the circuit, also trustees, and the first Sunday School superintendent. They have the exclusive authority to license men to preach, but are not permitted to do so unless they come recommended by the society to which they belong, or by a leaders' meeting. Then, after due examination on the subjects of doctrines and discipline, they can give the license, if they see cause, and recommend a local preacher to the Annual Conference, to be ordained or admitted to the travelling connection, or both.

They also receive and try complaints preferred against local preachers, and appeals of laymen from the action of a society by which they have been impeached. Besides, they appoint the stewards, and hold them to account for their doings, have an oversight of the trustees and Sabbath Schools, and, indeed, of all the interests of the society.

To these we may add what are known by the name of *Leaders'* or *Board Meetings*, usually composed of the preacher in charge and the leaders and stewards of his society. These are held frequently, and take cognizance of every thing pertaining to the temporal and spiritual interests of the society with which they are connected. And, generally, as is this body, so is the society. Being usually composed of a number of the most intelligent and influential men of the church, it operates as a balance wheel, and regulates the whole body. Stewards and trustees hold occasional meetings by themselves, but these are only for the more convenient performance of their respective duties.

Thus, our highest officers are under law, and our law-makers under a constitution they may not infringe. Each man is clothed with power equal to the work assigned him; but is bound to exercise it by specific rules, and with reference to a given purpose, and may be called to a strict account if he does not. But as the peculiar advantages of this system are to be considered in another place, we will not enlarge upon the subject here.

CHAPTER III.

METHODIST EPISCOPACY, BOTH SCRIPTURAL AND WESLEYAN.

FROM the two preceding chapters, the uninitiated will be able to form something of a correct idea of our government, and the points of difference between it and the other systems. He will, therefore, be able to appreciate the objections and arguments which have been urged against particular parts of it, and what we are about to say in its defence. Among the most ancient objections, and one which is quite formidable in certain communities, is, that our episcopacy *is not valid;* in other words, that our bishops are *no bishops*, and consequently we have *no valid ministry or church.* The argument in support of this sweeping allegation is, in substance, as follows: To be a scriptural bishop, one must have received his ordination in a direct and uninterrupted line of succession from the apostles: but Methodist bishops have not thus received their ordination; therefore, Methodist bishops are not scriptural bishops.

This argument, it will be perceived, is based upon the *fiction* of uninterrupted succession, which is too *fanciful* to merit sober treatment. When we consider the divisions that early occurred in the church; that various and conflicting claims to supremacy were pressed to the greatest extremes; that during the *Dark Ages*, embracing more than a thousand years, the church was sunk in the deepest ignorance and corruption, so that it is exceedingly doubtful whether there was a valid bishop on earth, it is manifest that such a *succession* could not have been maintained without one continued *miracle*. But could it be proved, it would not establish its validity, since many of the popes, each of whom is assumed to be a link in the chain, are known to have been so basely profligate, and utterly unworthy of the titles they bore, that, had they received a genuine ordination, they were not in a condition to transmit it to others. This is not the writer's opinion, only; it is the sentiments of wise and pious Episcopalians, who have something more than a mere succession to rely on for their authority.

Bishop Hoadly says, "I am fully satisfied that, till a consummate stupidity can be happily established and universally spread over the land, there is nothing that tends so much to destroy all due respect to the clergy, as the demand of more than can be due them; and nothing has so effectually thrown contempt upon a regular succession of the ministry, as the calling no succession regular but what was uninterrupted; and the making the eternal salvation of Christians to depend upon that uninterrupted succession, of which the most learned must have the *least* assurance, and the unlearned can have *no notion, but through ignorance and credulity*." Eusebius was one of the earliest historians, and in attempting to trace the succession, declared it to be "a matter of much doubt, — that he had but slight authority to depend on respecting the definite fields of the apostles, if they had any, and that was *mere report*." Who their successors were, he says, it "is no easy thing to tell." Hence, says Bishop Stillingfleet, "If the successors of the apostles by the confession of Eusebius are not certainly to be discovered, then what becomes of that unquestionable line of succession of the bishops of the several churches, and the large diagrams made of the apostolical churches, with every one's name set down in his order?" Other bishops have seen the folly of these pretensions, and repudiated them, but we have not room to quote their words. Nor is it necessary. The facts that the least deviation is allowed to make a breach in the imaginary chain; that there have been two, and even three popes at the same time, excommunicating and denouncing each other, — that some of them were officially declared to be schismatics, Arians, *magicians*, and *heretics*, and that the succession, if there be any such thing, has come down through these very men, seems to be sufficient to brand it as a miserable fabrication.

And still there are other objections to it, not less formidable. It attributes a virtue to mere ceremonies, that they do not possess. "Christianity has its rights, simple, and hallowed, but teaches them with a latitude, in respect to their mode, which shows that their spirit, not their letter, constitutes their importance. The genius of Christianity is spiritual, not formal. This tenacity for modes destroys its spirituality; it is the source of Puseyism, and the infinite corruptions of Popery. The doctrine of a special mysterious virtue inherent in the acts of a man, because of a specific mode of appointment to his office, is but a step from the doctrine that he imparts a special virtue to the sacraments, by which, independently of the moral temper of the recipient, they save his soul; a religion of forms without morals — transubstantiation — the adoration of the host — implicit reliance on the mediation of the priest — and numerous other delusions follow in the train." — *Stevens' Church Polity, p.* 74.

To say nothing of the uncharitableness of a doctrine that unchurches the Christian world, and leaves them to hope only in the uncovenanted mercies of God, our final remark is, that it is not supported by one single passage of Scripture.

which is equivalent to the most positive declaration against it. If the doctrine be true and important, as assumed, surely there is nothing Christ and the apostles would have taught sooner, or more explicitly. It is, therefore, false, or those teachers sent from God were recreant to their high calling.

We accord with a writer in the Edinburg Review, who says: "Whether we consider the palpable absurdity of this doctrine, its utter destitution of historical evidence, or the outrage it implies on all Christian charity, it is equally revolting. The arguments against it are infinite; the evidence for it absolutely nothing. It rests not upon *one* doubtful assumption, but upon *fifty*. First, the very basis upon which it rests — the claim of episcopacy itself to be of apostolic origin — has been most fiercely disputed by men of equal erudition and acuteness, and, so far as can be judged, of equal integrity and piety.

"Again, who can certify that this gift has been incorruptibly transmitted through the impurities, heresies and ignorance of the Dark Ages? Is there nothing that can invalidate orders? The chances are infinite that there have been flaws somewhere or other in the long chain of succession; and as no one knows where the fatal breach may have been, it is sufficient to spread universal panic through the whole church. What bishop can be sure that he and his predecessors in the same line, have always been duly consecrated? or what presbyter, that he was ordained by a bishop who had a right to ordain? But the difficulties do not end here. It is asked, how a man, who is no true Christian, can be a Christian minister? how he, who is not even a disciple of Christ, can be a genuine successor of the apostles?"

How Episcopalians can make up their minds to criticize their more successful neighbors, on a point upon which they are so much exposed themselves, is unaccountable. Yet they do it, and urge their silly pretensions with an air of self-security that is hardly paralleled. Such an example of boasting weakness is not upon record, unless it may be found in some of the adventures of the knight of La Mancha, in the assumption of the prince of darkness when he attempted to purchase the homage of Christ, or in the lordly dictation of the maniac, when he fancies himself some extraordinary personage. If we were in their confidence, we should suggest that they "examine themselves." When they can satisfy the world that a *lay woman* is the legitimate *head of the church*, and explain the power of national lines to *extinguish* episcopal orders; in other words, how their bishops are out of the succession the minute they touch English soil, and enlighten the community on other similar questions, their pretensions will appear to better advantage.

The term *bishop*, (*episkopos*,) signifies an overseer, or one who has the direction of any thing. It is employed in the Scriptures to designate pastors of churches; as in Acts xx. 28, and several other places. Christ is called the "*Bishop* of our souls." As used by the apostles, in reference to pastors, it signifies the same as *presbyter* or *elder*, and the terms are applied to the same men, and the same office. When St. Paul came to Miletus, "he sent to Ephesus and called the elders (*presbuteroi*) of the church, and charged them, Take heed to all the flock, over the which the Holy Ghost hath made you overseers," (*episkopous.*) St. Peter says, "The elders, (*presbuterous*,) which are among you, I exhort, feed the flock of God which is among you, taking the *oversight* (*episkopountes*) thereof. And says Paul to Titus, "For this cause I left thee in Crete, that thou should set in order the things that are wanting, and ordain elders, (*presbuterous*,) in every city," provided he should find any suitable. "For," says he, ' a *bishop* (*episkopon*) must be blameless," &c., showing that bishop and elder mean the same thing.

The testimony of the fathers sustains this view of the subject beyond a doubt. They knew no difference in the meaning of the terms. Clement, Polycarp, Justin Martyr, Ireneas, and others, used the terms interchangeably, and avowed this to be their legitimate import. Those who wish to consult them further are referred to *Bang's Original Church*, and *Coleman's Primitive Church.*

Neale says of the reformers, under King Edward, that they "believed but two orders of church men in Scripture, bishops and deacons; and, consequently, that bishops and priests were but different ranks or degrees of the same order." Therefore, "they gave the right hand of fellowship to foreign churches, and to ministers who had not been ordained by bishops." In a work prepared by Cranmer, Latimer, and eight other bishops, at the command of the King, it is affirmed, that in the New Testament, there is no mention made of any degrees or orders, but only of deacons and of priests, or bishops." This was the prevailing doctrine, then, but times and plans have altered. In a work called "The Necessary Erudition of a Christian Man," approved by parliament in 1715, the King says, in his preface, "that priests [or presbyters] and bishops are, by God's law, one and the same, and that the powers of *ordination* and excommunication belong equally to both." Lord King, Archbishop Usher, Bishop Stillingfleet, and others, attest to the same, particularly that the power of *ordination* lays with the presbyters, and that they did ordain.

Stillingfleet says, "In the primitive church the presbyters either did or might *ordain* others to the same authority with themselves; because the intrinsical power of order is equal in them, and in those who were afterward governors over presbyters. And the allocation of orders doth come from the power of order, and not merely from the power of jurisdiction. It being likewise fully acknowledged by the schoolmen that bishops are not superior to presbyters as to the power of order."

"The terms bishop and presbyter," says Dr. Mason, "in their application to the first class of officers, are perfectly convertible; the one pointing out the very same class of ruler with the other, is as evident as the sun shining, in his strength. Timothy was instructed by the apostle Paul in the qualities which were to be required in those who desired the office of a bishop. Paul and Barnabas ordained presbyters in every church which they had founded. Titus is directed to ordain, in every city, presbyters who are to be blameless, the husband of one wife. And the reason of so strict a scrutiny into character is thus stated, for "a bishop must be blameless." If this does not identify the bishop with the presbyter, in the name of common sense what can do it? Suppose a law, pointing out the qualifications of a sheriff, were to say, "A sheriff must be a man of pure character, of great activity, and resolute spirit; for it is highly necessary that a governor be of unspotted reputation," &c., the bench and the bar would be rather puzzled for a construction, and would be compelled to conclude either that something had been left out in transcribing the law, or that governor and sheriff meant the same sort of officer; or that their honors, the legislature, had taken leave of their senses.

Whence, then, it may be asked, originated the distinction between bishops and elders? Writers have traced it to various sources. It seems to us to have arisen, at first, from different causes. One, probably, was a manifest distinction in the endowments and circumstances that existed among them. The probability is, that they possessed the same diversity of talent and adaptation, that is observed among spiritual and holy ministers of the present age. Some were peculiarly adapted to be "apostles, some prophets, some evangelists, and some pastors and teachers." And all were necessary "for the perfecting of the saints, for the work of the ministry, for the edifying of the body of Christ."

Another cause was the necessity of a president, superintendent, or leader, which all associations of equals feel, especially when they meet in conventions, and undertake great achievements, which require powerful executive skill, and energy. It was a dictate of wisdom then, as now, to place some one or more in command, to direct the movements of the enterprise, and see that all parts of the plan were carried into successful operation. This might have been done by lot, or by vote, or by common consent. It sometimes happens that one is providentially so distinguished, that a formal appointment from the body would seem almost ridiculous. The apostles, for instance, would have shown themselves wanting had they attempted to elect Christ to be their leader, because he manifestly held that relation from higher authority. And the infant churches, collected and organized by St. Paul, would have indicated a want of proper respect for him, had they assumed to be equal with him, and to assign him his field of labor and jurisdiction. He had begotten them through the gospel. Subsequently, ambition and the love of power, contributed, no doubt, to elevate the leading spirits of the church, to the depression of others. And as piety declined, and the church became entangled with the state, they were enabled to assume and maintain unwarrantable authority; and hence arose the *prelatical episcopacy*, of which the world has had so much reason to complain.

If one is the pastor of a flock, and watches, guides, and

feeds it with the bread of life, he is, scripturally, a bishop, whether his flock consist of ten or ten thousand,—whether it be limited to a single village, or scattered over a continent. Mr. Wesley became convinced of this, more than thirty years before he ordained any one, by reading Lord King's Account of the Primitive Church, when the authority of prelatical episcopacy stood in a different light with him from what it did before. Still he reverenced it, and would not interfere with its prerogatives any further than the interests of souls required. But, having been ordained first a deacon, and then an elder, he regarded himself a bishop in the proper sense of the word. He was an elder, not only by ordination, but by virtue of his age and experience, to which the term originally refers. And he was a bishop, not merely by virtue of the same ordination, but by reason of having an important charge of souls. Thousands, yea, tens of thousands, looked to him for spiritual direction. Under God, he was their father. He had called them by the gospel, and they had run after him, and looked to him for watch-care and guidance. They knew no other, nor would many of them follow any other. Had he forsaken them, they would, probably, have been scattered to the winds. He could not do it without being recreant to the high trusts Providence had imposed upon him. To have turned them over to the English Church would have been no better than placing a living child in the bosom of a dead mother, and in many cases it would have been more like casting lambs into a den of wolves. The church was dead, and not in a condition to appreciate the views and operations of Mr. Wesley, or to sympathize with his children. Its bishops would not ordain his preachers, nor its priests administer the sacraments to his numerous people. Indeed, they repelled them from the Lord's table for no other reason than that they were qualified to approach it properly. They repelled him, also, and otherwise treated him so unkindly, that we have wondered at his patience.

We say, therefore, that he was a bishop, not only in ministerial order, but in jurisdiction, — a bishop of two hemispheres, made such by Almighty God, who called him, by the Holy Ghost, to the office and work of the ministry, and called hundreds and thousands to follow him as their spiritual guide. Hence he was under obligation to watch over these souls, and supply them with the means of grace to the extent of his ability. Not only to send them pastors and teachers, bnt such as were endowed to administer the whole gospel, its sacraments as well as its precepts and promises. This he tried to do for many years, without exercising the ordaining prerogative which he believed to be vested in himself, as much as in any other man in England, *jure divino*, to avoid creating unneccessary prejudice, and keep the farthest possible distance from schism. But his followers, multiplying by the thousand, both in Europe and America, and becoming clamorous for the ordinances, especially in this country, he submitted to the pressing necessity, and, with the aid of Mr. Creighton and Dr. Coke, both presbyters of the Church of England, he ordained Thomas Vasey and Richard Whatcoat elders or presbyters, and then he ordained Dr. Coke superintendent of the Methodist societies in America.

That he did his duty, exercised and conferred all the authority legitimately involved in the two offices, we cannot doubt. 1. Because he and his associates were regular presbyters, and therefore authorized to ordain others, as we have already shown. 2. Many thousands of his followers were destitute of the ordinances. Their own preachers were not authorized to administer them, and of others there were few.

The Episcopal Church had been about broken up by the Revolution, and they were, at that very moment, seeking episcopal prerogatives from English bishops. The Methodist societies were also getting divided on this very subject. They had urged Mr. Wesley so long to send them ordained ministers, some were determined to wait no longer. How could he have done less than he did, and been true to his God and his followers ? 3. But using the term bishop, as a mark of official distinction and jurisdiction, Mr. Wesley, in the providence of God, was the only bishop of the Methodist societies, and the only man on earth that was qualified to provide them with the ordinances. What had the prelates and priests of the English Church done for them, but to persecute and despise them ? What had they done for their leader, but to hinder him in his work ? What right had they to ordain Methodist superintendents and elders for America ? Mr. Wesley was their acknowledged leader, and was endowed to do all for them that was necessary, as really as Moses was the leader of the Israelites from bondage. Not to construct and organize them, merely, but to furnish them with all the means of grace. 4. But these prelates would do nothing, had they been authorized. Mr. Wesley had desired them to ordain some of his preachers for the home service, but they would not. He knew how difficult the Episcopalians of this country found it to get a bishop ordained, and that if he asked for the ordination of a man of his selection to the superintendency of American Methodism, he should only be delayed and spurned. Besides, he knew this country was free from English law, and open to him as to any other man. 5. He was earnestly solicited by his followers to exercise his right to ordain, and assured that nothing short of this could hold his societies together. What could he have asked more ? Had he still resisted their wishes, he would have shown himself more careful of English *ceremonies* than of American *souls*. It would have been a stain upon his theological and religious character to all generations.

But some will say, supposing it to be true that presbyters are authorized to ordain presbyters, it does not justify Mr. Wesley in ordaining Dr. Coke a bishop, thus making him superior in office to himself. Episcopalians think it quite laughable; and others, to avoid the reproach, deny that he ordained Dr. Coke a *bishop*. But we see no difficulty in the case. Is it an uncommon thing for men to elevate others above themselves, and induct them into their office by appropriate ceremonies? The President of the United States is a very high officer, yet he is chosen by men, most of whom never enjoyed any higher office than that of a *voter*. Indeed, most offices in a free country, are conferred by those who are far below them, and may never rise so high as to share their honor.

But how does it appear that Mr. Wesley made an officer superior to himself? Dr. Coke was a presbyter of the Church of England when the ceremony commenced. In this respect he stood on a par with Wesley, and was as well qualified to ordain. But observe, Mr. Wesley does not pretend to elevate Dr. Coke to a *higher order in the ministry*. He denies that there is any higher. He ordained him rather to an *office*, — the office of *bishop or superintendent* of the Methodist societies in America, — and authorized him to ordain elders, deacons, and other superintendents. He did not make him an officer *superior* to himself, but conferred on him a part of his own great authority, in a part of his own parish, "the world," still holding him, and the people placed under his episcopal watch-care, in subordination to himself. In other words, he appointed him to go and do in America, what his other duties would not allow himself to do, still being the father and governor of the whole connection, as before. And the propriety of his ordaining Dr. Coke, instead of Dr. Coke ordaining him, is seen in the fact that he was the acknowledged *father* of the people to be provided for, whereas Dr. Coke was but a *younger brother*. And further, he had long been desired by them to provide for their necessities in this respect.

The letter he gave Dr. Coke, to introduce him to his new field, explains his views and the grounds of his authority in the clearest manner. It is as follows: —

"BRISTOL, *September* 10, 1784.

"TO DR. COKE, MR. ASBURY, AND OUR BRETHREN IN NORTH AMERICA.

"By a very uncommon train of providences, many of the provinces of North America are totally disjoined from their mother country, and erected into independent States. The English Government has no authority over them, either civil or ecclesiastical, any more than over the States of Holland. A civil authority is exercised over them, partly by the Congress, and partly by the Provincial Assemblies. But no one either exercises or claims any ecclesiastical authority at all. In this peculiar situation, some thousands of the inhabitants of these States desire my advice; and, in compliance with their desire, I have drawn up a little sketch.

"Lord King's account of the Primitive Church convinced me, many years ago, that Bishops and Presbyters are the same order, and, consequently, have the same right to ordain. For many years I have been importuned, from time to time, to exercise this right, by ordaining part of our Travelling Preachers. But I have still refused, not only for peace sake, but because I was determined, as little as possible, to violate the established order of the National Church to which I belonged.

"But the case is widely different between England and North America. Here there are Bishops who have a legal jurisdiction. In America there are none, neither any parish Ministers. So that, for some hundred miles together, there is none either to baptize or to administer the Lord's Supper. Here, therefore, my scruples are at an end; and I conceive myself at full liberty, as I violate no order, and invade no man's right, by appointing and sending laborers into the harvest.

"I have accordingly appointed Dr. Coke and Mr. Francis Asbury to be joint Superintnedents over our brethren in North America; as also Richard Whatcoat and Thomas Vasey, to act as Elders among them, by baptizing and administering the Lord's Supper. And I have prepared a liturgy, little differing from that of the Church of England, (I think, the best constituted national church in the world,) which I advise all the Travelling Preachers to use on the Lord's day, in all the congregations, reading the litany only on Wednesdays and Fridays, and praying extempore on all other days. I also advise the Elders to administer the Supper of the Lord on every Lord's day.

"If any one will point out a more rational and Scriptural way of feeding and guiding those poor sheep in the wilderness, I will gladly embrace it. At present, I cannot see any better method than that I have taken.

"It has, indeed, been proposed, to desire the English Bishops to ordain part of our Preachers for America. But to this I object, 1. I desired the Bishop of London to ordain only one, but could not prevail. 2. If they consented, we know the slowness of their proceedings; but the matter admits of no delay. 3. If they would ordain them *now*, they would likewise expect to govern them. And how grievously would this entangle us? 4. As our American brethren are now totally disentangled both from the State and from the English hierarchy, we dare not entangle them again either with the one or the other. They are now at full liberty simply to follow the Scriptures and the Primitive Church. And we judge it best, that they should stand fast in that liberty wherewith God has so strangely made them free.

"JOHN WESLEY."

Could any thing be more reasonable? And was it not equally Scriptural? Who does not see a striking analogy between this transaction and that which occurred at Antioch many years before. "Now there were in the church that was at Antioch, certain prophets and teachers; as Barnabas, and Simeon that was called Niger, and Lucius of Cyrene, and Manaen, which had been brought up with Herod the tetrarch, and Saul. As they ministered to the Lord, and fasted, the Holy Ghost said, Separate me Barnabas and Saul for the work whereunto I have called them. And when they [the three presbyters, Simeon, Lucius and Manaen,] had fasted and prayed, and laid *their hands* on them, they sent them away. So they, being sent forth by the Holy Ghost, departed unto Seleucia; and from thence they sailed to Cyprus."

But, as these remarks are designed to meet high church objections, let us hear Bishop White, who was trying to get the Episcopal Church duly organized in this country after the Revolution, but was much embarrassed by English prelates, who hesitated, to confer episcopal ordination. The good man was in a similar condition to that of Mr. Wesley, though not half as deeply involved in responsibility. He says: —

"The conduct meant to be recommended, as founded on the preceding sentiments, is to include in the proposed frame of government, a general approbation of episcopacy, and a declaration of an intention to procure the succession as soon as conveniently may be; but, in the mean time, to *carry the plan into effect without waiting for the succession.*" * * * "Are the acknowledged ordinances of Christ's holy religion to be suspended for years, perhaps as long as the present generation shall continue, out of delicacy to a *disputed* point, and that relating only to *externals?*" To relinquish the worship of God, and the instruction and reformation of the people, from a scrupulous adherence to episcopacy, he says, is "sacrificing the *substance* to the *ceremony.*"

Bishop White did not believe that God's ordinances should be neglected, merely because the bishops were not pleased to ordain. Neither did Archbishop Tillotson, Bishop Patrick, or Stillingfleet. They were for ordaining in the best way possible, and go forward. So thought Mr. Wesley. And so thought Roger Williams and his deacon, in commencing baptism by immersion in this country. According to their own principles, they were neither of them qualified to baptize; but there must be a beginning somewhere. So they went down into the water, and the minister first baptized the deacon, and then the deacon baptized the minister. How could they have done better in exile, as they were? And who will deny the validity of baptism in Rhode Island, on account of this beginning. Necessity is the highest law of nature.

Do not Episcopalians provide for *lay* baptism in certain cases on this principle? And what do they mean by that article our church has adopted from their creed, in regard to ceremonies, if we may not vary from prelatical notions, without getting out of the succession? They say there, "It is not necessary that rites and ceremonies should, in all places, be the same, or exactly alike; for they have been always different, and may be changed according to the diversity of countries, times, and men's manners, so that nothing be ordained against God's will," &c. "Every particular church may ordain, change, or abolish rites and ceremonies, so that all things may be done to edification."

We say, then, in view of these considerations, that our episcopacy is *valid*, and that we *are in the succession*, our enemies being judges. And we might add, if the old test of character is still in vogue, "by their fruits ye shall know them," that its claim is not exceeded by any other in the world. For, it will not be denied, that our bishops strikingly imitate the apostles in their travels and labors, and the success of our endeavors comes nearer to the achievements of the gospel under their ministration, than any thing which has occurred in modern times.

Our Episcopacy is also Wesleyan. A few remarks upon this point will suffice. In the first place, Mr. Wesley him self lived and died an Episcopalian; and published to the world that he *believed the "episcopal form of church government to be scriptural and apostolical."* Of course he would not recommend any other to his followers.

2. He ordained Dr. Coke a superintendent, or bishop, for the reason, as he declares, that the Methodists in this country desired "*still to adhere to the doctrine and discipline of the Church of England.*" Does this look as though he meant to exclude a prominent feature of the discipline of that church?

3. If he did not ordain Dr. Coke a bishop, what were all his "*scruples*" about, which had embarrassed him so long, and which were only relieved by our country becoming independent? And to what order, or office, did he ordain

him? He was a presbyter before. And what was it that "startled" Dr. Coke, when the thing was suggested to him, and led him to a thorough investigation of the subject before he was satisfied of Mr. Wesley's authority to ordain him? He had submitted to Mr. Wesley's *appointment* before, as had others, Mr. Asbury in particular, who was then acting under a special commission in this country; but we hear nothing about his being "*startled*" till his ordination is mentioned.

4. If Mr. Wesley did not ordain Dr. Coke a bishop, and thus authorize him to ordain others, why did he apologize for the act by saying that he "had been importuned, from time to time, to exercise this right by *ordaining* some of our travelling preachers," and by saying, that in America, there are no "*bishops who have legal jurisdiction?*"

5. We ask, too, wherein the ordination of Dr. Coke differed from that of Messrs. Whatcoat and Vasey, who were ordained elders at the same time, if Dr. Coke were not ordained a bishop?

6. And why did Mr. Wesley prepare a prayer-book, "little differing from that of the Church of England," embracing episcopal forms for the ordination of deacons, elders, and superintendents, and a solemn injunction that all elected to either of these offices should be presented to the superintendent for ordination in this form? And why did he put this into the hands of Dr. Coke to bring to this country, if he did not intend to establish an episcopal form of government?

7. Why did Dr. Coke request that Messrs. Whatcoat and Vasey should be ordained presbyters, if he did not understand that he was to be made a bishop? and why assign this reason for the request, viz., "*propriety and universal practice make it expedient that I should have two presbyters with me*

in this work?' Those who deny that our episcopacy is Wesleyan, cannot give any satisfactory answers to these questions whatever. And there are other facts equally opposed to their position. For instance: 1. The prejudices of Charles Wesley against the whole proceeding. He understood it to be designed as a *bona fide ordination.* John knew his brother's hostility to his exercising episcopal authority so well, he thought it expedient to conceal his intentions from him till the work was done. If he did not mean to *ordain*, properly speaking, and lay the foundation of an *episcopal* government, why did he not relieve his brother by stating the facts, and explaining his purposes? And why did he not explain the matter afterwards, as the seceders have done since, and especially when Charles accused him of arming Dr. Coke with authority to ordain his preachers, and make them all dissenters? Who can answer? 2. Mr. Wesley was informed of the organization of the Methodist *Episcopal* Church, in 1784, soon after Dr. Coke's arrival in the country, — was accused of approving of it, and of consecrating Dr. Coke a bishop in view of effecting it; but never denied it. Is not this remarkable, if it were not true? 3. Soon after the organization, the minutes made their appearance, entitled "General Minutes of the Conferences of the Methodist *Episcopal* Church in America," declaring that said Conferences had formed an *episcopal* church by the "*recommendation*" of Mr. Wesley. These minutes were transmitted to Mr. Wesley, and printed in England. But did he ever object, or deny that he recommended such an organization? Never; though he was not a little persecuted on the account. Dr. Coke defended himself against the abuse of the press, by saying "*he had done nothing but under the direction of Mr. Wesley.*" Did Mr. Wesley ever deny this? His brother said Dr. Coke had acted rashly in the premises; but, instead of conceding it, Mr. Wesley replied that he "had done nothing rashly."

The American Minutes of 1789 spoke of Mr. Wesley as exercising "the episcopal office." This fact was immediately published in England. Was Mr. Wesley offended? Did he deny it? Never; but, when accused of it, he justified himself by saying, "I firmly believe that I am a Scriptural *episkopos*, as much as any man in England, or in Europe. For the uninterrupted succession I know to be a fable, which no man ever did or can prove."

We are aware that Mr. Wesley objected to applying the name *bishop* to our superintendents, and that three years after the organization of the church, when they were distinguished by this title, he wrote Bishop Asbury a very pointed letter, remonstrating against it. But he did not deny that they were bishops, nor did he object to their exercise of episcopal powers; he had ordained them for this very purpose. He objected to the title, from prudential considerations. He knew the jealousy of the Episcopal Church, and did not wish to interfere with its claims any further than was positively necessary. The term bishop, as then used, too, involved various civil and social dignities, not intrinsically implied in it. He might have thought that the title, without its adventitious honors and benefits, would be construed into vanity and ambition, and thus become a source of disgrace to himself as well as the bishops, and, by consequence, a hindrance to the work of God. And, so far as his own country was concerned, there was, probably, some danger. We insist, it was not the thing itself which he opposed, but the *title* given it. The Methodist Episcopal Church, with its name emblazoned upon its front, and its superintendents in the full exercise of episcopal prerogatives, had been in operation more than three years, before Mr. Wesley made the least objection. But when the Conference took the liberty to call their superintendents *bishops*, though they added not one *iota* to their duties or authority, Mr. Wesley demurred. The title might do harm, — it might excite to vanity, and be misused, — it might be construed to the injury of the cause.

These are the views entertained on the subject by our Wesleyan brethren, both in Europe and America; and several of their ablest writers have argued the question at considerable length. Indeed, none but offended seceders from our church, and carping sectaries and bigots, by their suggestion, have presumed to regard the subject in any other light. But the case is so clear, and the arguments hinted at so conclusive, it is not necessary to extend the discussion. We have said enough for all general purposes. If the reader has occasion to canvass the matter more fully, he will find Bishop Emory's "Defence of our Fathers," Stevens' "Church Polity," and Dr. Bangs' "Original Church of Christ," of great service to him in prosecuting the investigation.

We will only suggest, further, that Mr. Wesley, in constructing our excellent system, exchanged the terms *priest* for *elder*, *church* for *chapel*, &c., and, probably, for the same reasons that moved him to reject the title of bishop. He also complained to Mr. Asbury for applying the term *college* to a collegiate institution he and Dr. Coke had established. "I found a school," said he, "you, a *college*. O, beware! Do not seek to be *something*." But was Mr. Wesley opposed to colleges? No one believes it. The *name* was what he disliked. So, neither, was he opposed to our episcopacy, but only the *title* by which our superintendents came to be distinguished.

CHAPTER IV.

METHODIST EPISCOPACY, WITH ITS POWERS AND APPENDAGES, NECESSARY TO ITINERANCY.

THERE is no feature of our economy more highly prized among us than its *itinerancy*. It is believed by many that much of our extraordinary success in saving souls is attributable to this peculiarity of Wesleyanism, more than to any other one thing. We have seldom seen a minister, or private member, who would be willing to exchange it for the local system. Even those who cry out against our bishops, and complain the most clamorously of our government, still insist on maintaining the itinerancy. This is one of our peculiarities, which seceders of every class have been pleased to retain, though they have often crippled its operations by leaving too much choice to individual ministers and societies. If the question were to be submitted to the vote of the whole church, to-day, we doubt if one in two hundred would consent to its abandonment.

Itinerancy is, then, a settled arrangement, and must be maintained. But there are difficulties in the way. It is laborious and trying to the preachers and their families to be moving about the world among strangers, without any certain abiding place, and it is unpleasant to the people to lose ministers they esteem, and receive strangers in their place. Under these circumstances, it is necessary, to its efficient maintenance, *that it be subjected to rather stringent regula tions that may not be repealed or evaded in emergencies.* Men are seldom better than they determine to be beforehand, though they often fall short of their firmest resolves. Itinerants, having no established plan of action, will be liable to great instability. Governed by no system, — pledged to nothing, — the offer of a fine situation, and a fat salary, — the reproach of the settled clergy, or the prospect of long and tedious journeys and scant fare, will be likely to divert them from those fields which most need their services. If the matter is left to themselves, many, like the twenty thousand of Gideon's army, when they came near to the contest, will "be of a fearful heart," and turn back. The highways and hedges, publicans and sinners, especially those who are poor and scattered over new countries, will almost surely be neglected.

To meet the difficulties incident to itinerant life, there must, then, be a plan of operation devised and agreed to in the outset, by all the parties involved; by the ministers — or, when they are called upon to occupy a position of trouble and danger, they will flinch, and the cause be left to suffer; by the people — or, when they become numerous and rich, and able to sustain a preacher well, if they are not gratified, they will renounce the itinerancy, and provide for themselves. Bind them all to a plan in advance; and though they may sometimes feel afflicted by its operation, and strongly inclined to retreat, yet, "for their oath's sake," they will go forward and bear the burdens of a system which has brought them many blessings, and will not now forsake them, though, at the present, it demands a painful service. A plan, to be effective, must involve three things, namely: —

1. The relinquishment of the personal right on the part of the ministers to *choose their field of labor.* Ministers

are but men; they are subject to the infirmities of humanity, and naturally love ease, and honor, and plenty, like other men, and prefer places where these may be most fully enjoyed, in preference to those of an opposite character. Hence, the necessary result of ministers retaining and exercising the right of determining their own settlements, is, that some places will have ministers, and some none, — some will have those that ought to occupy other places, and powerful men will confine themselves to narrow circles, who ought to electrify the nation.

2. The plan should also embrace the relinquishment of the right of the people *to choose their own ministers.* We concede to the people the abstract right of choosing their own preachers, as we concede the right of the preachers to choose their own fields. While they retain this, it is reasonable to believe that they will use all honorable means to procure a minister of talent, and otherwise agreeable to their taste, and retain him indefinitely, irrespective of his adaptation to any other place, or the necessities of any other people. They must provide for *themselves.* Hence, by the operation of Independency, the circulation of ministerial talent, beyond occasional exchanges, is utterly precluded. Talent will be distributed according to the demands of *selfishness* rather than the interests of the cause, and will change under the direction of the same sordid principle. There have been sufficient experiments upon this point, we should judge, to satisfy the most incredulous.

3. The third necessity of such a plan is, that these rights, thus relinquished, *be vested in a third party*, who shall survey the field, study the qualifications, circumstances, and wishes of the preachers; the conditions, tastes and desires of the people; and then make such distribution of the various talents submitted, as it may judge most for the glory of

God, and the benefit of all concerned. How many individuals should compose this third party, or from what department of society it should be selected, admits of an honest difference of opinion. All, however, will agree that it should be composed of men who are interested in the general cause, are above *sectional prejudices and personal animosities*, of sound judgment and noble bearing, who are willing to set an example of labor and sacrifice. Persons of a different character could not be expected to apply themselves sufficiently, to make judicious appointments. Besides, they would lack the example of self-denial, necessary to their influence and success in stimulating and inspiring the whole body, under the trials incident to the enterprise. They must not only be wise to command, but brave to face the dangers and share the toils and privations of the conflict. Like a valiant general, they must be ready to thrust themselves into the hottest of the battle, and hazard all for the victory.

It is also desirable that they be placed in circumstances the least liable to party bias. If it were possible, it would be well that they should belong to neither party, and yet be capable of entering fully into the interests of both. Preachers, to be stationed, would unavoidably be tempted in relation to their own appointments. At all events, they would have the credit of taking special care of themselves, however disinterestedly they might act. And hearers would, no doubt, feel a special interest in their own and neighboring societies. They could not avoid it. If they were to be made dependent on individual contributions for their support, they might be influenced to favor the rich of both parties from selfish considerations. They should, therefore, be supported in another way, that they might be entirely free from the hope of gain, and the fear of want. It is important, too, that they be holden *amenable* for all their conduct, or they may become indifferent, and abuse the powers entrusted to them. Finally, to obtain the necessary information, and maintain a proper sympathy with the parties concerned, they need to travel through the whole territory embraced in the plan, become acquainted with the men to be appointed, and the fields to be occupied.

Good men, men of God, who feel a holy interest in the salvation of souls, and love their brethren, thus guarded against all the evil passions and liabilities of fallen humanity, and acquainting themselves with the various talents in the ministry, and the wants of the membership, can certainly judge better what is for the good of the cause, in regard to the appointments, than the parties themselves, who are necessarily blinded by individual interests, and limited views of the facts in the case. The parties may know what will please them most, and may dispose of themselves profitably, so that the preacher shall not preach in vain, nor the people hear in vain. But while the talented minister and the wealthy church are *pleasing* themselves, they may be enjoying less *profit* than would fall to their lot under a more benevolent arrangement; and others, less fortunate, are suffering for the means of grace, or for the peculiar qualifications enjoyed exclusively by their wealthy neighbors. Hence, we think, high Christian magnanimity requires that the parties make common stock of themselves, and submit to whatever sacrifice may be necessary for the general good. Till they do this, and put their own fortunes out of their own hands, it is impossible to establish a permanent itinerancy; selfishness forbids it. Entertaining these views, Mr. Wesley declined a settlement, and preached, like the apostles, "*every where*." When God raised up men of like heart and purpose, and they came to assist him, he received them only on the condition that they would *travel* and preach under his direction, and watch over the souls that had been pleased to submit themselves to his pastoral care. When individuals asked for his fellowship and spiritual oversight, he required their acquiescence in certain principles and measures involving the *itinerancy*. When he erected his first chapel, he took good care to secure and dedicate it in a way that it should always be open to him and his itinerant assistants, whoever might wish to divert it to other purposes. Indeed, he guarded this peculiarity of his system in all his movements.

That our bishops are clergymen is admitted; but we trust this does not disqualify them to understand the true interests of the people, or to feel a proper sympathy for them. If, however, any offset to this is necessary, we have it in the fact that the preachers have to bear the brunt of the itinerant battle. They must go when and where sent; they must take up with such fare as the people please to give them, or none at all; while the people hear and pay, or not, as they may choose. To make the very best of it, even where the people do their whole duty, it is a laborious and trying business, which few will follow, who are not impelled by a solemn sense of obligation to God and their fellow men. If either party is, therefore, to have any advantage in this respect, the preachers have the higher claim.

In all other respects our bishops answer the description given. They are required to travel through the connection *at large*, not a mere conference or diocese, "and oversee the temporal and spiritual business" of the whole church. This gives them an opportunity to see many of the circuits and stations, and form some judgment of the people, their wants and necessities; and to become personally acquainted with the ministers they are to appoint. By this means, too, they set an example of sacrifice and labor that inspires others, and enables them to say to the trembling and fearful ones, "follow me, as I follow Christ." A lordly, idle bishop could do nothing with the preachers. They would not endure him, nor submit to his direction, while they would glory to follow one who himself is "more abundant in labors" and self denials. They would follow him even to martyrdom. Wise men have often wondered at the courage of the fathers, who traversed the country from end to end, on horseback and on foot, sleeping in wigwams, on the hard floor, and even in the open air, and often hungry, and almost naked. The matter is explained in part by their religion; but the whole secret is not out, till we contemplate the immortal Asbury, and mark his career of peril and of glory. Who could not suffer for God under such a leader? Like a mighty hero, he rode from camp to camp, inspiriting the feeble bands he found associated, and then away he would plunge into new and untried scenes, and in the name of his master rear the banner of the cross, and sustain it alone, till God sent him relief from the gaping crowd, who, catching his spirit, would join in valiant fight, and battle mightily.

By having a general charge, and travelling "through the connection," our bishops feel a general interest, without those local prejudices and partialities which blind and warp the judgment. And being provided for from *general* resources, they are comparatively incapable of being bribed, or unduly influenced by pecuniary considerations. And to bind them still firmer to the discharge of their high trusts, their official conduct is carefully recorded by those over whom they preside, sent up to the General Conference and reviewed; for every part of which, as well as for their more private deportment, they are holden to a strict account.

But to help them in their work, and secure a more critical

superintendence of each preacher and society, and afford every officer of the entire church all possible assistance in the discharge of his peculiar duties, it was long since found necessary to institute the office of *presiding elder.* Methodism being new in the country, and, by consequence, our preachers and societies all young, and generally inexperienced in the management of church matters, it was important that they should have frequent correspondence with preachers of higher attainments. This might have been provided for by the multiplication of bishops; but, for good reasons, we think, it was judged better to have only enough of these to take the *general* superintendence, attend the conferences, &c., and provide them with coadjutors, under the title of presiding elders, who should be required to visit each circuit once a quarter, and take the oversight of all the preachers and societies in their districts. Whether the necessities for this office still exists, is questioned. The writer, however, does not see how it can be abandoned with safety to the cause at the present, without increasing the number of bishops, so as to have one or two to each conference, which would make them too common, and too much entangle them in local difficulties, to exert the influence needed in the appointing officer.

Our bishops, at present, are twelve in number. Allowing them all to be effective men, they cannot possibly exercise a very particular supervision over so many ministers and members, spread out through so much territory. It it be possible for them to see all the *preachers*, they cannot form any particular acquaintance with them, much less visit all the societies. Hence, to make intelligent appointments, without having other means of knowledge, is utterly out of the question. But let the conferences be districted as at present, and appoint efficient men to act the bishop in his absence, report every thing to him at the Conference, and at other times as may be necessary, advising him about the appointments, and twelve bishops may be sufficient, and do the work more carefully and even better than a larger number. By travelling through his district once a quarter, the presiding elder becomes familiar with all the preachers, their habits, health, qualifications, peculiarities, usefulness, and standing among the people. Holding Quarterly Conferences with official members of each society, and mingling with private members, as he necessarily does in love-feasts, and other associations, he becomes acquainted with their circumstances. He is often found consulting the stewards about the support of the preachers; examining the leaders, instructing, exhorting, advising and reproving the preachers, and sometimes changing them; examining candidates for the ministry; writing licenses, deeds of churches and parsonages, and contracts for building them; hearing complaints, and trying appeals; indeed, doing every thing he can do to advance the cause. Pursuing this course, if he be a good man, and a man of sound judgment, he will not only "pay his way," by his labors in the societies, but he will be able to give the bishops and the Conference information and advice in reference to every appointment, and every preacher, of inestimable value to all concerned.

"By keeping a watchful eye over all the travelling and local preachers in his district, administering advice and admonition as occasion may require, a presiding elder may restrain irregularities in their early stages; correct small offences before they ripen into evils which would disgrace the church and injure the cause; and thereby prevent many of the charges and trials which otherwise would fall upon individuals, to their injury, if not their ultimate ruin.

"By an accurate knowledge of the gifts, grace, usefulness, and general character of all the travelling preachers under his care, the same officer may be prepared to give such a representation of them at the Conference, as shall provide for a wise determination of the following points, to wit: who shall be advanced in the ministry; who shall be set aside for want of talents or piety; and where each man shall be appointed. And with respect to the local preachers, a solemn obligation rests upon the presiding elder to use his influence to encourage and help forward those of them who are pious and useful; but especially to arrest, restrain, or dismiss, according to discipline, those who may be found otherwise. He should be well prepared to give an enlightened and true representation, at the Conference, of every man under his care who may be recommended for a travelling preacher, or for orders in the local ministry; that no one may be improperly put forward, through the influence or indifference of the presiding elder. It is exceedingly culpable in presiding elders, except in extraordinary circumstances, to come to Conference unacquainted with these great church interests, so as to leave the Conference to act in the dark respecting matters of so much importance." — *Hedding on Discipline, p.* 31.

Presiding elders, therefore, need to keep the farthest distance from *personal prejudices and predilections.* At least, they should not allow such influences to warp their judgment, or inspire their representations of *societies* or of *individuals.* They need to be as *impartial* as judges upon the bench. The least show of *dislike* or *favoritism* in this officer, however merited, creates alarm. He may have *friends* and *enemies* — he cannot well avoid having more or less of both; but when he comes to give an *official* opinion, *he must have neither.* He must then see men and things as *they are,* and speak as the *cause of God* and of souls requires. No *narrow*, *party man*, is, therefore, fit for the office. Nor one who is highly *susceptible* of being swerved from right and duty by personal considerations. It requires a noble, generous, benevolent mind, divinely imbued with the magnanimity of the gospel.

To make judicious appointments without the aid of such an officer, would be utterly impracticable. Our bishops, however good or great, can judge no better than others without ample and correct information. Presiding elders are expected to furnish that information; and to obtain it in a cheaper and less exceptionable way is, to say the least, very difficult. We can conceive of no way that it can be done. To multiply the number of bishops so that they might visit all the societies, might secure the necessary knowledge, but it would not lessen the expense, or save important men for the stations. To make a stationed preacher a kind of presiding elder over several societies in his neighborhood, and let him perform the double duty of pastor and presiding elder, would not be well. No preacher would want the office, and no society would willingly take the officer. The time may come when something of this kind may succeed; but "it is not yet." Because the Wesleyans of England make it work under their system, it does not follow that it is adapted to this country.

In the first place, in some sections of the work, there are not half a dozen societies within fifty miles of any one point. To put twice that number under the care of a pastor any where, would impose on him the necessity of being absent from home and from his pastoral work beyond what societies generally would endure. What station would wish to have a preacher oppressed with such a burden? Tell about supplying his place with local preachers, and young, inexperienced itinerants; would our larger societies, nay, would any society, submit to it? Would they be willing to have him absent during the week, even, as he must necessarily be to considerable extent, particularly in cases of trial and difficulty? We have no hesitancy in saying it would not be endured patiently. Nor would the preachers be willing to take such responsibilities upon themselves.

But the great difficulty would be in making out the appointments. The stationed presiding elders, or "*Chairmen*," if you please, must be the bishop's counsel, and represent the preachers and people of their respective districts. Of course, they would have to represent *themselves*, their own feelings and wishes, since *they* are to be stationed as well as others. Would it not be very *unnatural* for them not to feel a little extra interest in their own cases? Could they avoid it? They would be suspected in any case, and particularly if they should not receive their full share of the inferior appointments. Should they happen to be stationed among those who could not be pleased with them, they would unavoidably be suspected of procuring their own appointments. The experiment, we apprehend, would be any thing but pleasant, and would probably result in both preachers and people desiring to return to the presiding eldership, which excludes selfishness from the cabinet, except when one is leaving the office to return to the ranks.

If any ask why this plan may not work here as well as in England, we reply, 1. In England the whole work lies within a narrow compass, in a dense population, and is, therefore, accessible and manageable, as our's is not, and can never be. They have one Conference, only, embracing the ministerial talent of the entire connection, and need but one president, who can take an appointment at any place in the Conference, and superintend the whole work more critically than our five bishops can superintend the work under their supervision. 2. Their chairmen of districts are not *necessarily* connected with their stationing committee, and need not be, because the work is so condensed information can be promptly obtained from any point. 3. There is not the difference in their appointments which exists among us. Our appointments pay their ministers from *fifty* dollars per annum to six thousand, averaging, perhaps, from six hundred to two thousand dollars. The same difference exists in regard to *localities*, stretching all the way along from the Atlantic Ocean to the Rocky Mountains, and so on to California and Oregon. Some are easy of access and very agreeable, while others are distant and dreary, not approachable by public conveyance, if, indeed, some of them may be reached by any conveyance, unless it be a horse or a mule. Consequently, it is a matter of great interest to a minister here where he is to be stationed, in more respects than one, and especially if he is blessed with a family. It is sometimes a question of life and death, and in a majority of cases it is one of competence and incompetence, of poverty and suffering. But it is not so in England. The distance there is hardly an item of thought, roads and conveyances being nearly perfect, no furniture to move, (it being furnished by each circuit,) good domestics provided for, and the disciplinary travelling, and other expenses, making up the entire salary, which is ample, being paid to the last farthing, whether the society be rich or poor, great or small. The only choice among healthy men is, therefore, a mere matter of *taste*. Place us in the condition of our English brethren, financially, to say nothing of other things, and we could well afford to be represented by chairmen, however they might look after their own interests. Assure us of a competent support, of the payment of our travelling expences, and of sufficient domestic assistance, and what would we care about our appointments? We could refer this matter to a committee, and go into Conference, and debate the appointments in as good temper as Englishmen. But as things are, to adopt their policy, either in regard to the chairmen of districts, or the appointment of the preachers by a committee, would be extremely hazardous.

This is philosophy demonstrated by fact. The failures of experimenting seceders admonish us to beware how we attempt to imitate our trans-Atlantic brethren. Their system, no doubt, serves their purpose better than our's would, but, like every other, it sometimes "*rubs hard.*" Our presiding eldership has worked well, and seems to us an indispensable appendage to our episcopacy. And we have yet to learn that it is not doing well now, and have no doubt it would be still more useful, if, instead of trying to expunge it, we would honor it with the incumbency of our *best and wisest men*, and *respect* their office, as essential to the harmony and efficiency of our system. We do not now refer to the most *popular* preachers, or the most *profound.* Such men often lack important qualifications for it. But we speak of men who, on the whole, are best *adapted* to it. There is an *adaptation* which every great and good preacher does not possess, and may not acquire. This may be found in brethren who are not *sought*, as stationed preachers, and, if we may say it, who are hardly passable in that capacity. Indeed, some of the best presiding elders we have known were not distinguished as *preachers.* They either lacked the *life*, *tact*, versatility of talent, *manner*, or something else, to command the admiration of the same congregation for two years; and yet they made excellent presiding elders. A presidential mein, a pretty thorough knowledge of Methodism, and attachment to its various arrangements, a *sound judgment*, a *kind*, *pious*, *and sympathetic heart*, are a pretty ample atonement for almost any defect in the pulpit. Besides, it often (not to say always) happens that a man who is *moderate* in a pent up station, where he has to preach to the same handful of hearers Sabbath after Sabbath, when loosed from his bondage, and brought under the inspiration of new circumstances every week, will preach in demonstration of the Spirit and with power. Hence, the remark that a man is not "fit for a station, and is, therefore, appointed to the presiding eldership," may be true, and yet he may be the very best man for the office in the Conference to which he belongs. But no man should be appointed *merely* because he "is fit for nothing else." One society had better suffer than many. Nor because he is very *desirous* of the office. This is pleasing a good man at too great a sacrifice. Nor because he has held the office a year or two, and will be afflicted if removed. Many may be afflicted if he is not removed, and mildew blast the office and its functionaries. Nothing excites a hue and cry against it, or in favor of making it elective, or modifying it, so quick.

But the expense is one of the strongest grounds of objection. We are aware that it costs something, but not half what it is really worth. Presiding elders often give advice in difficulty that is of more value to a preacher, or a church, or both, than all they pay him twice told. It is through them that the people receive their preachers, and the preachers their appointments. And, if we may be pardoned for divulging the secrets of the cabinet, we will say they generally *make* the appointments, while the bishop only accedes to them, and decides where elders disagree. They are the men, too, to correct errors in the appointments, and to adjust difficulties by changing preachers, where it becomes necessary, so as to improve their situation, relieve the people, and further the cause. And they often do it with excellent effect. And yet the societies relieved, or especially helped, do not pay their presiding elder so much in several years as it would cost them, on the Independent system, to effect a single settlement or removal. One *ordination or dismission* costs some congregational societies more than they would pay a presiding elder, as Methodists, in five or ten years. And yet Congregationalists are not generally better satisfied with the preachers they settle, than our people are with those who are sent them, according to our system. This is an interesting fact, which the disaffected and incredulous are invited to consider. The writer has been astonished at the result of his own investigations in the premises.

But it is objected that quarterly meetings are not as interesting as formerly. This may be, but it must be remembered our circumstances have changed. When Methodists were few and far between, and had but little preaching in any one place, few meeting-houses, and no Sabbath Schools to require their attention at home, and especially when they were persecuted and treated as outcasts by other sects, quarterly meetings were important occasions. Brethren assembled from a great distance, exchanged sympathies, heard the word of the Lord, and rejoiced together as fellow-sufferers, bound for the same heavenly country. Their religion was the same as our's. The *peculiar* zest of their quarterly meetings was attributable to the circumstances. Restore those circumstances, and old fashioned quarterly meetings will follow as a matter of course. But this is not desirable, good as old times were. We prefer to be more numerous and influential, have regular preaching and other religious privileges at home, though they may deprive us of the warm and happy greetings of other days.

Still, however, we admit these great occasions are important, and we are happy to know that in some parts they are maintained. They exert an excellent influence in counteracting our tendency to localism, and create a sympathy between adjoining societies, both pleasant and profitable. Besides, they have a good *appearance*, which strengthens our influence in community.

But we are wandering from the point. Our object is to show the importance of the episcopacy, aided by the presiding eldership, to the efficiency, stability, and perpetuity of the itinerant system. It seems to have been contrived and endowed with special reference to it. Less power would not have answered the purpose — more, might have been dangerous. The happy medium seems to have been discovered. Preachers now entering the itinerancy, surrender the abstract right of choosing their own places of labor, and submit to the appointment of the bishops. They do it voluntarily — *nobly*. Thus devoting themselves to the system, they are bound by their own choice to conform to its regulations, and occupy such fields as are assigned them. They are not at liberty to select for themselves, or enter into any negotiations with the people, with a view to obtain a particular appointment. This is at variance with the system, and is dangerous to its existence. Yet it is perfectly consistent for them to represent their situation to the bishops, and "ask what they will." The only difficulty about this practice is, brethren are liable to be more *emphatic* than is suitable, and if their wishes are not gratified, to be offended and complain. They do not consider that other preachers have claims, or that the wishes of the people are to be consulted as well as their own. They view the subject in one aspect only, and thus are deceived. If in imagination they would exchange places with the bishop a few moments, they might conceive many reasons why they should not be indulged.

On the other hand, the people coming into the church surrender the right of choosing their own preachers, and engage to take their chance with others. They accordingly secure the use of their pulpits to the ministers of the church duly appointed, reserving the right of representation and petition, similar to that enjoyed by the preachers in regard to their appointments. As it is improper for the preachers to enter into any negotiations with them, so the least attempt on their part to negotiate with the preachers, contrary to the stipulations of the system, is a breach of solemn contract. It is clandestinely attempting to exercise a right they have relinquished openly, and may be characterized as "*pious fraud.*"

Our itinerant system is, therefore, one of *compromise*, involving a mutual sacrifice for a general good, and vesting the executive or motive power in our bishops. That it is powerfully effective will not be denied. We believe it is equally *safe*. But take away the executive power from our bishops, the rights now surrendered revert to their original owners, our system is dissolved, and our appointments, like our breakfasts, become a matter of "*truck and dicker.*"

If any are disposed to deny this, we refer them to *history*. What has become of Lady Hundingdon's itinerancy? How have seceders prospered in renouncing the "*terrible power of episcopacy*," and standing upon abstract rights? A father and a leader in the experiment has just called to consult about his return to the direction of that power; and ere the words we are writing will see the light, that brother will probably be restored to the itinerant ranks. He has learned by experiment that an efficient itinerancy cannot co-exist with Congregationalism — that nothing short of *moral sovereignty* in the appointing power is equal to the undertaking, and, therefore, he submits to it again for conscience sake. What he has learned by experience, we have long since been convinced of by other means ; and never witness any serious attempts to remodel our episcopacy, either in its principles or subordinate agencies, without trembling for the result.

CHAPTER V.

THE GOVERNMENT OF THE M. E. CHURCH WELL BALANCED. ITS DANGERS AND SECURITIES.

THE principal objections urged against our system converge to this one point, viz., *the power of the ministry*. It is assumed that it is too great, and, therefore, dangerous to the rights and liberties of the people. A brief consideration of this general charge is essential to our object. Preliminary, however, to the main question, we beg leave to remind the reader,

1. That we do not pretend that our system is absolutely perfect; nor, if it were so, that it would never fail of securing the proper objects of government; since so much imperfection of knowledge and judgment attach to its administrators, to say nothing of its subjects. Melancholy results have sometimes occurred under the safest and best of systems.

2. That this power, whatever it be, has settled upon the ministry *providentially*, and by a sort of necessity, rather than by the ambition and self-seeking of its incumbents. God first raised up a Wesley, and endowed him with peculiar grace. A few individuals, being awakened, came to him for advice, and submitted themselves to his direction. Here his power commenced. He could do no less than to suggest certain rules for them to observe, such as he deemed necessary to secure the great object of their pursuit. Nor was it reasonable for him to continue the relation of spiritual guide

to them, if they would not yield to his advice. As the number multiplied, and new difficulties arose, his responsibility increased, and further advices and rules became necessary, which he, as the teacher and guide of the flock, must make. When his charge became too great for him to supervise alone, and Providence raised up other men of his own spirit, he employed them to aid him, and gave them the part of his own authority their new duties required. Here was the beginning of *their* power. Some of his children, emigrating to this country, and commencing religious operations, as we have shown, solicited the extension of his episcopal and fatherly watch-care to them, also, which he could not refuse. But how should he guide and govern them, but by the same means he had adopted at home? Hence the introduction of his *minutes*, which constituted our discipline at the first, and the preachers he sent to act for him, and, therefore, clothed with his authority, to do his work, and report to him. Hence, also, his ordination of Dr. Coke, and the arrangements for an episcopal form of government, and the organization of the societies into a church. There was no planning, — no preconcert, — no "stealing the march of the people," — no "jesuitical contrivance to establish another hierarchy," — nothing of the kind. Things came along as they were needed. The *want* was first seen, and the *supply* was fitted to it. And thus it has been through our whole history, and none have been better pleased with the little additions and subtractions which have occurred from time to time, than the people themselves; and we believe the day has not yet dawned when they would not have been deeply afflicted by a radical revolution, though it had imposed on them twice their present authority in the government. For proof of this, we refer to the two incontestable facts of history, viz., 1. That every effort that has been made to effect such a revolution has been limited to comparatively few individuals. And, 2. That all these efforts have originated and been chiefly conducted by disaffected preachers.

3. We think it important, also, to be remembered, that this power, however great, is of *Wesleyan descent*, and is vastly less than that exercised by our venerated founder No little prejudice has resulted from misapprehension on these points, which is our apology for their introduction at this time.

4. We would suggest, finally, that the existence of great powers and trusts in a public officer does not prove, *per se*, that they are peculiarly dangerous. To make out an alarming case, it must be shown, 1. That there is, or may be, a peculiar want of *interest* in the officer. 2. That he is wanting in the wisdom necessary to the duties devolving upon him. 3. That he lacks the requisite time and opportunity. 4. That peculiar motives operate to influence him to betray his trusts, and abuse his powers. And, 5. That he is not guarded by suitable checks.

But who will undertake to prove any one or all of these things, in relation to the ministry of our church? Their business is to convert, organize, discipline and save the people. That good men may attempt this work, who are not suitably informed, is admitted. But then no minister is alone ; he is under inspectors, tutors, and overseers, and if not qualified for the task, it will soon be discovered, and he will be discharged, or placed in a position suited to his capacity. Injury, therefore, from this source can only be temporary. As to time and opportunity, our travelling preachers have every possible advantage. This is their peculiar business, with which they are to let nothing interfere. That they will either enter or continue in the work without inter est, is incredible ; for the motives which affect an uninterested heart are on the wrong side. Worldly honor is not found here, nor wealth, nor ease, nor convenience ; but persecution, reproach, poverty, incessant labor and sacrifice, are its universal accompaniments. And, beside, our disciplinary checks to indifference, and the misuse of ministerial functions, are severe beyond parallel.

To demonstrate these points, let us consider,

1. The powers and circumstances of our bishops. Their powers are considerable, but greatly inferior to those exercised by Mr. Wesley. He presided in the Conferences, — appointed preachers to all the Methodist pulpits in England, — adopted rules and regulations for the government of the connection, — had the entire management of all the Conference funds, and the produce of the books, — received, ordained, and dismissed whom he pleased, and was responsible to no earthly tribunal for his conduct.

But it is far otherwise with our bishops. They have no legislative authority whatever, other than what may be involved in the right of giving advice, — have no control of church funds, — can neither receive nor exclude a minister or member, except by a disciplinary process, — have no power of appointment to our pulpits, but what is delegated by the General Conference, — and are strictly amenable to that body for all they do or leave undone, — and are liable to be arraigned, disfranchised, and expelled for improper conduct.

Their powers are considerably less than they were at the organization. According to the minutes of the Conferences for 1784, which, with the English minutes, then constituted the discipline of the church, no one could be ordained superintendent, elder, or deacon, without the consent of a superintendent, however unanimously elected by the Conference ;

nor was any brother allowed to print his own or another's writings, without the approbation of one of the superintendents. They also received and decided appeals. But it is not so now. They ordain such as the Conferences elect, — have no other than an advisory jurisdiction of our printing, — and decide no appeals, except on questions of discipline, this power being transferred to the Conferences.

Nor are their powers and privileges equal to those exercised by the bishops of the Protestant Episcopal Church. They have a veto power on the action of the house of delegates, in their General Convention, so that no man can be put into the episcopacy without their consent, nor can a bishop be tried and deposed except by bishops. They may also originate or arrest any measure they please ; so that their relation to the lower house is similar to that of the English House of Lords to the House of Commons. Their official duties are comparatively easy and pleasant, and their pecuniary compensation double that of our bishops, whose onerous labors require them to be from home most of the time, and appropriate all their energies.

Our lamented Bishop Hedding, from whose opinion there will be no appeal, says : "The superintendents now have no power in the church above that of elders, except what is connected with presiding in the Conferences, fixing the appointments of the preachers, and ordaining. They have no voice in any question to be decided by vote in any Conference, — no vote even in making the rules by which they themselves are to be governed. They are the servants of the elders, to go out and execute their commands.

"At the same time they are held rigidly responsible, not only for their private conduct, but also for their official acts. The General Conference appoints 'a Committee on Episcopacy,' consisting of one delegate from each Annual Conference, to examine the conduct of the superintendents, both private and official, for the four years next preceding the session, and to present to the Conference any thing they find exceptionable.

Since this was written, provision has been made for trying bishops, during the intervals of the General Conference, both for immoral and imprudent conduct, and also for giving them an appeal to the General Conference. This places them on a par with other ministers, and gives them a fair chance for defence, should they be accused. It also gives the church the means of protecting itself against any misconduct on their part *at once*, whether moral or official, and is thus a benefit to both parties. A bishop is liable to be falsely accused, and may need a fair trial to vindicate himself; and, however wise and good, he may fall into personal or *official* imprudence, which will prove disastrous to the church if continued. So that, whether the arrangement is the best that could be devised or not, it supplies a manifest want in our former jurisprudence, that time may show to be of the utmost importance.

Thus the bishops, though higher in office and responsibility than ordinary ministers, are not above law, and may be arraigned, expelled, reproved, or suspended by their subordinates. Should they appeal to the General Conference, their case would be adjudicated by a mixed court composed of ministers and laymen, from whose decision there is no appeal.—*Discipline*, ¶¶ 313–318.

Under these circumstances, where is the danger from our episcopacy? Entirely subject to the body of the elders, restricted and regulated by specific statutes, and *declining* rather than increasing in its powers, who can feel any great alarm? The idea is ridiculous! Those who object to their appointing the preachers, should consider that, if we will maintain our itinerancy, the power to do this must be lodged somewhere. Nothing short of it will suffice. To whom, then, shall it be intrusted? Who are wiser, better, more interested, freer from the influence of selfishness and other impure motives, and in a condition to judge more discreetly, than they? Give it to the preachers and people in general, and it would soon have an end. Vest it in a committee, or in the Conference, and the result will be the conflict of opposing feelings and claims, confusion if not destruction.

As it is, it is equally safe and fair for both laity and clergy, endangering neither the liberty nor prosperity of one or the other, and securing spiritual results the most magnificent and encouraging.

Others may complain that the bishops *decide law questions*. But is not this a wise arrangement? Such questions will arise, and must be settled. Who is better qualified to decide them than our bishops? Selected from among our first preachers, travelling through the Conferences, and conversing with our oldest and best informed men, and being in a position requiring them to study and understand every part of our economy, they are expected to combine the disciplinary wisdom of the whole church. Besides, being *public* men, not the bishops of *my* Conference or of *yours*, not of *sectional* itinerancy but of *general*, they are necessarily free as erring mortals can be from sectional prejudices and predilections, which warp the judgment and elicit one-sided decisions. If this power was lodged with the Annual Conferences, what would become of our union? A single year would not pass, before different Conferences would be in open conflict with each other on law questions. The discussion would be carried into our pulpits and papers, and what would be the result? The reader cannot mistake.

With whom, then, could this power be better intrusted?

Is it not safe? If a decision be made which any brother considers erroneous, he has the right of appeal to the General Conference, and may go before that body and argue the case at length; and if he can convince a majority that he is right, said decision will be reversed. But "it is not democratic!" Possibly not; but what is democracy on this subject? The American constitution declares "the judicial power shall extend to *all cases* arising under the constitution, the laws of the United States, and treaties made, or to be made, under their authority." "This," says Mr. Bayard, with the endorsement of Chief Justice Marshall, Judge Story, Chancellor Kent, and other distinguished jurists, "necessarily gives to the courts authority to declare an *act of Congress, an article in a State constitution*, or a *State law*, which is inconsistent with the constitution of the United States, *void*. When a question of this kind arises, and is brought before the Supreme Court for adjudication, its decision must be final, and conclusive; because the constitution gives to that tribunal power to decide, and has given *no appeal from its decision*."

This is democracy; and yet the Supreme Judges of the United States Court are authorized to declare not only State constitutions and laws, but the laws and treaties of Congress, void; and there is no appeal or redress. The President of the United States, Congress, and all the people, must submit. So says the constitution, which is the supreme law of the land, and so says history, and every day's experience. Is it a great thing, then, a dangerous feature of our economy, that the bishops decide questions of law for us, subject to an appeal to the General Conference? We think not.

2. A similar process of reasoning will show that the powers exercised by the *presiding elders* are equally safe.

They are, generally, men of information and experience We see no object a bishop can have in appointing unsuitable men, or men who have not the *confidence both of the preachers and the people.* Nor do we conceive of any motive calculated to influence this officer to abuse his authority in reference to any part of his flock. He may err, and thus give offence; but he must be a very unsuitable man for the office, and, withal, an odd genius, to oppress his brethren, where all the motives bearing upon the case impel to a different course.

But should he get warped, and become conceited, sour, or one-sided, so as to decide disciplinary questions erroneously, or otherwise act inconsistently with his proper dignity or our economy, the remedy is at hand. If the case requires immediate attention, it may be laid before the bishop having charge, whose duty it will be to examine the matter, and remove, reprove, or advise him, as he shall judge necessary, and take such other measures as the arrest of the evil may require. Otherwise, the offender may be arraigned at the ensuing Annual Conference, his administration reviewed and corrected, and himself punished according to our discipline and usage. If these are not sufficient guarantees for the good behavior of presiding elders, and for the rights and liberties of brethren under their supervision, we mistake their importance.

And is not all the power they possess necessary to protect both preachers and people, from unintentional or other injuries they are liable to experience from each other? Suppose the people attempt a wrong course toward the preacher, who is to check them and protect him? And suppose he should intrude upon their rights and interests, who is to arrest him and defend them? The bishops are too far off, or otherwise occupied, to investigate all such cases; and if they were not, the details of difficulty had better be attended to by a subordinate officer. Then, should a case prove to be serious, and come before him by appeal, he will be prepared to adjudicate it without prejudice or partiality.

We have been surprised to hear some preachers, and societies, too, complain of the *power* of our bishops and presiding elders. What would have become of them had it not been for this very power, is a sober question. It has plucked them out of trouble more than once. But so it is; the most obliged are often the most forgetful of their obligations. The words of our first two bishops are full of import. We commend them to the consideration of all candid minds: —

"Is it not strange," say they, speaking of presiding elders, "that any of the people should complain either of this or of the episcopal office? These offices in the church are peculiarly designed *to ameliorate the severity* of Christian Discipline, as far as they respect the people. In them the people have a refuge, an asylum to which they may flee on all occasions. To them they may appeal, and before them they may lay all their complaints and grievances. The persons who bear these offices are their fathers in the gospel, ever open of access, ever ready to relieve them under every oppression."

3. These remarks apply with equal force to preachers in charge of circuits. They are judges of law in their respective stations, as the presiding elders are in their districts, and as the bishops are in the whole church; but any brother may appeal from their decision, and, if it be wrong, he can have it corrected, and all the action based upon it reversed. In this respect our jurisprudence answers well to that of the States, though more democratic even, as in the other particular already mentioned. The decision of the Supreme

Judges of the United States Court is *final*. The decisions of the Supreme Courts of the different States are also final in most cases, but not in all. In questions relating to the Constitution and United States law, with many others of high importance, but which need not be named, an appeal may be taken to the Supreme Court of the country. Appeals are also allowed from all the lower Courts, in specific cases, to those which are higher, sometimes to the highest. But with us there may be an appeal, in one way or another, in every case, sufficient, at least, to secure a fair and impartial decision from our highest judicial authority; so that every member has security, not only for his character as a member of the church, but for his opinions of our church polity.

Some have objected that preachers in charge appoint our class leaders, as though it were a very dangerous arrangement. But the alarm is not general. The operation of this part of our system has been so satisfactory, it is difficult to create a panic about it among the people in the most exciting times. One experimental fact weighs more with them, and with all sober-minded men, than a hundred fine-spun arguments. But the arguments against this are as weak as the facts in favor of it are potent. To prove that a public officer is particularly in danger of using his authority so as to offend and injure his constituents, some probable motive must be shown. But what motive can operate upon a preacher in charge to induce him to appoint unsuitable leaders, or leaders he knows to be disagreeable to the classes? It is impossible to conceive of any. The danger is greater in the opposite direction. The love of approbation is usually so strong in ministers, as well as others, they are more liable to be *indulgent* than *oppressive*. Besides, if one was inclined to be more independent than prudence would allow, a moment's reflection would suggest that to be so in such a case would be the height of folly. Preachers cannot compel their members to attend the classes of offensive leaders; and they know it. Nor would they be willing to answer for disciplining members for neglecting to attend class under such circumstances. One, therefore, who has the spiritual prosperity of the church at heart, will endeavor to select such leaders as are suitable and most agreeable to the members. If a different character should happen to obtain charge, he will soon reveal his unfitness for the pastoral office, and receive his discharge.

There is another consideration that comes in here, not to be overlooked. The appointment of leaders is not so arbitrary as has been represented. Though classes are seldom called upon to vote in reference to it, their wishes are generally known and respected. The other leaders and stewards are also consulted, and often make nominations by the preacher's request. He is anxious to appoint the best men possible. He would naturally please all parties, and at the same time consult the interests of the cause; therefore, he takes advice. But should he neglect this precaution, or appoint an unsuitable man notwithstanding it, the class will decline, and both leader and members will naturally covet a change, when the error may be corrected. Should he exercise "this power in a capricious or tyrannical manner, the people may lay their grievances before the bishops, or presiding elders, or before the yearly Conference, which may proceed even to his expulsion, if he grossly offend against that wisdom which is from above, and which is first pure, then peaceable, gentle, and easy to be entreated, full of mercy and good fruits, without partiality, and without hypocrisy." — *History of Discipline, p.* 304.

But why allow the preachers to appoint the leaders at all? Why not let the classes or society choose them?

For this reason, if for no other: Their work is strictly *spiritual and pastoral* — the work of the minister, so far as he can do it, and the work for which he is responsible to his Conference, to his people, and his God. The leaders are his "*helpers*" in watching and guiding the flock, and who is in a condition to judge what kind of help he needs so well as himself? He understands the qualifications of the candidates, and the real necessity of the classes, as no other person can understand them, and is likely to be free from many local prejudices and false notions, that might operate disastrously in the election of a leader. Take away from him the power to appoint the leaders, and you lessen his responsibility in regard to the spiritual condition of the church one half, at least, and lay it upon the leaders. Then, if religion wanes, he may charge it to the leaders, and the leaders may charge it to him, and the church may take sides with which they please. Thus, there would be confusion in the elections, contention in the administration, and failure where we now have peace and prosperity. So long as the preacher in charge is the responsible executive officer, he must have authority to select his own cabinet. To make him responsible, and deny him this, would be an anomaly in legislation.

Some have objected that the preacher in charge is authorized to appoint committees to try accused members, and preside in such trials. But who can do it more impartially, or with greater wisdom? If we try members by committees, the committees must be appointed, and some one must preside. The president should be responsible for the proceedings of the trial, that they be disciplinary and correct. He should, therefore, understand the Discipline, the general principles of civil jurisprudence, and be unbiased by party connections and party feelings. Who is so likely to possess the necessary qualifications as the preacher in charge? But he may err. It is not impossible that he may administer discipline in a partial and oppressive manner. These are contingencies to which we must always be liable. But the security of the membership against injustice from this source lies, *first*, in their right of appeal to the Quarterly Conference, where the whole case will be considered and decided by another court. But should the appellant still think injustice done him, he has one other resort. He may, *secondly*, follow the preacher to the next Annual Conference, and there arraign him for *mal-administration*, and thus obtain the judgment of that body upon the subject, the effect of which will be either to establish or reverse the preceding decisions in his case.

Under these liabilities, and what to a preacher is a matter of the highest concern, under the liability of being *censured*, and even expelled for wrong, and especially for *malicious*, administration; liable to a civil suit also from the injured party, it seems to us very unlikely that a preacher in charge will allow himself to depart widely from Christian propriety, either in the appointment of committees or in presiding over them in church trials. But allowing that he may do so, who could be more safely *trusted*, or more promptly and effectively *arrested?*

In relation to the right of nominating the stewards, it is sufficient to say, that if a preacher does not nominate one at first that the Quarterly Conference approve, he must "try again," and again, till he gives satisfaction. And so also in relation to the nomination of trustees. In forming a *new* board of trustees, it is true, he is left to his discretion. When the section of Discipline referring to this subject was adopted, it could not well have been otherwise, however it might be now The preachers had the plan to conceive, the money to raise, and the work to oversee. Who had a better right to appoint trustees? This is still the case in a large portion of our work, though in the more established societies the people have taken much of this responsibility on themselves. What still rests on the preachers will probably be transferred in due time to those upon whom it more properly devolves. But whether it ever should be so or not, so long as the preacher's interests are identical with those of the people, no harm can be done by it. It will generally be exercised as it has been, in the united wisdom of both parties, and with pure regard to the cause of God. We see no advantage a preacher can take of it in any event; and where there can be no *motive* to the *abuse* of power, there is nothing to be feared from its existence.

In reference to the *rule making* power of the ministry, we have, *first*, to remind the reader again of our origin, which was such, if the preachers had not made the rules, we should have had none. *Secondly*, that most of our rules have descended to us from Wesley himself. *Thirdly*, that those which have been made since the organization of our church, are more particularly for the government of the preachers than the people. *Fourthly*, that this power is so restricted by civil law, by our *constitution*, and the acknowledged rights and relations of the people, that there was not the slightest danger of its being abused. Still, it was never entirely satisfactory. Early and numerous efforts were made to limit it by introducing laymen into the General Conference, but were successfully opposed until of late. Soon after the South separated from us, many of the former opponents of lay-delegation came to see it to be of the highest importance to the welfare of the church, and inaugurated measures to introduce it in the General Conference, which resulted in its adoption as before detailed.

The checks of our people upon the ministry are ample. 1. It lies with them to determine who shall assume its high prerogatives. To become a minister among us, one must be recommended by the *society* to which he belongs, or by the *leaders'* meeting. Without this, there is no authority in the church to constitute a minister. After such recommendation, the Quarterly Conference, composed chiefly of laymen, may vote the license, when it becomes the presiding elder's duty to *write* it. Should the experiment prove unsuccessful, and indicate that they have endowed the wrong man, they may refuse to renew the license, and restore the brother concerned to private life. On the other hand, should he satisfy them of his call and adaptation to the office, they may recommend him to the Annual Conference for admission into the travelling connection ; without which, the Conference cannot receive him. Nor can they ordain him as a local preacher, till he shall have held the office four years, and been recommended to the Conference as a suitable person to receive that distinction. If this is not placing a very strong *lay* guard at the entrance to the ministry, we mistake. We know of nothing equal to it in other Christian churches. But since the people have relinquished the right of choosing their own pastors, in the common acceptation of the phrase, it is, perhaps, none too strong. They ought to have an important part in constituting the ministers they may be required to receive. It will help their patience in bearing their infirmities, and save the episcopacy from much censure.

2. But the main security of the people lies in their *sovereignty over their own purses.* We cannot touch the *property* of our members. We have no authority to levy a tax on them, nor to collect one. Our people determine the *amount of our allowance*, and then pay it or not, as they

please. If they do not, we have no redress. Our Discipline denies us the right of collecting our dues by a legal process. We can only lament our failure, and hope to meet a better fortune in another appointment. We may, indeed, preach in their churches, the pulpits of which they have been pleased to secure to our occupancy, but they may leave us to address the bare walls, and pay our own expenses. How long we should endure such discipline we leave others to conjecture. If the power, however, of thus withholding temporal supplies, is not a sufficient guarantee against oppression, our preachers must possess more obstinacy, and less attachment to "filthy lucre," than falls to the lot of ordinary good men. Highly as we think of them, considering their poverty and dependence on the people for their daily bread, we are constrained to believe that this power is nearly equal to that of choosing and rejecting preachers at discretion. *Clerical oppression*, under these circumstances, is impossible. Ministers are but men. They can no more subsist without food than other men; and when this is withheld, from dissatisfaction with their labors, they will be very likely to construe it into a *call* to seek another and more promising field.

Speaking on this subject, says our lamented Bishop Emory: "The interests of the preachers as men are not only co-incident, but identical with all the interests which bind them to be good pastors; and that these again are identical with the interests of the people. They cannot possibly have any earthly motive for setting themselves in opposition to the people. All human motives are on the other side. And the far greater danger is that their sense of dependence, and the pressure or apprehension of want, may tempt them, in the general state of our poor, fallen nature, to lower the gospel standard, and to *relax* its holy discipline, in accom modation to the common frailities of those who hold over them, and over their wives and children, and all most dear to them, the fearful power of feeding or starving them at discretion. For the sober truth is, that there is not a body of ministry in the world more perfectly dependent on those whom they serve, than the Methodist *itinerant* ministry. In those churches which have a lay representation, the pastors make legal contracts with their people, and have legal remedies to enforce their fulfilment. We make no such contracts, and have no such remedies. In this, our system is more Scriptural, and renders us more dependent. It places us, in fact, not only from year to year, or from quarter to quarter, but from week to week, within the reach of such a controlling check, on the part of the people, as is possessed, we verily believe, by no other denomination whatever; and which is considered, both by them and us, as a relinquishment of what might be claimed on our part, fully equivalent to the relinquishment on their part of a direct representation in our General Conferences."

But, lest disaffected and parsimonious individuals should take advantage of these remarks to refuse to aid in the support of their preacher, a word of explanation is here necessary. While we allow that the people *as a body* may withhold their preacher's support, and that this is justifiable in case of *oppression*, and as a last resort, when redress cannot be obtained by the milder means of remonstrance and petition, we deny the *moral* right of *individuals* to indulge their private spleen against a preacher in this way, when a majority of the society incline to sustain him. The tendency of such a practice is disastrous. Generally adopted, it would keep our societies in perpetual agitation, and reduce them to a worthless mass of discords. Being young, and not wealthy, union is indispensable to existence. All must act in concert, or the cause will decline. If one may refuse to support *this* preacher because he is not a favorite, or because of some prejudice against him, others may refuse to support *that*, for the same reason. And if this should be recognized as a correct principle, no year would pass without more or less difficulties from this quarter, as no one preacher can possibly be the favorite of all. Besides, there are some covetous persons, no doubt, who would not scruple to invent objections to a preacher, if by so doing they could honorably refuse to support him. The principle furnishes a strong temptation to the avaricious to disaffection, and is, therefore, wrong and ruinous. We believe it to be strictly anti-Methodistical. To adopt it, is an attempt to control by our *money*, what we have submitted to the direction of other causes, and is putting *ourselves* in the place of God, and the best interests of the church. The true Christian policy is, to support the preacher, and make the most of him, whether *we* are particularly pleased or not, provided the society, as such, does not see cause to adopt the extreme measure of withholding his support. It is *the cause of Christ* and the church, which is to be consulted, and not our *prejudices*. Will my withholding support from God's minister be the best I can do for the *cause?* is the question, and not whether it will gratify *my feelings*. If others are pleased and profited by his labors, that is reason enough why I should sustain him, though, as an *individual*, I may dislike him. This is the true magnanimity of Methodism, and is fatal to that narrow selfishness which supports the gospel only so far as may be necessary to gratify personal prejudices and predilections. And every departure from this practice is hazardous to the itinerancy, since it is calculated to embarrass the preacher financially, and necessitate him to resort to some different system, under which his support will not depend upon so many contingencies.

It should be remarked, also, that this confidence of the preachers in God, and the magnanimity of the people, should never in the least influence the latter to follow a narrow and contemptible policy. When it has been determined what a preacher's claim shall be, stewards, and, indeed, the whole church, should exert themselves just as much to meet that claim as they would if it were collectable by law. It is not only a *debt of honor*, in the highest sense, but it is a religious debt. And the insinuation that it is "no matter whether it be paid or not, since the removal of the preacher will cancel it," is too dishonest and mean to be countenanced for a moment. If there be a steward in the church capable of acting on such a principle, the sooner he leaves it the better it will be for the cause. On the same principle, when the people have fully done their duty, the preacher must patiently submit to the result, though his receipts have not met his claims, or supplied his necessities.

But these explanations do not invalidate our argument. They are designed to prevent the abuse of the system at two different points, and secure to the preachers their proper claims where it is at all practicable, and to societies the exclusive privilege of starving preachers off, against the usurpation of covetous individuals.

Societies have this pecuniary check upon the ministry, and it is right they should have it; but brethren cannot be good members of those societies while they refuse to act in concert with the majority, and withhold their pecuniary assistance in meeting expenses, to gratify a personal prejudice.

The people hold other influences over their minister. They may smile or frown upon him, encourage his plans or frustrate them, and make him happy or miserable. He is a "lone pilgrim" and stranger, without friends or influence; they are at home, surrounded by associates who are accustomed to sympathize with all their views and modes of effort. Let them attempt to harass the preacher, and his condition will be unpleasant, indeed. He has every thing that is desirable in their friendship, therefore, to induce him to conduct toward them like a gentleman and a Christian. In such a contest, he has every thing to lose — nothing to gain. He cannot be so reckless of his own peace as to do them injustice.

He is, however, liable to mistake. We have known some to exceed their legitimate powers, through ignorance, but were corrected under the natural operation of the system, which provides not only for the correction of wilful wrongs, but for others. So the people have sometimes gone beyond their rights, and experienced the appropriate restraints. The system does not preclude errors, but it corrects them when they occur with wonderful facility. It aims high, requires great sacrifices and achievements, and endows its officers accordingly. There is no collision of one part with another. Its various forces operate in admirable harmony, and secure the interests of all who submit to its arrangements.

Finally, the best argument for the system is, *it works well.* If eagle-eyed complainers have found oppression in it, the people have not experienced any in its operation. We have had occasion to ask men who had renounced it with a view to the establishment of something better, if it ever oppressed them, but they all, with one consent, answered in the negative. It has also been efficient. Look at its history. What system ever effected so much in so short a time, with such feeble means, and against such formidable opposition? The like has never been witnessed before, since the days of the apostles. Systems which claim more democracy, and have learning, and wealth, and age, and political influence, have been out-stripped by it, a hundred to one. Hopeful competitors and antagonists have fallen down, and perished by the way, notwithstanding their numerous advantages, while this has gone on from strength to strength, working "righteousness," subduing "kingdoms," stopping the mouths of lions, waxing valiant in fight, and turning to flight the armies of the aliens. But a few years since we were no people; but we are now the people of the Lord, spread out over the whole land. A little more than a half century ago we numbered our flocks by scores and hundreds; now we number them by millions. How is this? Where is the secret of our success? Would an ill-contrived system, though hard worked, have done so much? We think not. Would a system oppressive to the people, such as this has been represented, have been so cordially received? The people have never complained. Let us be judged by our works, and we will abide the issue.

CHAPTER VI.

THE GOVERNMENT OF THE M. E. CHURCH CONTRASTED WITH OTHER SYSTEMS.

THUS far we have said little of our polity by way of com parison, preferring to present it on its own merits. The discussion would, probably, be more acceptable to brethren of other sects, were we to maintain this policy to the end. But considering the assumptions of other systems, and especially the numerous objections their friends and supporters have seen fit to urge against our own, we cannot do justice to this department of our work, without referring to a few particulars, in which the former are wanting in virtues that abound in the latter. We shall treat the subject as delicately as possible, and hope to give no offence.

Of the different forms of episcopacy, we have little to say. Not for the reason that they are more agreeable to us, so much as that they are less in our way. Romanism is an absolute monarchy. The priesthood is the master, the people the slave. But this abuse of episcopacy does not invalidate it. Those who declaim against bishops, because they have figured so abhorrently in the Romish Church, seal their own condemnation. They practice many things that have descended to them through this same medium. They might reject the Bible on this principle. But, muddy as is the channel through which it has been transmitted, they receive it as the pure word of God. They erect churches, also, keep holy days, preach and pray, all of which things Romanists have abused from time immemorial.

Nor would we be understood as having any particular friendship for the system of Protestant Episcopalians, though we leave them out of this account. Their episcopacy is altogether over-strained, and not properly guarded. They assume too much for it, and concede too much to Romanists, to maintain a very stable and protracted existence, except where they are identified with the State; and there, even, they will be subject to infinite trouble, since the administration will, probably, vary in its predilections, as heretofore; now inclining toward Rome, and now, again, toward liberty and religious toleration.

We shall speak principally of Independency and Presbyterianism, and on general principles. Three points of comparison will be sufficient to indicate the grounds of our preference for the Methodist Episcopal system.

I. The first we shall name relates to pastoral and ministerial authority.

The difference between us and Independents and Presbyterians, on this point, is considerable. We believe the Christian ministry, however established, to be invested with certain prerogatives that are not to be exercised or controlled by any other body. That is, that when a man is duly called of God to the ministry, he is authorized to discharge certain functions that other men should not undertake; and, therefore, when he is recognized, by any people, as thus called, this authority should not be subordinated to their control. If they do not dare to trust him, and want *security* for his prudence and fidelity in using it, they may provide for it as they and he can agree; but while he is among them as a minister of Christ, to represent his master's cause, and do his work, he should be untrammelled in regard to every part of ministerial duty. We refer now more particularly to the ministry of the word and the administration of the sacraments.

If we mistake not, both Presbyterianism and Independency (we use the latter term, without meaning any offence, to designate all Congregationalists of whatever sect) theoretically and practically deny this authority, and place their ministers under a guardianship in the discharge of their peculiar duties, which can but prove a serious impediment to the success of any man who attempts achievements worthy of the office, — to say nothing of the care with which they supervise the utterances of the pulpit, complaints of which are becoming more and more multiplied and emphatic every day. How is it in regard to the ordinances? Is a minister allowed to baptize such as he deems worthy? By no means. He may preach the gospel to them, teach, and conduct them safely through the process of repentance and regeneration; but there he must stop. Before he fulfils the other part of his commission, "baptizing them in the name of the Father, and of the Son, and of the Holy Ghost," he must call a meeting of the "church session," if among Presbyterians — of the church, or the church committee, if among Independents — and have them canvassed to the satisfaction of the body, when, if they judge proper, and give their consent, he may proceed; but if they, in their *prudence*, decide for postponement, whether it be for good reasons, or no reason at all, he must withhold the ordinance, however assured of the worthiness of the candidate to receive it. The same is also true of the Lord's supper. He may "travail with them in birth, until Christ be formed in them," and feel an unutterable solicitude to have them baptized, and admitted to the Church and the sacrament, but he must wait the motion of the ruling elders, or of the committee, who may have no sympathy for the work, and are just in the right spirit to perplex candidates with knotty questions of doctrine, ungrounded suspicions and delays, to "see if they are not deceived, and are *going to backslide.*"

Now the question is not whether ministers of these denominations are not often as cold as the people, and realize no difficulty from this source, nor whether they do not frequently gain *influence* enough over their constitutional managers to control them in such matters, nor whether the people are not sometimes more spiritual than their preachers. There is no doubt on either of these points. Nor do we assume that there is any particular difficulty in these arrangements, where society is formally established, and possesses little religious enterprise beyond the weekly routine of settled service. But where a minister is properly engaged in his work, and is connected with a church whose leading spirits do not harmonize with the legitimate objects of the ministry, he may find them a burden more grievous to be borne than poverty or persecution. One who was many years a Presbyterian, and honored with various offices of responsibility, speaking of this system of overseership, says, "It embarrasses the ministry, in all its forms and modes of operation, and disappoints its aims and ends; it sets up a complicated, inconvenient, unmanageable machinery, which is hard to keep standing, so as to command respect, much more to keep going, so as to do good. * * * This machinery has absorbed all controlling power, and the ministry is an accident. That which was first has come to be last. Christ gave his sacraments to his ministers — to the apostles — that in the use of them they and their successors might maintain the visible forms of his kingdom. But, in this system, the sacraments are held by organizations of laity, and the ministry are obliged to ask leave to take and use them." It was to this kind of control that an old non-conformist minister referred, when he remarked, "I left England to get rid of my lords, the bishops; but here I find in their place my lords, *the brethren and sisters;* save me from the latter, and let me have the former." And we find frequent allusions to it in the communications of Congregational and Presbyterian ministers, in speaking of revivals. It is when they undertake to accomplish something for God and souls, that the system embarrasses them.

We object to this aspect of it,

1. That it is *unscriptural.* If the commission under which all ministers profess to act means any thing, it requires those who receive it to "baptize," as much as it requires them to "preach," or to "teach." And they must be their own judges both as to the one and the other. They have no right to agree to refuse baptism to such as, in their opinion, ought to be baptized, to gratify the prejudice, or extreme prudence, or, it may be, the ignorance, of a committee, whose opportunity of understanding the merits of the case is not half equal to their own; and the people ought not to require such subordination at their hands. If they do not think their minister competent for the work, let them dismiss him, and obtain one they can trust.

Is it reasonable to believe that the apostles, and their immediate successors, were subject to such a regimen? Where is the proof? Is it likely that Jerusalem and all Judea passed through the hands of a committee to John the Baptist, before they received the ordinance? Or that St. Paul called the ruling elders to examine the jailer? Was Cornelius, or the eunuch, or the thousands baptized on the day of Pentecost, tested in this manner? The apostles acted on their own responsibility, and required repentance, and such "fruits" in the candidate as satisfied themselves. And since ministers are answerable to the Chief Shepherd for the fulfilment of their commission, why is not this right? "As I live, saith the Lord God, surely, because my flock became a prey, and my flock became meat to every beast of the field, because there was no shepherd, neither did my shepherd search for my flock; therefore, O, ye shepherds, hear the word of the Lord. Thus saith the Lord God: behold I am against the shepherds, *and I will require my flock at their hand*, and cause them to cease from feeding the flock."

2. Another objection to this arrangement is, *it degrades the ministry.* It assumes that ministers are unsuitable judges in such cases, and need to be directed when to exercise their commission. If we add that the pastor is required to be a member of his own church, and subject to discipline and exclusion at their discretion, his degradation is complete. "We maintain," says the Congregational Manual, p. 24, a book of high authority, "that among ministers there should be no distinctions of rank, but that they are all equal, and that ministers have no right to exercise lordship over the brethren of the church; that the brethren of the church [embracing the minister] *are all equal;* and that no church, or body or council of churches, can have any inherent power to control particular churches." An Independent minister informed the writer, within a few days, that he was required to be a member of his own church; but he thought were he to be accused and tried, they would allow him a counsel, though the final determination of the case would lie with them.

3. We object to it, also, that it is inconvenient. It is so, 1. In that it leaves the churches without a *visible head*. Every society needs a head, possessing powers that belong to no other member. Hence we give our Union a President, each State a Governor, each court a judge, and assign

them duties, which they are to discharge under constitutional restrictions, on their own responsibility, without the liability of being overruled in each case by the popular voice. But here, though the minister is moderator in church meetings, his order may be countermanded by a bare majority, whether it relate to theology or discipline. The Church is supreme, and he must submit. 2. It is inconvenient in that it requires proceedings that must, in many cases, be very difficult, if not impracticable. Look at the Congregational manner of organizing a church, which is only a single development of the system. In the "Manual," before named, we read: "The organization of a church is a step which should not be taken without much caution, and due consultation with those whose judgment in the case can be well relied upon. Whenever a decision has been made upon the expediency of such a movement, the first thing to be done is to have the articles of faith and covenant by which the church is to be bound together, drawn up and agreed upon by those who propose to become members. The next thing is to fix upon a time and place for the assembling of the council, and the formation of the church. Then, by what is called a 'Letter Missive,' some of the neighboring churches are requested to be present, by their pastors and delegates, to assist (if *they* shall judge it to be expedient) in the organization of the proposed church. The 'Letter Missive' states some of the more important circumstances of the case, — the number of persons expected to constitute the church, — the churches that have been invited to aid in forming it, — the time and place of the meeting of the council, and of the public services of the day.

"When the day arrives, and the members of the council have come together, (the persons desirous of being formed into a church being present,) they are called to order by one of their number, who reads the 'Letter Missive,' as an explanation of the object of the meeting. The business then proceeds by choosing a moderator and a scribe, and the offering of prayer for the divine assistance in the performance of the duties that are to follow.

"The whole subject of going forward in the accomplishment of the purpose for which the council has been called, is then deliberately considered; all desired information in relation to the number and circumstances of the candidates for membership in the new church is presented, and the articles of faith and covenant, and letters of dismission and recommendation of such as belong to other churches are examined.

"If the council decide upon going forward, arrangements are then made for the public exercises; and, at the time appointed, all concerned proceed to the house of God, where the solemn transaction is to take place.

"The public services are usually in the following order: 1. Reading of the doings of the council. 2. Invocation. 3. Reading of the Scriptures. 4. Singing. 5. Prayer. 6. Singing. 7. Sermon. 8. Reading of the articles of faith, and giving assent to them by the persons about being formed into a church (who, at this time, are standing together.) 9. Administration of the rite of baptism to those who have never received it. 10. Reading and acknowledgment of the covenant. 11. Consecrating prayer. 12. Fellowship of the churches. 13. Singing. 14. Prayer. 15. Benediction. The persons who in these exercises have associated themselves together, are thus constituted a church, possessing all the powers and privileges of a church of Christ."

That this may work respectably in a dense population,

where societies are numerous, enlightened and enterprising, is not questioned, though it seems to us heavy and cumbrous for any circumstances. But its inadaptation to a world lying in wickedness, superstition, and ignorance, is manifest. What could the apostles have done with such a system? How could Wesley have managed it? And where would have been the millions that have been gathered into the fold of Christ by him and his successors, had he adopted it? It reminds one of Saul's armor. The machinery requires too many individuals to work it, takes too much time, and costs too much. But where there is a want of harmony or of enterprise, it becomes unmanageable, and proves to be any thing but *Independent* in its operations. Let us refer to a single case by way of illustration.

A portion of an interesting Orthodox Congregational Church, at A., became dissatisfied with their pastor, and desired him to ask his dismission. The pastor saw no good reason for his doing so, and was sustained by a bare majority of the church in his position. After much discussion, and many unpleasant transactions, he united with the church, for the gratification of a respectable minority, in calling a council to sit upon the question of the propriety of his asking to be dismissed. The council was convened, and displayed many ministers and lay delegates of distinguished ability. The whole question was discussed, both parties speaking all that was in their hearts. After a day or two the bell was rung, and the parish came together to hear the report, which was, in substance, that the pastor was entitled to great credit for his labors and success, and ought to retain his position; and the disaffected minority were advised to be peaceable, and to coöperate with him. This, of course, was not very pleasing to some of the members. Passing the church, about that time, one issued forth, and in no very pleasant mood denounced the council for their *ex parte* proceedings, declaring that there was *one* thing the minority could do, viz., they could form a new church, and they should do it immediately. Reminding him that all systems have their hard bearings, we suggested that he might find that as difficult as to get rid of his minister. "How so?" he inquired. "In the first place," we remarked, "you must get letters of dismission and recommendation from your church to a council, to be formed into another and a separate church. But your church will give you no such letters, until a majority are convinced it is best to have another church in the place, and the same majority that retains the preacher will not be likely to indulge you in this way. But, suppose you get your letters, and call your council, the council may judge as the church do, that it is inexpedient to have a second church, when, of course, you are 'all up' again, for they will not organize you till they are convinced on this point." "Well," said he, "we'll go without letters, and form a church without a council!" "This," we replied, "you *can* do, but the church will probably *expel* you for neglect of duty and disorderly conduct, which they will have a right to do. But," we asked, "who will you get to be your preacher? Congregational ministers will not serve you, because you will not be in the regular line. But should one be found who would consent to be as disorderly as yourselves, you could get no council to sit upon the question of his settlement; ordain, install, or give him the right hand of fellowship. But should all these difficulties be surmounted, every regular association and convention of the denomination would disown both you and your preacher as spurious coin."

This was a new idea. Of course, he reported it to his copartners in *reform*, and it was as strange and new to them as to him; and, finding themselves tied hand and foot, so that they could not move but at the will of the *sovereign majority*, they hammered away upon the afflicted pastor, as the only thing they could do, till he was compelled to compromise, and call another council to permit him to leave, and determine how much the church should give him for going. This done, the agitators settled down quietly in their old position, wiser than they were before; but they have been in a quandary ever since, to learn why such a system should be called *Independent*, or *Congregational;* and they have not yet discovered wherein it is better to be under the lordship of *unrestricted majorities* and foreign councils made up for the occasion, than to be subject to bishops and other ecclesiastical functionaries, whose authority is limited by constitutional stipulations.

We might refer to other inconveniences for which the system is peculiar. Where the desire for another church is the result of Christian enterprise, the difficulty of organizing it may be equally formidable. The church may refuse the letters, the covenant and creed may not suit the council, or the candidate preacher may be offensive, and the undertaking consequently fail. But we will not go into particulars. The system is better adapted to *permanence* than *progress*, and the more quiet it is kept, the less awkward will it appear.

4. We think it *prejudicial to ministerial independence.* Any minister thus encompassed with committees, and other appointees, having the direction of *his* appropriate work, must feel more or less embarrassed. If he be a man of talent and *courage*, he may manage *them* and the church to his liking, (an occurrence that often happens,) and not become a slave to his people. But where there is only an ordinary man, and his overseers chance to be men of con-

siderable consequence, and high notions of the rights of the laity, he will eventually succumb to their dictation, and instead of *making* society what it ought to be, he will become its mere *echo*.

5. It evidently *fails of its object.* This we suppose to be the protection of the members, and the advancement of the work of God. But the system, by taking much of the responsibility from the minister, and vesting it in ruling elders, or in the church, destroys not only an important *means of usefulness*, but one of the most powerful incentives to effort that *regenerated* humanity can have. When one feels that he is *alone* responsible for a work, he will think of it, and acquit himself with honor. But divide that responsibility among a dozen, in such a way that it will not be generally known who does, and who does not attend to it, and it will probably be neglected. This is as true in regard to disciplining members as baptizing them. If the writer were to be tried, he would prefer to have the minister, or some *one* man, to be his *judge*, and decide the law and order in the case, under proper restrictions, than to have the *whole society*. Knowing that his act would decide the case, and incur for *him* praise or blame, he would feel the necessity of coming to a proper decision, that, if arraigned before the bar of public opinion, or any other bar, he might vindicate his conduct with boldness and success. But a church is *nobody*. "Corporations have no souls," and, of course, no *individual* responsibility.

Besides, who does not know the power of neighborhood gossip to beget jealousy, envy, and evil surmising, which create prejudice and warp the judgment. In a popular trial, before an excited church, an innocent man has no chance at all, though the crime alleged may be no more than that of giving "aid and comfort" to reputed heretics, or visiting the meetings or communion of another sect. They have no specific law to keep or to break. Their will is sovereign, their action final. But if they were under a constitution and laws, subject to the ruling of a responsible *judge*, and liable to be reviewed and condemned by a higher court, they would have reason to be cautious.

On the other hand, the church would be defended against improper characters. As *good* men are liable to be wronged through popular *prejudice*, so *bad* men may be preserved in the church, to its great dishonor, through popular *favor*. *Merit* is by no means the criterion of the estimate the public place upon men. A hard way into the church makes a hard way out of it. Those who claim to examine candidates, and test them by a popular vote before they are received or admitted to the ordinances, also claim to retain them to their liking; so that persons are often kept in the church by *favoritism*, who in justice ought to be excluded. If the policy of England is right in not allowing its judges to preside in the district where they were born, and if the method of empanelling juries so as to exclude all improper influences, is important, Independency is wanting at this point.

Is it said that the desideratum indicated is supplied, by the association of the churches under different names for counsel and advice? We believe this association is *designed* to supply it, and, therefore, we regard it as a practical acknowledgment of the imperfection of the Independen system. But, however it may operate to protect the ministry (for it benefits them more than others) and the people, in specific cases, in application to the matters in question we think it an entire failure. If we err in this opinion, we are certainly correct in saying, that just so far as it is effective, it diverges from Independency. If the parties advised are *bound* to acquiesce in the advice given, on pain of being excluded from the association, consociation, state convention, or the like, Independency is abandoned, and a modification of Presbyterianism is adopted, which is no doubt an improvement. This we believe to be the case in certain sections and among certain Congregationalists, but others claim the right of rejecting advice if it does not suit them, without damage to their denominational reputation.

In distinction from all this, under our economy, a minister goes forth preaching the gospel; and when he is successful, and the people repent and become converted, he receives them on *trial*, baptizes them, and administers to them the sacrament of the Lord's Supper. Whenever three or four persons desire his watch-care, he forms them into a class, and attaches them to the main body, and then adds to their number as he is able. Thus most of our churches commenced, and thus they have been nursed, and enlarged, and multiplied. The first blush of our history indicates to every rational man that the other system would have proved an incumbrance. Our churches have been *disciplined*, too, with the same ministerial authority; but in all cases under such guarantees as to secure the people against oppression.

II. We believe our government preferable also in *its legislation*. Not that we have better moral rules than our Christian neighbors; we will not insist on this, but that we have come nearer the happy medium in respect to the number and extent of them. There are two extremes to be avoided, viz.: *paucity and redundancy*. In our opinion, the Independents have fallen upon the first, and the Presbyterians upon the last. The former have few rules. They agree to very little in advance, and leave almost every thing to be settled at the time. They doubtless have *customs* that in part supply this necessity, but they evidently lack for constitutions and laws defining the rights and duties of the several parties concerned in their organization. Therefore, matters of whatever nature turn a good deal upon the fancy or current of feeling that may happen to predominate. Hence, when we inquired of an Independent minister as to the government of his denomination, preparatory to writing this chapter, he replied that it was "a *perfect mobocracy.*" The explanation that succeeded did not modify the statement, but developed his entire dissatisfaction with it. He said they lacked a *head*, a *constitution*, *authority*. That prejudices often operated to turn out worthy members, and retain those who were a disgrace to the Christian name, and there was no redress. Still it was his intention to abide in the body, and make the best of it.

The Presbyterians have evidently gone to the other extreme. They have left little to discretion. Matters of great simplicity, and not of the highest importance, are drawn out with particularity, so that one needs to be something of a lawyer, and a pretty thorough student, to understand the whole. This exposes them to many difficulties. It gives troublesome characters a chance to annoy the min ister and his flock, where, if there were less of rules, and more of discretionary authority vested in the pastorate, under proper guarantees for its legitimate exercise, the machinery would operate with less *friction* and more *force*.*

We may have erred in the same direction. Excess is the tendency of legislators generally. Though we admire the *smallness* of our Discipline, next to the system it graphically delineates, still we are inclined to think it may be too

* A glance at the "*Assembly's Digest*," a large volume composed of reports of cases, precedents, and commentaries, will be sufficient to substantiate these remarks.

large. That it restricts both preacher and people at points where they had better be left to their own discretion, is highly probable. *Religion is one and eternal,* and must not be altered to accommodate the king. But there are a thou sand little out-of-door matters — matters of finance or of taste — having no particular moral bearing, that may be varied according to the judgment of the brethren concerned in different localities. If we were to be consulted, we should advise that all such matters be left discretionary, holding the officers concerned amenable for their action in the premises to the tribunals having the supervision of their administration.

III. We think our government a little superior, too, in its *jurisprudence;* that is, in its process of dealing with offending and delinquent members. While it is impossible to avoid the necessity of such proceedings, it is important that they be conducted in the best manner. There are two objects to be provided for in a system of proceeding in such cases. One is *promptness* and energy, without public agitation; the other is *security* against wrong and oppressive action, into which the most sincere are liable to be precipitated by improper influences. The *first* is necessary to the protection of the *church,* that it may not be dishonored by immoral and scandalous characters, or crippled by an accumulation of dead and unfruitful members. The second is necessary to the protection of *individuals,* against whom processes may be instituted, that they may be fairly tried, whatever the state of feeling against them, and have ample opportunity to defend themselves on every point. If we are not deceived, Independency is faulty in both these particulars.

1. In regard to the church, it lacks the requisite *provision* for such proceedings. Its fundamental principle is that

of strict *equality* among members, and its covenant binds them to mutual "watch and care," so that one has originally as much authority in the premises as another. Now, what is every body's business is generally neglected. No one feels particular responsibility. Each thinks it more suitable for another to move in the case, and thus the evil is suffered to remain; whereas, if the responsibility was devolved upon an *individual*, and it was made his *duty* to attend to it, it would not be so.

We concede that these churches often appoint committees on such cases, and that these committees exercise discipline; but, then, *will* they appoint them in all *proper* cases, or will they be *warped* by the circumstances of consanguinity, friendship, wealth, &c., and suffer the cause to be reproached? Will they sustain such a committee when appointed, and inflict the appropriate punishment, or will they evade the issue, and cover up iniquity? Human nature is such that, where we have no constitutions and laws binding us, we are very apt to consult our convenience, to the neglect of duty.

The disposition to do the right thing being admitted, other questions arise, such as, what conduct is to be considered censurable? Here is a chance for much difference and discussion. This settled, it must then be determined when and how the process shall be commenced, and how conducted. Next comes the verdict. Can these questions be settled where all are prosecuting officers, *judges*, *jurors*, *counsel, and witnesses*, with sufficient despatch and impartiality to protect the church? Or is there a strong chance for party feeling, discord, electioneering, personal crimination, inefficiency and delay? How would a town succeed in managing its judicial affairs in this manner?

To say that "Christ is our *head*, and his word our *law*,"

does not relieve the difficulty. What that law requires on many of these and collateral points, is to be determined by a majority. Nor does the fact that you are Christians, looking for the honor of the cause of God, remedy the evil. Christians are liable to be blinded and swayed by the various influences that operate upon the human mind, as well as others. If you say that this whole business is done by the minister and a few leading men in the church, we think this is decidedly better; but it is a departure from the main principle of Independency.

Understand us, we do not complain. This is a free country, and we may all please ourselves. We speak of things as we understand them. And the inefficiency we charge upon the system is frequently conceded by those who ought to know. One good minister in this city, who was groaning under the incubus of unworthy members in his church, remarked to the writer, "*we lack your discipline.*" Another averred to painful facts, in relation to members in his denomination, which they could not touch without throwing the church into a perfect tumult. And another, still, referred us to disgraceful circumstances, which Independency cannot reach, and from which, therefore, his church is doomed to suffer, if not to perish.

2. That it protects individuals better than it does the cause, is not likely. Having no constitution and well defined laws, and no properly constituted expounder of law and order to preside in such proceedings, they may fall upon a member, in a fit of prejudice, and hurl him from among them in the most summary and unjust manner. Hence, the phenomenon, that is not unfrequently witnessed, of a church retaining members of the most unsatisfactory character; while it excludes others of acknowledged piety, for a slight difference of opinion on some *nice* point of doctrine, or for

favoring another denomination, or because the tongue of slander has created a prejudice which the church is afraid to resist. Is it said that the church is bound to do right, and act according to the gospel? We reply, that does not help the case, so long as *they* — the excited, bigoted, and prejudiced members — are to decide what right requires. Bind them by a constitution and laws, to be explained and administered by intelligent and impartial judges, and then the case will be different. But that will not do; they must be their own judges in all these matters.

Hence, we say, there is no security for individual character. A member may be disgraced by expulsion, at the option of a majority, and he has no redress, unless he can obtain it by an appeal to the civil courts, which is exceedingly doubtful; for "where there is no law there is no transgression," and where there is no transgression [violation of contract] no damage can be recovered. If Independent societies have no constitution and rules in reference to such things, of course they violate none in following their passions in the premises, and cannot be punished. The suffering member may regret that he surrendered himself so entirely to their hands; but it is too late to correct the mistake.

Is it said that he may call a council? True, — *if he can obtain one;* but here is the difficulty. Nobody is obliged to serve, and few would be likely to accept the call of an excommunicated member to attend to such business. But suppose he should succeed in getting a council, and the council should advise the church in his favor? What then? Will not the church do just as they please, after all? The advice of *ex parte* councils is not very powerful with majorities. Majorities are often the most inexorable tyrants. Is it said, let him call a mutual council? That he cannot do without the consent of the church, which they will give or not, as they please. The probabilities in the case cannot be mistaken. But should they consent, and the council be called, it can only *advise;* so that, in any case, redress is exceedingly uncertain. The presumption is, 1. That the church, in most cases, would not consent to a *mutual* council. 2. That an *ex parte* council could not be obtained. 3. If it should be, that its advice would avail nothing. And, 4. That the labor, difficulties, loss of time, and expense of creating such a court, and prosecuting the investigation, would discourage ninety-nine hundredths of the denomination from undertaking any such project. The excommunicated member, therefore, is practically doomed to submit to his fate, however unjust. If it were not for being personal, we might furnish numerous facts illustrative of all these positions.

Presbyterianism we think less exceptionable, in that it provides regular judicatories, with full powers to attend to such business; and not only requires them to be faithful, but places them under such restrictions as not essentially to endanger the rights of individual members. If the court below is delinquent, or misjudges in a given case, the next above may correct it, so as to repair the damage. But, like Independency, it wants a head. In the "church session," the pastor and ruling elders stand on a par, except the former is the moderator. All may give their opinions; but every question is to be settled by the majority. Hence, they are liable not only to a difference of judgment as to the merits of the case, but also in reference to the law of the church bearing upon it. Their trials may, therefore, lead to an extended discussion of legal questions, and occasion much perplexity, and the loss of much time. The same is true in regard to the higher judicatories of the church. But if the "general assembly" would appoint men to preside in these several courts, and decide all questions of law and order, like a judge upon the bench, making them amenable for their decisions and administration, it would lessen the difficulties of enforcing discipline very much. And if they would endow them still further, and permit them to exercise certain discretion, in resisting and suppressing vexatious suits, holding them to the same responsibility as in the other case, it would be still better; but they have not seen fit to do it.

Under our economy, a large discretion is vested in the preacher in charge, in reference to complaints. He is made judge of law and order, subject to an appeal, and is required to discipline the church in a prompt, prudent, and energetic manner. Should an excommunicated member believe he has been improperly treated, — that his trial was not disciplinary and fair, — he may appeal to the Quarterly Conference, where the whole matter will be considered and determined, under the direction of another president, and by another body. If the trial was misconducted below, or the verdict was more the result of prejudice than evidence, it is corrected here, and the decision reversed. Local preachers, condemned by this court, may appeal to the next Annual Conference having appellate jurisdiction, where their case will be adjudicated by a body of strangers, having no prejudices or predilections to serve. This would seem to be a sufficient guarantee to the members concerned; but still they have another resort. Every member of an Annual Conference is responsible to his Conference for the right administration of discipline. Should he be thought, by a censured or excommunicated member, to have exceeded his authority and taken an unwarrantable course, he may be charged with mal-administration, and, if the charge be sustained, the case may be thrown back, on the ground that "what is not done correctly, is not done at all." We think of an instance to the point. There was a difficulty in the church at R., and parties were formed. The preacher, taking sides with the less reliable members, had charges preferred against the principal man on the other side, on which he was condemned and expelled. Believing the proceeding to be *ex parte*, and contrary to discipline, he sent a complaint to the next Annual Conference, charging the preacher accordingly. The charge was examined with such evidence as was at hand, and sustained. With this decision, the complainant demanded of the next preacher to be recognized as a member in the same standing he held when the suit was commenced. The preacher stated the case to the church, and informed them, that the trial having been condemned, he should be obliged to regard it as null and void, and accede to the brother's request. "But," said he, "if any of you see cause to prefer charges against him, he shall be duly tried." Here the matter ended. The source of difficulty being removed, all soon came right again, and peace ensued.

This is the protection which our members enjoy against hurried, irregular, and unjust prosecutions. Though it goes beyond any thing to be found in other churches, we believe it to be proper. Its effect is to beget such care on the part of the ministry to have business done correctly, that Conferences are seldom troubled with complaints of this nature

CHAPTER VII.

DISCIPLINARY QUESTIONS OFFICIALLY DECIDED.

SINCE our bishops have been constituted judges of disci pline during the intervals of the General Conference, their decisions have become valuable, though not authoritative, unless delivered in some case in course of adjudication. We present a few of them here, together with others, for the benefit of our younger brethren. But the reader must not forget that many of them which relate to Quarterly Conferences are now somewhat modified by District Conferences where they are held.—*Discipline*, ¶¶ 113–127.

I.—OF ANNUAL CONFERENCES.

1. "When, in the interim of an Annual Conference, a preacher, being a member of the Conference, has been tried, and the case adjudicated by the presiding elder and a committee, according to the provisions of the discipline, and the individual acquitted of the charge, or punished for the offence, is it competent for the ensuing Annual Conference to take up the case and pass on it another adjudication, unless an appeal be made from the decision by one of the parties?"

Ans. "The investigation of an accused preacher's character, in the interim of the Annual Conference, is for the purpose of determining whether he shall be suspended until his Conference meets, and is not properly a trial, it being fully considered and determined only before the Annual Conference. The Annual Conference may try said preacher, whether the committee find him guilty or not; the Conference having original jurisdiction. The case never goes up from the committee by appeal, and all proper testimony in any church trial is admissible." — *Bishop Hamline.*

2. "Does the Conference year terminate on the opening of the session of the Annual Conference, or at the close of the session?"

Ans. "The current Conference year has its commencement at the close of the Conference, when the appointments are announced, and terminates at the close of the next session following." — *B. Waugh.*

II.—OF PRESIDING ELDERS, QUARTERLY CONFERENCES, AND LOCAL PREACHERS.

1. "Has the Quarterly Conference original jurisdiction in the case of local preachers, on the charge of immorality?"

Ans. "In the Discipline there is a distinction made between *charges and mere reports.* When a local elder, deacon, or preacher is reported to be guilty of some crime expressly forbidden in the word of God, it is made the duty of the preacher in charge to call him before a committee of local preachers, by whom he shall be acquitted, or, if found guilty, suspended until the next Quarterly Conference. The design of this rule is, first, to relieve the character of an innocent persecuted brother from the influence of evil reports; or, secondly, to relieve the suffering church, by preventing a wicked man from preaching till he can be regularly tried. It requires the preacher in charge to proceed on mere report, whether there be any formal charges or not; to call a committee, which is of the nature of a court of inquiry, to ascertain whether or not there be cause of trial; and, if so, it must go to the Quarterly Conference, the only tribunal that has authority to try the case. And in all practicable cases, the preacher in charge should inquire into complaints against local preachers by a committee, before they come into Quarterly Conference, or be held responsible for this neglect of duty. But if he neglect it, or fail to obtain a committee, or fail for want of time, that neglect or failure does not deprive the Quarterly Conference of its legal authority to try a local preacher on charges of immorality. The rule is definite and clear. 'The Quarterly Meeting Conference shall have authority * * * to try, suspend, expel, or acquit, any local preacher in the circuit or station, against whom charges may be brought.' * * * It is, therefore, my opinion that the Quarterly Conference has original jurisdiction in the case of local preachers on a charge of immorality, and may proceed directly to trial, provided always that the accused has had proper notice." — *Bishop Morris.*

2. "Suppose a local preacher to be charged with immorality, and brought before the Quarterly Conference for trial, whereupon a motion is adopted to strike out the first specification, which is only for *imprudence*, the previous labor required by Discipline not having been performed, has the Quarterly Conference exceeded its authority in the premises?"

Ans. "If any illegality is found, the Conference may reject any part of the bill." — *E. S. Janes.*

3. "Are the characters of local elders subject to examination in the Quarterly Conference?"

Ans. "Most certainly they are. The difference between the accountability of a local preacher and that of a local elder, in Quarterly Conference, is, the license of the former may be withheld for mere want of qualifications, but the office of the latter cannot be taken away until he is tried and convicted of some offence against the Discipline. One rule requires every local elder, deacon, and preacher, to have his name recorded on the journal of the Quarterly Conference of which he is a member, and also enrolled on a class paper, and meet in class; 'or, in neglect thereof, the Quarterly Conference, if they judge it proper, may deprive him of his ministerial office.' Another rule says: 'No elder, deacon, or preacher among us shall distil or vend spirituous liquors, without forfeiting his official standing.' Now, these rules need no comment to show, that the characters of local elders are 'subject to examination in the Quarterly Conference, as much as those of travelling elders are in the Annual Conference. And what is said of elders is equally true of deacons." — *Bishop Morris.*

4. "When a Quarterly Conference has determined that a local preacher is guilty of some offence, who is to determine the amount of punishment?"

Ans. "Not the presiding elder, but the Quarterly Conference." — *Hedding on Discipline, p.* 33.

5. "Suppose, at the examination of an appealed case, the presiding elder discovers that the trial below was conducted contrary to rule, has he a right to throw out the case, prevent the decision of the Conference, and declare the person not expelled?"

Ans. "On this question there have been differences of opinion to a wide extent, and great debates in Conferences. But I should say, no; the appeal is to the Quarterly Conference, not to the presiding elder." — *p.* 34.

6. "Is it right for the Quarterly Conference, on the ques-

tion, 'Are there any complaints?' to hear complaints against the travelling preachers, or any other member of the Quarterly Conference?

Ans. "This question admits of division. I will first answer what pertains to travelling preachers. If this refers to travelling preachers of the circuit who are on trial, the answer is furnished by the Discipline. 'A preacher on trial, who may be accused of crime, shall be accountable to the Quarterly Conference of the circuit on which he travels. But if the question refers to travelling preachers who are members of the Annual Conference, then the Quarterly Conference has no jurisdiction of their case. Members of the church who are grieved with the delinquencies or improprieties of their preachers, have a right to state their grievances to the presiding elder who has charge of them; and, in many cases, it may be proper for the presiding elder to hear that statement in Quarterly Conference, to afford the preachers an opportunity of explanation and amicable adjustment; also, in case it cannot be settled there, to enable the presiding elder to represent the case understandingly at the Conference. It may, also, be prudent for the presiding elder to inquire, at the last Quarterly Conference for the year, whether there is any thing against the travelling preachers of the circuit, so that he may be fully prepared to represent the preachers, and the business of his whole district. But the Quarterly Conference has no authority to try any member of an Annual Conference on any charge or complaint whatever.

"The second part of the question refers to 'any other members of the Quarterly Conference.' Besides the travelling preachers of the circuit, the other members of the Quarterly Conference are local preachers, exhorters, stewards, and class-leaders. What a Quarterly Conference may do with local preachers, has already been stated. As to exhorters and stewards, there is no rule by which to try them on charges of immorality different from the rule for trying private members of the church before the society, or a select number. But complaints respecting their official acts are perfectly within the jurisdiction of the Quarterly Conference, by which their official authority was conferred. If an exhorter makes a bad use of his license, the Quarterly Conference may refuse to renew the license. If stewards act illegally in the appropriation of funds, or neglect to perform the duties of their office, the Quarterly Conference, on complaint being made and sustained, 'shall have power to dismiss or change them at pleasure.' [*Dis.*, ¶ 311.] Respecting class leaders, it is enough to say, they are appointed and changed by the preacher in charge, without any agency of the Quarterly Conference, and for their official acts as leaders are accountable only to him. [¶ 255.] Thus the question asked in every Quarterly Conference, 'Are there any complaints?' takes a broad range. It includes not only complaints of members dissatisfied with the awards of arbiters of their disputed accounts, &c., but whatever lies against the official or moral character of its members under the above named restrictions." — *Bishop Morris.*

7. "When a decision on a point of law is made by a presiding elder in a Quarterly Meeting Conference, and action in the Conference follows, which affects the membership of a member of that Conference, and no appeal is taken by the parties concerned from the decision of the presiding elder to the bishop presiding at the next Annual Conference, is the decision of the Quarterly Conference *final?*"

Ans. "If in the case presented an appeal is not taken by one of the parties to the president of the next Annual

Conference, before the close of the next succeeding session, the action of the Quarterly Conference above referred to is final." — *Bishop Hamline.*

8. "When a local preacher is before a Quarterly Conference for the renewal of his license, the Conference voting by ballot, does a tie vote decide the case against the renewal of the license?"

Ans. "We answer in the affirmative." — *B. Waugh and E. S. Janes.*

9. "Is a Quarterly Conference competent, after having licensed a local preacher for a series of years, to take away that license without impeachment of *moral* character, or finding any decrease of piety, talent, or usefulness?"

Ans. "We answer affirmatively." — *B. Waugh and E. S. Janes.*

10. "Can the Quarterly Conference adjourn to a distant day to take up new articles of business which cannot come before that body now?"

Ans. "An adjournment from day to day to finish pending business is certainly regular, but it cannot be proper to adjourn to a distant day to take up new business which would properly belong to a future Quarterly Conference." — *Hedding on Discipline, p.* 36.

11. "Has a presiding elder a right to call a fifth quarterly meeting in the year to do special business?"

Ans. "I know of no such authority. I see not how there can be five quarters, or five quarterly meetings in a year." — *Hedding on Discipline, p.* 36.

12. "What are the relations of a superannuated preacher?"

Ans. "A superannuated preacher, whether a member of your Conference, or any other Conference, is not a member of your church. If he lives within the bounds of his own Conference, he is a member of the Quarterly Conference where he resides. If he lives beyond the bounds of his own Conference, he is not a member of any Quarterly Conference."*— *E. Hedding.*

13. To whom is a preacher on trial amenable for his *administration* when he is in charge?

Ans. "He is amenable to the presiding elder and the Conference. The presiding elder can correct his errors and reprove him, and change his relation by putting him under another preacher; and the Conference can drop him for that cause." — *E. Hedding.*

14. Can a local preacher be licensed for a less time than a year?

Ans. "No. The license of a local preacher runs for a year, unless the Quarterly Conference, for cause, in due form, deprive him of his ministerial office." — *E. S. Janes.*

III. — OF PREACHERS IN CHARGE.

1. "When a local elder, deacon, or preacher, is reported to be guilty of some crime expressly forbidden in the word of God, and a committee is called on his case, who is to preside?"

Ans. "The preacher in charge." — *Hedding on Discipline, p.* 49.

2. "When the committee find the accused guilty of a crime, who is to suspend him?"

Ans. "Not the preacher, but the committee." — *p.* 49.

3. "When the evidence is all presented, and the pleadings closed, ought the preacher to remain with 'the select number' while they are making up their judgment?"

Ans. "Certainly he ought, for he is pastor of the flock; and he would greatly neglect his duty were he to be absent, and consequently not know on what law or evidence the

* Since modified. See *Discipline*, ¶ 296.

judgment is rendered." —*p.* 63. But "no judicious administrator of Discipline will let the committee, or any other person, know his opinion of the case, either before the trial, or during its progress, till the committee have made their decision, and signed their names to it." — *T. Morris.*

4. "Who is to decide whether the case is to be brought before the whole society, or a select number?"

Ans. "The preacher." —*Hedding on Discipline, p.* 63.

5. "When the judgment of guilt is rendered, who is to award the punishment?"

Ans. "The preacher. For when the authority of deciding on the guilt or innocence of an accused member was taken from the preacher, and given to the people, that was all that was taken from the one, or given to the other. All the other powers referred to in the above questions and answers remain with the preacher as they were before, when the preacher was the judge of the guilt or innocence of the accused person." —*pp.* 63, 64.

6. "What is to be understood by 'the society?'"

Ans. "The word society is used in different parts of the Discipline to mean sometimes the members of our religious community in general; sometimes those in one Annual Conference; also, those in one city or town; and again, those who usually meet in one place for public worship; and, likewise, those of one circuit or station. It may include both the latter in the present rule; but except necessity require to extend it to the circuit, for the want of suitable members for the 'select number' in the neighborhood where the accused belongs, it seems most proper to limit it to those members usually meeting in one place for public worship." —*p.* 64.

7. "Suppose the accused should object to one or more of the select number, what shall be done?"

Ans. "If the objection appear to be reasonable, the person should be changed for another. But if the objector appear to be captious, or to object with a design to evade justice, the preacher shall overrule the matter and proceed in the trial." —*p.* 66. *Discipline,* ¶ 336.

"In selecting the committee, however, for the trial of a member, a preacher ought to be very careful to obtain wise, pious, and candid men, who will do justice both to the accused person and to the church. There should be a sufficient number of them to form a respectable court; for the decision of so important a matter should not be left to two or three individuals. A fit time and place should be appointed for a fair investigation; time enough should be taken for that object, even if it require an adjournment from day to day; nothing should be done in a hurry where so important an interest is pending as membership in the church. The accused person should be furnished in season for preparation with the matter of which he is accused; and if he be ignorant, or incapable of managing his own cause, a capable and honest member should be employed to assist him, that no advantage be taken of one of the least of the children of God." —*p.* 65.

8. "When the 'select number' decide that the accused is guilty of the *act* alleged, who is to determine whether said *act* is a crime, in the sense of the rule; the 'select number,' or the preacher?"

Ans. "The 'select number;' for *crime* is *included* in the judgment of guilty." —*p.* 66.

9. "When a verdict of 'guilty' is rendered, is the preacher in charge obliged to expel the member, or may he pardon?"

Ans. "For scandalous crimes, expulsion should undoubtedly take place; but for crimes of a moderate degree, and when the offender is suitably humble and penitent, forgiveness and forbearance should be exercised, and a repentant brother may be retained in the church. 'Brethren, if a man be overtaken in a fault, ye which are spiritual restore such one in the spirit of meekness.' That the rule is to be so understood, is evident from a clause in the General Rules: 'If there be any among us who observe them not, who habitually break any of them, let it be known unto them who watch over that soul as they who must give an account. We will admonish him of the error of his ways. We will bear with him for a season. But if then he repent not, he hath no more place among us. We have delivered our own souls.'

"In exercising mercy in this case, the preacher will need great prudence, to avoid doing it in a way to grieve and afflict the members, or cast a stumbling-block before the world. On this question he should take counsel with the select number, or the leaders' meeting, or in some cases with the society in the place, that it may be understood the offender is restored by general consent."—*pp.* 66, 67.

10. "When a member of the church shall refuse to refer, &c., a disputed case to arbitration, as proposed in the section of the Discipline relating to the duties of those who have the charge of circuits or stations, can he be lawfully expelled without further trial?"

Ans. "No; the preacher must bring him to trial before the society, or a select number of them, that they may judge whether the accused person *has broken* the rule. There is no case in which a preacher may expel a member, except a judgment of 'guilty' be first rendered by laymen."

"The following rule has been supposed to be an exception to this opinion:—'To prevent scandal, when any of our members fail in business, or contract debts which they are not able to pay, let two or three judicious members of the church inspect the accounts, contracts, and circumstances of the case of the supposed delinquent; and if he have behaved dishonestly, or borrowed money without a probability of paying, let him be expelled.' But here is no trial, only an inspection of accounts, &c. All this rule provides for can be regarded only as furnishing a *bill of charges.* The 'two or three judicious members' named, are not the society, nor a select number of them, to try a member. They may be 'members of the church' from other places. But the delinquent must be brought before the proper tribunal, and found guilty of 'behaving dishonestly,' or of borrowing 'money without a probability of paying,' and that by the decision of the proper authority, before he can be expelled."—*pp.* 68, 70.

"The two cases mentioned in the following paragraph, [*p.* 56,] are of the same character. 'And in case the debtor refuses to comply, he shall be expelled.' But who is to judge here whether the debtor *refuses to comply?* Not the preacher, nor the above named committee, but the *society* of which he is a member, or a select number of them. This principle is carried out in the following clause: 'And if the creditor refuse to comply, he shall be expelled.' The Quarterly Conference has said what the creditor ought to do; but if he be charged with refusing to comply, that point must be determined by the members of his own society; otherwise he would be expelled without trial before the society of which he is a member, or a select number of them, and also would be denied the 'right of appeal.'"—*pp.* 68, 70.

11. "When a preacher, differing in judgment from the society or the select number, refers a case to the Quar-

terly Conference, as provided for in the Discipline, page 92, is that reference an appeal?"

Ans. "No; it is a new trial. 'The trial may be referred,' &c., is not the language of an appeal, but that of removing a trial from one court to another. But as there are difficulties in the minds of many concerning the constitutionality of this rule, as it is not seen how there can be an appeal from the decision of the Quarterly Conference in this case, it is advisable that the preachers should not use it. But if, in any case, the preacher should refer such a trial to the Quarterly Conference, I should advise the Quarterly Conference not to decide the case, but to refer it back to the society for a new trial."—*Discipline,* ¶ 348.

12. "Who shall decide whether a person absents himself from trial in the sense of the Discipline, ¶ 338?

Ans. "The select number." — *Bishop Hedding.*

13. "Has a preacher a right to receive a person into the M. E. Church living within another charge, when it is known to him that there are objections to that person of such a nature as would prevent his being received in the charge where he lives?"

Ans. "It is unfavorable to good government in the church for a preacher, under any circumstances, to receive into membership in his charge a person living in the bounds of another pastoral charge. Yet established usage justifies it under some circumstances, especially in cities where there are several separate charges, and where it is very difficult to define them geographically. But in these circumstances comity and Christian courtesy should be strictly maintained. The general peace and prosperity of the church, as well as the golden rule of doing to others as we would be done by, requires this. In some cases it would be a palpable violation of Discipline to receive a person from within another charge, when objections were known to exist against him by members of that charge. As, for instance, in the case of an expelled person, who cannot be again admitted to membership without contrition, confession, and satisfactory reformation. Reformation satisfactory to the society aggrieved. Or, if a person is under any disciplinary liabilities or disabilities whatever. It is possible there may be cases of mere prejudices, without any tangible cause, that might render one society unwilling to admit a person to membership, which would not be a sufficient reason for preventing him from joining another society. But where the objection is specific, and is made by responsible members of the society where the person lives, and especially if the objection grows out of former church relations, or disciplinary actions of the church, or antagonism to the authority of the church, in our judgment it would be wrong for a preacher to receive such person or persons into membership. The adage, 'Better one suffer than many,' is applicable to this question."

14. "If charges are preferred against a probationer of such a nature as would, if proved, exclude a member in full connection, can a preacher be justified in refusing or neglecting an investigation of such charges, and continue the person on trial?"

Ans. "In such cases as is described in this question, if the charges are preferred or presented by responsible members of the Methodist Episcopal Church, it is the duty of the preacher in charge to investigate the case, and if the charges are found to be true to drop the person."

15. "Has a preacher in charge the right, on his individual responsibility, to decide on the credibility or disciplinary correctness of a local preacher's credentials, and cause his name to be entered upon the official list of the Quarterly

Meeting Conference, without consulting or presenting said credentials to said Conference ? "

Ans. "As the Discipline directs that a preacher in charge may individually give a sufficient certificate to dismiss a local preacher from one church, and introduce him to another, it seems reasonable that he may also receive such a certificate and judge of its legality for the time being, so far as to admit, or refuse to admit, the name of the said local preacher on his class book. But the proper time to enter his name on the official list of the Quarterly Meeting Conference is at the first session of, and after the opening of, said Quarterly Meeting Conference; when, if any question is raised as to the sufficiency or legality of the certificate, it must be decided as a question of law by the presiding elder, subject to an appeal to the president of the next Annual Conference."

16. "How long may a letter be retained by a member of the church ?"

Ans. "I am not certain that I understand this question, but presume it has reference to what is called, in Discipline, 'a note of recommendation,' or 'a certificate of membership, given to members of the church who remove from one circuit to another.' If this is the sense of the question, my answer is, there is no limit prescribed in the Discipline. Of course, as the rule now is,— and it is not for me to say what it should be, — a preacher in charge may receive a member on such certificate at any time, and hold him responsible, when he is received, for any thing he may have done while he retained the certificate." — *Bishop Morris.*

17. "When a person that has been expelled from the church comes forward and confesses his wrong, and is penitent, and gives satisfaction, may he be restored to full membership, or must he be received again on trial ?"

Ans. "He should be restored to the standing he had previous to his expulsion." — *E. Hedding.*

18. "Who is chairman of the trustees? the Committee on Missions?"

Ans. "Where the trustees are appointed according to the rule of Discipline, the preacher in charge is chairman of the meeting. The preacher in charge is also chairman of the Committee on Missions." — *Bishop Hedding.*

19. Is an administrator of discipline at liberty to refuse to entertain a bill of charges, when signed by respectable members of the church, and a trial is demanded by the accusers?

Ans. "He is at full liberty. There may be various reasons why he should not entertain charges, and a preacher in charge is bound in duty to call a member to trial against whom there is credible report that he is guilty of a crime, even if there be no charges presented." — *E. Hedding.*

20. "Should an administrator decline to entertain a bill of charges, what redress can the accuser have, if any?"

Ans. "He can complain of the preacher to his presiding elder, or to the Conference, for neglect of duty; and if he be found culpable, he can be punished as his offence deserves." — *E. Hedding.*

21. When a charge of high imprudence is preferred, with various specifications involving immoral and unchristian conduct, may the accused be punished for such conduct, if found guilty, or can he only be punished for high imprudence?

Ans. "He may be punished for any thing of which he is found guilty. It is not the design of the Methodist Discipline to limit the trial to the charge, but to deal with a man as his works deserve. It is true, if a different crime is proved from the one alleged in the charge, and the accused pleads that he is not prepared for trial on that point, the court ought to adjourn, and give the accused fair time to defend himself." — *E. Hedding.*

IV. — OF EVIDENCE.

1 "In trying an appeal of a private member to the Quarterly Conference, are we limited to the record of the testimony in the trial below, or are we to admit new testimony?"

Ans. "On this question different opinions and different administrations prevail. But, as in the appeal of a travelling preacher to the General Conference, and that of a local preacher to an Annual Conference, the trials proceed on the minutes of the evidence in the preceding trials, so, it appears to me, consistency requires we should proceed in such cases in the Quarterly Conference." — *Hedding on Discipline, p.* 35.

2. "Should it be found that accurate minutes have not been taken in the trial before the society, or the select number, what shall be done?"

Ans. "The case should be referred back for a new trial, that those who did their work carelessly, at first, may have opportunity of doing it properly, and of being admonished to avoid such errors afterward." —*p.* 35.

3. When a local elder, deacon, or preacher, has been tried and condemned by a committee, and the case is taken up in the Quarterly Conference having jurisdiction, can new evidence be admitted, or must the Quarterly Conference proceed upon the evidence recorded in the minutes of the trial?

Ans. "New evidence may be admitted if necessary; for it is a new trial, not an appeal. The Conference has origi nal jurisdiction in the case, and the best evidence should be admitted, whether the minutes or personal testimony.—*p.* 49.

4. "Can an accuser be a witness?"

Ans. "In cases of personal dispute, in the issue of which the accuser has a direct interest, he cannot; but in cases where he has no other interest than is common to all the members of the church, he may be permitted."—*E. S. Janes.*

V.—OF WITHDRAWING FROM THE CHURCH.

1. What is our discipline and usage in regard to withdrawing from the church?

Ans. "The subject of withdrawing from the Methodist Episcopal Church, having, since the last General Conference, engaged the attention of our ministers, and there appearing to be a difference of opinion leading to diversity of practice, it has been judged proper by the superintendents to embody their views, and govern their administration by the opinions stated in this paper.

"'Is a member of an Annual Conference withdrawn from the church, when he says to a bishop or presiding elder, "I withdraw from the church?" or is it the province of the Conference, of which he is a member, to decide whether he is withdrawn or not?'

"This question was proposed to the General Conference of 1848, and referred to the Committee on Questions of Law. The Committee having had it under consideration, reported the following resolution:—'Resolved, That when a person, whether a preacher or a private member, declares to the proper authority of the church that he withdraws from the Methodist Episcopal Church, he thereby forfeits all privileges in said church, and places himself beyond her jurisdiction.' The resolution led to considerable discussion, and various amendments and substitutes were offered, on which action was earnestly pressed on the General Conference, but which was invariably avoided by that body; and, finally, after protracted debate, and various efforts to obtain the decision of the Conference thereon, the whole subject was laid on the table. (*See the Printed Journal of said Conference, pp.* 19—30, 31, 32, 33, 38.)

"From this succinct history of the question of withdrawal from the church, as mooted at the late General Conference, it is apparent to us that the right of a minister or member of the Methodist Episcopal Church to withdraw at his option, and without the consent of the proper authorities to whom he is amenable, was neither held nor conceded by said General Conference. We cannot but think that it would have been not only anomalous, but fearfully ominous, if such unqualified right had been admitted. Such a doctrine would have been at variance with the general usage of the church from the beginning of its organization. In our opinion, the admission of the right to withdraw at option, without the consent of the church, especially when under imputation of gross and scandalous offences, would operate most injuriously to the maintenance of wholesome discipline and sound morals. In accordance with this view, we deem it to be our duty to say, that it is contrary to the economy and usage of the Methodist Episcopal Church to allow ministers or members, when guilty of gross violations of the Discipline, to evade its salutary authority and force by declaring themselves withdrawn from the jurisdiction of the church." * *

* This decision was inserted on the authority of a distinguished name. But learning that the bishop, on reading it, could not remember having given it, and that he doubted its correctness, we feel bound by our regard for his excellent memory, to withdraw his authority; which we hereby do, — leaving the question undecided. — THE AUTHOR

PART FOURTH.

PRUDENTIAL ARRANGEMENTS PECULIAR TO DIFFERENT SECTS OF WESLEYANS.

CHAPTER I.

MANNER OF RECEIVING MEMBERS.

To receive members into the church hastily, is to endanger the purity and reputation of the body; to delay candidates too long, may injure them. In trying to avoid these two extremes, Methodists have adopted arrangements peculiar to themselves. Our church receives none on trial "until they have met twice or thrice in class," unless we are assured that they are suitable persons to be received. Our rules being explained to them, they are then placed under the watch-care of a class leader, and instructed as it is found necessary; and giving satisfactory evidence of piety, they are baptized and admitted to the Lord's supper. Though we occasionally receive one on trial as a *seeker*, we have never known such baptized before being converted; nor, indeed, does a seeker remain on trial long without realizing this great change.

The time of continuing persons in this relation has varied at different periods. In 1789 it was "extended to six months." If, after this term of probation, they have been baptized, and, on examination, it appears that they are Methodists in faith, and are disposed to observe the rules of the church, they may be admitted to full membership, and be entitled to the privileges, and subject to the discipline, of other members. In being received on trial, they only profess a "desire to flee from the wrath to come." They do not say they are Methodists, and believe our doctrine or Discipline. They may know nothing about either. But they do believe they may derive essential benefit to their souls by coming among us, and mingling in our devotions. When they become weary of our company, or requirements, they *leave* us; and when we become weary of them, on account of their indifference, or misconduct, and cannot reform them, we mark them "dropped," without bringing them to trial. But having been received into full connection, they stand in quite a different relation. They now profess to believe both our doctrine and discipline, and are governed by them. In case of defection, therefore, they are liable to be tried and expelled according to our rules. Before, they were only *candidates; now*, they are *members*. But still, should they wish to change their church relations, while in good and regular standing with us, they will not find it difficult to get excused. We are not so *bigoted* as to believe that there is no salvation out of our church, or so *foolish* as to wish to retain members whose hearts are with another people.

Whether this probationary arrangement is on the whole expedient, is a question about which good men may differ. We believe it is founded in wisdom. In the first place, it keeps no Christian from the sacraments for a day, as delays do in other denominations. They debar their candidates from the ordinances until they receive them into the church. But with us, the ordinances are not mere *church* rites. They lie back of the church, with preaching and prayer, and belong to all God's people. We doubt our right to withhold them from those who, in our judgment, are converted, and desire them, for a single week. And we doubt their right to neglect them any longer than is necessary to decide as to the *mode*, &c. The question of joining *this* church or *that*, is a different thing, and cannot be intelligently settled without time for examination. The sentiments and policy of churches are matters in which the unconverted take little interest. If they think of them at all, their investigations seldom reach beyond the denomination in which they have been educated. But multitudes have never been religiously educated, and know little about these things. To ask them within a few weeks of their conversion, if they believe in Calvinism, or any other denominational system, is like asking a blind man if he is pleased with certain colors. They have *no* faith beyond mere elemental principles, the verities of which they have experienced. And before they can determine whether they are Calvinists or Arminians, they must have time to examine the two systems, and compare them with the Bible, and what they already feel and know.

Another fact to be considered in this connection is, that an enterprising and aggressive church will often find itself as little acquainted with its converts as they are with theology and church government. They are strangers; belong, perhaps, to another nation, and have been the vassals of various habits and associations, that may entangle them again. To receive others into the church, and put them off, to "see whether they are going to *hold out*," will not be likely to help them. They will infer that the church has no confidence in their piety, and become discouraged. They need to be brought under all the kind influences and restraints possible If there be any advantage in intimate association with Christians, or in the sacraments, they should have it. And yet, to receive them into the church at once, seems rather premature. Heartless churches will, perhaps, experience little difficulty from either of these sources. They have few converts to dispose of, and those few belong to the parish, and are well known. They can plod along as their fathers did before them ; but it is not so with churches which are favored with revivals. They can neither bring converts right into the church, nor suggest to them that they are probably deceived, and had better wait. Hence, they are often embarrassed. But our plan obviates all these difficulties. It gives strangers an opportunity of becoming acquainted with us, and it gives us an equal opportunity of becoming acquainted with them. If either party is not satisfied at the expiration of the six months, further time can be allowed, or the connection may be dissolved.

No *specific* form of receiving probationers into full connection has been maintained among us, further than to examine them before the church as to their faith and willingness to observe our rules. In other respects preachers have followed their own judgment and taste, and in some cases have given them the right hand of fellowship. This is a wise and useful arrangement, and is *now* provided for by our ritual, which is substantially followed, though not with verbal uniformity. It is well, perhaps, to have some printed form for those who need one, and equally well not to insist on its rigid observance. Circumstances often call for peculiar utterances unknown to forms. Heart religion, and its most efficient propagation, sometimes require great liberty of speech, which should not be denied. We have seen crowded assemblies melted to tears during these services, and doubt not that they have been sanctified to the salvation of many souls.

Till 1840 our Discipline contained no exception to the rule requiring a probation. Persons coming to us from other denominations, however intelligent and pious, had to join on trial, and graduate in due form. Though this was in perfect keeping with the spirit and example of older denominations, it looked too exclusive and Pharisaical, particularly where persons came well recommended. A rule was, therefore, introduced, providing that a member in good standing in any Orthodox church, who shall desire to unite with us, may be received at once into full fellowship, "giving satisfactory answers to the usual inquiries." (*Dis.*, ¶ 49.) Observe, it does not state what evidence of "good standing" shall be required. A letter from the pastor or church certifying it is desirable. But, however worthy the member, this cannot always be obtained. Close Communion Baptists will not give such a letter to a member leaving them to join us. At least, we have never heard of their doing so, and we have known of their refusing in numerous instances. But, when they find that a member has left them, they *expel* him, or, in their own denominational dialect, "withdraw fellowship" from him, which is the same thing. And they treat letters from us with as little respect as they treat members leaving their communion to unite with Methodists. They make not the slightest account of them, but proceed precisely as if the member had come from the world, and receive him on his experience, unless they may in some instances recognize his baptism, which is not very common. Some Congregationalists, Presbyterians, and others, give letters, which we receive with unqualified respect. Many, however, sympa thize with the Baptists, and pursue a similar policy. But it will not always be so.

If persons propose to come from others to us, we prefer that they should bring letters of character and dismission, at least. We always recommend that they ask for them, unless we know that it is inconsistent with the practice of their church to dismiss members in this way, and are persuaded that such a request would be followed by a protracted and vexatious assault. In such cases, we think it better for them to send their minister a note certifying their intention to join another church, and their consequent withdrawal. When a member has been refused a letter, or has withdrawn in this way, and furnishes evidence of recent good standing in an evangelical church, we receive him into full fellowship upon his giving satisfaction in the examination.

We receive ministers, also, in like manner, not only from all churches of the Methodist family, but from all evangelical churches, recognizing their orders on their taking upon themselves our ordination vows, without the imposition of hands, provided we find them properly qualified, and they accede to our doctrines, discipline, and usages.

CHAPTER II.

LAY PREACHERS, AND OUR STYLE OF PREACHING DEFENDED.

THOSE who assume to find the secret of our success in any one or two particulars, take limited views of the subject. Our peculiar doctrines and government have had their influence. They have formed a sort of substratum in our system of agencies, but avail little alone. Those who well understand us, must not only "tell the towers" of our economy, and "mark well its bulwarks," but extend their investigations to its minuter details, some of which we propose now to consider.

LAY PREACHING.

The origin and success of this agency has already been noticed. But we have said little in its defence beyond what is involved in the necessity which called for it, and the strong providential indications connected with its origin. Its necessity appeared in the facts that the people were perishing in their sins, and the regularly authorized clergy were doing little or nothing to save them. They either did not understand their condition, and the adaptation of the gospel to relieve it, or they had no interest in the subject.

Hence, when certain of the "*common* people" became converted, and felt a burning love for souls, they were constrained to "cry aloud and spare not." They had no intention of infringing on the priestly office, but only to give vent to the mighty emotions of their own souls, and do good. But God wrought such wonders in the conversion of sinners by their instrumentality, they were constrained to continue their efforts. Mr. Wesley was amazed at first, but what was he that he "could withstand God?" Hence, he directed the unexpected agency he did not dare to oppose, and succeeded in making it an engine of moral power and usefulness. As the work spread, others were moved by the same Spirit to take upon them the ministry of the word, and were compelled by the force of circumstances to do it, if at all, contrary to the religious custom of the times. Many had no means of obtaining a regular education; others were too old to undertake it; while such was the necessity for their immediate services, and the power of the Spirit urging them to the work, they would hardly have *dared* to delay, had they been younger, and amply furnished with means. Besides, the efficiency of many, who had not been "disobedient to the heavenly vision," so far exceeded that of most of the regular clergy, there was no encouragement to pursue the ordinary course, had it been practicable. Hence, the ministerial office was early filled with men who, like the apostles, had not been favored with a liberal education. The necessity for this class of men still continues, and God, therefore, calls them into his vineyard, both by powerful impressions and providential openings. And it is matter of thanksgiving, that the church is yet simple-hearted enough to receive and ordain them, notwithstanding their deficiencies.

This part of our policy has given other denominations much apparent amusement. They have spoken flippantly of our ignorance and inefficiency, and reported many silly falsehoods in confirmation of their assumptions. They have, however, been compelled to witness our success, and, for one cause or another, have seemed quite disposed to gather the fruit of our labors into their own churches. And when our ministers have become tired of the itinerancy, and applied to them for admission to their fraternity, we have never known them refused. The Episcopal Church received several of Mr. Wesley's lay preachers, and other sects have shown similar courtesy to their successors; since which, little has been heard of incompetency.

That there are advantages in having a thorough literary and theological education is not denied. But it by no means follows that none should enter the ministry till they have become thus qualified. Nor is there any authority for such a conclusion, either in Scripture or reason. The Scriptures certainly do not authorize it, and reason, in our opinion, is opposed to it.

What are the facts in the case? Why, the gospel, embracing repentance toward God, and faith in our Lord Jesus Christ, justification, holiness, heaven, &c., is to be preached, and its ordinances administered. The topics are few. Most of them come within the range of Christian experience. To preach repentance, justification, regeneration, and various other Scripture doctrines, is, therefore, to preach what every Christian knows by experience, and often feels the importance of, like fire shut up in his bones. Hence, so far as these things are concerned, and they are the main points in gospel preaching, one possessing an active mind and a tolerable utterance is prepared to illustrate and apply them with interest. If he labors under the disadvantage of not *knowing* some important things, he is also saved from the perplexity of *fearing* many others. He enters the work, not because he is learned and eloquent, but because God has called him to it. If he has but little information, he has no reputation to serve, and may save much time and breath in apologies. If he elicits less applause from the fastidious and fashionable, he has less temptation to change his church relations, and to diverge from fundamental and effective truth into metaphysical speculations.

But we are reminded that "the gospel is opposed by learned and arch enemies, and must be defended." True: but because we are occasionally met by an opponent of peculiar learning and sagacity, shall every candidate for the ministry prepare himself to resist his attack, or be accounted incompetent to fill the sacred office? A greater blunder could not be committed. The "*defence* of the gospel" against such opponents is of rare necessity, and requires rare talent. A Goliath has never yet appeared without finding a David somewhere to match him. The ordinary business of ministers is to preach the gospel; that is, proclaim or declare it. There is only now and then a man who is naturally endowed to become an able polemic, if he should apply himself ever so closely; but most Christians, and especially Christian ministers, who give themselves to reading, meditation, and prayer, are altogether sufficient to meet the ordinary objections with which they are molested.

It is said, too, that "a minister ought to be able to read the Scriptures in the language in which they were written." We allow it is desirable, but, if it be necessary to ministerial efficiency, most ministers are in a pitiable condition, for few are able to do it. Much less are they able to read them *critically*, so as to point out the errors of our common version, or of the criticisms of learned commentators. But no such necessity exists. Our wisest men exhort us to adhere to the English translation of the Scriptures, as the best we can have. They condemn the miserable attempts at verbal criticism we often hear in the pulpit, as foppish and contemptible. They tell us to "*preach* the word, not *mend* it;" to enforce it, not explain it *away*. This, a man of ordinary intelligence may do with effect, particularly if he be called of God. The thing he cannot do, is what all sensible men concede should seldom be undertaken.

The idea that one must compass the whole realm of science and literature to be a useful minister, is as false in theory as it is impracticable. The connection between certain studies and the ministry, is perfectly inconceivable. They have no more adaptation to the ministerial work than botany has to the manufacture of steam engines. Hence, as one may be a good mechanic who knows nothing of agriculture; and a good physician without being able to do a sum in the "Rule of Three;" so one may be a mighty man of God, and a powerful minister of Jesus, who never read the first line of Homer, or became acquainted with the first letter of the Greek alphabet.

We make these remarks defensively, and would not be understood as disparaging any part of a regular collegiate course. Each has its place and its importance; but the knowledge of certain parts is no more necessary to ministerial competency, than a black hat, or a white cravat. Yet as it is desirable to know a little of all knowable things, and quite important to become acquainted with some of them, we insist on keeping the fountains of knowledge open and accessible to all, particularly to our pious young men, whom we have reason to believe the Lord will call to the sacred office.

EXTEMPORANEOUS PREACHING.

The Wesleys were trained to *read* sermons. But they had not advanced far in the progress of reform before they found manuscripts an incumbrance. Their helpers extemporized generally, as have their successors in all countries. The spirit of Methodism has been too *earnest* and emphatic to be hampered in this way. If the business of the ministry was merely to announce the truth, the case would be different. But an *impression* is to be made, and an *effect* secured, which requires the soul's deepest sympathy, and the fullest manifestation of it. It is not enough for the hearer to see his minister weeping over the touching language of a studied manuscript, written he knows not when. He wishes to hear him speak in the expressive language of his present emotions. There is always a sort of distrust connected with the sight of a manuscript, chilling to the sensibilities. Besides, it is impossible for a minister to *read* with as much emphasis and power as he can preach. He needs to see his hearers, and have them see him. The Maker of the "human face divine" gave a tongue to every feature. Reading distorts the whole, so that it is impossible to appear natural. There is power, also, in proper gestures; but who can make them with his eyes fastened on his book? One may keep up a kind of mechanical motion, but it must be inexpressive, except he has the rare faculty of remembering the most he has written, and only needs to glance at the beginning of his paragraphs to recite the whole without hesitating.

Extemporary preaching has equal advantages as a mode of instruction. True, one may, if he pleases, state a proposition on paper as intelligibly as he can extemporize it. But he is not likely to do so. Every writer seems to have an idea that he must write in a different dialect from that he employs in extemporary speech. And then, he must *dole* it out in about such a measure and tone till all is finished, whether it be understood or not. He has little opportunity to observe the countenances of his hearers, to ascertain how his message is received, or to revolve it before them till he sees conviction in their eyes. He has something else to do.

If written discourse is the more instructive, why do not teachers write? Why do not judges read their charges, and advocates their pleas? But this will not do; a reading lawyer would soon be abandoned by his clients. They want an advocate who can *talk*, and make himself *felt* by the jury. They will have no other. Even sermon-reading ministers would not employ a reader. They know the difference between reading and speaking too well. But aside from all these considerations, we add, extemporary preaching has the sanction of high authority. Jesus, the great exampler of ministerial conduct, was never suspected of reading a sermon. He spake from other influences than that of a manuscript. The message was in his *heart* and mind, and he preached from the intensity of his love for a perishing world. And the apostles imitated his example. Reading sermons is a modern invention, the product of political jealousy. With that jealousy it should have passed away.

We are aware it is a labor saving arrangement. It would be especially so to us who are changing our position so frequently. A few sermons would serve us for a whole life, and save us the study and perplexity of originating new ones, or calling up and remodelling the old. It is equally true that sermon reading saves one from much painful anxiety and frequent mortification. How shall I succeed? is often an inquiry of overwhelming interest to extemporizers as the hour of their effort approaches. It leads them to God in earnest prayer, and to close and hard study. And, after all, if the mind does not happen to be in a fruitful state, they come very far short of their wishes; by reason of verbal mistakes, which happen with the most correct of speakers, and perhaps a want of consecutive order, and exact finish in every point, they fail of a high reputation they might enjoy in community, if they would consent to the fashionable practice of reading.

But notwithstanding these, and all the other advantages connected with sermon reading, Methodists repudiate it. They believe it inconsistent with that free and full flow of soul the minister should enjoy in the sacred desk, and those powerful effects he should anticipate, and strive to produce. And they have been encouraged in this course not only by the attention of the people to their word, but by the conversion of many to God; and by the fact, that when other denominations really set out to preach the gospel *effectively*, they follow their example.

We are sorry to say, however, that some of our ministers are strangely falling away from original Methodism in this respect, and taking to *reading*. And what appears most remarkable is, that this defection is largely confined to those who have had the best opportunities to learn to *preach*. But as they do not increase their popularity or power by the means, and as other denominations are coming to preach extemporaneously, there is reason to believe that the evil will be limited to a small minority.

CHAPTER XII.

ITINERANCY BOTH "LAWFUL AND EXPEDIENT."

ONE of the most striking and permanent features of Methodism is its itinerancy. It found the clergy generally settled, both in Europe and America. "A permanent ministry" was the established doctrine of the church, and settlements were understood to be for life. That Mr. Wesley had any radical objections to this arrangement, at first, is not certain. But either from reflection, or from personal experience, he soon found that something was to be effected by preaching the gospel "every where," as did the apostles, that was impracticable under the local policy. He therefore put himself in lively circulation, and invited his coadjutors to join him. Some did so; and, as they wandered from place to place, the Lord worked with them, and many were reformed whom the regular ministry had little prospect of benefiting. Thus, the importance of an itinerant ministry was established; and it has been transmitted to all branches of the Wesleyan family as a permanent arrangement.

Our reasons for its maintenance are,

I. *That it is Scriptural.* The imperial founder of the ministry itself, set his followers an heroic example of the manner in which they should exercise it. He "went about doing good." When persecution interrupted his course in one place, he resorted to another. And when his popularity had reached such a height that the people were about to proclaim him "king," he departed and exercised his ministry in other and more promising fields. The obscure village was not so unimportant as to escape his notice, nor the magnificent city so attractive as to monopolize his efforts. He "sent the apostles forth into every city and place, whither he himself would come." The great commission given to them after his resurrection places this matter in the clearest light: "Go ye into all the world, and preach the gospel to every creature." "Go," — not settle down, — go into all the world. They were not permitted to stay to bury a father. "Let the dead bury their dead," said he, "but go thou and preach the kingdom of God." "And they went forth and preached *every where*," showing how they understood their instructions. The itinerancy of St. Paul is a matter of imperishable record. The map of his long and tedious journeys by sea and land is found in almost every Sabbath School, and is a silent rebuke to the local system. Timothy and Titus were travelling bishops. Indeed, itinerancy was a stamped feature of the early Christian ministry, but was soon interrupted by the selfishness and ease-loving spirit incident to human nature.

II. Another general reason for this feature of our economy is, that it is *expedient*. Some, who will not deny that Christ and the Apostles itinerated, think that it is *inexpedient* for ministers to do so now. But we vindicate the measure,

1. By the fact there is such a diversity of gifts and grades of talent in the ministry. Men probably differ more in their mental and moral constitutions, than in their physical. Christ, in his sovereignty, selects his ministers from all ranks

and conditions of men. Some he calls from the field,—others from the fishing boat,—the receipt of custom,—the study of the law,—from the lowest peasantry to the highest aristocracy; so that we find among them all degrees of refinement and of intellectual caste,—men of oratory, logicians, poets, and historians, sons of "consolation," and sons of "thunder."

Now, is it reasonable to believe that the Saviour would have ministers, thus diversified, confine their labors to a single congregation? In the divine economy every thing is fitted to its appropriate place and use. The light is adapted to the eye, and the eye to the light. The food to the animal, and the animal to the food. Is it not the same here? Every minister is not a logician, nor is all the heresy in any one place. No minister is adapted to please all, yet every one has an adaptation to some part of every community. The defender of the gospel will find business every where, for error is wide-spread. And the same is true of all the gifts that God has called into the work. To confine any one gift to a single place, is to surfeit that place with a good thing; to overdo an important service. Certainly, the Master never designed Boanerges should lavish his thunder upon one little community. Are there not others who need it as much? And is there but one city where the mourner needs comforting, that the son of consolation should shut himself up within its walls? And is all the taste and refinement in one neighborhood, that elegant Apollos should shed all his splendors there? We believe there is necessity for these several talents in every community; and that to circumscribe their application, as is done by the local policy, is entirely opposed to the divine economy. Besides, it puts it in the power of selfish men, who have pecuniary means, to bottle up the thunder, and lightning, and logic, and tears of the pulpit, and appropriate them to their own exclusive use.

2. *There are different tastes among the people.* It is impossible for one minister to please every body. Every minister is too profound, or too superficial, too refined, or too coarse, to gratify a portion of his hearers, as would be most profitable for them; and yet each is a perfect model in the view of some of them. One man as naturally admires the reasoning of Paul, as another does the eloquence of Apollos. Another, who takes but little interest in either, is overwhelmed by the energy of Peter; while his neighbor, indifferent to them all, is charmed and melted by the sympathy of Barnabas, the son of consolation. Accordingly, there is a corresponding difference in our capability of usefulness to individuals. A minister is not so likely to be useful to those who are not pleased with his style and manner. We have to attract the people to hear us before we can benefit them by our preaching; and then, if they are interested in the manner, they may heed what is said.

This point is illustrated by a single fact in the history of itinerancy, viz., that its revivals are comparatively frequent. By a frequent change of ministers, all the talents of the vocation are brought to bear upon the several tastes and susceptibilities of the people. All, in their turn, are pleased and profited. Paul wins some by learned argument,—Apollos wins others by the power of his eloquence; while other classes are affected and saved by their successors, who, though less attractive in some respects, are, nevertheless, able ministers of the New Testament. Thus, by the blessing of God upon the labors of his itinerant servants, the work advances with something like uniformity, and is not limited to revivals of from *five* to *fifteen* years' intermission; — the preachers all become revivalists; and all ranks in community, from the most hopeful subject to the reckless reprobate, are modified, if not converted, by the preaching of the gospel.

3. A proper system of itinerancy limits the ministry as to time, and thus *keeps them more closely to the subject matter of their mission.* To preach to the same congregation for a succession of years, one must necessarily take a wide range to avoid sameness, and keep the attention of his people. Various subjects will need to be discussed, and each amplified with great particularity. It will not do to consider theology alone; philosophy, natural and intellectual, astronomy, mathematics, politics, and history, cannot be overlooked. That these subjects have any direct tendency to awaken and convert sinners to God will not be pretended. Though they may attract more attention than the doctrines of the cross, they are not calculated to subdue the heart. The truths upon which heaven has conferred the distinguished honor of accomplishing this wonderful work, are few and simple. The being and perfections of God, — the depravity of man, — the atonement made by Christ, with its causes, designs, and consequences, necessary and contingent, — repentance, — holiness, — the resurrection of the body, — judgment, — heaven and hell, — embrace the substance of them. Thus, John preached repentance and faith in the Saviour at hand. Jesus opened his ministry by proclaiming repentance, as an imperative duty. The "twelve" preached the kingdom of heaven near. Peter and Paul preached these soul-stirring truths with the Holy Ghost sent down from heaven, and with power. And wheresoever salvation has come through preaching, whether by itinerants or settled

pastors, it has come through the preaching of these truths, and not by the thousand novelties and abstractions of this or any other age.

Few men have such rare talents as to be able to confine themselves to these topics, and closely apply them to the heart and conscience, year after year, without incurring the charge of tautology, and preaching their hearers to sleep. Said Mr. Wesley: "Should I preach to one congregation steadily for two consecutive years, I would preach myself, as well as the people, dead as stones." But by a change of gifts, these difficulties are avoided, and the interest is kept up. Old truth, being presented in a new dress, is more attractive and energetic than ever. Those who rejected it in prose, embrace it in poetry; while others, who turned from it as infinitely dull and dry in close-jointed syllogisms, are alarmed when it breaks upon them in an avalanche of impassioned eloquence. How else can we account for the remarkable success of certain ministers, called evangelists? Are these the brightest lights — the profoundest men — the world ever saw, or that now live? We do them no injustice in saying, that for intellectual and literary strength there are hundreds in the land who exceed them. And yet, judging from the best data the subject admits, these men, after making a fair deduction from their labors for spurious converts, accomplish more for the salvation of men in one month, than some of their settled superiors do in a whole life. The fact is, they ply their new hearers with these burning truths, till they make an impression. They have nothing to fear from the charge of sameness, for their stay is short. The object is to win souls to Christ, *now*, and not merely to keep on good terms with the people; and, therefore, they preach directly to the point, and succeed. And if their local brethren would show less opposition, and pay more respect to the obvious meaning of the commission under which they act, we believe it would be better for all concerned.

4. It has the advantage of a *natural love of novelty*, which pervades the race. Whether right or wrong, we do love new things. This passion is, no doubt, stronger in some than in others, but it is co-existent with humanity. We see it every where and in every thing with which our predilections are concerned. Even the firmest advocates of a settled ministry are infected. They want new houses, new furniture, new equipage, new lawyers, doctors and teachers, and, indeed, many of them want *new divinity*, and will have it. Now, since this is the case, and since it is optional with people to attend upon the preaching of the gospel or not, it is desirable to present all the attractions possible, to draw them. A new preacher is not one of the least. Many who would lounge away the Sabbath rather than hear an old sermon repeated, or a new one in a familiar tone and style, might take an interest in hearing a stranger. It is on this principle that strangers are sought as speakers in political campaigns, and in moral reforms, and also that the parish congregation is larger when it is known a stranger will officiate. The people wish to hear a new gift. Itinerancy, taking the advantage of this feeling, charms those to the house of God who, otherwise, would not come. And many, thus attracted by curiosity, are awakened, and retire to pray, and not a few instances are recorded of their returning home praising God. The church-going bell summoned them to the house of prayer in vain. All interest in their worthy pastor's pulpit performances was gone. But when it was announced a stranger was coming, they were attracted, converted, and saved.

5. It is *highly conducive to piety*, both in the ministry and membership. The truths which awaken the sinner, and

induce him to submit his heart to Christ, are directly calculated to nourish and strengthen devotion in the believer. The minister who faithfully explains and enforces them, must feel more or less of their divine influence upon his own heart. To be constantly holding up Christ, from place to place, preaching faith in his name, and the glorious results which follow, must inspire him with a holy fervor, especially if he succeeds in bringing sinners to repentance. Besides, there is great difference in the spiritual condition of churches. Some are engaged and full of enterprise, and they wish their minister to be as much, or more so. They, therefore, pray for him. The influence of such a society upon its minister is remarkable. It gives him more efficiency, and makes him a better man. Thus, itinerancy, bringing its various subjects within the hallowing influence of the most devoted churches, becomes a source of spiritual interest to them, and prepares them to communicate the heavenly inspiration to others. Its tendency, in this respect, is virtually admitted by its enemies. It is a known fact, that when they desire a revival of religion, they procure the labors of other men, — of strangers, — men, if possible, fresh from a revival. The old familiar gift, now that something is to be done, is superseded by a new one, and this is considered indispensable to success.

6. An itinerant ministry *is less liable to difficulties with the people.* Where a man is settled for an indefinite term, it is difficult for the people to remove him without contention. They may think his usefulness is at an end, but he does not. As the matter is to be decided by a vote, *they* go about to make proselytes to their views, and *he* to fortify himself as firmly as possible. *They* talk of his faults, and *he* of their abuses. Prejudice is created on the one side, and sympathy on the other, till the parties become fully formed. Then

comes the crisis — the ballots are cast, and he triumphs. But the minority is not satisfied, and the contest is not ended. Another campaign may come to a different issue. So, on they rush, to prepare for a new trial. A settled minister (and an estimable man he is) informed the writer, a few years since, that there were six lawsuits then pending in his society, some of which he commenced himself. He fought the battle through, and remained in town the pastor of the minority. Similar scenes have been witnessed in other places, where ministers have remained years amid a storm of opposition, which has neutralized their influence, and, finally, left, to escape the violence of their enemies. The judicial records of New England are *black* with the quarrels of settled pastors and their people. And the drama is not yet closed. Many societies are now in trouble, and will not probably find peace without resort to the law. An itinerant ministry, subject to proper regulations, escapes these evils. Where a minister is stationed for a year or three at most, and is to be removed at the close of this term, any thing like a long and bitter contention is impracticable. And the *least* is impolitic ; for, though the parties may be dissatisfied with each other, the best and most natural remedy of the evil is to wait patiently till the expiration of the term, when a separation *must* take place. It is a pleasing reflection, and a truth, the language of which cannot be mistaken, that amid all the litigation that has been witnessed in the courts of New England, between preachers and their people, the Methodist Episcopal Church has been only a spectator. Her first suit is not yet filed ; and such is the nature of her arrangements, it is not probable that she will soon need the intervention of law to adjust any differences that may occur. Her ministers rather depend on the magnanimity and affection of their people to support them, than on *law:* and leave for other scenes, when their usefulness is at an end, rather than remain in contention. And this we believe to be more in accordance with the instruction of the Saviour, who said to his apostles, "when they persecute you in this city, flee ye to another;" and it certainly is more becoming a minister of the gospel of peace.

7. It is indispensable to the *general spread of Christianity.* However successful stationary ministers may be in our cities and more densely settled portions of the country, they are not adapted to meet the exigencies of a sparse population. To wait for a *call* from new and unenlightened parts of the country, would be to consign the people to everlasting darkness. The ministry that will regenerate such members of the human family, must go among them *uncalled*, and travel from town to town, preaching and teaching as Providence may direct. If there were no other argument in favor of an itinerant ministry, this would be sufficient, not only to prove its expediency, but its absolute necessity to the objects of preaching in the larger part of the world.

8. The history of itinerancy furnishes one of the strongest proofs of its expediency. Rev. B. B. Edwards, a Congregationalist, speaking of the early history of the church, says, "The *travels* and ministry of the apostles and other missionaries soon spread Christianity through the Roman empire. Palestine, Syria, Natolia, Greece, the islands of the Mediterranean, Italy, and the northern coast of Africa, as early as the first century, contained numerous societies of Christians. At the end of the second century, Christians were to be found in all the provinces; and at the end of the third century, almost half of the inhabitants of the Roman empire, and several neighboring countries, professed the faith of Christ." Another eminent writer, speaking on the same subject, says "Destitute of all human advantages, protected by

no authority, assisted by no art, not recommended by the reputation of its author, not enforced by eloquence in its advocates, the word of God grew mightily and prevailed."

The modern history of itinerancy is identical with Wesleyan Methodism, under its various modifications. We have seen something of its operations in the foregoing pages, and need not enumerate them here. There is, however, one other view of the subject that should not be overlooked. We refer to the influence of our itinerancy upon other churches. We take no undue credit when we say, there are thousands and tens of thousands in their communion who were awakened and converted through our instrumentality. Many things contributed to draw them away from their spiritual relations, and they settled down in church fellowship with those who never "travailed in birth" for them. But these churches have been more especially benefited by itinerancy in another way. It has "provoked" them to love and good works. Their ministers are better preachers, better pastors and better Christians, — they have more zeal and enterprise, — preach less error and more truth, — and otherwise labor more appropriately than when Methodism was first introduced among them. And their people have improved proportionably. Where the family altar was entirely neglected, it now smokes with acceptable incense. Where there were but two meetings in a week, and those on Sunday, in the parish church, there are now several, in various places, to accommodate the people. Where there was pride and worldly amusement, with little piety and enterprise, there is now Christian activity and devotion to God. Such has been the effect of itinerancy upon them, that churches which feared and trembled at the approach of the itinerant, have become firmer, more united and spiritual than they ever were before, and have reason to bless God for the Providence which brought so useful an agency among them. Had we not succeeded in forming a single church, or in doing any other good, the influence we have exerted on surrounding denominations is an abundant compensation for all our sacrifices. This is a high source of encouragement to feeble churches. Though they gain very slowly, if at all, they are doing a great work, and should hold fast and struggle on in good cheer. But, O, what a multitude, gathered from all ranks and countries, by the sacrifices and sufferings of itinerant men, have gone home to heaven! Many of them were as sheep having no shepherd, and many had only a hireling shepherd. They were formalists, or infidels, or common sinners, till they heard the voice of the stranger calling them to repentance and to God; "warning them day and night with tears." Then they were arrested, found peace in believing, and have since yielded their spirits to God who gave them, with exceeding joy.

From these considerations, to say nothing of others which might be mentioned, an itinerant ministry is evidently expedient. He who established it at first, and sent out his apostles "into all the world to preach the gospel," acted, no doubt, in the light of infinite intelligence. He adopted the best means for the world's conversion. And who that looks at this question impartially, will not discover substantial reasons for his action? If the world's conversion to God in the shortest time possible, were the supreme object of all ministers of the gospel, would any settle down and confine their exertions to one place? Impossible! When settled ministers wish to accomplish much for temperance, missions, moral reform, &c., they fly from town to town, and from city to city, proclaiming the most pungent truths they have at command touching their subject. Ask them why they do not settle and advocate their favorite cause, and they will think you are joking. Yet such a policy is supported by nearly the same arguments which are urged in favor of a settled ministry. A distinguished writer in the "Encyclopædia of Religious Knowledge," of the settled order, says: —

"Notwithstanding the prejudices of mankind, and the indiscretions of some individuals, an *itinerant teacher* is one of the most honorable and useful characters to be found upon earth; and there needs no other proof than the experience of the church in all ages, that, where this work is done properly and with perseverance, it forms the grand method of spreading wide, and rendering efficacious, religious knowledge; for great reformations and revivals of religion have uniformly been thus effected; and it has been especially sanctioned by the *example* of *Christ* and his apostles, and recommended as *the divine method* of spreading the gospel through the nations of the earth."

But there are objections. For instance, we hear it said, 1. That it is *unpleasant to the people* to part with a minister they love. But in estimating this, we are reminded that the unpleasantness of a religious measure is no valid argument against it. It is unpleasant to repent, to break off our sins. It is like the plucking out of a right eye, or the amputation of a right hand. If a minister be a man of peculiar power and effectiveness, and has been especially useful in one place, it is a good reason why that people should release him, and let him go and do a similar work in another place. The reason why they love him, and would retain him among them, is the very reason why he should go to another field. But a minister is sometimes esteemed for other reasons. It may be that he is eloquent, and companionable, and prophesies smooth things. One of this description generally finds many friends. He treats his hearers tenderly, and they reciprocate the favor, and extol him as a worthy man, though there is not one converted, and religion is on the decline. To lose such a minister would be very painful, but is it not *best* that he should leave? He will do nothing if he remains. He needs to go among a people of more devotion to God, and a flaming herald of truth is best fitted for usefulness in the place he vacates. Such a change would be mutually beneficial, and ought to be made, however disagreeable to personal feelings.

2. It is objected, that it is *laborious for ministers.* This will not be denied, and especially where the country is new, the roads rough and difficult, and the support insufficient to meet the actual necessities of life. But laborious as is the work, and unpleasant as it is to break up our associations so frequently, and form new acquaintances, the itinerancy of the Master was much more so. He had not "*where to lay his head.*" So was that of the apostles. "In journeyings often, in perils of water, in perils of robbers, in perils by the heathen, in perils in the city, in perils in the wilderness, in perils in the sea, in perils among false brethren; in weariness and painfulness, in watchings often, in hunger and thirst, in fastings often, in cold and nakedness," they pursued their divine mission, and died martyrs to their work. And is it becoming their successors to talk of ease and convenience? Those who have entered the ministry at their own suggestion, uncalled of God, may do so; but shame on us if we can put such considerations in opposition to any plan of gathering the lost sheep into the fold of Christ. Though by this policy we are torn from the graves of our fathers, and are compelled to bury our wives and little ones among strangers, in different and distant parts, it ill becomes

us to complain of hardship, while we claim Christ for our leader, or his apostles for our brethren.

3. It is objected, that an itinerant minister *cannot know the circumstances of the people*, like one settled, and, therefore, cannot *adapt his instructions to their necessities*. In reply to this, it is important to remind the objector, that if a minister is successful, it is in vain to talk of the disadvantages of his system. Itinerancy has succeeded beyond all precedent. It, therefore, is the system for all practical men, though its theory were a perfect paradox. But it requires only a short time for an industrious man to form all the acquaintance with the largest societies that is necessary to a proper adaptation of his labors. A minister does not need to know every thing about his people. There is scarcely less danger of knowing too much, than of knowing too little. The success of the pulpit depends on the illustration and enforcement of the fundamentals of Christianity. These are adapted to every community, of every possible condition. He, therefore, who confines his pulpit discourses to these, is always appropriate, but never *personal*. To know more of his people — to understand their various notions, and petty differences, real and imaginary faults — may help him to preach more *personally*, but not more appropriately. But personalities in the pulpit are always impolitic, and out of place. They seldom fail to offend, and rarely benefit any one. Yet the same truths, uttered by a stranger to the circumstances, so that the idea of personality cannot come into the account, may be useful. When the eccentric Lorenzo Dow described the character of one of his hearers, who had defrauded in the matter of *measure*, she resolved on immediate reform, and retired to restore the bottom of her half bushel to its proper place. Had she supposed him to be personal, the result would probably have

been different. But he was an entire stranger, and knew nothing of her affairs. Too much knowledge of the people is also sometimes very perplexing to a minister. For these reasons, itinerants have often refused to hear more of a society to which they have recently come than what was indispensable. They wished to feel no impediment to the discharge of their whole duty, and, therefore, determined "not to know any thing among" the people "save Jesus Christ, and him crucified." All ministers might do well to exercise the same precaution.

4. It is objected, that the piety of those who profess religion under the labors of itinerants is *evanescent and worthless*. This is an old objection, but has no foundation in fact. Its falsity is sufficiently obvious from the avidity with which settled pastors receive converts from this quarter. That some who profess religion under the labors of itinerant ministers apostatize from the faith, is admitted. But that the proportion of such converts is larger than is found under the stationed ministry, cannot be proved. If there are more in number, there are also more converted. If many fall away, many also persevere. But it is a lamentable truth, to which we can but advert in this place, that not a few, who make shipwreck of their profession, do so by the proselytism of sectarian relatives, and others, who have taken no part in their conversion; or by the cold and faithless treatment they receive from those who ought to take them to their arms, as brethren beloved, and guide them in the way to heaven.

5. It is objected, that such a system may impose a minister upon a people *who is not adapted to their wants, and one they do not like.* This is not denied; but it should not be forgotten that it also removes him at the end of the first year, or indeed before, if good and sufficient reasons can be

given for so doing; and that without contention. This is an advantage which a well regulated system of itinerancy holds over the settled system. But it is important to inquire, whether the most rigid Congregationalists never have a minister they do not esteem? The truth is, all their precaution in settling ministers does not screen them from mistakes. Certificates of competent education, and other ministerial qualifications, with several trial sermons, the most satisfactory, are not sufficient. They often settle men, who, after a little better acquaintance, prove themselves unadapted to their wants. But it is now too late — they have no itinerant arrangement to take them off their hands, and must submit, or hazard a difficulty among themselves in attempting to remove them.

These, we believe, are the most serious objections that are urged against our system, but they have little weight with those who "seek not their own." Their foundation is *selfishness*. And in this respect they tally well with the holiest conceptions of many intelligent men. "Well," says one, "I should not *like* this moving about so much." And another, "Do you *like* to move so often?" Just as if our *like* or *dislike* were the only thing to be consulted. We wish all such inquirers to know that we have no more fancy for moving than other men — that we should enjoy a "sweet home," pleasant houses and lands, and old friends, and relations, as well as they; and that we only deny ourselves of these pleasures in subordination to what we regard a high obligation imposed upon us by Him who hath put us into the ministry. Take this away, and many would not preach at all, much less expatriate themselves, and wander abroad, without any "certain dwelling place."

CHAPTER IV.

DISTINCTIVE SOCIAL MEETINGS VINDICATED.

OUR regular Sabbath services differ very little from those maintained by other evangelical Christians. We, however, hold several meetings peculiar to ourselves, in reference to which it may be proper to give a word of explanation.

QUARTERLY MEETINGS

Are holden in each of our circuits and stations, once a quarter, from which circumstance they derive their name. They are usually commenced on Saturday, and continue through the Sabbath. The presiding elder is generally present to take charge. Saturday afternoon is occupied with preaching, or a love-feast, and the Quarterly Conference; and the evening with a prayer meeting. The Sabbath often embraces a love-feast, several sermons, and the Lord's supper. The services, however, are not the same in all places, though generally interesting, particularly in large circuits. Whatever may become of them as our home privileges multiply, it must be conceded that they have been eminently useful. They are still anticipated in many places with holy satisfaction, and effectively improved in promoting the Redeemer's kingdom.

CLASS MEETINGS.

Of the general character and origin of these meetings we have already spoken. Their management and utility are matters of equal interest. With a view to these points, the Discipline requires that the leaders "be not only men of *sound judgment*, but men *truly devoted to God.*" To find a sufficient number of such men is not always practicable. The cause has often suffered for the want of them. But still, class meetings are of infinite value to us as a denomination. They furnish a natural and easy mode of approach to the church, bring the members and inquirers together, away from the presence and sneer of the world, where they may indulge in free communication concerning their spiritual interests, and mingle in prayer and praise. Such meetings must, therefore, be beneficial, even under the direction of an indifferent leader. But with one who labors to prepare himself for his work, and deals faithfully, but kindly, with every member, they are especially so. Other denominations have seen their operation, and coveted their advantages. Some ministers have established meetings of the kind among their people, but they have usually run a brief and feeble race. The truth is, they are not a part of their *system;* they do not belong to their economy, they rather come in collision with it; and can never be engrafted into it, we fear, so as to work efficiently.

Those who really *enjoy* religion, or are *earnestly* seeking it, instinctively incline to meetings of this kind, more perhaps, than to any other. They desire to be closely questioned, and personally advised and prayed for. Indifferent professors *need* them, and often find them sources of great spiritual excitement to duty. They should never neglect them. Where all other means fail of stirring their hearts into life, this may succeed. Nor should our members cease to invite all serious-minded persons to accompany them to these holy convocations. "Through the grace of God," says Dr. Coke, "our classes form the pillars of our work, and are, in a considerable degree, our universities for the ministry." They are generally opened by singing and prayer, after which the leader gives some account of his own experience the past week, and then inquires of each concerning their spiritual state, giving them such advices, as he proceeds, as appear to him most suitable. They may rise and speak, or remain on their seats and answer such questions as the leader may propose. Some pursue one course, and some the other, according to their respective tastes and states of mind. The main point is to find out where they are, and to help them to work out their salvation. The less formal, and the more social and conversational the exercises, the more satisfactory and profitable.

Thus we "consider one another, to provoke unto love, and good works: not forsaking the assembling of ourselves together, as the manner of some is; but exhorting one another; and so much the more as we see the day approaching." — Heb. x. 24, 25. We "confess our faults one to another, and pray one for another, that we may be healed." — James v. 16. And we "exhort one another daily, lest any be hardened through the deceitfulness of sin," — Heb. iii. 12, 13; "teaching and admonishing one another in psalms, and hymns, and spiritual songs, singing with grace in our hearts to the Lord." — Col. iii. 16. Or, in the language of a more ancient worshipper, we invite all who fear God to come and hear, and "declare what he hath done for our souls." — Psalms lxvi. 16. Thus we endeavor to imitate the good of other days, who "feared the Lord, and spake often one to another;" of whom it is written, "the Lord hearkened

30

and heard; and a book of remembrance was written before him for them that feared the Lord, and thought upon his name. And they shall be mine, saith the Lord of hosts, in that day when I make up my jewels." — Mal. iii. 16, 17.

GENERAL CLASS MEETINGS,

Sometimes called church meetings, are holden in many of our societies once in a month or two, on an evening in the week preceding the administration of the sacrament. Here all the leaders and their classes meet, with their preacher in charge, and state in a few voluntary remarks how they are prospering in spiritual things. If any have been received into the classes since the last meeting, some preachers take this opportunity to read their names and introduce them to the church, at the same time stating to them what they may expect of the church, and what the church will expect of them. Some think it expedient, too, to read the names of those who are about to be baptized or received into full connection, that if any member knows good reason why the proposed step should not be taken, he may privately communicate the same to the preacher in charge. But these arrangements are not enjoined by the Discipline.

LOVE FEASTS

Were established by Mr. Wesley in reference to the *Agapæ*, or feasts of charity, observed in the apostolic age. The celebrated historian, Augustus Neander, D.D., says:—

"We will now speak of these feasts of brotherly love, as they were when they went under the particular name of *Agapæ*. At these all distinctions of earthly condition and rank were to disappear in Christ. All were to be one in the Lord; rich and poor, high and low, masters and servants, were to eat together at a common table. We have the description of such a feast of Agapæ by Turtullian. 'Our supper,' he says, 'shows its character by its name; it bears the Greek name of love; and, however great may be the expense of it, still it is gain to make expense in the name of piety, for we give joy to all the poor by this refreshment. The cause of the supper being a worthy one, we estimate accordingly the propriety with which it is managed, as its religious end demands. It admits of no vulgarity, nothing unbecoming. No one approaches the table till prayer has first been offered to God; as much is eaten as is necessary to satisfy the demands of hunger; as much is drank as consists with sobriety. The conversation is such as might be expected of men who are fully conscious that God hears them. The supper being ended, and all having washed their hands, lights are brought in; then each is invited to sing as he is able, either from the Holy Scriptures or from the promptings of his own spirit, a song of praise to God, for the common edification." — *History of Religion, vol.* 1, *p.* 325.

"The celebration of the Eucharist was originally accompanied by meetings, called Agapæ, or *Feasts of Love.* Every Christian, according to his circumstances, brought to the assembly portions of bread, wine, and other things, as gifts, as it were, or oblations to the Lord. Of the bread and wine, such as was required for the administration of the sacrament was separated from the rest, and consecrated by the bishop alone; its distribution was followed by a frugal and serious repast. Undoubtedly, these assemblies acted not only as excitements to ardent piety, but also as bonds of strict religious union and mutual devotion, during the dark days of terror and persecution. It was probable on those occasions, more than any others, that the sufferers rallied their scattered ranks, and encouraged each other, by one solemn act of brotherly communion, to constancy in one faith, and association in the same afflictions." — *Waddington's Church History, p.* 46.

These views are confirmed by still higher authority. An apostle records of the early Christians, particularly those who were converted on the day of Pentecost, "They continuing daily, with one accord, in the temple, and breaking bread from house to house, did eat their meat with gladness and singleness of heart, praising God and having favor with all the people." — Acts ii. 46. But this interesting service, like every thing else with which man has had to do, was abused. Wicked men crept in, and perverted it to purposes of drunkenness and gluttony. St. Jude speaks of them thus: "These are spots in your feasts of charity, when they feast with you, feeding themselves without fear; clouds they are without water, carried about of wind; trees whose fruit withereth without fruit," &c. Hence, after a time, the *agapæ* was laid aside, and had no place among the services of the church, until revived by the Moravians and the Wesleyan Methodists.

In the revival of this venerable institution, Methodists have so far varied the elements employed as to secure it against the abuse it received at the first. They have excluded wines, and all the rich and costly viands that formerly made it attractive to persons of intemperate and gluttonous tendencies, and supplied their places with water, and a bit of common bread. They, however, endeavor to retain its spirit and secure its object, — the increase and perpetuity of brotherly love; and we rust they are not altogether unsuccessful. Our love-feasts are designed to embrace all the members of the church, and other serious minded persons, and no others. (Triflers should never be admitted.) They. are opened by singing an appropriate hymn, and prayer for the divine blessing. The president of the occasion then gives a brief explanation of the nature of the feast, and the stewards pass the bread and water, while he proceeds to relate such matters of experience, instruction, and advice, as he may judge proper. When he closes, some one strikes a familiar tune, and all unite in singing a verse; after which, the services consist of brief experimental remarks from the different members present, interspersed with thrilling songs of praise to God, and sometimes with more thrilling shouts of joy and exultation.

On the whole, these meetings are among the most profitable the church enjoys. They generally bring us encouraging information from the district, through the presiding elder, who ordinarily presides; they bring the members of different classes, and often of different societies and towns, to look each other in the face, and feel each other's influence; sometimes they bring together several preachers of the same circuit or neighborhood, and elicit the best feelings, plans, and purposes of the church, in a manner to electrify and encourage many hearts. They are peculiarly interesting to the poor and degraded. Here they meet their superiors on common ground, and feel that all distinctions are laid aside; here they can open their minds freely and fully, and tell how much they love God, and the church, and the cause of religion; here they can praise the Lord without the restraint important to be exercised in a promiscuous assembly; and here, too, they have an opportunity of letting their light shine on the church, so as to stimulate colder hearts to "glorify their Father which is in heaven."

WATCH MEETINGS.

The same zeal which stimulated St. Paul to continue "his speech until midnight," and to pray and sing praises unto God at that late hour, has sustained these meetings, and will sustain them so long as it prevails among us. They have, however, been complained of, and opposed with great boldness and energy. Formalists have read us mournful homilies on the evil of late meetings; while the rabble, encouraged by their religious disapproval, have often taken the liberty to disturb our devotions, and otherwise endeavor to counteract their effect. Had they been as careful to prevent other late meetings, such as balls and parties, which not unfrequently extend to a still later hour, even to the rising of the sun, their motives would have been more highly appreciated. But the opposers of watch meetings have not generally appeared very scrupulous on these points; so that their opposition has been suspected of arising more from enmity to God, than from any great concern for our health and reputation, or for the maintenance of religious prosperity. But if it was proper for Jacob to wrestle with an angel "until the breaking of the day," and then refuse to let him go, unless he would bless him, and for Jesus to continue in the mountain "all night in prayer to God," why may not Christians occasionally "watch and pray" till midnight? Why? Can any good reason be assigned? So long as they cherish the emotions incident to ardent piety, such meetings will sometimes seem necessary to relief, and to the attainment of the holy objects of their pursuit. Paul was an orderly man; yet he continued his speech, at Troas, till a late hour. Souls were at stake. What he could not accomplish "in season," he felt compelled to effect "out of season;" and every Christian should do the same. This tying religion up to a set of cold, time-serving forms and rules, which leave its friends little or no discretion, is not right. Christians ought tc consult the providence as well as the word of God, and seize upon every facility to do good, and save souls from death. It has been said of the reforms of England, that "they begin with breaking the law." Whether this be so or not, all spiritual reforms have been effected by infringing upon regulations, suggested by decline and adopted by apostacy. The reformation, under Luther, was a series of innovations. So was that which originated with the Wesleys. The institution of watch-meetings was one of them, and, like most of its associates, it created no small stir, but resulted in great good.

These meetings are more commonly holden upon the last evening of each year, and continued until a little past twelve o'clock. They are usually commenced by singing and prayer; after which the time is occupied in preaching, singing, exhortation, and prayer; in reviewing the year past, the excellencies and defects by which it has been characterized, and suggesting purposes for the year to come. Sometimes the Lord's supper is administered, and, not unfrequently, a part of the evening is devoted to love-feast exercises, praying for mourners, &c. A little before twelve o'clock, the time is announced, and all present are invited to kneel before God in silent prayer, and thus remain until the knell of the departed year is rung, when the presiding officer commends the congregation to the divine guidance and protection in vocal prayer, and closes by singing the covenant hymn, and the benediction. These exercises are generally followed by an affectionate shaking of hands, and exchange of Christian salutations, accompanied with many "I wish you a happy new year."

Watch-meetings have, undoubtedly, been very useful. The *occasion* of them is full of interest. The vows of the past, and the awful contingencies of the future, crowd upon the mind, and command reflection. It is a period, too, when great changes are taking place in society; changes in life, in business, in prospects. The merchant takes account of his stock; old bills are paid, and new contracts effected. How appropriate for the sinner to square his account with sin, and enter into covenant with his Maker; for the wanderer to return to his father's house, and the Christian to grapple higher achievements than he has ever dared to anticipate! And how appropriate from another consideration! This evening is generally employed by the gay and fashionable in dancing, and other folly. The friends, sometimes the children, of Christian parents are active in these amusements. O, how befitting the children of God to meet and endeavor to counteract their influence. They may be useful, too, on other occasions, as a special means of grace, particularly in promoting a revival of religion.

CHAPTER V

CAMP MEETINGS.—OBJECTIONS TO THEM ANSWERED, AND THE GROUNDS OF THEIR DEFENCE STATED.

CAMP MEETINGS are supported by the purest philosophy. This will appear by referring to a few particulars.

1. Every enterprise needs to have great occasions, when friends may meet and encourage each other in their work. Among the Catholics these are numerous, and they exert an incalculable influence. Indeed, all sects and parties have them, at great expense and trouble, and are satisfied of their importance to success. A pleasant meeting of brethren, from different meridians, strengthens affection and confidence, and qualifies for the more cheerful and efficient operation of their system.

This accounts for the appointment of the various festivals under the Jewish economy. God saw that such associations were necessary to consolidate the *social union* of the tribes and families of his people. And so long as they observed them, they were united and active. They were the means, too, of their restoration, when they had fallen. Thus, when Hezekiah sent out the posts " from Beersheba even to Dan," to summon the apostate people to Jerusalem to solemnize the passover, " they laughed them to scorn, and mocked them." The proposition seemed ridiculous, at first. But when they came to journey with other tribes, and especially when they arrived at Jerusalem, and saw the devotional spirit of Hezekiah, the priests and chief men of the city, where there had recently been a powerful revival, and heard the law, the mighty shouting and singing of inspired hearts, the fires of devotion kindled within them, so that, contrary to all their plans and to the astonishment of every one, they continued their meeting *fourteen* days, celebrating the "feast with gladness;" while the "Levites and priests praised the Lord day by day, singing with loud instruments unto the Lord." Then they separated, but not without reluctance, and spread the zeal and fellowship of their own replenished minds throughout all Israel.

As Methodists, we need these occasions for *all* the people. Our General and Annual Conferences embrace the preachers chiefly, but they exert a salutary influence. Though the meetings of these bodies are principally for business purposes, they subserve mutual friendship, and strengthen the members for their arduous work. But few of the people enjoy the privilege of attending them. This loss was formerly recompensed by the Quarterly Meetings, which convened a large number of preachers and people from different parts of an extended circuit. But, as great occasions, Quarterly Meetings have no existence in a considerable part of our country. Few attend them beyond the limits of the society where they are held, and we see no prospect of restoring them to their former greatness. We are left, therefore, to supply this necessity of the people to our camp meetings. Take these away, and the strongest bond of social union among us is sundered.

2. The importance of camp meetings appears in the *advantages of protracted devotion.* The ordinary services of the church are interrupted by frequent intermissions. The Sabbath, with other occasional meetings, is soon past, and gives place to duties of a less spiritual character. The

mind, jaded and perplexed with worldly interests, hardly gets fixed on the subject before it must be diverted. Where one has relapsed into indifference, the Sabbath is too short to abstract his thoughts from the world, and concentrate them on Christ, so as to secure his recovery. This suggests the reason why the Jewish feasts were extended to such lengths. Infinite wisdom saw that one day was not sufficient to bring the cold and alien tribes into a right state. It was clear enough that minds so dead to moral and religious interests would need to be held in contact with better spirits, and listen to the law day after day, and be drilled by a protracted effort. The masters of Israel also understood this. When Hezekiah had succeeded in getting a mighty multitude to the temple, he saw it was for their good to retain them in its services, till they were entirely recovered from their wanderings, and re-attached to the proper object of worship.

These remarks are no less applicable to unbelievers than to Christians. It is more needful, indeed, for them to be excluded from care; and, in many cases, unless they are there is little hope. They are attached to the world, and must be taken away from it, broken off, and held to the closest contemplation of eternal things. Not for an hour, or a single service, and then turned out to plunge again into business; but for days and weeks, even. We have known of meetings continued for forty days in succession, in which little was done till toward the close. It took most of the time to bring the public mind to the *acting point*. But camp meetings, taking men off many miles from their business and sinful amusements, and holding them to pointed and pathetic preaching and exhortation, and bringing them into immediate contact with the most effective Christians, some of whom were similarly situated to themselves when they were converted, they can but become sources of powerful conviction and impulse, and often of sound conversion.

3. Camp meetings afford also an opportunity for profitable Christian intercourse. The tendency of Christians to backslide is remarkable. It is a lamentable truth, that a large proportion of all who are converted to God, sooner or later lose some degree of their first love, while many turn entirely back to their old sins. It is true, too, that they frequently become shaken in mind, in regard to important doctrines and measures. Another fact is, that when this deterioration commences, it usually continues its ravages till the particular branch of the church in which it appears is generally infected. Where the infection becomes universal and virulent, it exhausts the recuperative power of the body. Thus they lie under the dominion of profound stupidity, and enjoy the union of the dead, if any, rather than the active pleasures and hopes of the living.

Now when churches relapse into this condition, they need to come in contact with other and better society than they find in the regular routine of their ordinary formalities. They need to see and hear a higher order of Christians, and feel their regenerating influence. Camp meetings bring together the best spirits within a large circumference. Those who possess most of the divine influence, and are best informed in the science of salvation, are much inclined to such meetings. They love to retire from the world, to commune with God and his people. They delight to talk of his word and works; of the blessedness of religion; to sing his praise, and tell of his goodness. How appropriate, then, is the place for the stupid and the impenitent! Many such have found it the place of awakening and spiritual transformation. They have been constrained to say, as they listened to the streaming eloquence of living hearts, and saw the beauty of religion exemplified in its possessors, "How miserably I have lived! I will return to my Father's house! I will sink into the will of God! The Lord helping me, I will be an entire Christian!" And, like Paul, on meeting his brethren from Rome, they have "thanked God, and taken courage."

4. Camp meetings are emphatically adapted to the conversion of sinners. To the remarks made in the last paragraph, it is important to add several others. That sinners are generally convinced of sin, and of the necessity of becoming pious under ordinary training, is demonstrable from common experience. But they are hindered from using the necessary means by various circumstances. One is, their relation to others. They are connected in business, or pleasure, or educational pursuits, or in some of the domestic relations, with persons whose influence is against religion. To change their course in favor of it, so as to obtain its enjoyments, would expose them to persecution from their dearest friends. Here is a difficulty which, taken in connection with the apathy of the church, and the low state of religious interest in the community, is quite sufficient to deter them from duty. But at a camp meeting these impediments are, in part, removed. Many of their companions are not present, nor are most of their neighbors and acquaintances, whose scorn they dread. The public services are calculated to arouse their feelings, and induce them to immediate action. Besides, many of the most devoted Christians are kindly pressing them up to the work; by which means an excitement is created, sufficient to carry them over their difficulties, and bring them out in open pursuit of the desired object. The action of others in a simi-

lar direction, is no little advantage to them. Many have been induced to do their duty in connection with others, who would not have been persuaded to do it alone.

5. *The relation of such meetings to the subject of holiness, furnishes another powerful argument* in favor of their continuance. The doctrine of entire sanctification is the brightest star in the doctrinal constellation of Wesleyan Methodism. Yet, it is opposed by other denominations as peculiarly false and fanatical. Another obstacle is found nearer home. Some of our own people have their doubts; while many, who allow the possibility of the thing, entertain different views of its conditionality and manifestations. Particularly do they differ in regard to the latter; some attributing to the sanctified, powers and perceptions little short of miraculous; while others only allow them more of the same spirit they experienced in their conversion. This makes the open and vigorous pursuit of the blessing not a little perplexing. But the fact that some brethren possessing it have run into enthusiasm and extravagance, renders it still more so. The result of these circumstances, in many places, is the almost entire neglect of the subject. Most have not *interest* enough to speak of it, and those who have lack the necessary courage.

6. *The influence of camp meetings on revivals of religion* furnishes a strong argument in their favor. Revivals are generally brought about by human instrumentality; but many of the most effective means are forbidding to our fallen nature. Hence, Christians often modify their movements, so as to avoid reproach, or at least to mitigate its severity. How many have been to camp meetings precisely in this condition, cold and timid, and been so divinely inspired as to overcome their fears, and make the successful

effort? The work of the Lord has often broken out immediately among them, and spread as by miracle.

7. But *our chief reliance is upon facts.* Multitudes of our ministers were converted at camp meetings, and owe their ministerial standing to their influence in reviving and stimulating them to duty. When called to preach, they had their cherished plans of life laid, and disliked to abandon them. They saw more sacrifices involved in an itinerant ministerial career than they had grace to grapple. So they deferred or positively refused, and incurred guilt and spiritual darkness, terribly dangerous to their souls. But the camp meeting broke the fatal spell. They *heard*, *felt*, and submitted their whole being to God, and were restored, and endowed for their calling. Many, too, have been sanctified on these occasions. The biography of the lamented Dr. Fisk presents us with a brilliant instance of this kind. Who can estimate the full value of that single case to our connection? Our membership has derived similar advantages. Converted, received, and sanctified in the tented grove, many have lived far better than they would have done but for this means. But the fruit of these meetings is not confined to our own church. Thousands, of other sects, and of no sect, are greatly benefited.

But there are objections.

I. It is said, "we have *churches now to accommodate the people.*" But this only meets one of the least of the reasons originally urged in favor of such meetings. II. Another objection,—and it is the strongest that can be urged,—is, that camp meetings are the *occasion of much evil.* In reply, we allow that many wicked people attend them, and sometimes conduct disgracefully. But it should be considered these persons were wicked *before the meeting was called*, and would have drunk and caroused, and been pro fane, had they been any where else. Mere *pretenders* to good character expose their hypocrisy more fully, at such times; and it is well, perhaps, that they do. It may open the eyes of some blind one they are leading to ruin. It is a good place to study character, and see who are really upright, and honest, and reliable — who are gentlemen and ladies. We say *ladies*, because women are actors in the scene as well as men, and, we are sorry to remark, often expose the utter emptiness of their pretensions to good sense and good manners, and, what is worse, the baseness of their principles and their hearts.

We repeat, and it should be remembered, that those who prowl about our camp meetings, and commit the sins referred to in this objection, are the *moral filth* and *offscouring* of all the region round about. They go wherever they can find companions, and get an opportunity to drink, and gamble, and steal, and disturb the peace of others, with the least exposure to penal consequences. They are *criminals* wherever they be; and the only difference the camp meeting makes with them is, it changes the scene of their crimes. Even in the far-distant days of Job, " when the sons of God came to present themselves before the Lord, *Satan* came also among them;" but *they* were not blamed on the account, nor did they see cause to abandon their meetings.

2. It should also be considered, that if this is a valid argument against camp meetings, *it is equally so* against every other religious movement which is the occasion of sin. And what one is not? If God had never revealed his name, it would not have been profaned; therefore, that revelation has been the occasion of great sin. If he had not given us his word, we should have had no infidels; and thus the world had been saved from a great moral nuisance. But for

the institution of the Sabbath, this country had been free from the dreadful sin of Sabbath-breaking. Thus, every religious arrangement our heavenly Father has made is an occasion of sin, and, generally, in proportion to the zeal and fidelity exerted to carry it into operation. What sins were the coming and preaching of Christ the occasion of among the Jews! And how many shocking murders, and other crimes, did the preaching of the apostles occasion! Wherever religion is promulgated in its spirit and power, it will be the occasion of more or less evil. It will arouse the carnal mind, and bring down the wrath of the enemies of God upon those who are interested in his work; breaking up family and other friendships; inflicting persecutions and oppressions, and calling out curses and imprecations too blasphemous to be repeated. But who thinks of giving up Christianity, or blaming it, for these things? The objection, carried out, would banish the religion of the Bible from the world.

But it seems to be applied to camp meetings only. Generally, if people see the wicked driving and hallooing along the street, they blame *them*, and not the occasion or its patrons. But when they see them doing the same thing in connection with a camp meeting, they blame the Methodists, and their meeting. Why is this? Where is the justice or consistency of it?

3. Finally, brethren who make this objection should consider whether the evils named, great as they have sometimes been, are not more than compensated by the good effected. Who can estimate the value of one soul! But we never heard of a camp meeting that was not instrumental in the conversion of several; and, says inspiration, "he which converteth the sinner from the error of his way, shall save a soul from death, and hide a multitude of sins."

III. It is also objected to camp meetings that they are *nurseries of enthusiasm.* Taking the term in a good sense, we admit the assumption, but question its application. Enthusiasm, to a certain degree, is indispensable to success in any enterprise. An eminent writer says, "There is no man excellent in his profession, whatever it be, who has not in his temper a strong tincture of it." It implies vigor of thought, fervor of spirit, vivacity and strength, that elevate the soul to higher aspirations than unimpassioned reason ever attains. In this sense it is a glorious acquisition, and the tendency of camp meetings to promote its attainment, in special application to religion, is one of the strongest arguments in their favor. The human mind is inclined to grovel, to lose sight of heavenly interests, or pursue them with indifference, unbecoming their nature. Camp meetings are calculated to quicken and elevate; of the truth of which there are many witnesses. But the objection employs the term in an *offensive* sense, to mean religious deception and extravagance, particularly in relation to personal experience. That persons under strong religious excitement are more liable to extremes, in this direction, is undeniable. An engine without fire seldom runs off the track. Lifeless professors have no enjoyment or communion with God, to *suggest* the idea that they possess peculiar endowments. Nor are they so elated with their possessions and prospects as to indulge in unreasonable exclamations. Dead men are not the material for enthusiasts of this stamp. Christians of the highest excitability, and the most sincere devotion, are more exposed. Whatever, therefore, contributes to elevate their emotions, increases their liability. Hence the objection lies with equal force against every other means of grace, in proportion to its adaptation to awaken and strengthen religious interest.

But we deny that the objection, thus far admitted to be true in fact, is of any validity. The truth is, every acquisition, whatever its nature, increases our liability to one evil or another. The *beggar* is in no danger of being robbed or envied. Raise him to opulence, and you expose both his reputation and his life. Nor is the mere professor liable to become an enthusiast. There is no element of spiritual life in him. He is equally indifferent to the agony of the publican, and the transport of assured faith.

There is another kind of enthusiasm which, in our opinion, is most dangerous of all. We refer to a *sleepy* and *inoperative* profession of religion, that does but little for the cause, and that little in a spiritless way. Much as we deprecate wild-fire, we prefer it to no fire at all. For, say what we will, it is an *active* principle, and hits the mark more frequently than indifference.

IV. It is objected to camp meetings, also, that *they are expensive.* Brethren have figured up their cost, and calculated the amount of good it might do if applied to the payment of church debts, the extension of missions, &c. But such close reckoning always reminds one of the "precious ointment" poured upon the head of Jesus. "When his disciples saw it, they had indignation, saying, To what purpose is this waste? For this ointment might have been sold for much, and given to the poor." But Jesus rebuked them, and pronounced the work of the woman a good one, because he was only an occasional visitor, whereas they had the poor with them always. So we say of camp meetings; they come but once in a year, whereas other claimants upon our resources are "always with us," and we have the other fifty-one weeks of the year to supply them. This objection often appears more benevolent than it really is. With many it originates in sheer avarice. They have no care for the poor, more than Judas, and will not give a farthing from the savings of camp meeting week.

But it must be observed that this objection lies equally against all other means of grace that are not entirely expenseless. For, as to the divine authority of camp meetings, it is not wanting, and in utility they will not suffer in comparison with any other in the entire calendar.

V. It is also objected that the spiritual results of camp meetings *are not valid.* This may be true in particular cases. Persons naturally excitable and unstable, often make an ado, at such times, to little purpose. Like land floods, they move with a rush, and then disappear, till the recurrence of another similar occasion. This has been a stupendous reproach to such meetings; but it should not be. The truth is, were it not for some such exciting occasions these people would not pray at all. If they are influenced to live religiously a month or two in a year, it is clear gain. But it must not be overlooked that many others take a different course. They get converted "*for life.*" Their experience is sound and thorough. Many such are to-day in the ministry and membership, doing valiantly. They obtained pardon, and revival, and sanctification, at camp meeting, and maintain Christian deportment with unwavering stability. A temporary quickening is a blessing of vast utility; but a permanent, genuine, conformity to God is invaluable. Both are obtained at camp meetings, when, perhaps, neither would have been sought at home.

We should be glad to discuss this subject more fully; but, as we have done this in another work, we forbear.*

* Essay on Camp Meetings. Published by Messrs. Nelson & Phillips, New York.

CHAPTER VI.

FORMS OF WORSHIP AND MODES OF USEFULNESS, NOT GENERALLY MAINTAINED BY OTHER DENOMINATIONS.

THOUGH the *forms* of religion are of less consequence than the *spirit* and power of it, they are entitled to particular consideration. As it is by the use of the former that the latter is obtained and developed to the gaze of the world, it is important that they be conformed to the gospel rule, and of a character to exert the best influence on all who use or witness them. Guided by these objects, Methodists have been led a little out of the common path, and distinguished themselves by certain forms of worship or religious practices, which demand a word of remark.

1. *Kneeling in prayer* is one of them. This is as old as the denomination, and as universal as class meetings or itinerancy. It is a strange thing to see a Methodist *stand* to pray. We have seen them do so in crowds where kneeling was impracticable; and sometimes on wedding, and other popular occasions, where they might and ought to have kneeled; but it is not common. Those who are called upon to pray in courts, legislatures, and other promiscuous assemblies, generally treat the divine Majesty with the reverence which becomes his character. We doubt whether it is proper for us to pray where, being convenient, it would be improper to kneel.

Kneeling in their religious worship was a common prac

tice among the Hebrews. Hence, when Solomon prayed in the temple, he "*kneeled* down upon his *knees* before all the congregation of Israel." Says the prophet Ezra, in relating a fact of himself, "I *fell upon my knees*, and spread out my hands unto the Lord my God." Daniel "*kneeled upon his knees three times a day and prayed.*" When Peter would raise Tabitha to life, "he *kneeled down upon his knees*, and prayed." Stephen, also, when he was stoned, "*kneeled down*" to pray for his murderers. When Paul had finished his discourse at Ephesus, "he *kneeled* down and prayed with them all." — Acts xx. 36. In Tyre, he "*kneeled down on the shore and prayed.*" — Acts xxi. 5. But above all, when Jesus was approaching the time of his great conflict, he "*kneeled down* and prayed;" "and when he *rose up from prayer*, he found his disciples sleeping." Is not this enough? So much cannot be said in favor of standing in prayer. Hence, when we seek associates in our devotions, we adopt the emphatic language of the Psalmist, and say, "O, come, let us worship and *bow down;* let us *kneel before* the Lord our Maker."

There is nothing figurative or hyperbolic in all this. These examplers of religion did just as we have stated — "*they kneeled upon their knees.*" They did not stand, and, addressing their Creator, say, as many have said most falsely, "we *bow down before thee*," or "we *prostrate our selves at thy feet*," or even, "we come into thy presence upon the *bended knees of our souls.*" These are all miserable apologies for neglecting their example, and imitating the Pharisee, who "*stood and prayed*," and thanked God that he was not as other men were. Yet we do not question that they often come from an humble and honest heart; a heart much better, perhaps, than many that inspire bodies of humbler attitude. But still, we insist with Dr. Clarke, that, "according to the Scriptures, in all our private and public addresses to God, we should *kneel*, as the most suitable, the most humble, and the most becoming posture for persons who have nothing to bring, possess no merit, and who have every thing to receive from God's *mere mercy*."

The *appearance* of kneeling in prayer is certainly more becoming the characters concerned, and the business involved. It makes a better impression, and commands more reverence and attention. How affecting to see a whole congregation on their knees, while their minister is commending them to God. To see ten men standing or sitting about the groves we pass in journeying, makes no impression; but the sight of one on his knees with his hands stretched toward heaven, though he utters not a syllable, is not so easily forgotten. The great and good Rev. John Angell James has publicly stated, that "all his usefulness in the ministry and the church of God may be traced to the *sight* of a companion who slept in the same room with him, *bending his knees in prayer on retiring to rest.*" We recollect to have heard a gentleman remark several years since, that the sight of his wife on her knees in prayer affected him to tears. It is taking some pains to speak to God. When outward circumstances are not contradictory, it goes far toward convincing observers of the Christian devotion and sincerity of the suppliant, and consequently contributes greatly to his moral influence.

The practice of kneeling in silent prayer on reaching our seats at church, is a most excellent one. God forbid that it should be done away. In his name, reader, let us determine it shall not be while we live. Sitting down on our seats, and covering our faces, or leaning forward, is better than nothing; but it is a sort of dodging the point — a lazy mode of running round the cross, which seems to say that the prayers we have to offer are so short or unimportant they will hardly pay for the trouble of kneeling. We also admire the practice of spending a moment in the same way at the close of the service; but this has never been very common among us. Except in some very rare cases, we should always kneel in time of prayer, not only when we pray ourselves, but when we unite with others, and let the prayerless world see that we are trying to walk "humbly with God."

2. But Methodists were originally distinguished less by kneeling in prayer than by some other circumstances connected with it. They had been trained to *read* prayers prepared to their hand, however inappropriate. As the fire began to burn, it generated emotions which demanded more emphatic and expressive utterance than these forms provided for. It also led them into situations never contemplated by the prayer writers, and subjected them to the mortification of praying inappropriately, or not praying at all. For example, Mr. Wesley went to visit a man who was under sentence of death, and in great humility and sorrow of heart. True to his church, he first exhausted all the forms having any squinting toward the case in hand; but nothing being effected, he poured out his soul in such words as the circumstances required, and the Lord heard and blessed the poor convict with pardon and peace. At another time his heart was "so full" he broke over again, and determined to be fettered no longer. One who prays merely to obtain a livelihood, naturally prefers *reading prayers* to *praying*. A good man may read devotionally, and if timid and slow of speech in extemporizing, he may prefer it; but one who feels the intense love of God "shed abroad in his heart by the Holy Ghost," or is overwhelmed with desire for

some spiritual attainment, will regard the best forms as an incumbrance. And if it be true, as the devout Brooks remarks, that "God looks not at the *oratory* of our prayers, how *elegant* they may be; nor at the *geometry* of them, how *long* they may be; nor at the *arithmetic* of them, how *many* they may be; nor at the *logic* of them, how *methodical* they may be; but at the *sincerity* of them," we cannot doubt that those which are truest to the gracious impulses of the heart are the most natural and most effective, however imperfect in their verbal composition.

This peculiarity of Methodism arose, as did others, from its *spirituality*, rather than from any disposition to dissent from church order. It was at first a source of much complaint, both from friends and foes, and adopted from a sense of duty rather than inclination, but soon became pretty general throughout the connection. The practice of *social prayer* among the laity followed; when *prayer meetings*, not less new and odd than the piety which suggested them, sprung up in every direction. This agency of carrying on the work in the hearts of believers, and in extending it to others, attracted much attention, and demonstrated that those who were not able to read might, nevertheless, *pray* with good effect. And it was little less strange in this country than in England. Most of the praying at that age was done here by the clergy, and on the Sabbath. And now, even, though prayer meetings are maintained by all the evangelical denominations, in most of them they are under embargo; the exercises being limited not only to the stronger sex, but to a few select individuals, instead of being free to all, of whatever sex, on whom the spirit of prayer may rest. If our policy subjects us to hear some prayers that are mis-shapen and disjointed, it often saves us from those which are *heartless*, the greatest deformity a prayer can possess, and secures us many of the richest and best we should never hear under the book and aristocratic systems.

3. Methodism is still more peculiar in the *liberty* it allows its members in *public speaking*. At its first appearance, little was ever heard of religion in public, except from the clergy. They offered most of the prayers, and communicated most of the instruction, for which the Sabbath was found to afford ample opportunity. Methodism, originating in a divine impulse, and developing itself in all the graces of the Spirit, inspired its subjects to hold frequent meetings for speaking and prayer. Hence, breaking over the restraints of custom, they began to tell what the Lord had done for their souls, and the world was presented with the phenomenon of ignorant men, and even *women*, addressing promiscuous assemblies concerning their souls' salvation. The effect was good; and the practice has continued to the present day. Whether it be *proper*, is another question. We believe it is. The desire to talk and communicate our thoughts and feelings to others, is *natural*, and, therefore, universal. It is a source of personal satisfaction. It increases our pleasure, it mitigates our pain. And as our emotions, so is our tendency to speak. "I am full of matter," said Job, in his affliction; "the spirit within me constraineth me; I *will speak*, that I may be *refreshed*." This is one of nature's own methods of giving vent to the emotions of the heart, and of corresponding with others. To speak, therefore, is not wrong, nor to speak on any subject upon which we feel an interest. The wrong, if there be any, is found in *what we say*, and the time and manner of saying it. The most fastidious churchman will not deny the weakest Christians, not even females, the privilege of talking about religion, or talking to the other sex. The complaint urged against us is, that we let

them talk *in meeting*. But to talk implies that we have an audience. Of course, then, the wrong consists in the *number*. But how many are necessary to constitute it? If it consist in the *position* of the speakers, what is the position in which they may speak innocently? Who can tell? To us it seems there is no wrong. Religious *experience* tends to religious conversation. A soul under conviction pants for personal instruction, as the hart pants for "the water brook." A soul happy in God desires to communicate the fact to others. One under trials is anxious to report his sorrows, that he may be relieved. A Christian who is oppressed with anxiety for the salvation of sinners, will long to give utterance to his emotions, and secure his object. In all these cases we say, *speak*, give vent to your feelings in stating them to one, two, or more, as the case may be, and strive to improve them so as to secure the best results. Not only in our class meetings, love-feasts, and other church gatherings, therefore, do we allow our members to exercise their gifts, but in our prayer meetings also. We wish them to speak "often one to another," and "pray one for another, that they may be healed;" to "exhort one another daily," "warn them that are unruly, comfort the feeble-minded, and support the weak."

Such endeavors exert the happiest influence. They promote union, increase the spirit of prayer, advance the work of grace in believers, awaken and convert sinners, and keep up a public interest in religious things. And if we would always have the right object in view, pray, speak, and sing *short* and to the *point*, and not try to be too *nice*, and do too much, and do every thing at the proper time, and yet *voluntarily*, without being called upon or urged, so as to have every instant occupied, they would be still more powerful and effective. But long and stupid exercises, without point or purpose, accompanied with silent *interludes*, and many entreaties that brethren will bear the cross, are killing. The less we have of them the better.

4. But many complain of so much liberty. They think it infringes upon the priestly office, and begets pride and insubordination in the membership. Especially do they demur at *our women speaking*. Not but what many know enough, and have interest enough, and exert a powerful influence, but they ought not to speak or pray in public. However happy, they must keep it to themselves; however intelligent, and whatever need there may be of instruction in the community, they must hold their peace, though the very "stones cry out." No matter if they can talk and pray better and more acceptably than any man in the neighborhood, not excepting the minister himself, a circumstance that often occurs, they must put their light under a bushel; at all events, they must not let it shine in the presence of the other sex. So say most Christian denominations, but we demur.

The whole strength of the argument on the other side lies in the words of St. Paul: "Let your women keep silence: for it is not permitted unto them to speak, but they are commanded to be under obedience, as also saith the law. And if they will learn any thing, let them ask their husbands at home; for it is a shame for women to speak in the church." — 1 Cor. xiv. 34, 35. And again, "Let the women learn in silence with all subjection. But I suffer not a woman to teach, nor to usurp authority over the man, but to be in silence." — 1 Tim. ii. 11, 12.

That these quotations forbid a certain kind of public speaking is not denied. But do they forbid that under consideration? We think not. Whatever else may be said of the speaking here condemned, it involves *disloyalty* to the man, and is condemned for this reason only. "Let your women keep silence:" that is, not enter into controversy with men, "for it is not permitted unto them to speak" in this way, "but they are commanded to be *under obedience*," and not in *hostility and controversy*. But if they differ from others in any matters of dispute in the church, and "will learn any thing, let them ask their husbands at home," and not enter into public strife and debate with the other sex, "for it is a shame for women to speak in the church" in this manner. The passage to Timothy is to the same effect. *Speaking* is placed in *opposition* to *authority*: "Let them learn in silence, *with all subjection*." She must not assume to dictate the other sex in these things. "I suffer not a woman to teach, nor usurp authority over the man," and clamor for the mastery; "but to be in silence," quietly to submit to his judgment and authority. "For Adam was first formed, then Eve. And Adam was not deceived, but the woman being deceived was in the transgression."

We insist, therefore, that the thing opposed here, is not the exercise of devotion, such as prayer, the relation of Christian experience, &c.; but interference with certain matters of difference and debate, such as were common in the Jewish synagogues. "It is evident from the context," says Clarke, "that the apostle refers here to asking *questions*, and what we call *dictating*, in the assemblies. It was permitted to any *man* to ask *questions*, to *object*, *altercate*, *attempt to refute*, &c., in the synagogue; but this iberty was not allowed to any woman. St. Paul confirms this in reference also to the Christian church. He orders them to *keep silence;* and if they wished to learn any thing, let them inquire of their husbands at home, because it was perfectly *indecorous* for *women* to be contending with *men* in public assemblies, on points of doctrine, cases of conscience, &c. But this by no means intimated that when a woman received any particular *influence from God*, to enable her to teach, [or speak to the edification and comfort of others,] that she was not to obey that influence. All the apostle opposes here is their *questioning*, *finding fault*, &c., in the Christian church, as the Jewish *men* were permitted to do in their synagogues; together with the attempts to usurp any authority over the men, by setting up their judgment in *opposition* to them." — *Commentary on* 1 *Cor. xiv.* 34.

That women did not hold their proper rank among the Jews, will not be denied. It was the doctrine of the Rabbins, that "a woman should know nothing but the use of her distaff." Rabbi Elieser only recorded the feeling of his nation when he wrote, "Let the words of the law be *burned*, rather than they should be delivered to women." But the prophets intimated that the gospel would place them on terms of spiritual equality, so that in Christ there should be neither male nor female. Eight hundred years before the advent of Christ, it was declared: "It shall come to pass afterward, that I will pour out my Spirit upon *all flesh*, and your sons and your *daughters* shall prophesy;" "and upon the servants and upon the *handmaids* in those days will I pour out my Spirit;" "and it shall come to pass that *whosoever* shall call on the name of the Lord shall be delivered." — Joel ii. 28, 29, 32. Peter, on the day of Pentecost, referred to this, and declared that the developments of that day were only the fulfilment of this prophecy. And, sure enough, women did *prophesy* as well as men, and the apostles did not think proper to forbid it. St. Paul did, indeed, forbid their "*usurping authority* over the men," as we have seen. He also forbid their prophesying in a *masculine* and *immodest* manner. "Every man," said he, "*praying* or *prophesying*, having his head covered, dishonoreth his head. But every *woman* that prayeth or prophesieth with her head *uncovered*, dishonoreth her head."

Now, the praying and prophesying in both cases means the same thing. The apostle evidently refers to that which was *vocal* and *public*, since it could make little difference to either sex, in private, whether they were covered or not. And hence he recognizes the public exercises of women in prayer and exhortation as both right and proper, though it was unsuitable for them to do it with an uncovered head,— a condition, by the custom of the times, indicating *immodesty and prostitution*, utterly inconsistent with the Christian character. If it was wrong for them to take a part in these exercises, why had he not said so outright, instead of directing *how they should do it?* And how absurd the idea adopted by certain commentators, that, after having given *directions* to women for the exercise of their gifts in the *eleventh* chapter, he commanded them in the *fourteenth not* to exercise them at all, but to maintain profound silence! These writers evidently mean to bend the Bible to their creed, rather than conform their creed to the Bible. They are equally unreasonable in other respects. The instructions of Paul to Timothy, which they understand to refer to devotional speaking in public, are intimately connected with certain rules in relation to female *attire*, to which they seem to pay little attention. "In like manner, also, that women adorn themselves in modest apparel, with shame-facedness and sobriety; not with *broidered hair, or gold, or pearls, or costly array*, but (which becometh women possessing godliness) with good works." That they would soon exclude females who should pray or prophesy in their meetings, needs not the least proof. Are they as particular in respect to "*costly array*," &c.? But while they forbid females to speak or pray among them in their social meetings, they do allow them to "*teach*," nay, even appoint them to the work; to teach not only *letters*, but *religion*, and that in public, and in the presence of the other sex, notwithstanding St. Paul has said, "I suffer not a woman to teach." They do most of the teaching in their Sabbath Schools, and do it often better than it is possible for the men of the same community to do it. Why may they not be equally competent and effective in social meetings? They are so. They are more likely to be deeply pious than men; are more susceptible of suitable impulses, and naturally more touching and eloquent in their appeals to the heart. And they frequently feel constrained to speak. Why forbid them? Thank God, Methodism does not. Like St. Paul, she corrects them when they err, and speak too long or too loud, but still retains them as a powerful auxiliary in carrying on the work. This is one of our peculiar advantages, and one to which we owe much of our success.

5. *Singing* has always been a part of divine worship; but, like every other, has waxed and waned with the vitality of the worshippers. As the enslaved Israelites could not sing the Lord's song in a strange land, so heartless and formal professors cannot "sing with the Spirit and with the understanding."

> "In vain they tune their formal songs,
> In vain they strive to rise."

But when they "wake to righteousness and sin not," and feel the "mighty comforts" of religion, rejoicing "in the hope of the glory of God," singing is as easy and natural as weeping in affliction and sorrow. Hence the early Methodists were great singers. One of the first charges against them was that they were continually singing and praying, and many were attracted by their music to listen to their other exercises.

But another circumstance to which we are more indebted than to the abstract tendency of religion to stimulate and inspire singing is, that our founder and guide, under God, understood the true philosophy of music, and how to make it serviceable to the grand object of his mission. It was easy enough for him to see that the miserable *flummery* of the orchestra needed reforming as much as the pulpit and the people. Hence, he introduced a new style of singing suited to the spirit and aims of his followers. "Sing all," said he; "join with the congregation as frequently as you can. Let not a slight degree of weakness or weariness hinder you. If it is a cross to you, take it up, and you will find a blessing. Sing *lustily*, and with good courage. Beware of singing as if you were half dead, or half asleep, but lift up your voice with strength. Be not afraid of your voice now, nor more ashamed of its being heard than when you sung the songs of Satan. Above all, sing *spiritually*. Have an eye to God in every word you sing. Aim at pleasing him, more than yourself or any other creature. In order to this, attend strictly to what you sing, and see that your heart is not carried away with the sound, but offered to God continually."

These instructions, together with the ardor of deep experimental piety, introduced a wonderful change in this part of public worship. In order that all might sing, the most easy and familiar tunes were selected, and the hymns were "*lined*." These measures, in a great degree, superseding note and hymn books, the influence of which is much like a manuscript in preaching, and a formula in prayer, enabled the people to concentrate their whole souls on the sentiment, and rise up to God in every strain The result was harmony, spirituality and power; qualities for which our singing has ever been peculiar, except when we have been too ambitious of new and fashionable tunes, and have enslaved ourselves to *fiddles*, and other follies, which have gradually encroached upon our simplicity, and encumbered us with performances that are often more laughable than religious The singing at our camp meetings, love-feasts, and other spiritual convocations, has excited universal admiration, and does now. On these occasions we sing our old tunes and hymns, that are familiar to all, and all sing; sing "*lustily*," yet in harmony, but with little regard to the *niceties* of modern music, and it kindles the holy fire on many hearts. God has made our singing little less effective than our prayers, and our preaching. Thousands have been awakened and converted under it, and have gone up to sing the song of Moses and the Lamb. If we will continue to be useful, we must not only maintain our peculiar freedom in prayer, preaching and exhortation, but we must continue to sing with spirit and power.

6. *Coming forward for prayers.* The custom of inviting those who would be Christians to manifest it in some way, has prevailed among us from the beginning. For many years we have practised inviting them to rise up, or come forward to the altar or front seats, and kneel, while we commend them to God in prayer, that they may be converted. This measure has been adopted to a limited extent by others, but many denounce it as impolitic and extravagant.

In our opinion it is both philosophical and Scriptural. In the first place, to be converted, sinners must repent. This implies conviction of sin, confession, and reformation. The two latter are as important as the former. Conviction will never save one without *confession*, and the confession must be '*before men*." The divine economy is very explicit on this point. Those who have spent their whole lives in open rebellion against God, cannot be let off with mere private confession. No; they must come out from the world, take up their *cross* and follow Christ, though it may be to them as the plucking out of a right eye, or the amputation of a right hand. They must abandon father, and mother, and wife, and children, and brethren, and sisters, yea, and life itself, rather than not become Christians, or they will never be converted. And it is important that they be tested on this point. Hence, under the Levitical economy, which was the same in spirit with the gospel, if a man sinned he was required to confess his sins, and bring a trespass-offering unto the Lord, and have the priest make an atonement for him. — Lev. v. 5, 6. "Whosoever," said Christ, "shall *confess* me *before men*, him will I confess before my Father which is in heaven." "He that *taketh not his cross* and followeth after me, is not worthy of me." — Matt. x. 38. And says St. Paul, "If thou shalt *confess* with thy mouth the Lord Jesus, and shalt believe in thine heart, thou shalt be saved." And all this is in harmony with the general declaration of Solomon, uttered long before: "He that covereth his sins shall not prosper; but whoso *confesseth* and forsaketh them, shall have mercy." Rising up or coming forward for prayers is a practical confession of sin, and an open renunciation of the world in favor of Christ and religion, and is one of the best tests of sincerity that can be devised.

And have we not examples in the gospel strikingly analogous to it? As Jesus entered the synagogue on a certain Sabbath, he saw a man there "whose right hand was withered." He knew the Scribes and Pharisees were watching him; he knew also that to heal that hand *openly* would subject the afflicted man to much reproach and persecution; and if he had thought best he might have healed it privately, and saved himself and the poor sufferer much inconvenience, and the public much agitation. But his first measure was to command the man to "*rise up and stand forth in the midst.*" This was no doubt a great cross, but it was borne, and all eyes were fixed upon him. Now, says Jesus, "*stretch forth thy hand.*" And he did so, and "his hand was restored whole as the other." Can any one inform us what was the use of all this parade? Yet it was ordained in infinite wisdom.

When Saul fell to the earth, and tremblingly said, "Lord, what wilt thou have me to do?" why was he not converted then and there, and the scales taken from his eyes? The reasons are obvious. He was a persecutor, full of prejudice; it was necessary that he should be subjected to a process of humiliation and instruction that should fully demonstrate his sincerity to those with whom he was to be associated, and secure him a better acquaintance with the nature of their religion. It was not enough, therefore, that he was under conviction, that he was *deeply* awakened, and humble, or that he prayed and trembled; he should submit to the mortification of being led to Damascus, and of coming under the tuition of the despised disciples. And when God saw that he was not disobedient to the heavenly vision, which required him to show himself to the disciples a poor penitent, desirous of their counsel and prayers, he took the scales from his eyes, and filled him with the Holy Ghost. Who will pretend that he was not a better and more useful man for these measures? Coming forward for prayers, in our opinion, tends to the same blessed results? It humbles and brings inquirers directly to the point, so that they soon have the witness in themselves that they are new creatures, and evince the same to all who have marked their conduct. If any fail to see the *philosophy* of these results, we refer them to the facts in the case, thousands of which might be adduced in attestation of the truth of our remarks.

Another advantage of the measure is, it brings out and improves occasional convictions. Many have been awakened to no purpose, who, if they could have had an opportunity of manifesting their feelings, and receiving proper instructions, would have become the subjects of converting grace, and perhaps the means of saving many others. But no one suspected them, neither the minister nor his people being upon the look-out for such things; so they kept it to themselves, grieved the Spirit, and became more wicked than before. Not to make inquisition for such cases in some way, nor to provide for them, very strongly suggests that we have little faith in the gospel we preach, and expect nothing special as the result of our labors.

But we are not very tenacious about *forms* where the word of God is not explicit. We have none that may not be modified to meet the demands of any time or place. The best of *human* rules should admit of many exceptions. Any service run on the same line from month to month, and from year to year, will lose its interest. A wise administrator will vary his movements in some minor respects, at least, every month, if not at every meeting. Revivals will not run long without some modification of measures. While general uniformity is desirable, *variety* is not less so. Methodism is systematic, but it is still *elastic* enough to admit of the employment of all desirable agencies.

CHAPTER VII.

MISCELLANEOUS PECULIARITIES; EMBRACING OUR GENERAL APPEARANCE, DRESS, AUDIBLE RESPONSES, ETC.

METHODISM was born in a laughing age. All classes were upon full tilt for frolic and fun. Not to joke, and dance, and play cards, and go to the theatre, &c., was to be odd and vulgar. Hence, the general appearance of the early Methodists attracted little less attention than their doctrines and measures. They could do none of these things with a good conscience. They could no more *trifle*, than they could cheat or lie. The divine command, "watch and be sober," is as imperative as that which requires us to "believe and be baptized." They, therefore, denied "ungodliness and worldly lusts," and lived soberly, righteously, and godly, denying themselves all diversions, except such as they might use "in the name of the Lord." They also discarded the use of spirituous liquors, the reading of books and singing of songs which would not tend to the glory of God, and accounted all needless self-indulgence sin.

But in no respect were they more singular than in their style of dress. Setting out to be Bible Christians, they could not overlook the divine prohibition of all gaudiness and extravagance, and adopted a plain, economical habit, traces of which are still to be seen in our ranks. That individuals were too fastidious is not impossible; but that our obligations extend to dress, as well as to our words and actions, cannot be denied. We are specifically restricted. "Whose adorning," saith St. Peter, "let it not be that outward adorning of *plaiting the hair*, and of *wearing of gold*, or of *putting on of apparel;* but the hidden man of the heart, even the *ornament* of a meek and quiet spirit, which is, in the sight of God, of great price." The practice proscribed is objectionable on two grounds. 1. It engenders vanity and pride. It is nearly impossible for one to indulge in it, without thinking more highly of himself than he ought to think. The pride which demands the indulgence is strengthened by it, till the heart becomes intoxicated with vanity and overwhelmed by worldly influences. 2. It requires an expenditure of time and money that is inconsistent with our spiritual improvement and the duty we owe to the morally and physically destitute. We should be plain and modest in our apparel, in self-defence against the world, as well as to set an example to others; we should be economical, that we may have time and means to relieve distress, and extend the blessings of religion. But in all these things, we are to avoid extremes. We should not be so odd as to attract attention, or so coarse or untasteful as to merit disgust. As "there is no religion in dirt," so there is none in the mere color or cut of a garment. But cleanliness, simplicity, economy, and Christian modesty, are all virtues, without which our piety will appear deformed, and lose much of its influence both on ourselves and others.

Audible responses to appropriate expressions in public prayer and other exercises, have been common in all ages, both among Jews and Christians. They are common even now, except with certain Protestants, whose aversion to Popery has led them to repudiate many excellent customs. *Amen*, meaning *true*, *certain*, *faithful*, and indicating, at the close of a prayer, or sentence, the concurrence of the respondent in it, has been much in use on such occasions. When David closed his psalm at the removing of the ark, "all the people said *amen*, and praised the Lord." — 1 Chron. xvi. 36. St. Paul, urging the importance of speaking understandingly in public exercises, inquires, "how shall he that occupieth the room of the unlearned say *amen* at thy giving of thanks? seeing that he understandeth not what thou sayest." — 1 Cor. xiv. 16. Responses of this nature were common in his day, and formed a part of public worship, as much as singing and prayer.

The practice of responding in terms of exultation and praise is equally authoritative. When God appeared in his temple at the dedication, the children of Israel "bowed themselves to the ground, and praised the Lord, saying: For he is good; for his mercy endureth for ever." As Jesus was entering Jerusalem his disciples shouted "*Hosanna:* blessed is he that cometh in the name of the Lord. *Hosanna in the highest!*" When Nehemiah had the walls of Jerusalem dedicated, the people rejoiced; "the wives, also, and the children, rejoiced," in so tumultuous a manner "that the joy of Jerusalem was heard afar off." At the laying of the foundation of the temple, the people "*shouted* with a great shout, and praised the Lord." But some, who had seen the first house, "wept with a loud voice, so that the people could not discern the noise of the shout of joy from the noise of the weeping; for the people shouted with a loud shout, and the noise was heard afar off." — Ezra iv. 11, 13. Singing is another Scriptural mode of expressing the same thing. "When ye come together," saith the Spirit, "every one of you hath a *psalm*, hath a doctrine," &c. — 1 Cor. xiv. 26; indicating different states of feeling and modes of communication.

The utility of suitable responses is manifest. They are

true to nature, — are the proper expressions of real *feeling*, which is not only cherished and increased by them, but transferred to others. One who is happy in God *feels* "*amen!*" and "*glory to God!*" and "*hallelujah!*" and "*hosanna in the highest!*" whether he utters it or not. To speak it out, without the fear of *offending*, gives him increasing comfort. And it stimulates and comforts others, particularly the speaker. It often convinces sinners, too, and they are induced to seek the same blessed boon. That there is danger of overdoing it, and getting into confusion, is admitted. Some people have little consideration, and may speak out of time. This has often been done; but if they have religion enough to justify their shouting at all, they will stand corrected, and be more prudent in future. If they have not, the sooner they are silenced the better. Our troubles from this source have not been half equal to those which have arisen from spiritual coldness and death. This is the most fatal enthusiasm that can get into the house of God. If one is engaged, but wild and fanatical, he may be managed and employed to some good purpose; but dead men are a positive encumbrance. We hope, therefore, that the church will continue to cherish the practice, and respond and praise God on all suitable occasions, in the full assurance of hope. And if it be done with modesty, as unto God, and not to men, it will continue to prove a blessing to the cause; but if any err let them be corrected in love, however it may grieve them. One had better suffer than many. Thus, avoiding the stupid responses of Churchmen, and the squeamish and formal timidity of dissenters, we shall maintain the peculiar freedom and whole-souled earnestness by which we have been characterized in other days. If our opponents do not see the philosophy of it, we will refer them to their own political and other conventions;

—to the English Parliament, if they please, whose cries of "*hear! hear!*" and "*hurrah!*" will suggest to them topics of profitable meditation. We have been particularly struck with the noisy clapping and shouting of such fastidious critics, on these occasions, who cannot endure an *amen*, in the minor key, much less a thorough outburst of religious joy. But such is the prejudice of education, and of party interest. The philosophy of the thing is the same in both cases; it is according to the nature of things, and is, therefore, invulnerable.

But "such responses lead to noise and extravagance." Not necessarily. Few Christians are so destitute of good sense, or good manners, as to disturb brethren with their extravagances; and when any such appear, they may be checked without difficulty. But some *professors* are too easily disturbed. They can hear noise about any thing else except religion. But is it any worse to praise God aloud, than to praise the president? to clap and shout for joy when we are happy in God, than for others to do so when they are pushing for political victory? Yet the latter is all right, and even popular. We say this, not to justify the evil referred to, so much as to show the unreasonableness of certain complainants. We despise a senseless and improper noise in any meeting; but a hearty "*amen*," or "*glory to God*," when it comes from a pious spirit, and is well timed, we believe both reasonable and Scriptural. And we hope the church may not soon become so cold, or nice, as to account it disorderly.

THE END.

www.ingramcontent.com/pod-product-compliance
Lightning Source LLC
LaVergne TN
LVHW021319110826
845150LV00003B/619

9781425557324